At Play in the Fields of Consciousness

Essays in Honor of Jerome L. Singer

At Play in the Fields of Consciousness

Essays in Honor of Jerome L. Singer

Edited by

Jefferson A. Singer
Connecticut College

Peter Salovey
Yale University

Ψ Psychology Press
Taylor & Francis Group

NEW YORK AND HOVE

First published by Lawrence Erlbaum Associates, Inc., Publishers
10 Industrial Avenue
Mahwah, NJ 07430

This edition published 2013 by Psychology Press
Psychology Press   Psychology Press
Taylor & Francis Group   Taylor & Francis Group
711 Third Avenue   27 Church Road
New York, NY 10017   Hove
                                  East Sussex BN3 2FA

Psychology Press is an imprint of the Taylor & Francis Group, an informa business

Cover design by Kathryn Houghtaling Lacey

Library of Congress Cataloging-in-Publication Data

At play in the fields of consciousness : essays in honor of Jerome L.
    Singer / [edited by] Jefferson A. Singer, Peter Salovey.
        p. cm.
    Includes bibliographical references and indexes.
    ISBN 0-8058-2637-8 (alk. paper).
    1. Consciousness. 2. Mental representation. 3. Cognition. 4.
Personality. I. Singer, Jerome L. II. Singer, Jefferson A. III.
Salovey, Peter.
BF311.A744   1998
153—dc21   98-35308
                                                       CIP

10   9   8   7   6   5   4   3   2   1

Contents

PART II: COGNITION AND PERSONALITY

**PART III: CONSCIOUSNESS AND PERSONALITY
IN CONTEXT**

Preface

The study of consciousness includes research about ongoing thought, dreaming and daydreaming, autobiographical memory, and fantasy. For the first 60 years of this century, research in these areas was relegated to a minor status in psychology by adherents to the two major theoretical paradigms of the time—behaviorism and psychoanalysis. Behaviorists considered the covert products of conscious experience—thoughts and feelings—to be epiphenomenal and unnecessary to explanatory models of behavior. Psychoanalytic theorists viewed the products of consciousness as mere screens for more critical aspects of personality, submerged in the unconscious.

With the information-processing revolution of the late 1950s and early 1960s, the role of conscious thought in the construction of personality and identity, described by James in the previous century, again became a matter of central concern for researchers in psychology. The innovative theorizing of Simon and Neisser about cognition, Tomkins about emotion, and Kelly and Klein about personality began to be integrated by cognitively oriented researchers who brought the rigor of experimental methods to the study of ongoing conscious experience. Anticipating the present-day excitement about the influence of cognitive interpretation on social behavior and social cognition, these investigators relied on the collection of verbal protocols, the analysis of mental chronometry, and computer simulation to get inside the head in a systematic and experimentally verifiable manner.

Jerome L. Singer was a pioneer during this period. Trained in experimental psychopathology at the University of Pennsylvania and in psychoanalytic psychotherapy at the William Alanson White Institute, J. L. Singer was part of the first wave of psychoanalytically oriented therapists who put the assumptions of psychoanalytic thinking to empirical test. Although his earliest work in this area used projective tests as the method for understanding individual differences in the richness of fantasy life, he soon recognized that imaginative processes could be studied more reliably through controlled laboratory methodologies. His seminal research with Antrobus, his first doctoral student, about daydreaming and what they called Task Unrelated Imagery and Thought (TUIT) represented a testing of the waters in the stream of consciousness. These early experiments revealed that conscious experience was not merely the province of poets and philosophical speculation, but lent itself to the creation of lawful models that could withstand empirical scrutiny and componential analysis. This programmatic line of research revealed the power of human imagination, which J. L. Singer captured in the first scientific book about daydreaming (J. L. Singer, 1966). Monographs discussing the implications of this work for understanding the child's world of make-believe (J. L. Singer, 1973), as well as the use of imagery techniques in psychotherapy (J. L. Singer, 1974), soon followed. All of these writings helped to articulate J. L. Singer's eloquent argument for the power of private experience over human attentional processes. J. L. Singer proposed an ongoing competition for attentional resources between the demands of external sensory stimuli and an internal world of thoughts, feelings, fantasies, and daydreams. Far from being mere distractions or desultory wanderings, private experience, as his research demonstrated, offered opportunities for rehearsal and constructive planning, as well as an unlimited source of internal pleasure.

A growing collaboration with his wife, Dorothy G. Singer, a child psychologist, fostered the application of his research about consciousness to children's play, the development of aggressive behavior, and the impact of television on families. Their work in this area demonstrated the pervasiveness of children's imaginary playmates and, to the relief of many parents, the normality of childhood fantasy (D. G. Singer & J. L. Singer, 1990). An analysis of children's television programming, such as *Mister Rogers' Neighborhood*, *Sesame Street*, and *Barney & Friends*, revealed that developmentally appropriate television that encourages sustained attention so necessary at school is possible, but requires parental mediation to maximize its benefits. Perhaps, most importantly, the Singers articulated a vision of family-oriented television as a vehicle for promoting prosocial values, healthy behavior, and the development of imagination and creativity.

In recent years, J. L. Singer found himself in the midst of a revolution of sorts, seeking to understand psychodynamic concepts in the context of a cognitive–affective view of personality that applies the methods of social cognition. These scholars have made clear that so-called unconscious phenomena such as repression and transference can be explained through cognitive models invoking concepts such as schemas, scripts, selective attention, and implicit memory. For example, his 1990 edited volume about repression continues to be a widely cited bridge between experimental psychology and clinical phenomena.

J. L. Singer's former students and collaborators, others who were in the vanguard of consciousness research, and fine newer researchers (e.g.,

Andersen, Glassman, and Mayer) contributed the chapters to this volume. These chapters express the continuity of self and of consciousness as the integrative agents of personality, while organizing cognition, motivation, and behavior. Part I contains a series of chapters about consciousness and mental representation. Antrobus describes the neural–cognitive underpinnings of ongoing thought and discusses the interface of his work with J. L. Singer on TUITs and contemporary cognitive neuroscience. Klinger next describes the flow of thought, especially its importance in a construct he calls *current concerns*, which are latent states that extend from initial commitment to a goal to its termination. Klinger offers an empirically derived articulation of the major dimensions that contribute to the content of conscious experience. Congruent with J. L. Singer's efforts at revisiting psychoanalytic theorizing about mental phenomena, Epstein applies his cognitive–affective theory of personality (Cognitive-Experiential Self-Theory) to a new view of dreaming. Epstein argues that the seeming symbolic coherence of dreams is due not to the manifest representation of latent conflicts, but to the operation of the experiential system of thought that naturally fashions narratives from imagistic and affectively intense material. These experiential narratives have more to do with the ongoing concerns of the day than with repressed wishes that cannot be articulated except through disguised symbolic content. Izard refocuses attention from cognitive systems to affect. His chapter presents the relation of emotion to consciousness and how emotion organizes attention, learning, and memory. He and his colleagues provide a distinctly developmental approach in looking at the acquisition of empathy and social competence through the building up of increasingly elaborate cognitive–affective structures within the personality. The final chapter in Part I describes how research in social cognition can be used to understand transference, a more general cognitive phenomenon, which has traditionally been couched in psychoanalytic terms. Transference, according to Glassman and Andersen, is essentially the process by which past experiences, wishes, fantasies, and expectations emerge in a current relationship with a new person. They clearly demonstrate empirically that transference influences all interpersonal relationships, not just the relationship of client and therapist.

The chapters in Part II describe the study of conscious processes in personality. Mayer offers a framework for organizing the study of individual differences at various levels of analysis. Essential to his scheme is the internal personality, reminiscent of J. L. Singer's private personality (J. L. Singer, 1984), serving as an interface between brain and culture. The subsequent three chapters focus on the three traditional major divisions of the internal personality: cognition, emotion, and conation. The cognitive aspects of consciousness are the special focus of Kreitler's chapter. She describes the importance of a theory of meaning in accounting for individual differences in the content of consciousness, in the processes of consciousness, and in the experiential awareness of these mental activities.

Feshbach studies the relation between conscious and unconscious processes by looking at attempts to self-regulate emotion. His chapter focuses on the suppression of fear, the inhibition of positive affect, and the modification of vicarious and actual aggression. Pervin's contribution turns attention to conation or volition, the third traditional dimension of personality. His chapter focuses on the inability to do what one intends or wants to do and the inability to stop oneself from doing what one does not intend or want to do. James refers to these as the challenges of obstructed will and explosive will; Pervin describes them as problems of inhibition and addiction.

The third and final part of this volume extends the study of consciousness into psychotherapy, creativity, and the development of imagination in children. The chapters by Bonanno and Siddique, and Horowitz explore conscious representation in the context of psychotherapy. Bonanno and Siddique study dispositional tendencies to shift attention away from undesirable and unpleasant emotions, and the consequences of this kind of dissociation and self-deception for mental health. Horowitz describes the different modalities in which mental experience can be rendered. He then demonstrates how these modes of representation can be elucidated by studying individuals who are working through problems such as depressive rumination and social anxiety in psychotherapy. Morrison provides an intriguing look at similar imaginative processes in the life of Jack Kerouac. He portrays the interplay between the private personality, so important to Beat poets and novelists, and their creative products. Morrison emphasizes, in particular, the effects of childhood bereavement on Kerouac's later artistic imagery and themes. The final chapter in this volume is fittingly contributed by D. G. Singer. She delineates a program of research about imagination and children's play spanning 3 decades, and connects this work to the study of television programming as a tool to enhance positive products of consciousness and adaptive social behavior.

In assembling these chapters, the broad reach of J. L. Singer's scholarship was once again obvious. Of course, this was not a new discovery on our part because he was a favorite graduate school mentor and a fatherly influence on both of our lives (in one case literally so and in another symbolically so). As he approaches his 75th birthday, we are proud to place in a single volume a cross-section of the intellectual concerns and passions that have inspired his research across 5 decades. Just as important as the substantive aspects of his scholarship, however, is his commitment to the study of the whole human being, providing an integration across the subdisciplines of psychology. This dedication to general psychology, in the face of pressures toward overspecialization, is a quality that we learned from him and seek to emulate in our own writings and professional activities. Although this book inevitably calls for a retrospective emphasis on J. L.

Singer's work, we nonetheless look forward to the play of his imagination and creative process in the new millennium.

ACKNOWLEDGMENTS

The editors extend their most sincere gratitude to the outstanding contributors to this volume, especially for their collusion in keeping it a secret from J. L. Singer for nearly 2 years. The editors also thank the staff at Lawrence Erlbaum Associates: in particular, Judi Amsel, for graciously helping to plan this volume, and Kathleen Dolan and Dorothy Gribbin, for shepherding it through its various stages. Finally, we acknowledge Nancy MacLeod, Richard Lally, and Roberta Mouheb for their invaluable assistance in manuscript preparation.

—Jefferson A. Singer
—Peter Salovey

REFERENCES

Singer, D. G., & Singer, J. L. (1990). *The house of make believe: Children's play and the developing imagination.* Cambridge, MA: Harvard University Press.

Singer, J. L. (1966). *Daydreaming.* New York: Random House.

Singer, J. L. (1973). *The child's world of make-believe: Experimental studies of imaginative play.* New York: Academic Press.

Singer, J. L. (1974). *Imagery and daydream methods in psychotherapy and behavior modification.* New York: Academic Press.

Singer, J. L. (1984). The private personality. *Personality and Social Psychology Bulletin, 10,* 7–30. (Presidential address, Division of Personality and Social Psychology, American Psychological Association)

Singer, J. L. (Ed.). (1990). *Repression and dissociation: Implications for personality, psychopathology, and health.* Chicago: University of Chicago Press.

At Play in the Fields of Consciousness

Essays in Honor of Jerome L. Singer

I

CONSCIOUSNESS AND
REPRESENTATION

1

Toward a Neurocognitive Processing Model of Imaginal Thought

John S. Antrobus
The City College of the City University of New York

This volume celebrates the first half century of the research that has grown out of Jerome Singer's conception of the imaginal stream of thought as a cognitive process that contributes to the psychological enrichment and well-being of the individual. The origin of Singer's interest in the study of imagination and fantasy lies, I think, in his regard for the rewards of a rich imaginal life—rewards that, I also think, he hopes we share. We are fortunate that he has been so successful in persuading us, his friends and colleagues, to join him in this research endeavor.

Singer once told me that he outlined his research program as part of his PhD preliminaries at the University of Pennsylvania. The originality of his conception is remarkable for its independence from those of his contemporary theorists who regarded fantasy only for its role in psychopathology. Clinical psychologists and the research funding agencies tended to assume that pathological processes could be understood with little comprehension of normal or healthy processes. Fantasy, daydreaming, and mindwandering were pathological because they represented underlying intrapsychic conflict, and their primary value to the clinician was the information they provided for the diagnosis of such conflicts and disorders. They were also regarded as escapist because they implicitly denied reality.

Singer's interest in psychopathology was always secondary to his concern with the inner life of the normal healthy individual. He has insisted that pathology cannot be understood without first appreciating the normal state. His conception of fantasy and imaginal thought, therefore, is that they are an essential part of a healthy, integrated, and satisfying mental life. During the course of a demanding day, there is never enough time to consider fully the consequences and implications of all that one does and sees. Therefore, the free minutes between external tasks, even those brief moments while responding to external demands, afford the opportunity to both look back, reconsider, and anticipate better future events and possible responses to them. This style of considering and anticipating is beautifully portrayed by one of Singer's favorite characters, the title character of Saul Bellow's *Herzog* (1964), who carries on continuous conversations and imaginary correspondence about the things in life that matter with everyone from his demised mother to the president of the United States.

However, many people have no patience for this Walter Mitty style of life. They consider fantasy the antithesis of achievement in the real world and question whether imaginal thought can contribute to effective solutions to real problems. Planning ahead may be desirable, but it can be done only with conscious deliberation. Nothing is lost if these idle thoughts and images are ignored or suppressed in favor of external sources of information. If people have free time, they prefer theater, film, and television, which are created so as to be maximally competitive with spontaneous thoughts and fantasies. However, the price of being continuously wired into external sources of information, whether for work or entertainment, may be that the cognitive resources that are needed to create a satisfying inner life, to be able to explore alternative solutions to a problem, and to anticipate future events in one's life may never develop and flourish. With such limited cognitive resources, many people cannot sit on a train without the assistance of a portable audio device, and many cannot eat lunch without the distraction of a magazine, television, or both.

Although it may be of paramount importance to many of us, concern with the quality and the richness and satisfaction of the private mental life has not been a concern of academic psychology, much less an area for research funding. American professional psychology has emphasized the functional or instrumental value of a given process. We needed to direct the theory and research about imaginal thought to the study of its utility, of its integrative function in personality development, and of its role in exploration, expectation, and planning.

In proposing that imaginal thought is a cognitive skill (Singer, 1966) that participates in exploration, expectation, and planning, Singer anticipated a theme of the emerging area of cognitive psychology and its contribution to the understanding of human development and adaptation. This concept also anticipated a research and development program in the high-tech application of artificial intelligence to aeronautics. At a recent neural-network symposium on the topic of consciousness, I was struck by the similarity of Singer's conception of the adaptive function of imagination, thought, and imagery to a proposal by Werbos (1994), a codis-coverer of the neural-network "back propagation" algorithm and leading computer science engineer at NSF. Werbos suggested that costly computer-controlled machines such as aircraft would fare much better if, like human beings, they had the ability to imagine risky events that had not yet happened. He has, in fact, actively solicited research proposals for such designs. For example, suppose that while in flight an aircraft loses a piece of a wing. There would not be sufficient time to compute and put into effect a possible solution if the plane were seconds from disaster. However, if the aircraft's computer, when not occupied with demanding assignments such as takeoff and landing, had applied its idle computational resources to imagining possible threats and developing solutions, the plane might have a chance of surviving. We can anticipate the personal concerns module (see Klinger, 1971) of a future aircraft being activated by flying over mountain ranges and wondering, that is, computing, whether its ground-level detectors would give it sufficient warning if the approaching peaks were even higher, the cloud cover even heavier, and the headwinds even stronger. With more sophisticated cognitive skills, the craft might imagine where it would attempt to land if its deicing device failed or if an engine caught on fire.

Thirty years earlier, Singer (1966) had introduced the human application of this model, namely that people use imaginative thought and fantasy to anticipate complex situations and responses to them. He proposed that much of what most people disparagingly refer to as mind-wandering or daydreaming are unplanned cognitive processes that attempt to solve important personal problems. Singer suggested that some of these attempts at personal problem solving might yield implausible solutions and that cognitive exploration of unsuccessful paths would facilitate the search for other more successful alternatives.

Singer's view of the function of imaginal thought included precisely the function described by Werbos (1994). It is particularly ironic that the adaptive or survival value of this cognitive process Singer promoted for so long in the psychological community should be championed by an engineer who is almost completely uninformed about psychology. Sensing the need for such a field, Werbos suggested that bioengineers might create it under the title of computational biology. Although ignorant of psychological research, many bioengineers like Werbos have superb training in mathematical modeling. In attempting to incorporate this most human of cognitive processes into advanced aircraft design, bioengineers and computational neuroscientists may someday contribute significantly to our understanding of imaginal processes.

Computational and neurological models have begun to make important contributions to the understanding of imaginal processes. One challenge for theories of both waking imaginal processes and dreaming has been to account for how novel images and imaged sequences and meanings are created. What is novel must be constructed or computed from features that have been acquired by prior learning. In order for features from diverse sources to be combined in a seamless fashion to form a novel image, it is necessary to assume that the features themselves are constructed from more elementary "microfeatures." This allows novel images to be constructed from subsets of the microfeatures of different features. For example, although the concepts *person, horse, table,* and *journey* are not novel, each makes use of a common feature, *leg*. But each *leg* feature consists of a different subset of *leg* microfeatures, namely, those microfeatures that make a seamless fit to the other features of the concept. Neural networks provide a conceptual and computational basis for representing such relationships. The schema model of Rumelhart, Smolensky, McClelland, and Hinton (1986) describes a plausible neurocomputational model of how novel cognitive objects and events can be constructed in a systematic fashion from networks of simpler features or microfeatures, whose interconnections are well learned. This capability is essential to a model of imaginal processes. Because of the large number of microcognitive units that potentially contribute to such a novel imaginal schema, large high-speed computers are required to model such processes. The increased availability of these computers has now made the study of such neural-net models possible for psychologists. I have recently applied neural-network models to imaginal sequences that might occur during dreaming sleep or daydreaming (Antrobus, 1991). These introductory models are intended only to demonstrate the feasibility of applying neural-network models to imaginal processes, however, and are not in any sense proposed as complete models.

It is one thing to describe a plausible verbal model of imaginal processes, but quite another to translate the components of a verbal model into a working computer model. Verbal models of very complex cognitive processes are often described in metaphoric language. They make use of hypothetical intermediate processes, which can be measured only indirectly so that they are defined in a vague fashion. They invariably make use of implicit assumptions that the theorist may not define explicitly unless he or she builds a computational model. A computer model is much less forgiving than a verbal model. In building his excellent computer model of content sequences in daydreaming, Mueller (1989) frequently found that he had to explicitly define many assumptions that were only implicitly defined in the psychological literature. The construction of an accurate working model is not, of course, *prima facie* evidence that we have a valid theory. Mueller's model is able to "imagine" sophisticated psychosocial sequences, but it cannot create the novel imaginal objects and events that are characteristic of creative imagination nor, as

Fookson and Antrobus (1989) demonstrated in a preliminary model, can it model the switching back and forth between fantasy and perceptual-motor activity that occurs in real-time fantasy. Our present inability to construct a comprehensive model of imaginal thought is evidence that, despite the enormous amount we have learned in past decades, we still have much to learn about how imaginal processes are produced and about their individual usefulness.

Singer's research began in earnest about 40 years ago with a National Institute of Mental Health research project titled "Dimensions of Fantasy and Imagination." As the title suggests, Singer wanted to reduce the many characteristics of fantasy, imagination, creativity, mind wandering, and rumination to a smaller number of independent dimensions and to determine how they related to the dimensions of personality. The initial work on this issue was described in Singer and Antrobus (1966, 1972) and was further developed by Huba, Aneshensel, and Singer (1981) and Huba and Tanaka (1983–1984).

It was one thing to find that the imagery and thought people reported on a questionnaire could be summarized using a finite number of dimensions, and it was quite another to assume that these dimensions would be confirmed in live samples of reported thought. Indeed, there was no empirical basis for assuming that the magnitude of total fantasy reported on a questionnaire would be isometric with time sampling of imaginal thought. Although we developed some satisfactory ways of coping with questionnaire response sets such as social desirability—the tendency to affirm or deny any statement about oneself—we had no means of validating a questionnaire as a measure of private events. If there were no way to measure private experiences such as fantasy, how could one validate the questionnaire? From a late 1990s perspective, it is difficult to appreciate that in the late 1950s, at least at Columbia University, one dared not make any assumptions about private events from a subject's report of them. It was no accident that it took two naive physiologists, Aserinsky and Kleitman (1955), to ask people to report their mental experience after being awakened from sleep, and so discover the relation between rapid eye movement (REM) sleep and dreaming. It was this measurement validation question that brought us to the experimental laboratory.

We described a simple theory of how imaginal thought should vary under specific experimental conditions, and of how participants' reports should vary as a consequence of the hypothesized changes. If participants' indices of imaginal thought supported our predictions, then not only would the theory be validated, but the measure of fantasy would be validated as well. Our next step was to describe a theory about imaginal process that would yield clear, testable, experimental predictions—both across individuals and across time.

Modern cognitive psychology was in its infancy when we began our research on imaginal processes. We thought that if we integrated our conception of imaginal processes with those of the new cognitive psychology, we could build a better model of imaginal processes than if we confined our database and theoretical assumptions to those derived from research about imaginal processes alone. Rather than creating an independent model of imaginal thought, we wanted our model to become part of a more comprehensive model of cognition. Broadbent (1958) provided an easy introduction to cognitive psychology because many of his studies included a dimension of individual differences, namely thinking introversion, which was popular with English psychologists and which could be seen as related to imaginal thought. However, Broadbent's primary contribution was his limited capacity channel or "bottleneck" model of attention, an interference model for the analysis of dichotic listening in which attention to information in one ear caused a decrement in processing information in the other. Later, Moray (1967) suggested that interference might occur at the point of a limited capacity common *processor* and subsequent investigators developed the late-selection theory in which initial levels of two cognitive processes proceed in parallel but compete only at later levels such as the production of conscious images, short-term memory storage or motor production (Meyer & Kieras, 1997; Norman, 1968; Posner, 1978).

Even before Moray's paper we had applied this common processor model to determine what perceptual processes suppress imaginal processes (Antrobus, 1968; Antrobus, Singer, & Greenberg, 1966). Interference implies competition for shared neurocognitive processing resources. If a perceptual or cognitive task interferes with the production of imaginal processes, then imaginal production must share some of the same neurocognitive processing resources that task performance utilizes. In order to study this simple question we needed a measurement procedure that could accurately quantify imaginal processes over time. We assumed simply that any perceptual or cognitive process that interfered with the production of imaginal processes must share the same processor, or same processor module(s). That is, the processor could produce either perceptual or imaginal imagery and thought, but not both. This model was simply a more formal way of saying that when one is paying attention to external events, one cannot let one's mind wander; or conversely if one's mind does wander one isn't paying attention. We thought we would start by seeing if our measures of imaginal processes were good enough to support this common everyday assumption.

Our initial model had two input channels: the first sensory; the second, input from memorial sources. Processing the sensory source yields perceptual events; processing the memorial source results in imaginal qualia and meanings. Because of the limited capacity of the processor it could accept information from only one source at a time. Our primary interest, of course, was in the conditions under which it accepted input from memorial sources. We assumed that, within the constraints of processing capacity, choice of input was determined by the estimated payoff or value to the individual of processing the two alternative input channels. If the environment was novel, unpredictable or associated with highly valued events, the processor would select the sensory channels over the memorial ones. On the other hand, if the environment was highly predictable, that is familiar, there might be material in the memorial modules that were of greater value to the individual and the central processor might therefore select input from this channel. Following computer lingo, we called this selection, "going *offline*." For example, if one is traveling on a visit to an old friend, it might be of greater personal value to reminisce about the friend than to look at the scenery.

Initially, we posited a payoff in which going offline was some kind of, perhaps, low-grade problem solving. Subsequent research, described later, suggested that this offline process might be limited to problem defining rather than actually working out plausible solutions to problems. Singer suggested that these imaginal processes also have a playful entertainment value. They help maintain the positive feeling tone of the individual. Later, we extended this payoff model to include fantasy about painful images that elicited negative affect. Although the emphasis of the model was on the positive function of imaginal processes, the model also included depressive and neurotic imagery and thought (see Gendrin & Werner, 1996–1997).

The development of both our measuring instruments and theoretical models of imaginal processes has been greatly influenced by concurrent developments in the neurocognitive sciences. The imaginal processes we call daydreaming, fantasy, and mindwandering are neurocognitive processes. In this respect, there is every reason to assume they are functionally related to the entire neurocognitive apparatus.

At the time we started this work, models of cognitive processing were largely inspired by the architecture of digital computers that have a single processor. With the development of increasingly precise models of localized cortical functions, it became apparent that the single central processor metaphor was inappropriate. This argument became the basis for the development of neural network models of cognition (Rumelhart & McClelland, 1986). But developments in the field of cognitive neuroscience also demonstrated that different characteristics of imaginal processes might be carried out in different cortical regions. Much later, Kosslyn (1994) described a comprehensive localized cortical model for the production of visual imagery. In his research, however, visual imagery is generally elicited in response to verbal instruction. Singer's interest, by contrast, has been in the function of visual and other imaginal processes that are not controlled by deliberate verbal instructions or explicit goals. For this reason, the neurocognitive architecture that produces spontaneous imaginal events is different in important respects from Kosslyn's model. Neurocognitive models have come a long way since we described our early imaginal model and we attempt to take advantage of continuing developments in cognitive neuroscience to improve our models.

The evidence from brain imaging studies showing that different brain regions are selectively activated in different tasks fits nicely with the late selection theories of cognitive theorists. This suggests that brain regions whose processes do not compete or conflict with one another might process different classes of cognitive information in parallel. If the outputs of two regions compete for processing in a subsequent neural region their outputs might be processed in that region by rapid switching back and forth between the two inputs. In contemporary cognitive parlance, the earlier processes might be called implicit. For the implicit processes to be rendered explicit they would need to be accepted into brain regions that could represent some of their characteristics as sensory-like images, meaning, or speech. Although this conception of a shared neurocognitive processing region is a quite plausible replacement for the common processor model, the precise operation and control of these shared neurocognitive resources is not yet well understood. To the extent that the production of imaginal thought is driven by personal goals and concerns we assume that this control is represented in the frontal lobes. These cortical regions may be able to activate other regions that have the neurocognitive resources appropriate for addressing a particular problem. For example, the frontal lobes might activate prefrontal and temporal cortical regions that can represent the goal processes in a symbolic or verbal format. Indeed, Courtney (1997) described a functional magnetic image (fMRI) visual perception study that supported this neural model. She employed a visual encoding task in which brief signal intervals were alternated with brief intervals with no stimuli. We have shown (see later) that the likelihood of imaginal thought in these latter intervals is high. Courtney found cortical activation moved rapidly from occipital and parietal regions during signal encoding to the frontal lobes in the intervals where imaginal thought normally occurs. Although Courtney suggested that the occipital activation represented memorial processing of task information, she presented no direct evidence for that assumption. An equally plausible explanation might be that the frontal lobe activation could just as well be attributed to mindwandering activity between task stimuli.

The assessment of a person's subjective, private thoughts and images is vulnerable to response biases such as the tendency to please the experimenter by reporting more characteristics that are generally socially desirable particularly if the experimenter seems to be interested in them. Because it is extraordinarily difficult to measure such biases and because they may increase with the complexity of the required judgment, studies eliciting reports of imaginal thoughts are well advised to make the subject's judgment as simple as possible. In our own work, the participant was simply asked to make a binary "Yes" or "No" judgment as to whether an imaginal thought or image occurred within a specified time interval or trial. In our early papers we referred to imaginal thought as stimulus-independent thought, but people argued that no thought is truly independent of stimuli so we changed it to task-irrelevant thought and imagery, and then to employ a better acronym to task unrelated imagery and thought (TUIT).

Participants were placed in a standardized task environment consisting of sound- and light-attenuated cubicles that facilitated the subject's binary TUIT judgment and discouraged them from taking on any additional external "task" such as exploring the furniture or any form of tactile stimulation. The task itself occupied most of their attention so that by default almost any nontask cognitive event of which they were conscious was a nonperceptual event. In order to ensure that the TUIT response excluded all perceptual input, we classified proprioceptive and interoceptive sources as perceptual events as well as stimuli associated with the experimental task. The justification for this criterion was based on the binary late selection model in which the only two input sources for the common processor were the memorial antecedents to imaginal thought and perceptual stimuli—primarily the stimulus–response task—but including other nuisance inputs. The model assumes that attending to back pain or a stomach ache has the same interfering effect on imaginal processes as does attention to an external visual stimulus that is under the control of the experimenter.

With this definition of perceptual input we defined the source of any other cognitive event by default as memorial. By defining TUIT as thought or imagery produced from memorial input to the central processor we had to deal with the question of when a percept becomes a memory. Clearly, there is no discrete boundary between the two. Even the so-called sensory information in the sensory projection regions of the cortex is memorial information derived from a sequence of neural processors that transform the original information encoded by the sensory receptors. In defining TUIT as derived from memorial sources we are simply referring to sources that are older by some arbitrary criterion than the more recent memories we call *percepts*. From the viewpoint of cortical localization, these older memories are also located in different regions than the recent events.

We were concerned that in our effort to simplify our definition of fantasy and imagination we might inadvertently broaden the category so that TUIT might include deliberate or controlled forms of thought. In practice, however, the processing constraints of the external task were such that participants never reported such classes of thought. Deliberate planning and problem solving seem to require unconstrained cognitive processing resources. When cortical-cognitive processing resources are limited as they are by the heavy load of our sensorimotor task, access to relevant information in memory is limited so that deliberate thought is impossible. Under such processing constraints, cognitive "solutions" to personal matters may tend to appear improbable and unrealistic.

In order to ensure that the proportion of TUIT, p(TUIT), can be used as a dependent variable, it should vary between 0.2 and 0.8 across subjects. We found that 15- or 16-second trial durations satisfied this requirement. The only exception to this practice was one study described here in which we varied the interval from 2 seconds to 2 minutes.

Subjects made a fairly simple pair of judgments when they heard a tone that terminated each trial. "Did I experience any imagery or thought during the past trial?" If none, then press the key to indicate no perceptual ("outside") thoughts. If yes, did all of them correspond to external, proprioceptive or interoceptive stimulus? If yes, then press the "no outside thoughts" key. If at least one thought or image did not correspond to one of these stimulus sources, then press the outside thoughts—"yes" key (Antrobus, Singer, Goldstein, & Fortgang, 1970). The definition was followed by a number of typical yes and no TUIT examples furnished by the experimenters, and then followed by a set of borderline examples. For example, if the subject was thinking—during the trial—that a task error had been made, he or she was instructed to press "no"; but if thinking he or she performed badly on a previous trial, the subject was told to press "yes" because we arbitrarily defined cognitive responses to events in a concurrent trial as perceptual, and to those of an earlier trial, memorial. The participant was told to press "no" if he or she felt hungry; but if he or she imagined a hot, juicy cheeseburger, the subject was to press "yes" because the cheeseburger was not a stimulus event within the trial interval. We next followed the examples with a test that consisted of a number of additional examples. If the potential subject passed 9 out of 10 consecutive items, he or she was given preliminary training on the task and then on random trials queried on his or her basis for making yes and no responses. Agreement with the experimenter on 9 out of 10 successive queries allowed the subject to proceed with the experiment. When sessions ran for multiple days, reliability checks were made on each successive session.

Although training the TUIT judgment was complex, the judgment once learned was easy and fast. One of our reasons for not asking the participants to make a more complex judgment about the quality of her or his imagery and thought or to scale the magnitude of TUIT was that the decision process of satisfying a more complex criteria would surely have interrupted the ongoing flow of imagery and thought. Once the outside thought judgment became almost automatic for the subject, the entire session became like a single state from which multiple yes or no samples of TUIT were obtained and used to compute a single value of p(TUIT). One major advantage of this multisampled simple judgment was that once the task and judgment were well learned they proceeded with little apparent interference with the ongoing thought and imagery itself. Our personal impression was that once participants adapted to the experimental procedure there were no carry over interference effects from the act of reporting TUIT at the end of one trial to the resumption of TUIT about a second later on the subsequent trial. Indeed, the next study described here shows how we were able to test this assumption.

We may assume that if the neurocognitive processes that produce TUIT within a trial are constant throughout the trial then the act of making a yes or no TUIT judgment at the end of a trial interval will not interfere with the rate of producing TUIT at the beginning of the next trial. Conversely, if the judgment process does suppress TUIT production in the subsequent trial, then the reduction should be greatest at trial onset and be followed by a higher rate of TUIT production in the later part of each trial. In distinction to $p(TUIT_t)$ which equals the probability that TUIT occurs in a trial of duration t, we let λ_{TUIT} equal the probability that TUIT occurs in any given small interval. Although λ_{TUIT} has a Poisson distribution, the relation of λ_{TUIT} to $p(TUIT_t)$ may be illustrated with the binomial distribution of $p(TUIT_t)$ which approximates the Poisson. Consider that a 30-second trial consists of two consecutive 15-second halves, each with $p(TUIT_{15}) = 0.5$, and remember that if TUIT occurs in the first half, the second, or both, the TUIT response for the 30-second trial = 1. If λ_{TUIT} is constant throughout the trial, then, $p(TUIT_{30}) = 0.75$ $(.5 + .5 - .5^2)$ and $p(TUIT_{60})$—two consecutive 30-second trials = $(.75 + .75 - .75^2) = 0.9375$. One can see that if λ_{TUIT} is constant throughout a trial, $p(TUIT_t)$ is a negatively increasing function of trial duration, t, rather than a linear function.

Now return to the question of TUIT suppression at trial onset. The question translates to the suppression of λ_{TUIT} suppression at trial onset and the null hypothesis is that λ_{TUIT} is constant throughout the trial. We tested the hypothesis by varying trial duration over durations from 2 minutes, 1 minute, 30 seconds to 1/32 minute (1.875 seconds). Participants were run over 2 weeks to obtain 100 readings at each of the seven trial durations. Our data supported the Poisson model, namely that $p(TUIT-\lambda)$ is constant across time within the trial.

With respect to the original question, this means that the processes that generate TUIT generally start at the beginning of each trial and continue at a constant rate—depending on task information rate and individual disposition to produce TUIT. For one participant, however, TUIT production was delayed a fraction of a second into the new trial and for another, TUIT production started almost a second before trial onset. For that individual, TUIT was apparently sustained even during the brief reporting interval of approximately 1 second, leading to an erroneous reporting of TUIT within this interval. But the good news was that in asking participants to make a very simple judgment about TUIT there was little interference with TUIT production, at least at levels that we could measure. We were surprised by the kinds of questions that our results were forcing us to ask. Before starting the laboratory experiments we generally assumed that imaginal thought and fantasy started only after a long period of monotony. Now we were entertaining the idea of switching to such imagery in fractions of a second.

Now that we have described our procedures for defining TUIT, we can evaluate the cognitive model that TUIT is designed to test which, in turn, is designed to validate p(TUIT) as a measure of imaginal thought. Our initial model assumes that the common processor accepts input from only one source at a time. Therefore, accepting perceptual input is incompatible with accepting memorial input—the source of TUIT. The model was easily tested by varying the information rate of a visual or auditory encoding task and predicting that p(TUIT) equals a decreasing function of the task information rate. For our first perceptual task, we used an auditory task (stimuli of 1, 2, or 3 tones presented as independent binary digits or bits, $p = 0.5$ each, at one stimulus per 5 seconds, 1 second, or 0.5 seconds. The bit rate thus varied from 0.2 to 6 per second). As predicted, p(TUIT) was a negative linear function of task information rate (Antrobus, 1968). Our basic model was thus supported and the TUIT measure validated.

The study raised several questions that allowed us to start improving the model beyond the simple common sense conception with which we started. We noted that at the highest information presentation rate of 6 bits per second subjects were able to encode correctly only half of the information (i.e., 3 bits per second). But despite their inability to keep up with the task they still reported TUIT at a rate of 0.35 per 15-second trial. This observation suggested several possible alternative explanations. Although the reduction of p(TUIT) as a function of task information rate implies that TUIT interferes with task performance, the lower asymptote of p(TUIT) at 0.35 implies that the common processor apparently cannot or does not completely eliminate TUIT. Many processing units in the central nervous system are biased to respond to change. The response thresholds for these units, or rather networks of neurons, rise quickly when stimuli are repetitive. Despite the high information rate of our task, the superficial sensory features of the stimuli vary within only a small range. Under these circumstances the common processor may be unable to block out competing memorial sources that are less monotonous and associated with personal concerns and values, in a word, more interesting than the task.

Alternative explanations oblige us to make assumptions about the fine-grained cognitive processes within the brief interstimulus intervals within each trial. The simplest explanation for these results is that the central processor switches to the task at the beginning of each stimulus interval, makes a perceptual decision, then a motor response, and then switches back to producing TUIT. As task difficulty increases, response time should increase in an effort to minimize task error. But because stimuli vary in difficulty, difficult stimuli have longer response times, leaving briefer "free-time" intervals available for TUIT production.

Drucker (1969) reasoned that in order to make maximum use of the free time following the motor response to produce TUIT, the common processor should learn to estimate the interstimulus interval. That is, it should be able to anticipate the amount of free time it has before the next simulus. Obviously, this estimate should be more accurate when the interstimulus interval was fixed than variable. To test this assumption, Drucker compared TUIT rates on fixed and varied interstimulus intervals and found, as predicted, a large suppression of p(TUIT) in the varied condition.

Why precisely should stimulus unpredictability suppress TUIT? Does the arrival of the unpredicted stimulus mask the ongoing TUIT and prevent it from being stored in short-term memory? Or does the production of TUIT block recognition of the sensory task signal so that in the varied interval condition the processors must repeatedly switch to a sensory buffer to check whether a task stimulus has been presented? Or does waiting for the stimulus to arrive delay the switching of the processor from TUIT to the sensory task and therefore reduce the time available for processing the task response and leave less time for producing TUIT? If some central processor shared by both the task and TUIT switches back and forth continually between the two inputs, what happens to the TUIT while the task is being processed? Is TUIT really produced in a sequence of tiny discrete windows, each a fraction of a second in duration? If so, is there continuity from one window to the next? Subjects do report sustained fantasies as well as brief flashlike images. But our TUIT response did not distinguish the duration of an image or thought sequence.

If the switching model is correct and there is continuity from one brief interval to the next within a trial, then continuity may be provided by the implicit memory-based processes that are not interfered with by task-related processes. The extensive research on priming and word recognition of the past two decades has shown that auditory and visual stimuli automatically activate the features that represent their meaning and these activated features may facilitate the activation of other items that share some of these features. Moreover, there is substantial evidence that this spreading of activation can take place without conscious awareness (Carr, McCauley, Sperber, & Parmelee, 1982).

That priming can occur without consciousness suggests that the associative sequences that appear to support the continuity of imaginal thought may be similarly sustained even when portions of the associate sequence are not conscious. Such nonconscious associations provide the basis for the continuity of imaginal thought in our experiments where the opportunity for TUIT is continuously interrupted by the processing of sensorimotor task demands.

From a neurocognitive perspective, this nonconscious process may be explained by positing that the common processor is made up of many microprocessors that in turn can be assigned in different ratios to two concurrent tasks. In this model, the task and TUIT are processed in parallel. Performing the task suppresses TUIT by using a portion of the microprocessors that might otherwise be available for processing TUIT. In a more dynamic version of this model—which I favor—the common processor might, during high task rates, process task and TUIT in parallel, but when the task interstimulus intervals are as long as several seconds, switch exclusively to TUIT during those intervals. The lack of reliable online computing ability at the time we carried out these studies made it impossible to clearly support one of these alternative over the other. We did obtain fairly good evidence, however, that p(TUIT) was much higher during the interval between the motor response and subsequent stimulus. Furthermore, when this interval was reduced effectively to 0 seconds (i.e., there was no free time), p(TUIT) remained substantially above 0.0, which implies that task and TUIT also occurred in parallel. This evidence supports that dynamic parallel-switching model in which the rate of producing TUIT is a function of the available processing capacity—both parallel and sequential (Antrobus et al., 1970).

Unfortunately, it is extremely difficult to tell the difference between a pair of truly parallel processes and a single process that rapidly alternates between two tasks. Both may be true, as it appears in this case. A TUIT process may simply slow and save its current state during the fraction of a second when resources are needed for the task and then resume at a higher rate when the perceptual judgment is passed on for a motor response. After we had addressed this issue, Shiffrin and Schneider (1977) and Fisk and Schneider (1984) developed their model of automatic and controlled processes and developed improved criteria for identifying parallel versus sequential processes. It became clear that almost any apparently parallel set of processes might be serial if viewed through a finer temporal lense.

Shiffrin et al. also showed that regardless of the complexity of a task, if the mapping of stimulus to response array remains constant, task performance, with sufficiently long training, tends to become automatized. Translated to our task situation, this suggested that if we studied task and TUIT over an extended period of time, task performance would become so automatized that it would no longer interfere with TUIT, even at high task information rates. PET scan images of brain activation over time on the same task show that the patterns of activated brain regions change and that fewer regions are active as the task is better learned. It can be assumed that many regions of the brain are engaged with a novel task and that learning the pattern configuration of the task stimuli and responses involves learning the minimum brain resources needed to perform the task. As familiarity with the task increases, progressively smaller regions of the brain learn to achieve the same performance level that initially required large areas of the brain. The cortical regions that are most likely to be relieved from active participation in the well-learned task are those that involve sensory images, verbal production, and meaning—the basic elements of consciousness and the essential elements of imaginal thought. If these are the primary common processor regions that are necessary for imaginal thought, then it follows that p(TUIT) should increase as task performance becomes automated.

Two lines of research in our lab suggested some modification and elaboration of this model. The first was based on the time course of physiological activity during task learning and task performance. Like a number of our colleagues, we were looking for cortical and other physiological measures of attention and in some of our studies we were measuring every known physiological variable while the subject learned and performed the task. Observation of one of the first subjects who was encoding auditory signals in a pitch black room revealed that eye movements and eye blinks were totally suppressed when a trial began. Continuing the trial for 5 minutes, we found that the dampening of blinks and saccades gradually weakened and then released completely at the end of the trial. We asked the next subject simply to encode the signals but refrain from the motor response—and got the same effect, although perhaps weaker. Singer and I wanted to know whether the effect was limited to the oculomotor system or more general in scope, so we decided to measure heart and respiration rate, plethysmography, electromyography over the entire body, gross motor activity, and electroencephalography, in addition to blinking and eye movements. We found that every response system was damped when auditory stimuli were encoded (Antrobus, 1973). Although the initial dampening diminished over time, it was clearly observable throughout the hour sessions. Our interpretation was that when subjects are in the early stages of learning the characteristics of a new task, cortical systems that might possibly interfere with the learning process are initially inhibited, and subsequently released from inhibition as the cortical system determines the minimum cortical resources essential to task performance.

The suggestion that one brain region inhibits a second in order to reduce interference from the second requires further study. The inhibition could also function to distribute metabolic resources to where they are most needed. In a recent fMRI study, Schneider (1997) found that 95% of the brain regions that were active during skill acquisition had dropped out, or dropped below an arbitrary activation threshold, during skill performance when the skill was well learned. The drop was particularly pronounced in the frontal cortex that may play a major role in organizing a new skill. As suggested earlier, because of their role in representing personal goals and anticipatory behavior, the frontal cortices may be essential for the production of imaginal thought. This model is consistent with the automatization model later proposed by Shiffrin and Schneider (1977). Unfortunately, we did not measure TUIT concurrently with the shift in the physiological measures during the adaptation period, but we may I think, assume that TUIT was similarly suppressed.

Our one experiment that systematically studied TUIT over a number of sessions was initiated by the inadvertent observation that some of the content of TUIT described subjects' concerns with the experiment itself rather than with personal concerns that we had expected them to report. On further reflection, we realized that the novel characteristics of the experiment and its surroundings were indeed appropriate matter for our subjects' TUIT. As participants in the experiment their personal concerns might include the significance of the experiment, their relation to the experimenter, the implications of their competence, and so forth. We reasoned, however, that if a subject continued on the same task situation for an extended period, the imaginal thought would "work out" solutions to these novel concerns and turn to issues and concerns that were more remote from the immediate experiment.

Because p(TUIT) provided no indication of the content of imaginal thought, we developed an automatic procedure that interrupted the subject at random after making a TUIT yes response, once in each quarter of the session, and then recorded the subject's description of the mentation for that trial. Using a task of moderate difficulty we systematically collected these verbal reports over 11 one-hour sessions. We scored the reported mentation in three categories: the subject's performance on the task; the experimental context, including the purpose of the experiment, equipment design, and subject–experimenter relationship; and, what we called, experiment-remote concerns, such as relationships with family and friends, academic, and financial concerns. The first few sessions consisted of reports such as: "I was wondering how the signals are presented." "Am I doing OK?" "What is the purpose of this study?" "Does the experimenter like me?" But as expected, the imaginal thought in the first two experimental classes gradually diminished in favor of the experimenter-remote fantasies. In fact, the remote category changed from close to zero on the first session to almost 100% on the last. The observed ordering of these shifts answered the question that initiated the study and supported our assumption that the importance of an individual's personal implicit concerns are ordered in magnitude from most significant to least. In a novel situation such as our experiment, subjects are more concerned with the implications of the experiment than anything else; as these concerns are answered they can return to consider the broader spectrum of their interests.

The pattern over sessions did not, however, support the assumption that as the task is learned, some common set of resources initially utilized by the task is progressively freed up for the production of TUIT. Although we did not measure the extent of automatization achieved over the 11 sessions, certainly some substantial task learning took place. But p(TUIT) did not, as predicted, increase. On the other hand, if in defining TUIT we had set the time–space boundaries so that TUIT included only our Class 3 experiment—remote TUIT—which increased over sessions, then we would have found our hypothesis completely confirmed. This conclusion would have conformed to our everyday impression that our fantasies occur only when our surroundings and tasks are thoroughly routinized.

This analysis of variables that interfere with the production of TUIT has focused the consequences of task learning for conceptual content of TUIT. We assume that the features of imagery and thought like those of perception are represented concurrently across many regions of the brain. And we assume that some of the cortical neurons that generate the visual and auditory features of perception are the same neurons that generate these features in imaginal thought. It follows, therefore, that a perceptual encoding task should interfere more with imaginal features in the same rather than a different sensory modality. To test this assumption we (Antrobus et al., 1970) trained one group of subjects to make a TUIT response if and only if the TUIT included at least one visual feature; and a second group, only if the TUIT included an auditory feature. We then compared the p(TUIT) rates of the two groups under both a visual and an auditory encoding task. As expected, we found modality-specific interference with TUIT imagery—as well as the general interference with both classes of TUIT as a function of task information rate.

Recently Teasdale et al. (in press) extended the generality of this model by examining the relation between TUIT, or SIT, production and what Baddeley (1992) and his colleagues called central executive resources, two slave components, an articulatory loop-phonological store and a visual-spatial sketchpad. Similar in its basic conception to the central executive model of Antrobus (1968), Baddeley's central executive resources model (Baddeley, 1986, 1992; Baddeley & Hitch, 1974) is concerned with the pattern of short-term memory resources shared by a wide variety of cognitive tasks. The experiments of Teasdale et al. (in press) support the argument that TUIT production makes use of all three components, the central executive resources, the articulatory loop-phonological store and the visual-spatial sketchpad. Their interference task procedures and experimental designs focus on higher level perceptual processes than our auditory and visual encoding tasks. For example, they use digit span and digit repetition where we use the encoding of pure tone combinations. Our design also separated the sensory modality component from the central processor component. Further research will provide a more precise picture of the patterns of competition for resources. In general, however, the studies are consistent with one another.

Perhaps our greatest goal for the laboratory studies was to obtain evidence in support of the functional value of TUIT. In the discussion of the shift from task-related to experiment-remote TUIT in our 11-session study, we suggested that the subject matter of TUIT was determined by a hierarchial ordering of personal concerns by their importance or value to the individual. Subjects reported fantasy about their experiment-remote personal concerns only after they had spent considerable time producing TUIT about the experiment itself. But the probability that a task concern will be activated is undoubtedly higher when performing the task than when making dinner at home. Therefore, because performing the task increased the accessibility of task concerns over more remote concerns, the ordered shift away from experiment-related TUIT does not provide a good test of the assumption that TUIT is controlled by a hierarchial ordering of personal concerns. Because importance or value and accessibility are confounded, accessibility must be held constant in order to determine the effect of the personal value.

By first identifying personal concerns of particular importance to each of the subjects, and later in an experimental situation presenting background auditory material associated with these concerns, Klinger (1971) showed that matters of personal concern are more likely than is neutral material to modify the subject matter of imaginal thought. That is, fantasies are concerned with discrepancies between goal states and existing states of the individual. Klinger showed that environmental stimuli associated with these concerns are sufficient to initiate sequences of imaginal thought.

Like Klinger, Singer and I wanted to obtain experimental evidence that imaginal thought plays a role in finding solutions to personal problems and concerns. We wanted to test the assumption that when the cognitive system encounters a significant personal concern, it increases the effort to find solutions to this concern. We assumed that a significant personal concern would do more than displace the subject matter of other current concerns in the background. It would increase p(TUIT). From a neuro-cognitive perspective, this means providing more metabolic resources to frontal cortical areas that are processing information at a rate above some hypothetical resting level. The payoff for this increased effort is the increased likelihood in finding a solution to the problem of personal concern.

Our main procedural problem was to create a general personal concern that would have a sufficiently long-lasting effect to yield reliable measures of increased p(TUIT). We wanted to create in the laboratory a personal concern that could be sustained long enough for us to reliably measure its ability to increase p(TUIT)—about 35 minutes (100 trials lasting 15 seconds each). Imaginal thought rarely perseverates on a single personal concern, particularly in physically constrained situations such as sitting in our cubicle or driving home from work. One reason that such thought is not sustained is that the physical constraints of the task prevent the individual from either executing the behaviors that are cued by the imagi-nal thought or even engaging in more deliberate problem solving and planning. In these constrained situations, imaginal thought seems to as-sociate to one particular concern and then move on to another and then another. If many of these associations are related to one particular concern we may assume that concern has a memorial status that enables it to repeatedly capture a large portion of the associative sequences. Using today's neurocognitive concepts we suggest that this memorial status is accomplished by something like a long-term potentiation of a cluster of neurons that represents the concern. This potentiation lowers the response threshold for the cluster of neurons so that the cluster is more readily activated when any other neurons to which it is positively connected are activated. In this sense, the potentiated cluster of neurons, or mini-net-work, attracts associative sequences of thought whenever they come into its vicinity.

If an important personal concern is able to attract only intermittently the associative sequence of imaginal thought, then in order to measure an increment in p(TUIT) elicited by such a concern, the concern must remain in active memory for an hour's time. To accomplish this we created a concern—a stressor—that would be of significant value to everyone. We made the assumption that if a concern had implications for many aspects of one's life, then no matter where one's implicit associative sequence moved, it would activate items that reactivate the original con-cern, which in turn would construct a new schema around that concern. For example, when a close friend is married, the memory of the event may be reactivated every time anything that is associated with that friend—a friend of the friend, the friend's college, or the friend's vocation—comes to mind, so that the image of the marriage may continually reoccur, until all of the associates acquire links to the friend's wedding. Using this concept, we presented subjects shortly before measuring p(TUIT) with a simulated radio broadcast. Half of the subjects heard a broadcast that had extensive implications for their lives; the others received a neutral control broadcast.

The experiment was completed during the Vietnam War when college students were concerned about service in the war—for themselves as well as for their friends. For many students, the concern was a profound moral and life-and-death issue. Before the days of stringent subject review committees we created a broadcast announcing an emergency news bulletin to the effect that the Chinese were entering the war and had attacked our fleet. The U.S. Security Council was to meet in hours and anticipated a major draft announcement. The broadcast was presented after we had trained each subject on the encoding task and the TUIT response and allowed them 10 minutes to relax in a waiting area before returning to complete the 100 trials that we used to assess p(TUIT). Following the Vietnam broadcast, it was difficult to keep the subjects from calling their friends. As expected, p(TUIT) was significantly and substantially higher relative to a control broadcast condition throughout the subsequent session. p(TUIT) increased from 0.32 for the controls to 0.52 for the Vietnam broadcast condition, and the increment was constant across trials (Antrobus et al., 1966).

Postsession debriefing suggested that a wide range of plausible and not-so-plausible images were generated. One subject had a vivid image of enemy soldiers tying him to a tree and piercing his body with bamboo spears! Many reported imagining dramatic war scenes or leaving the country to avoid such a war. These reports suggested that imaginal thought may at least initially focus on the construction of potential threat scenarios as the cognitive system determines that the new information is a matter of personal concern.

Imaginal solutions cannot be generated until the personal threat is first identified. The broadcast did not identify the personal threat; it simply implied it. Although the potential implications of the broadcast were far reaching for each person, substantial cognitive work was necessary to generate the personal implications for each individual. And this cognitive work was carried out concurrently with an encoding task where the interstimulus interval was 1 second. Errors were slightly (.055 vs .045) higher in the Vietnam broadcast condition, which suggests that the added TUIT-producing work was accomplished by increasing the cognitive resources necessary to produce the TUIT rather than by simply crowding into the time normally devoted to processing the task.

Now that we have studied some of the variables that modify imaginal thought in the laboratory we can re-examine the dimensions of imaginal thought from a new perspective. The dimensions refer to individual differences in TUIT. One of our reasons for employing a standardized perceptual-motor task was to establish an accurate procedure for measuring TUIT as close as possible to the moment that it is produced. We did show that there is a significant association between p(TUIT) in the laboratory and our questionnaire measures of imaginal thought (Antrobus, Coleman, & Singer, 1967). That is, people who produced more TUIT in a free environment tended to produce more TUIT in a standardized environment. In developing the standardized measure, we have separated the individual-difference domain into two parts.

We have shown in the laboratory that task (i.e., environmental) characteristics can either diminish TUIT or allow it to flourish. In the real world, people are relatively free to select environments that either interfere with or facilitate imaginal thought. On the other hand, when environmental conditions are invariant as in our experimental conditions, substantial individual variation remains. Let us call the individual differences associated with variation in the environments, $\sigma^2_{TUIT:Env,}$ and individual differences that remain when environmental conditions are held constant, $\sigma^2_{TUIT:Ind \mid Env,}$ so that in a free environment $\sigma^2_{TUIT} = \sigma^2_{TUIT:Env} + \sigma^2_{TUIT:Ind \mid Env}$. It seems quite likely that the two components may identify rather different cognitive and conational processes.

The latter component, $\sigma^2_{TUIT:Ind \mid Env}$., identifies the individual differences in p(TUIT) that are observed when task conditions are held constant as they are in the laboratory. Cohen and Sandberg (1977) and Baddeley (1992) showed that these resources are correlated with general intelligence. For example, the concept of short-term memory developed from digit span memory, and digit span is a component of the Wechsler Adult Intelligence Scale (Baddeley, 1986). Similarly, individual differences in phonological span are correlated with short-term working memory and also with long-term language learning. For example, people who can hold more novel words in short-term memory are more successful at learning a second language.

The first component, $\sigma^2_{TUIT:Env,}$ which we studied in the laboratory by manipulating the information load of our experimental tasks is, in the natural environment, largely under the control of individual volition or preference, and in this sense, conation. The mental health relevance of this variance has emphasized the activities that people engage in to suppress disturbing thought. In one unpublished study we proposed that individual cognitive systems may be biased toward mentation that elicits either depressing or positive affect and that thought suppression achieved by means of interference from some continuous task should attenuate the affective bias. We found that 30 minutes of moderate load task information processing was effective in reducing both affective extremes toward a moderate level. Teasdale (1989) and Teasdale and Barnard (1993) also studied the relation between TUIT or SIT and depression.

Lost in this discussion is how TUIT is reduced by attractive environmental sources that constantly compete for attention. Some of us may prefer our own fantasies, plans, and problem-solving imagery and thought to the environmental alternatives available much of the time. But given the opportunity to sit down with a good book—that's a different matter. Other people tend to choose an environmental source at every opportunity as evidenced by the high rate of watching television. By identifying $\sigma^2_{TUIT:Env}$, we draw attention to the large variety of environments that compete with TUIT. Whether an individual produces TUIT surely depends on the value he or she assigns to attending to the alternatives available in the environment, corrected of course, for the cost of access to those environments. A large part of our economy, the advertising industry as well as the entertainment industry is devoted to capturing people's attention. The ubiquitous presence of electronic devices for communication and entertainment and the increased availability of high speed interactive computing devices is providing us with ever increasing ease, access to much of the world's recorded information. Although access delays currently permit ample time for imaginal thought, improving technology will gradually diminish these opportunities. Fortunately, one of the great advantages of TUIT is the ease with which it can be engaged in whenever and wherever needed.

Interaction with the external world provides us with the information necessary to learn the cognitive structures and knowledge on which all imaginal thought is based. Moreover, theater, movies, novels, and even the Web provide some of the cognitive and affective benefits, such as self-understanding and emotional enrichment, that we attributed to TUIT. Without discussing the specific merits of these alternatives, I suggest simply that an individual's choice, conscious or not, of TUIT versus an environmental source of stimulation is a preference based on some short-term calculus of gain minus cost over a set of alternatives. For example, for any given opportunity to engage in one's own imaginal thought, there may be some alternative environmental source that is equally attractive. By this token, one engages in TUIT only when it is more attractive than the environmental alternatives.

In a preliminary attempt to examine such a preference model, we determined the mean p(TUIT) rates for a small sample of individuals. We then introduced them to an environment they had two choices of how to spend their time. In the sound-attenuated and unilluminated laboratory cubicle they could either play a very simple electronic game or sit alone with their own thoughts. We found a strong association between individual mean p(TUIT) rates in the controlled environment and individual preference for the opportunity to produce TUIT in the free environment; subjects with low p(TUIT) rates preferred the game. It is easy to appreciate that a person who rarely has any imagery might prefer to play a simple game, and it is equally plausible that a person with a prolific mental life might eschew the game.

The preference calculus implies that there is some external source that is sufficiently attractive for the high TUIT subject to prefer that source over TUIT production—at least some of the time. A preference calculus must also account for the dynamic interaction of benefits and costs that determine the relative attractiveness of environmental sources and TUIT processes. One assumes that the benefits of either alternative saturate over time and further that the cost of responding to environmental sources accumulate over time so that preference should alternate between the two sources.

The increasingly convenient availability of attractive competitors for attention, competitors that reduce the time and effort we devote to producing our own mental thought raise again the question about the long-term consequences of the battle. Just as the invention of paper all but eliminated the reliance of our ancestors on rote memorization so too the media seems to be replacing much of our imaginal thought. Obviously, much of the knowledge from which imagery and thought are constructed derives from environmental sources and these include the media. We simply do not yet know enough about the cognitive abilities that produce imaginal and creative thought, anticipatory, planned, and problem-solving thought to predict the long-term effects of heavy dependency on these media.

The work of the Singers documenting the long-term consequences of television watching stands out as the major effort to understand the cognitive effects of passive media watching (see chapter 13). But we have many other electronic devices to ease our cognitive workload. They extend our knowledge bases and cognitive skills by eliminating other cognitive skills. Those who use electronic calculators are aware of some loss of some facility in mental calculation. One may speculate that the replacement of recall processes by recognition cues in window-driven choices on our computers not only weakens our learning of computer addresses and instructions but over the long term, our ability to learn the relations that we need to access memories unassisted. We need to know whether the long-term reliance on convenient recognition-based memory access will have, like the effect of paper on rote memory skills, a detrimental effect on our memory retrieval ability.

The bottom–up processes of perceptual recognition and top–down processes of memory retrieval, imaginal production, and thought appear to share many subsystems or modules, but they do not necessarily share the connections between those subsystems. To facilitate our use of electronic information systems such as the Web, the architecture of such information networks increasingly mimics that of human associative architectures and, among heavy Web users, private association architectures may increasingly mimic that of the Web. But the heavy reliance on external prompts to navigate the Web reduces the need to acquire one's own internal web or network and one's ability to navigate it without external aid.

Examining the neural structures and modeling their putative cognitive processes helps to understand their differences. The 10-to-1 ratio of top–down to bottom–up fibers between the visual cortex and lateral geniculate nucleus suggests that the two processes are not isomorphic. Hinton, Dayan, Frey, and Neal (1995) and Dayan and Hinton (1996) created neural net models of how the brain might generate as a top–down process, internal models of the outside world. Although they called their model of bottom–up perceptual processes, "wake" and their top–down processes "sleep," the latter is equally appropriate as a model of TUIT production. Although their work is still in progress and does not address some important characteristics of imaginal thought, it nevertheless provides a solid base on which future models of perception and imagination may be developed. But their sleep model does caution against assuming that the acquisition of perceptual processes is a sufficient condition for the acquisition of what Singer (1966) called the cognitive skills on which imaginal thinking depends.

The great advantages of paper, calculators, and computers for the enhancement of human knowledge cannot be denied. Nor can it be denied that knowledge itself has greatly enriched our mental experience. But we have yet to determine whether the great ease with which we can now access this knowledge will weaken our cognitive ability to access and creatively manipulate the knowledge in our own minds unassisted.

REFERENCES

Antrobus, J. S. (1968). Information theory and stimulus-independent thought. *British Journal of Psychology, 59*, 423–430.

Antrobus, J. S. (1973). Eye movements and non-visual cognitive tasks. In V. Zikmund (Ed.), *The oculomotor system and brain functions* (pp. 355–368). Bratislava, Czechoslovakia: Slovak Academy of Sciences.

Antrobus, J. (1991). Dreaming: Cognitive processes during cortical activation and high afferent thresholds. *Psychological Review, 98*, 96–121.

Antrobus, J. S., Coleman, R., & Singer, J. L. (1967). Signal detection performance by subjects differing in predisposition to daydreaming. *Journal of Consulting Psychology, 31*, 487–491.

Antrobus, J. S., Singer, J. L., Goldstein, S., & Fortgang, M. (1970). Mindwandering and cognitive structure. *Transactions of the New York Academy of Sciences, 32*, 242–252.

Antrobus, J. S., Singer, J. L., & Greenberg, S. (1966). Studies in the stream of consciousness: Experimental suppression of spontaneous cognitive processes. *Perceptual and Motor Skills, 23*, 399–417.

Aserinsky, E., & Kleitman, N. (1955). Regularly occurring periods of ocular motility and concomitant phenomena during sleep. *Science, 118*, 361–375.

Baddeley, A. D. (1986). *Working memory*. Oxford: Oxford University Press.

Baddeley, A. D. (1992). Working memory. *Science, 255*, 556–559.

Baddeley, A. D., & Hitch, G. J. (1974). Working memory. In G. Bower (Ed.), *Recent advances in learning and motivation* (Vol. 8). New York: Academic Press.

Bellow, S. (1964). *Herzog*. New York: Viking Press.

Broadbent, D. E. (1958). *Perception and communication*. Elmsford, NY: Pergamon.

Carr, T. H., McCauley, C., Sperber, R. D., & Parmelee, C. M. (1982). Words, pictures and priming: On semantic activation, conscious identification, and the automaticity of information processing. *Journal of Experimental Psychology: Human Perception and Performance, 8*, 757–777.

Cohen, R. L., & Sandberg, T. (1977). Relation between intelligence and short-term memory. *Cognitive Psychology, 9*, 534–554.

Courtney, S. (1997, February) *Functional MRI studies of visual perception and working memory*. Paper presented at the 22nd Annual Interdisciplinary Conference, Jackson Hole, WY.

Dayan, P., & Hinton, G. E. (1996). Varieties of Helmholtz machine. *Neural Networks, 9*, 1385–1403.

Drucker, E. (1969). *Uncertainty of signal presentation pattern and suppression of spontaneous thought*. Unpublished doctoral dissertation, City University of New York, New York.

Fookson, J., & Antrobus, J. (1989). *A neural network model for switching between task and personal concern imagery and thought*. Unpublished program.

Fisk, A. D., & Schneider, W. (1984). Memory as a function of attention, level of processing and automatization. *Journal of Experimental Psychology: Learning Memory and Cognition, 10*, 181–197.

Gendrin, D. M., & Werner, B. L. (1996–1997). Internal dialogues about conflict: Implications for managing marital discord. *Imagination, Cognition and Personality, 16*, 125–138.

Huba, G. J., Aneshensel, C. S., & Singer, J. L. (1981). Development of scales for three second-order factors of inner experience. *Multivariate Behavioral Research, 16*, 181–206.

Huba, G. J., & Tanaka, J. S. (1983–1984). Confirmatory evidence for three daydreaming factors in the short imaginal processes inventory. *Imagination, Cognition and Personality, 3*, 139–147.

Hinton, G. E., Dayan, P., Frey, B. J., & Neal, R. M. (1995). The "wake–sleep" algorithm for unsupervised neural networks. *Science, 268*, 1158–1161.

Klinger, E. (1971). *Structure and functions of fantasy*. New York: Wiley.

Kosslyn, S. M. (1994). *Image and brain: The resolution of the imagery debate*. Cambridge, MA: MIT Press.

Meyer, D. E., & Kieras, D. E. (1997). A computational theory of executive cognitive processes and multiple-task performance: Part 1. Basic mechanisms. *Psychological Review, 104*, 3–65.

Moray, N. (1967). Where is capacity limited? A survey and a model. *Acta Psychologica, 27*, 84–92.

Mueller, E. T. (1989). *Daydreaming in humans and machines: A computer model of the stream of thought*. Norwood, NJ: Ablex.

Norman, D. A. (1968). Toward a theory of memory and attention. *Psychological Review, 75*, 522–536.

Posner, M. I. (1978). *Chronometric explorations of the mind*. Hillsdale, NJ: Lawrence Erlbaum Associates.

Rumelhart, D. E., & McClelland, J. L. (Eds.). (1986). *Parallel distributed processing* (Vol. 2). Cambridge, MA: MIT Press.

Rumelhart, D. E., Smolensky, P., McClelland, J. L. & Hinton, G. E. (1986). Schemata and sequential thought processes in PDP models. In D. E. Rumelhart & J. L. McClelland (Eds.), *Parallel distributed processing* (Vol. 2, pp. 7–57). Cambridge, MA: MIT Press.

Schneider, W. (1997, February). *Brain imaging of circuits involved in acquisition but not execution of skills.* Paper presented at the 22nd Annual Interdisciplinary Conference, Jackson Hole, WY.

Shiffrin, R. M., & Schneider, W. (1977). Controlled and automatic human information processing: II. Perceptual learning, automatic attending, and a general theory. *Psychological Review, 84,* 127–190.

Singer, J. L. (1966). *Daydreaming.* New York: Random House.

Singer, J. L., & Antrobus, J. S. (1966). *The imaginal processes inventory* (filed with The Test Collection, #004304, Set C). Princeton, NJ: Educational Testing Service.

Singer, J. L., & Antrobus, J. S. (1972). Dimensions of daydreaming: A factor analysis of imaginal processes and personality scales. In P. Sheehan (Ed.), *The nature and function of imagery* (pp. 175–202). New York: Academic Press.

Teasdale, J. D. (1989). Daydreaming, depression and distraction. *The Psychologist, 2,* 189–190.

Teasdale, J. D., & Barnard, P. J. (1993). *Affect, cognition, and, change: Remodelling depressive thought.* Hove, England: Lawrence Erlbaum Associates.

Teasdale, J. D., Dritschel, B. H., Taylor, M. J., Proctor, L., Lloyd, C. A., Nimmo-Smith, I., & Baddeley, A. D. (in press). *Memory and Cognition.*

Werbos, P. J. (1994, June). *Neural nets, consciousness, ethics and the soul.* Paper presented at the World Congress on Neural Networks, San Diego, CA.

2

Thought Flow: Properties and Mechanisms Underlying Shifts in Content

Eric Klinger
University of Minnesota, Morris

This chapter sketches a brief history of modern investigation of thought flow, from the systematic introspective analysis of daydreaming by Varendonck (1921), to its placement on a modern behavior-scientific foundation by Singer (1966), to work on response organization, dreaming, and cognitive interference, and finally to its analysis within current-concerns theory. Evidence confirms that *concerns* (latent time-binding states that extend from the initiation of commitment to a goal pursuit to its termination) account for the control of attention, perception, and moment-to-moment changes in thought content through focus on, and processing of, cues related to current goal pursuits. The effects, which appear to be automatic and perhaps inexorable, may be mediated by emotional responses potentiated by the concerns. This chapter further describes both intraindividual dimensions and properties of thought flow assessed with thought-sampling methods, and individual differences in thought flow assessed with questionnaires.

Despite the popularity of James' (1890/1950) chapter and concept of the Stream of Consciousness, psychology has devoted relatively little solid research to describing and explaining the sequencing of thought content—to what starts and stops particular segments of thought or, more generally, of *mentation* (all mental content, regardless of its particular properties, verbal or otherwise). Nevertheless, enough data have accumulated to permit some statements about some useful dimensions of thought flow and of the factors that trigger shifts in its content.

A BRIEF HISTORY OF THOUGHT-FLOW RESEARCH

During much of the 20th century, psychologists adopted an associationist view of the sequencing of mentation. People were assumed to have learned associative links between words or other units, so that perceiving or thinking about one thing greatly increased the likelihood of next thinking about whatever was most strongly associated with it. This was a view propounded earlier by prominent associationist philosophers, beginning no later than Aristotle and emphasized again by empiricist philosophers including Hobbes, James Mill, John Stuart Mill, and Thomas Brown. This view was strengthened by Pavlovian and Ebbinghausian experiments, and was carried forward into the verbal learning subdiscipline that preceded psycholinguistics and the modern cognitive sciences. Verbal-learning investigators developed extensive catalogues of word associations, based on empirically derived word association norms, to lay the basis for predicting the order in which words would appear in both word-association experiments and natural language. It may have appeared to potential thought-flow theorists of that time that more research into thought sequencing would belabor the obvious.

The 1960s proved to be the Waterloo of simplistic associationism. For example, Chomsky (1959) devastated the Skinnerian position on language acquisition and production (e.g., Skinner, 1953), and the eminent, formerly associationist investigator Deese (1965) realized that word association norms completely lacked the ability to predict word order in natural language. Psycholinguistics largely abandoned simple associationism, and the question of what people will think of next became once again an open question. Meanwhile, data were beginning to accumulate in four subject areas relevant to thought flow: response organization, daydreaming, night dreaming, and cognitive interference.

Response Organization, Chunking, and the Nature of Behavioral Segmentation

After the abandonment of simple associationist views, the new look in theory of response organization was distinctly hierarchical. Older, prenetwork theory, especially stimulus–response and response–response associationism, viewed the unfolding of behavior as essentially a Markov process, in which each new response unit is determined by association with only the immediately preceding response unit or stimulus. For example, each word (or at least each meaning unit) in this sentence would be determined strictly by its association with the immediately preceding word or meaning unit. In the 1960s, however, theorists began to posit organizational brain events that controlled all of the units in a behavioral segment. Thus, all of the words in this sentence would be functionally dependent not on the immediately preceding words but on the grammar plan of the whole sentence (Miller, 1965), a brain event that must precede each sentence or other linguistic segment in order for it to occur.

Keele (1968), interested in musical and athletic performance rather than language, created a similar construct that he called the *motor program*. This construct continues to guide research and has begun to define a research area (e.g., Wulf, Schmidt, & Deubel, 1993). In a formal sense, the motor program closely resembles Miller's concept of grammar plans—an organizational response within the brain that encodes and controls the unfolding of a segment of behavior. I attempted to generalize these concepts under the rubric of *meaning complexes* (Klinger, 1971), a term that has not been adopted by other writers. Nevertheless, the concept of meaning complex serves to generalize the concepts of grammar plan and motor program to all realms of human response, including the covert responses of mentation. It also contains important theoretical consequences for theories of thought and dream flow, including the special case of schizophrenic inner experience and communication.

The concept of meaning complex incorporates the two English senses of meaning: *semantic meaning* in language (what an utterance is intended to mean) and *intention* (what an individual means to do). It implies that every behavioral sequence is chunked into naturally delimited segments and subsegments, with the response components of a particular segment controlled by a corresponding meaning complex. These meaning complexes are not themselves static units of a response repertoire but are assembled afresh for each act, although in patterns established through prior overlearning. (See Smith, 1996, for a contemporary view of the processes by which meaning complexes might develop and be assembled.) The concept also implies that every segment is defined by progression toward a preselected end point, a goal; it implies that all nonreflexive behavior is organized and guided, rather than ballistic.

In this conception, the thoughts and image sequences of mentation are organized into segments and are guided in a way similar to overt behavior. However, there are also important differences between the covert segments of mentation and the overt segments of action. Much of the time, mental segments are triggered by stimuli under conditions in which no useful goal striving is possible, at least in relation to whatever triggered the segment. In those circumstances, the segments manifest internal organization, but are neither controlled by the higher order guidance and constraints of operant goal striving, nor evaluated for how well they advance one toward a goal. They correspond to the inner experience of daydreaming (including mind wandering) or, in sleep, of dreaming.

Under the latter conditions and some others (e.g., great fatigue, certain drugged states, certain psychotic states), meaning-complex control over unfolding segments degenerates. Then, the normal inhibition of competing responses deteriorates. As a result, segments are often interrupted and prevented from reaching their normal end points. They may also fuse with competing tendencies. This interruption and fusion leads to the greater drifting, discontinuity, and symbolic fusion of psychotic thought and dreams.

Given these considerations, the foci of this chapter can be restated: What are the properties of mental segments, and what are the factors that determine their onset and content?

Daydream Research

The psychology of thinking has focused largely on its formal properties: the ability to solve problems; the steps necessary to do so; and the search for, uptake, and use of available information. Investigators have paid relatively little attention to the specific sequencing of content or the nature of segmentation in thought. One major exception to this generalization is the study of daydreaming, in which problem solving is at best an incidental benefit, and in which sequencing is presumably not governed by logical rules.

The systematic observation and investigation of daydreaming began most clearly with one of Sigmund Freud's disciples, Varendonck, whose book *The Psychology of Daydreams* (1921) laid out in exquisite detail his painstaking introspective observations, meticulously recorded over years, of his own daydream experiences. Varendonck arrived at conclusions about the properties of daydreaming that still appear valid (parenthesized references below are to subsequent data consistent with Varendonck's conclusions). For example:

1. Daydreams are composed of behavioral fragments already in the daydreamer's repertoire (Griffith's [1935] pre-established properties of play).
2. Daydreams come in clear segmental units, such that one can delineate the beginning and end of a daydream and also of subunits within it (Klinger, 1971).
3. Their content may be playful but is more often a quite sober treatment of serious themes (Klinger, 1977, 1990; Klinger, Barta, & Maxeiner, 1980; Singer, 1966).
4. Segments of fantasy are instigated by bursts of affective response, often to some secondary feature of the preceding thought segment.
5. The contents of daydreaming tend to drift, distinguishing them from working thought.
6. Although daydreaming is directly or indirectly about daydreamers' serious goal pursuits, it lacks a disciplined focus on working toward

a goal—the intervention of will—and is more an affectively toned reaction to preceding cues (what I have termed, borrowing Skinner's word, *respondent* activity [Klinger, 1971]) than a proactive attempt at goal attainment (*operant* activity).

7. By the same token, daydream segments are free of evaluations of how well they are advancing daydreamers toward their goals and are free of attempts to direct the daydreamer's attention back to a problem (Klinger, 1974).

The first substantial research program about daydreaming in the modern scientific–psychological tradition is J. L. Singer's, the first stages of which are brought together in his 1966 book, *Daydreaming: An Introduction to the Experimental Study of Inner Experience*. This groundbreaking book stimulated a large research literature about daydreaming (Klinger, 1990; Singer, 1975), both by J. L. Singer, John Antrobus, and their colleagues and by many others, including Leonard Giambra, Ruth and Steven Gold, Russell Hurlburt, and Steven Starker. This is not the place in which to review such a large, diverse literature, which also addresses assessment methods, individual and group differences, relation to sexual activity and to psychopathology, and possible functions and liabilities. However, it is worth noting two key research areas among the several to which Singer's and Antrobus' own joint research contributed. First, it delineated conditions governing the frequency of daydream (task-irrelevant) episodes: They declined with greater task-related stimulation, with more complex tasks, and with greater incentives for good task performance; they increased after emotionally arousing, threatening news (Antrobus, Singer, & Greenberg, 1966), and conflict (Klos & Singer, 1981). Second, their research produced a major questionnaire to assess individual daydreaming tendencies, the Imaginal Processes Inventory (Huba, Aneshensel, & Singer, 1981; Huba, Singer, & Aneshensel, & Antrobus, 1982; Singer & Antrobus, 1970), and established three reasonably replicable factors underlying individual differences in these tendencies (Huba, Aneshensel, & Singer, 1981; Tanaka & Huba, 1985–86).

One conclusion that might be drawn from these results is that daydream-like activity—unbidden, undirected, drifting—represents a kind of human mental baseline. This activity automatically fills in the mental spaces not pre-empted by directed, working thought. The greater the pressure to focus on particular tasks, the more the undirected activity is crowded out. The more the individual has pressing and emotionally laden issues separate from a task at hand, the harder it is to crowd out the undirected activity.

During the 1970s, the field was enriched by the addition of sampling methods, variously termed thought sampling (Klinger, 1978; Klinger, Barta,

& Mahoney, 1976; Klinger & Cox, 1987–88; Klinger & Kroll-Mensing, 1995), consciousness sampling (Hurlburt, 1979, 1990, 1993), and experience sampling (Csikszentmihalyi & Larson, 1984, 1987; Csikszentmihalyi, Larson, & Prescott, 1977). These all trained research participants to respond to investigator-controlled stimuli, such as beeps, with more or less detailed reports of their inner experiences just before the signal. They have made possible observation much less limited by memory or encumbered by generalizations about oneself that affect responses to standard questionnaires. They have provided detailed characterizations of the properties of conscious flow, which are described later. They also made possible detailed examination of the effects of experimental interventions on conscious experience, with strong implications for the mechanisms that shift mental content.

The 1970s also saw the advent of a comprehensive, systematic, integrated theory of fantasy (Klinger, 1971) and a formulation of motivational and emotional influences on thought content (Klinger, 1975, 1977). This work introduced the construct of *current concern* to label the hypothetical process active during the time that one has a goal. Any goal pursuit that is more than momentary requires some kind of underlying brain process that keeps behavior aimed at the goal, or that returns behavior to the goal following interruption. This brain process can also be regarded as a goal-specific state that lasts until the goal is either reached or relinquished. This is the process or state to which the term *current concern* refers. Thus, for each goal there is, theoretically, its own corresponding current concern that remains in force until the goal is reached or relinquished.

In colloquial English, the word "concern" connotes something happening in consciousness, but in this theoretical usage it has the status of a hypothetical construct, referring to a nonconscious brain process. It theoretically and demonstrably does influence the contents of consciousness— what people attend to, recall, and think about—but it does not itself refer to a conscious process. In fact, most of the time during which one harbors a long-lasting concern, one's consciousness is focused on something else. However, methods for assessing current concerns have so far relied on conscious self-reports elicited through interviews, ratings, or questionnaires such as the Motivational Structure Questionnaire (Cox & Klinger, 1988; Donovan, 1995; Klinger, 1978; Klinger, Cox, & Blount, 1995). This construct generated an increasing number of empirical studies, some of which are reviewed here.

Dream Research

Sampling approaches entered daydream research from their earlier successful use in the experimental study of dreams. Combined with measures of rapid eye movements (REM) and electroencephalographic (EEG) activity, one of their earliest yields was to show that the approximately 90-minute periodicity of REM was associated with marked differences in mentation: more vivid, dreamlike mental content during REM and more thoughtlike, less vivid content during non-REM periods (Aserinsky & Kleitman, 1953). This periodicity was subsequently found in measures of waking daydreaming as well (Kripke & Sonnenschein, 1978).

This finding, along with numerous others (Klinger, 1971, 1990), leads to the likely conclusion that mentation flows continually, during both waking and sleeping, in rather similar ways, modulated by physiological states such as sleep, but nevertheless responding to at least some of the same determinants and through at least some of the same mechanisms. Waking daydreams are more coherent and less bizarre (Williams, Merritt, Rittenhouse, & Hobson, 1992), but the differences are a matter of degree.

Cognitive Interference Research

Among the most powerful sources of cognitive interference are states of anxiety and depression. Both, although in somewhat different ways, interfere with ability to concentrate, and each is characterized by particular kinds of thoughts identified with it.

One kind of cognitive interference is *preoccupation*—thoughts about one thing that get in the way of doing or thinking about something else. When preoccupation takes the form of mulling perceived threats to one's goal pursuits, it is often labeled *worry* (Vasey & Borkovec, 1992). As a major component of anxiety, its dominant emotional responses are the negative ones such as fear or anger (e.g., Davey, 1994; Eysenck & Van Berkum, 1992). Overly repetitive thought, as part of worry or of other kinds of thought, is generally labeled *rumination* (e.g., Lyubomirsky & Nolen-Hoeksema, 1993; Martin & Tesser, 1996). Rumination is associated with goal pursuits that are mired down or in the process of disengagement, and its dominant emotional responses are anger, sadness, and fear. Rumination is a characteristic symptom of depression and other states related to major stressful life events (Tait & Silver, 1989), although it may also accompany positive moods, such as those associated with being in love.

Another kind of interference relates to attention and memory. Retrieval of material from memory has repeatedly been shown to be biased in the direction of mood-congruent content (Bower, 1992). This bias is not just a matter of valence—positive versus negative—but is specific to the type of negative affect: Depressed individuals tend to recall depressive content, and anxious individuals tend to recall anxious content (Ingram, Kendall, Smith, Donnell, & Ronan, 1987). A somewhat similar specificity can be seen in Stroop-like interference patterns (Carter, Maddock, & Magliozzi, 1992), in which research participants take longer to name ink colors of emotionally relevant words than of other words. Because such effects do not show up after depression has remitted (Lewinsohn & Rosenbaum, 1987), they are probably attributable to mood states rather than to more enduring cognitive traits of the individual.

In the case of attention, depressed individuals are more attentive to depressive cues than are nondepressed individuals (Gottlib, McLachlan, & Katz, 1988), and anxious individuals respond more quickly to threat-related than to threat-unrelated stimuli (using a probe method) in ways that indicate greater attentiveness to threat cues (Broadbent & Broadbent, 1988; Fox, 1993). This differential attentiveness presumably accounts for panic-disorder patients' selectively slower color naming of threat words in a Stroop-like task (Ehlers, Margraf, Davies, & Roth, 1988).

Without meaning to understate the complexities of these findings, it is possible to summarize the results using the following generalizations: If the emotionally arousing stimuli are central to the target task—and are therefore at the focus of processing—they facilitate perceptual and attentional responses. If, on the other hand, incidental stimuli are emotionally arousing, they distract from the target task and slow reaction time. In general, people also retain emotionally arousing stimuli better than other stimuli and experience more thoughts triggered by them.

DETERMINANTS OF THOUGHT FLOW:
MECHANISMS FOR SHIFTING MENTAL CONTENT

The data from these various research traditions suggested an evolving model of the determinants of thought flow (Klinger, 1971, 1990, 1996). The model focuses on the factors responsible for shifting content from one topic to another—in other words, the processes that shape segmentation in conscious flow. In summary, the current model asserts that thought content shifts when an individual encounters a cue that arouses emotion because of its association with one of the individual's current concerns, as already defined. The thought so triggered is likely to pertain to the respective concern. The cues may be either external, such as speech, writing, or nonverbal events, or they may be internal, such as features of the ongoing stream of thought, including mental imagery, either verbal or not. This model is capable of explaining the results described previously with emotionally evocative stimuli in cognitive interference.

The existence of emotional reactivity to cues associated with goal pursuits does not mean a full-blown emotional reaction to each cue that might be so associated. Rather, there are several points at which cues are screened. At the earliest point, the individual processes gross features of a cue and, if an association with a goal pursuit exists, responds with a purely central, nonconscious *protoemotional response*. It is too early to specify the brain processes involved in protoemotional responding, although, given the architecture of the brain (e.g., LeDoux, 1989, 1995), various limbic structures are likely candidates, especially the amygdala and hippocampus. A protoemotional response instigates further cognitive processing, which may confirm or disconfirm the relevance of the cue. In the case of disconfirmation, processing ends, whereas in the case of confirmation, processing proceeds further or is channeled into action, depending on the situation and on the extent of cognitive closure about the cue. At various points in this process, the cue may still be dismissed, terminating processing; or, as the meaning of the cue becomes clearer, the protoemotional process may gradually recruit other components of emotional response—glandular (e.g., adrenal, dermal), effector (e.g., facial, postural), and conscious components, including associated thought content.

Evidence of Current-Concern and Protoemotional Effects on Cognitive Processing

Initial investigations of this model employed dichotic listening to two similar, simultaneous, 15-minute narratives, one to each ear. At intervals, the narratives were modified by inserting words that would presumably be associated with one of the participant's own current concerns in one channel, and synchronously the opposite narrative was modified to allude to another individual's concern that was seemingly not among the participant's concerns. These conditions were balanced with respect to side, left or right. Participants used a toggle switch to signal the channel to which they were currently listening. A few seconds after each of these modified passages played, the tape stopped with a signal tone, at which point participants reported and rated last thoughts and also reported the last segments of the tape they could recall hearing. The effects of conditions were quite powerful (Klinger, 1978). Participants spent significantly more time listening to passages associated with their own concerns, recalled those passages much more often, and had thought content that (by ratings of blind judges) was much more often related to them than to the passages opposite them, which were related to another's concerns.

Other studies of both waking and sleeping participants indicated that these effects could not be attributed to a conscious process, such as deliberately focusing on concern-related stimuli. Rather, they are apparently nonconscious and automatic. In fact, concern-related stimuli seem to impose an extra cognitive-processing load, even when they are peripheral and participants are consciously ignoring them (Young, 1987), slowing reaction to a target lexical-decision task. Similar effects have been shown in yet other cognitive processes, Stroop and quasi-Stroop procedures, with slower reaction times in naming the color of the ink in which concern-related words are printed than that of nonconcern-related words (Johnsen, Laberg, Cox, Vaksdal, & Hugdahl, 1994; Riemann, Amir, & Louro, 1995; Riemann & McNally, 1995). Concern-related stimuli influence dream content during sleep much more reliably than do other stimuli (Hoelscher, Klinger, & Barta, 1981; Nikles, Brecht, Klinger, & Bursell, 1998). Data also link current concerns to electrodermal responses of the kind often identified as orienting responses, and they link spontaneous electrodermal activity to current-concern-related ideation (Nikula, Klinger, & Larson-Gutman, 1993). Taken together, these results confirmed that the effects of concern-related cues on cognitive processing are substantially automatic and are probably inexorable.

A number of indications from these and other data (e.g., Klinger, Barta, & Maxeiner, 1980) suggested that a critical property of current concerns is to dispose individuals to respond emotionally to cues associated with corresponding goal pursuits. The emotional response then induces a number of levels of cognitive processing, ending, at least in some conditions, with conscious thought. Because this hypothesis is difficult to test with naturally occurring thought flow, the investigations to which it gave rise addressed effects on attention, recall, and event-related brain potentials (ERPs). A reaction-time experiment (Schneider,1987) produced effects of emotionally evocative cues (which participants were instructed to ignore) on choice reaction time similar to those obtained with current-concern-related words by Young (1987). Furthermore, participants who scored high on the Affective Intensity Measure (Larsen & Diener, 1987) were slowed by emotionally arousing distractors significantly more than other participants were.

The ability of words to affect emotions (*emotional arousingness*) also affects recall. Words rated by participants as either relatively emotionally arousing or concern-related were later recalled significantly more often than other words (Bock & Klinger, 1986). Concern-relatedness and emotional-arousal value were strongly intercorrelated. Partialing emotionality and concern-relatedness of words out of each other (Klinger, Bock, & Bowi, 1990) suggested that the effect of current concerns on recall is mediated by the emotional responses largely potentiated by the concerns. This interpretation is consistent with other findings that people experience more emotion in relation to those autobiographical memories that are most closely associated with current goal pursuits and longer-term personal strivings (Singer & Salovey, 1993).

These findings help to make sense of the results described previously, in which emotional attributes of stimuli facilitate cognitive processing when the stimuli are central to a task at hand, and interfere with cognitive processing when they are distractors. Close examination of procedures used in such studies suggests that people respond to cues as emotionally arousing insofar as the cues are related to current concerns. Thus, patients suffering from social phobias attend differentially to socially threatening stimuli, but not to physically threatening ones, whereas people fearful of physical harm attend to the latter but not the former (Mogg, Mathews, & Eysenck, 1992).

To explore the timing of protoemotional effects on cognitive processing, we have begun to examine the effects of the concern-relatedness and emotional arousingness of words on visual ERPs. The logic underlying this work is that if stimuli differing in their concern-relatedness or emotional arousingness produce different effects on participants' EEG traces by a certain point in time, this must mean that the brain has already identified some aspect of concern-relatedness by that time. Our work built on previous findings by Naumann, Bartussek, Diedrich, and Laufer (1992), who showed that emotionally arousing stimuli elevated P300 components (positive EEG deflections about 250 to 700 ms after onset of the stimuli) of ERPs. Our findings (Klinger, Goetzman, Hughes, & Seppelt, 1996) confirmed theirs and indicated effects of concern-relatedness of words on the ERPs as well. The effects of concern-relatedness appear to extend to even earlier ERP components than the P300, at some sites even before 100 ms following stimulus onset, suggesting that these features of concern relevance may be detected at or near the outset of cognitive processing.

PROPERTIES OF THOUGHT FLOW

The model of thought flow described here primarily explains shifts in mental content, but it grew in interaction with emerging data. In the course of exploration and testing, the methods used also delivered considerable collateral information regarding other properties of thought flow. Some of these are described in the following section.

Intraindividual Dimensions and Properties of Thought Flow

Dimensions of Thought Flow. In two investigations student research participants were given an auditory signal (beep) on a quasi-random schedule as they went about their everyday activities. At each beep, participants noted down their latest thoughts and rated them on a series of scales. The results for the two investigations were similar. In the larger second study (Klinger & Cox, 1987–88), 29 students supplied 1,425 thought samples rated on 23 scales. These ratings were standardized within participants, thus eliminating individual differences in means and variances, and then were pooled across participants. The correlation matrix for the 23 scales was then factor analyzed. Because oblique rotations produced results much like those of the varimax rotation, the latter are presented here.

There are eight dimensions arising from this analysis worth discussing (i.e., the eight factors with eigenvalues greater than 1.0). In descending order of magnitude they are:

1. visual intensity (visualness, picture-like quality, color),
2. attentiveness to external stimulation (including relation of thought to the external environment),
3. operantness-specificity (directedness versus spontaneity of the thought segment, and specificity of its content versus vagueness),
4. controllability (sense of being able to modify or stop the thought if one wanted to),
5. auditory intensity (sounds, others talking),
6. strangeness (departure from reality; disjointedness),
7. future time orientation,
8. past time orientation.

The fact that these dimensions are orthogonal means that they are substantially independent of one another. Where a thought falls on one of these dimensions provides little information about where it falls on any other dimension. Clearly, even on such formal, abstract dimensions, thoughts vary greatly in complex ways.

Duration. A group of participants were provided with training in estimating the duration of their thoughts (Klinger, 1978). The median duration of distinct thought segments was 5 seconds; the mean duration was 14 seconds. These durations were essentially unrelated to other dimensions of the thoughts. Obviously, some thoughts are considerably longer than this, but many are brief flashes of content. Extrapolating from these figures provides the generalization that people who sleep 8 hours out of 24 entertain about 4,000 thoughts during the other 16 hours per day.

Interior Monologue. Most of the 23 scales loaded fairly highly on at least one of these dimensions. Only one loaded less than .30 on any of them. This scale was the presence of interior monologue. The reason was probably twofold: first, there was only one scale directly tapping this feature, and, second, interior monologues were a part of a majority of thought samples, with 74% containing some degree of self-talk.

Other Features of Thought. Analysis of the results revealed some other typical and occasional features of thought segments. The most prominent other features of thought segments were their *degree of relation to the external world* (64% could recall their surroundings "moderately well" or better), their *directedness* (on average, they contained "some directed thought," but also "some nondirected thought"), their *controllability* (on average, a sense of "moderate control"), and their *visualness* (on average, midway between "just a little" and "moderately visual," and between having a "trace of" and "fairly prominent" picture elements, with "probably a trace" of color).

On average, the thought samples also contained "just a little" sound and "one or a few words" of others talking. They contained on average "some disconnected things" but were "mostly coherent," and their content departed only slightly from "completely normal" and physically "probably possible." Nevertheless, activity departed substantially from appropriate role behavior in 13% of samples, and from physical feasibility in 10% of samples. Because these latter two variables are correlated at only .32, about 20% of the thought samples can be considered to be fanciful in the sense of departing substantially from reality.

These characterizations of thought were replicated with a sample of 184 students selected for high or low scores on measures of depression and anxiety (Kroll-Mensing, 1992), who contributed 4,145 thought samples. This investigation used some of the same rating dimensions as did the previously cited studies, although with a different number of scale points.

> Again, the majority of experience samples are rated as consisting of directed thought (58.7% above the midpoint) as compared to nondirected thought (33.1% above the midpoint). Ratings of the visual and auditory qualities of mental imagery, as well as RP's [research participants'] attentiveness to the external environment appear to be approximately equally distributed from low to high across the 7-point scales. . . . [A]pproximately 25% of thought flow is rated as colorful. . . . Again, the majority of thoughts are characterized as controllable (63.4% above the midpoint), modifiable (63.1% above the midpoint), and clear (64% above the midpoint). . . . The majority of thoughts are rated as positive (47.8% above the midpoint) and acceptable to the respondent (63.1% above the midpoint). However, approximately 20.5% (below the midpoint) of thoughts are rated as negatively valenced . . . 17.9% . . . are experienced as unacceptable or uncomfortable. . . . [C]ombining the ratings [of role-inappropriate and physically impossible behavior] . . . indicates that approximately 22% (ratings greater than 4) of mental imagery can be considered fanciful. Adopting a less conservative criteria [*sic*] (ratings of 2 and above), indicates that more than 50% of waking thought contains traces of fancifulness. (Kroll-Mensing, 1992, pp. 188–189)

Mindsets. Thought content varies—among other dimensions—according to its disposition to evaluate versus to prepare for action, and according to its objectivity in assessing the value of a potential goal or of the probability of successfully attaining it. There is now evidence showing that processing during the predecisional phase of goal striving (before a person becomes committed to a goal) differs systematically in these regards from processing during the subsequent phases, after deciding to pursue the goal.

The difference can be couched in terms of two kinds of mindsets. The *evaluative* or *deliberative* mindset accompanying the predecisional phase is on the average more realistic, attends to a wider range of stimuli, and is far more deliberative and less focused on action. The *implementational* mindset, which accompanies the subsequent phases, is more optimistic, more focused on goal-related stimuli, and is far more concerned with the specific steps required for goal attainment (Beckmann & Gollwitzer, 1987; Gollwitzer, 1990, 1991; Heckhausen & Gollwitzer, 1987). What is particularly remarkable about these phases is that, when they are induced experimentally, they influence processing across the board, even in regard to stimuli or tasks unrelated to the particular experimentally controlled goal pursuits that gave rise to the mindsets.

The concept of mindset was developed independently of the concept of current concern. However, it seems reasonable to infer that once a person is committed to pursuing a goal, and hence has a current concern regarding it, conscious thought about the goal will take place within an implementational mindset. Deliberation about whether to commit to the goal will take place within a deliberative mindset. However, what if one sets a goal of making a decision about committing to another goal, perhaps including gaining information and others' opinions about it? Here, one would predict that the individual will be in an implementational mindset with regard to gaining information and making the decision, and in a deliberative mindset with regard to the choice of goals. There is no evidence about what might happen to mental content in this situation.

When goal striving fails, the individual goes through a series of phases leading to disengagement from the goal. These successive phases—forming a cycle of invigorated behavior, anger, depression, and recovery—are each marked by characteristic moods and mental content (Klinger, 1975, 1977, 1987). When this cycle becomes sufficiently intense, it engenders psychopathological states of anxiety and depression.

Rate of Daydreaming. Stating a rate of daydreaming is complicated by the problem of defining it. There are at least three commonly used definitions of daydreaming in the literature: (a) fanciful thought that departs from reality, generally in a wish-fulfilling way (the traditional psychoanalytic view); (b) "task-unrelated imagery and thought" (TUIT; introduced as a more objective criterion by Singer and Antrobus [Singer, 1966] and given this name by Giambra [e.g., Giambra, Rosenberg, Kasper, Yee, & Sack, 1988–89]); and (c) undirected (spontaneous, respondent) thought, a definition that I formalized (Klinger, 1971) and that corresponds to de facto uses of the term when it includes mindwandering and related concepts. No one assessed the relation among these definitions until thought-sampling data became available. At that point, rather surprisingly, it turned out that the three definitions are substantially unrelated to one another (Klinger & Cox, 1987–88).

Daydreaming has never had a scientifically satisfactory independent definition. In view of these data, it is apparent that none is likely to be feasible. It is preferable to recognize that there are numerous intraindividual dimensions for characterizing thought, and to identify particular regions of the resulting hyperspace as roughly corresponding to popular conceptions of daydreaming. This is the approach I have taken.

Two overlapping classes of thought popularly accepted as daydreaming are thought that is predominantly undirected (i.e., spontaneous, respondent thought such as mind wandering), and thought that is at least partially fanciful. Thoughts that fall into these two classes, taken together, account for about half of all thought samples. It is, therefore, reasonable to assert that about half of human thought qualifies as daydreaming by one or the other of these definitions.

This rate varies according to the pressures of task difficulty and the incentives at stake in good performance. However, as Singer (1966) suggested, there may be a minimum rate of daydreaming (perhaps about 10%) across all but the shortest time intervals even when tasks are maximally demanding and the stakes are enormous. Given the evidence described previously, that undirected thought constitutes a kind of baseline for thought to which consciousness returns when not pressed into directed activity, one might even speak of a daydream imperative, at least in the sense of undirected working over of an individual's current concerns.

Combining stimulus-independent and fanciful-thought segments yields a rather similar estimate of rate. However, the samples included will be rather different because substantial amounts of thought unrelated to an individual's immediate environment represent directed thoughts about something else and hence constitute working thought, which I prefer to exclude from the daydreaming category.

Functions of Daydreaming. The fact that half of human thought can be considered daydreaming makes it highly likely that daydreaming performs important functions. It is, after all, hardly conceivable that evolution should have selected for an activity so biologically costly if it did not contribute substantially to survival. I have made the argument for its functions elsewhere (Klinger, 1990). Here I merely list some of the likely benefits of daydreaming.

1. Paradoxically, daydreaming is probably an essential tool for self-organization. By cycling through an individual's current concerns whenever immediate tasks require less than total concentration, daydreaming keeps individuals cognizant of their full personal agendas. Thereby, while absorbed in a particular activity, people need not lose sight of the other items requiring attention in their lives. In this way, daydreaming serves as a reminder mechanism and is probably essential to helping people keep their lives organized and their priorities intact.

2. Because daydreams often review past experiences or anticipate future ones, they serve as spontaneous tools for learning and planning. In working over the past—especially those past events that remain in part emotionally unresolved—people review their actions and past options, and gain fresh insights into their impact on others (or the perspectives of others) and into alternative ways by which they might have responded. By exploring future scenarios, be they job interviews, presentations, or romantic dalliances, people come to know better their options and the likely consequences of various alternatives. As they winnow out the less attractive courses of action and envision their most probable actions, they in effect rehearse their future behavior.

3. In performing these functions, daydreams may well also be "a way that individuals sustain an ongoing sense of identity, of connection between past, present, and future self" (J. A. Singer, personal communication, 1997).

4. A substantial anecdotal literature points to daydreaming states as fertile ground for creative ideas. They may even be essential for certain kinds of creativity. Unfortunately, there appear to be no systematic, controlled investigations of this possibility.

5. Adroit control of daydreaming enables individuals to entertain themselves when bored, stimulate themselves to sexual or hostile arousal, or relax themselves in the face of stress and pain.

6. Evolution probably did not select for utility in psychotherapy, but guided daydreams have shown promise as a tool in clinical intervention.

Interindividual Dimensions of Thought Flow

Daydreaming Styles. Individual differences in thought flow were investigated primarily with the Imaginal Processes Inventory (IPI; Huba, Singer, Aneshensel, & Antrobus, 1982; Singer & Antrobus, 1970), the Inventory of Childhood Memories and Imaginings (ICMI; Wilson & Barber, 1981), and the Action Control Scale (ACS; Kuhl, 1994).

The most enduring finding from the IPI studies, apart from age and group differences, is the delineation of three reasonably replicable factors underlying individual differences in imaginal processes: positive-constructive daydreaming, guilt and fear-of-failure daydreaming, and poor attentional control (Huba, Aneshensel, & Singer, 1981; Tanaka & Huba, 1985–86).

Fantasy-Proneness. The ICMI arose out of research about what makes an individual a good hypnotic subject (Wilson & Barber, 1981). The scale does in fact predict the ability to follow hypnotic suggestions (e.g., Rhue & Lynn, 1989); it was associated with a history of child abuse (Rhue & Lynn, 1987b); and very high scores were found to be modestly predictive of encounters with the mental health system and with dissociative phenomena (Rauschenberger & Lynn, 1995; Rhue & Lynn, 1987a). However, because the ICMI combines such a variety of items, tapping both childhood and adult experiences, and both preferences for fantasy and quasi-schizotypal phenomena, it is premature to conclude that any level of involvement in daydreaming as such is associated with psychopathology.

Action Orientation. During the 1970s, Kuhl became impressed with the fact that some individuals appear disproportionately preoccupied with memories, with uncompleted undertakings, and with their internal feeling states, whereas others focus disproportionately on taking action in pursuit of their goals. He labeled the two extremes *state orientation* and *action orientation*. These constitute a set of intraindividual as well as interindividual dimensions, but research has emphasized the interindividual implications. State orientation is not to be confused with deliberative mindsets, which focus on choices and are evaluative but are not inherently ruminative or perseverative. The orientation dimension of Kuhl and Beckmann is conceptually independent of the mindsets dimension and of the phases of goal pursuits.

The Action Control Scale, developed with Beckmann, assesses individual differences in three dimensions of state orientation: *preoccupation* (e.g., dwelling on a recent failure), *hesitation* (i.e., before making decisions or initiating actions), and *volatility* (versus persistence at pleasant, self-initiated activities; Kuhl, 1994). These dimensions have been implicated in a wide variety of other behavioral dimensions, from depression to confusion about the origins of one's goals. The ACS led to the development of the Volitional Components Inventory (Kuhl & Fuhrmann, 1996), which assesses individual differences in 30 facets of volitional control, with strong relevance to the qualities of thought flow.

The theoretical framework associated with this work gradually evolved into what, in its present form, Kuhl dubbed Personality Systems Interactions (Kuhl, 1996, 1997). This theory identifies four functions important for the effective exercise of will and is tied to neuropsychological findings.

It is entirely compatible with, and complementary to, current-concerns theory.

SUMMARY

We have learned much about thought flow over the past 4 decades. The accumulating evidence has confirmed some prior conceptions and has decisively refuted others. It is now clear that up to perhaps half of waking thought takes one form or another of daydreaming, that different definitions of daydreaming have addressed largely independent dimensions of thought, and that daydreaming is not only nonpathological but serves a number of psychological functions vital to living an adaptive human life.

Moreover, although association will always play a major role in human behavior, research has shown that thought flow cannot be understood as a purely semantically associative process. Instead, thoughts are, like more overt behavior, organized entities that depend on motivation and emotion. That is, they pertain to the goals to which people commit themselves, and are steered by emotional responses to goal-related cues. It now appears likely that these factors influence all cognitive processing, probably from the earliest stages in the processing of any stimulus to complex problem solving and creative thought.

Research also revealed a number of dimensions of thought segments and of thought flow, showing both intraindividual and interindividual differences. The evidence allows us to say much about normal conscious experience and how it varies, both through the phases of goal striving and from one person to the next. There is now incisive theory about the effects of mood on thought, and of how some individuals cope better than others with certain kinds of stress. Moreover, investigators have developed an impressive array of methods for assessing contents of consciousness, effects on cognition, motivational structure, and volitional dispositions, all pertinent to the study and determination of thought flow. It has been a rich 4 decades.

REFERENCES

Antrobus, J. S., Singer, J. L., & Greenberg, S. (1966). Studies in the stream of consciousness: Experimental enhancement and suppression of spontaneous cognitive processes. *Perceptual and Motor Skills, 23*, 399–417.

Aserinsky, E., & Kleitman, N. (1953). Regularly occurring periods of eye motility, and concomitant phenomena, during sleep. *Science, 118*, 273–274.

Beckmann, J., & Gollwitzer, P. M. (1987). Deliberative versus implemental states of mind: The issue of impartiality in pre- and postdecisional information processing. *Social Cognition, 5*, 259–279.

Bock, M., & Klinger, E. (1986). Interaction of emotion and cognition in word recall. *Psychological Research, 48*, 99–106.

Bower, G. H. (1992). How might emotions affect learning? In S.-A. Christianson (Ed.), *The handbook of emotion and memory: Research and theory* (pp. 3–32). Hillsdale, NJ: Lawrence Erlbaum Associates.

Broadbent, D., & Broadbent, M. (1988). Anxiety and attentional bias: State and trait. *Cognition and Emotion, 2*, 165–184.

Carter, C. S., Maddock, R. J., & Magliozzi, J. (1992). Patterns of abnormal processing of emotional information in panic disorder and major depression. *Psychopathology, 25*, 65–70.

Chomsky, N. A. (1959). A review of Skinner's *Verbal Behavior*. *Language, 35*, 26.

Cox, W. M., & Klinger, E. (1988). A motivational model of alcohol use. *Journal of Abnormal Psychology, 97*, 168–180.

Csikszentmihalyi, M., & Larson, R. (1984). *Being adolescent: Conflict and growth in the teenage years*. New York: Basic Books.

Csikszentmihalyi, M., & Larson, R. (1987). Validity and reliability of the experience-sampling method. *Journal of Nervous and Mental Disease, 175*, 526–536.

Csikszentmihalyi, M., Larson, R., & Prescott, S. (1977). The ecology of adolescent activity and experience. *Journal of Youth and Adolescence, 6*, 281–294.

Davey, G. C. L. (1994). Worrying, social problem-solving abilities, and social problem-solving confidence. *Behaviour Research and Therapy, 32*, 327–330.

Deese, J. (1965). *The structure of associations in language and thought*. Baltimore: Johns Hopkins University Press.

Donovan, D. (1995). Assessments to aid in the treatment planning process. In J. P. Allen (Ed.), *Assessing alcohol problems: A guide for clinicians and researchers* (pp. 75–122). Bethesda, MD: National Institute on Alcohol Abuse and Alcoholism.

Ehlers, A. M., Margraf, J., Davies, S., & Roth, W. T. (1988). Selective processing of threat cues in subjects with panic attacks. *Cognition and Emotion, 2*, 201–220.

Eysenck, M. W., & Van Berkum, J. (1992). Trait anxiety, defensiveness, and the structure of worry. *Personality and Individual Differences, 13*, 1285–1290.

Fox, E. (1993). Allocation of visual attention and anxiety. *Cognition and Emotion, 7*, 207–216.

Giambra, L. M., Rosenberg, E. H., Kasper, S., Yee, W., & Sack, D. A. (1988–89). A circadian rhythm in the frequency of spontaneous task-unrelated images and thoughts. *Imagination, Cognition and Personality, 8*, 309–314.

Gollwitzer, P. M. (1990). Action phases and mind-sets. In E. T. Higgins & R. M. Sorrentino (Eds.), *Handbook of motivation and social cognition* (pp. 53–92). New York: Guilford.

Gollwitzer, P. M. (1991). *Abwägen und Planen: Bewußtseinslagen in verschiedenen Handlungsphasen* [Weighing and planning: States of consciousness in different action phases]. Göttingen, Germany: Hogrefe.

Gottlib, I. H., McLachlan, A. L., & Katz, A. N. (1988). Biases in visual attention in depressed and nondepressed individuals. *Cognition and Emotion, 2*, 185–200.

Griffiths, R. (1935). *Imagination in early childhood*. London: Kegan Paul Trench, Trubner & Co.

Heckhausen, H., & Gollwitzer, P. (1987). Thought contents and cognitive functioning in motivational versus volitional states of mind. *Motivation and Emotion, 11*, 101–120.

Hoelscher, T. J., Klinger, E., & Barta, S. G. (1981). Incorporation of concern- and nonconcern-related verbal stimuli into dream content. *Journal of Abnormal Psychology, 49*, 88–91.

Huba, G. J., Aneshensel, C. S., & Singer, J. L. (1981). Development of scales for three second-order factors of inner experience. *Multivariate Behavioral Research, 16*, 181–206.

Huba, G. J., Singer, J. L., Aneshensel, C. S., & Antrobus, J. S. (1982). *Short Imaginal Processes Inventory Manual*. Port Huron, MI: Research Psychologists Press.

Hurlburt, R. T. (1979). Random sampling of cognitions and behavior. *Journal of Research in Personality, 13*, 103–111.

Hurlburt, R. T. (1990). *Sampling normal and schizophrenic inner experience*. New York: Plenum.

Hurlburt, R. T. (1993). *Sampling inner experience in disturbed affect*. New York: Plenum.

Ingram, R. E., Kendall, P. C., Smith, T. W., Donnell, C., & Ronan, K. (1987). Cognitive specificity in emotional distress. *Journal of Personality and Social Psychology, 53*, 734–742.

James, W. (1950). *The principles of psychology*, Vol. 1. New York: Dover (Original work published 1890)

Johnsen, B. H., Laberg, J. C., Cox, W. M., Vaksdal, A., & Hugdahl, K. (1994). Alcoholics' attentional bias in the processing of alcohol-related words. *Psychology of Addictive Behaviors, 8*, 111–115.

Keele, S. W. (1968). Movement control in skilled motor performance. *Psychological Bulletin, 70*, 387–403.

Klinger, E. (1971). *Structure and functions of fantasy*. New York: Wiley.

Klinger, E. (1974). Utterances to evaluate steps and control attention distinguish operant from respondent thought while thinking out loud. *Bulletin of the Psychonomic Society, 4*, 44–46.

Klinger, E. (1975). Consequences of commitment to and disengagement from incentives. *Psychological Review, 82*, 1–25.

Klinger, E. (1977). *Meaning and void: Inner experience and the incentives in people's lives*. Minneapolis: University of Minnesota Press.

Klinger, E. (1978). Modes of normal conscious flow. In K. S. Pope & J. L. Singer (Eds.), *The stream of consciousness: Scientific investigations into the flow of human experience* (pp. 225–258). New York: Plenum.

Klinger, E. (1987). Current concerns and disengagement from incentives. In F. Halisch & J. Kuhl (Eds.), *Motivation, intention and volition* (pp. 337–347). Berlin: Springer.

Klinger, E. (1990). *Daydreaming*. Los Angeles: Tarcher.

Klinger, E. (1996). Emotional influences on cognitive processing, with implications for theories of both. In J. A. Bargh & P. M. Gollwitzer (Eds.), *The psychology of action: Linking cognition and motivation to behavior* (pp. 168–189). New York: Guilford.

Klinger, E., Barta, S. G., & Mahoney, T.W. (1976). Motivation, mood, and mental events: Patterns and implications for adaptive processes. In G. Serban (Ed.), *Psychopathology of human adaptation* (pp. 95–112). New York: Plenum.

Klinger, E., Barta, S. G., & Maxeiner, M. E. (1980). Motivational correlates of thought content frequency and commitment. *Journal of Personality and Social Psychology, 39*, 1222–1237.

Klinger, E., Bock, M., & Bowi, U. (1990). *Emotional mediation of motivational factors in word recall*. Unpublished manuscript.

Klinger, E., & Cox, W. M. (1987–88). Dimensions of thought flow in everyday life. *Imagination, Cognition and Personality, 7*, 105–128.

Klinger, E., Cox, W. M., & Blount, J. P. (1995). The Motivational Structure Questionnaire. In J. P. Allen (Ed.), *Assessing alcohol problems: A guide for clinicians and researchers* (pp. 399–411). Bethesda, MD: National Institute on Alcohol Abuse and Alcoholism.

Klinger, E., Goetzman, E. S., Hughes, T., & Seppelt, T. L. (1996, May). *Microinfluences of protoemotional reactions and motivation on cognitive processing*. Invited paper presented at the annual meeting of the Midwestern Psychological Association, Chicago.

Klinger, E., & Kroll-Mensing, D. (1995). Idiothetic assessment: Experience sampling and motivational analysis. In J. N. Butcher (Ed.), *Clinical personality assessment: Practical approaches* (pp. 267–277). New York: Oxford University Press.

Klos, D. S., & Singer, J. L. (1981). Determinants of the adolescent's ongoing thought following simulated parental confrontations. *Journal of Personality and Social Psychology, 41*, 975–987.

Kripke, D. F., & Sonnenschein, D. (1978). A biological rhythm in waking fantasy. In K. S. Pope & J. L. Singer (Eds.), *The stream of consciousness: Scientific investigations into the flow of human experience* (pp. 321–332). New York: Plenum.

Kroll-Mensing, D. (1992). *Differentiating anxiety and depression: An experience sampling analysis.* Unpublished doctoral dissertation, University of Minnesota, Minneapolis.

Kuhl, J. (1994). Action versus state orientation: Psychometric properties of the Action Control Scale (ACS-90). In J. Kuhl & J. Beckmann (Eds.), *Volition and personality: Action versus state orientation* (pp. 47–60). Göttingen, Germany: Hogrefe & Huber.

Kuhl, J. (1996). *Psychologie des Willens: Von der Introspektion zur Funktionsanalyse (und zurück)* [The psychology of the will: From introspection to functional analysis (and back)]. Invited lecture, Universität Würzburg.

Kuhl, J. (1997). *Personality and volition: Centrally organized patterns of motivation–cognition interactions.* Unpublished manuscript.

Kuhl, J., & Fuhrmann, A. (1996). *The Volitional Components Inventory.* Unpublished inventory. Osnabrück, Germany: University of Osnabrück.

Larsen, R., & Diener, E. (1987). Affect intensity as an individual difference characteristic. *Journal of Research in Personality, 21,* 1–39.

LeDoux, J. E. (1989). Cognitive–emotional interactions in the brain. *Cognition and Emotion, 3,* 267–289.

LeDoux, J. E. (1995). Emotion: Clues from the brain. *Annual Review of Psychology, 46, 209–235.*

Lewinsohn, P. M., & Rosenbaum, M. (1987). Recall of parental behavior by acute depressives, remitted depressives, and nondepressives. *Journal of Personality and Social Psychology, 52,* 611–619.

Lyubomirsky, S., & Nolen-Hoeksema, S. (1993). Self-perpetuating properties of dysphoric rumination. *Journal of Personality and Social Psychology, 65,* 339–349.

Martin, L. L., & Tesser, A. (1996). Some ruminative thoughts. In R. S. Wyer, Jr. (Ed.), *Advances in Social Cognition* (Vol. 9, pp. 1–48). Hillsdale, NJ: Lawrence Erlbaum Associates.

Miller, G. A. (1965). Some preliminaries to psycholinguistics. *American Psychologist, 20,* 15–20.

Mogg, K., Mathews, A., & Eysenck, M. (1992). Attentional bias to threat in clinical anxiety states. *Cognition and Emotion, 6,* 149–159.

Naumann, E., Bartussek, D., Diedrich, O., & Laufer, M. E. (1992). Assessing cognitive and affective information processing functions of the brain by means of the late positive complex of the event-related potential. *Journal of Psychophysiology, 6,* 285–298.

Nikles, C. D., II, Brecht, D. L., Klinger, E., & Bursell, A. L. (1998). The effects of current-concern- and nonconcern-related waking suggestions on nocturnal dream content. *Journal of Personality and Social Psychology, 75,* 242–255.

Nikula, R., Klinger, E., & Larson-Gutman, M. K. (1993). Current concerns and electrodermal reactivity: Responses to words and thoughts. *Journal of Personality, 61,* 63–84.

Rauschenberger, S. L., & Lynn, S. J. (1995). Fantasy proneness, DSM-III-R Axis 1 psychopathology, and dissociation. *Journal of Abnormal Psychology, 104,* 373–380.

Rhue, J. W., & Lynn, S. J. (1987a). Fantasy proneness and psychopathology. *Journal of Personality and Social Psychology, 53,* 327– 336.

Rhue, J. W., & Lynn, S. J. (1987b). Fantasy proneness: Developmental antecedents. *Journal of Personality, 55,* 121– 138.

Rhue, J. W., & Lynn, S. J. (1989). Fantasy proneness, hypnotizability, and absorption. *The International Journal of Clinical and Experimental Hypnosis, 37,* 100–106.

Riemann, B. C., Amir, N., & Louro, C. E. (1995). *Cognitive processing of personally relevant information in panic disorder.* Manuscript submitted for publication.

Riemann, B. C., & McNally, R. J. (1995). Cognitive processing of personally-relevant information. *Cognition and Emotion, 9,* 325–340.

Schneider, W. (1987). *Ablenkung und Handlungskontrolle: Eine 'kognitiv-motivationale Perspektive'* [Distraction and action control: A cognitive-motivational perspective]. Unpublished diploma thesis, University of Bielefeld, Germany.

Singer, J. A., & Salovey, P. (1993). *The remembered self: Emotion and memory in personality.* New York: The Free Press.

Singer, J. L. (1966). *Daydreaming: An introduction to the experimental study of inner experience.* New York: Random House.

Singer, J. L. (1975). *The inner world of daydreaming.* New York: Harper & Row.

Singer, J. L., & Antrobus, J. S. (1970). *The Imaginal Processes Inventory.* Princeton, NJ: Educational Testing Service.

Skinner, B. F. (1953). *Science and human behavior.* New York: Macmillan.

Smith, E. R. (1996). What do connectionism and social psychology offer each other? *Journal of Personality and Social Psychology, 70,* 893–912.

Tait, R., & Silver, R. C. (1989). Coming to terms with major negative life events. In J. S. Uleman & J. A. Bargh (Eds.), *Unintended thought* (pp. 351–382). New York: Guilford.

Tanaka, J. S., & Huba, G. J. (1985–86). Longitudinal stability of three second-order daydreaming factors. *Imagination, Cognition and Personality, 5,* 231–238.

Varendonck, J. (1921). *The psychology of daydreams.* New York: Macmillan.

Vasey, M. W., & Borkovec, T. D. (1992). A catastrophizing assessment of worrisome thoughts. *Cognitive Therapy and Research, 16,* 505–520.

Williams, J., Merritt, J., Rittenhouse, C., & Hobson, J. A. (1992). Bizarreness in dreams and fantasies: Implications for the activation-synthesis hypothesis. *Consciousness & Cognition, 1,* 172–185.

Wilson, S. C., & Barber, T. X. (1981). Vivid fantasy and hallucinatory abilities in the life histories of excellent hypnotic subjects ("somnambules"): Preliminary report with female subjects. In E. Klinger (Ed.), *Imagery, Vol. 2: Concepts, results, and applications.* New York: Plenum.

Wulf, G., Schmidt, R. A., & Deubel, H. (1993). Reduced feedback frequency enhances generalized motor program learning but not parameterization learning. *Journal of Experimental Psychology: Learning, Memory, and Cognition, 19,* 1134–1150.

Young, J. (1987). *The role of selective attention in the attitude–behavior relationship.* Unpublished doctoral dissertation, University of Minnesota, Minneapolis.

The Interpretation of Dreams From the Perspective of Cognitive-Experiential Self-Theory

Seymour Epstein
University of Massachusetts at Amherst

It is a pleasure to be invited to contribute to a book on consciousness in honor of Jerome Singer because no one has contributed more to our understanding of fantasy and other forms of undirected thought. Not only has Singer elucidated the nature of fantasy in its own right, but, equally important, he has placed it both in a reasonable perspective in relation to directed conscious thinking and in relation to less accessible undirected unconscious thinking and imagery. He has demonstrated the importance of everyday undirected thinking and imagery and has revealed that there is much of importance in personality that is, at best, overlooked; and, at worst, misattributed with serious theoretical consequences, when the focus of investigations and observations is either entirely on conscious directed thought, or on deeper less accessible unconscious processes.

There is much I share with Singer's views. We both endorse a cognitive–emotional model of behavior, and, although both of us appreciate the psychodynamic contributions of traditional psychoanalytical theory, we remain highly critical of some of its other features. These features include its overemphasis on the repressed unconscious and its underemphasis on the preconscious, and the subjectivity of its procedures, such as determining the meaning of dreams by having those who are being analyzed free associate until they produce associations that support the analyst's views (Singer, 1997).

There is another, more personal reason that I welcome the opportunity to participate in this book. For more than a decade, I have been selectively collecting my dreams, primarily with the aim of elucidating the nature of displacement in the dream. No matter how edifying such research can be, it does not provide the kind of data that are welcomed in today's professional journals, which prefer carefully controlled studies in laboratory settings. Thus, I welcomed the opportunity to present this research in a freer medium. I believe the research has important lessons to teach about the nature of displacement in the dream, suggesting a critical misattribution about the prevalence of unconscious conflict in the early days of psychoanalytic theory, which may have influenced the entire course of its development. Singer (1997) has arrived at a somewhat similar conclusion about the overemphasis, in classical psychoanalytic theory, on the importance of unconscious conflict in human affairs from an entirely different database. I can think of no topic in the research I have conducted that is more fitting for honoring Singer than a study of the meaning of dreams.

How can one make sense of dreams? This question has occupied people since at least the beginning of recorded history (Van De Castle, 1971). Among the more well-known early examples of an attempt to decipher the meaning of dreams is Joseph's interpretation of the pharaoh's dream about seven lean cows and seven fat cows. Joseph's interpretation was based on the assumptions that dreams are prophetic and that they operate by metaphors. I have no doubt about the accuracy of the second assumption, but considerable doubt about the first, except insofar as the motivation of the dreamer can serve as a self-fulfilling prophecy. In any event, the challenge for Joseph was to make the correct interpretation of the metaphor. Considering the possible implications that the dream might have for the future, he made the reasonable interpretation that seven fat cows signified seven years of bountiful harvest, and that seven lean cows meant that seven years of famine would follow.

Freud's approach was somewhat more scientific. Rather than assuming that dreams are prophetic, he assumed they are expressions of unconscious processes that operate by principles he was determined to uncover, and which he finally believed he did. In fact, he regarded his presumed discovery of the principles of dream interpretation as his single most important accomplishment because he considered these principles to be the key for unlocking the mysteries of the unconscious mind, which was the foundation of his theory of personality and pathology. It is not surprising that among his voluminous publications about a wide range of topics, with his collected works running to 24 thick volumes, the contribution he was most proud of was his book, *The Interpretation of Dreams* (Freud, 1900/1965). Evaluating it 32 years after its publication, he commented, "It contains, even according to my present day judgment, the most valuable of all the discoveries it has been my good fortune to make. Insight such as this falls to one's lot but once in a lifetime" (p. xx). Freud's approach to unlocking the secret of the dream was to intensively examine the dreams of his patients as well as his own dreams. On the basis of free associations to the content of the dreams, he formulated the principles that he believed explained their meanings. He assumed that all dreams are motivated by wish fulfillment. The wish fulfillment, except in the case of children's dreams, is invariably disguised because the wishes of adults that are capable of generating dreams are always of a taboo nature and therefore guilt arousing. To express the wishes directly would generate so much anxiety that it would awaken the patient from sleep. Because an important function of dreams is to protect sleep, the wishes are disguised by presenting them as something other than themselves. Thus, he regarded displacement as among the most fundamental principles of dream interpretation. Other principles that he identified were symbolic representation, condensation (the convergence of more than one source on the choice of a symbol), and association.

A major problem with Freud's procedure for establishing the principles of dream interpretation is that, with the use of free association as the method for deciphering the meaning of a dream symbol, there is no objective way of determining which association should be regarded as correct. For this determination, Freud was guided by his theory of personality, which emphasized the importance of inhibited sexual impulses. Thus, there was a bias in Freud's procedure to interpret dream content, whenever possible, in terms of sexual symbols. Moreover, there is the complication that the dream content itself, as well as the associations it elicits, are influenced by the dreamer's beliefs about dreams, which in turn, are likely to be influenced by the beliefs of the dreamer's therapist. This can explain why Freud's patients reported dreams that he and his patients interpreted as confirming Freud's theory that dreams are motivated primarily by sexual needs, and why Jung and his patients reported dreams that they interpreted as confirming Jung's theory that dreams are motivated primarily by spiritual needs. Each believed that his own interpretations were objective and that the other's were biased. (For a similar criticism of Freud's procedure, see Singer, 1997.)

Given the lack of an objective criterion for determining the meaning of dream symbols, there is no entirely satisfactory way of establishing their meanings. However, there are ways of making the procedure simpler and of reducing its subjectivity. In this chapter, I present one such procedure. I make no claim that it is objective, but only that it is simpler, less subjective, and less theoretically biased than the procedure that Freud employed. My intent is to uncover the principles of dream interpretation that can be observed in the simplest, most readily interpretable representations in dreams. This will undoubtedly fall short of the kind of data required to support a complete theory of dream interpretation, but at least it is a useful beginning. Moreover, as will be seen shortly, it is adequate for certain purposes, such as demonstrating that displacement occurs for reasons other than avoidance of distressing thoughts.

This chapter is divided into three parts. The first presents a theory of dream interpretation that has much in common with Freud's theory, but differs in several important ways. The second illustrates the empirical procedure that was used to identify and subsequently test the principles described in the first part. Included in this part are examples of the application of the principles to dreams. The third part provides a general discussion of issues raised by the first two parts.

A THEORY OF THE MEANING OF DREAMS

The theory of dreams that I am proposing is part of a global theory of personality called cognitive–experiential self-theory (CEST; Epstein, 1994). Unlike Freud's approach, in which he first established the principles of unconscious information processing in dreams and then developed his theory of personality, CEST proceeded in the opposite direction. The principles of unconscious processing were established with reference to people's waking behavior, with emphasis given to findings in cognitive research and to broad theoretical considerations, such as evolutionary principles, and then incorporated in a general theory of personality. After the theory was developed, I considered its implications for dreams. As a result of proceeding from a consideration of normal mental processes to dreaming, the principles of unconscious information processing in CEST that are applied to dream interpretation are essentially adaptive. Singer (1997) has independently arrived at a somewhat similar position. He argues that night dreams, like daydreams, reflect the everyday concerns of the dreamer, albeit in altered form, and not necessarily deep, unconscious processes. My view, like Singer's, can be contrasted with the view of the unconscious in Freudian theory, in which the unconscious is regarded as an unrealistic, wish-fulfillment system. Neither human nor nonhuman animals could adapt to their environments solely on the basis of this system, which operates by the distorting principles of the primary process. They would starve to death amidst wish-fulfilling hallucinations of need gratification. Thus, the conceptualization of unconscious information processing in Freudian theory makes no sense from an evolutionary perspective. In order to account for people's ability to adapt to their environments successfully, Freud had to introduce another system, which he said operated according to the principles of the secondary process. The latter system is a rational, reality-oriented, conscious, primarily verbal system. The difficulty with this solution is that it is not feasible from an evolutionary perspective because nonhuman animals, who have no language and a very limited capacity for abstract reasoning, have no secondary process. It is difficult to understand how a system such as Freud's conceptualization of the unconscious could have developed in humans if it is fundamentally maladaptive. Moreover, modern cognitive psychology has demonstrated that most human information processing occurs unconsciously by a system that is essentially adaptive, and that, in fact, is far more efficient for adapting to the events of everyday life than the rational system. This system is generally referred to as the cognitive unconscious (e.g., Kihlstrom, 1987; Reber, 1993; Schachter, 1987).

The difficulty with the modern cognitive view of the unconscious for a psychodynamic theory is that it is a kinder, gentler processing system that is unable to account for the kinds of emotional and conflictual reactions that, until the introduction of CEST, has been the exclusive domain of psychoanalysis. By assuming that the cognitive unconscious is emotionally driven, CEST converts the cognitive unconscious to an unconscious that is a source of passion and conflict in a similar manner to the Freudian unconscious. Thus, CEST, like psychoanalysis, is a psychodynamic theory, but one that assumes that the unconscious operates by a set of principles that are essentially adaptive. The two systems in CEST that are analogous to Freud's primary and secondary process are the experiential and rational systems. The *experiential system* is an automatic, rapid, subconscious, holistic, concretive, associative, primarily nonverbal system, and has a very long evolutionary history. The *rational system* is effortful, relatively slow, conscious, primarily verbal, and has a very brief evolutionary history (see Table 3.1 for a more complete comparison of the attributes of the two systems). It is assumed that the experiential and rational systems operate in parallel, and are interactive. The experiential system was given its name because it is a system that learns from experience, and its schemata, accordingly, are primarily generalizations derived from emotionally significant past experience.

A particularly important assumption in CEST is that all behavior can be situated along a continuum of the degree of the relative contribution of the two systems. At one end of the continuum, behavior is completely determined by processing in the rational mode, and at the other end, it is completely determined by processing in the experiential mode. These two extremes are rarely, if ever, exhibited in pure form. As an example, consider someone working on the solution of a mathematics problem. At first glance, it might seem that such mental work is a pure example of rational processing. However, a moment's reflection indicates that this is

TABLE 3.1
Comparison of the Experiential and Rational Systems

Experiential System	Rational System
1. Holistic	1. Analytic
2. Automatic, effortless	2. Intentional, effortful
3. Affective: Pleasure-Pain oriented (what feels good)	3. Logical: Reason oriented (what is sensible)
4. Associative connections	4. Logical connections
5. Behavior mediated by "vibes" from past events	5. Behavior mediated by conscious appraisal of events
6. Encodes reality in concrete images, metaphors, & narratives	6. Encodes reality in abstract symbols, words, & numbers
7. More rapid processing: Oriented toward immediate action	7. Slower processing: Oriented toward delayed action
8. Slower and more resistant to change: changes with repetitive or intense experience	8. Changes more rapidly and easily: Changes with strength of argument and new evidence
9. More crudely differentiated: Broad generalization gradient; stereotypical thinking	9. More highly differentiated
10. More crudely integrated: Dissociative, emotional complexes; context-specific processing	10. More highly integrated: Context-general principles
11. Experienced passively and preconsciously: We are seized by our emotions	11. Experienced actively and consciously: We are in control of our thoughts
12. Self-evidently valid: "Experiencing is believing"	12. Requires justification via logic and evidence

Note. From "Cognitive-experiential self-theory: An integrative theory of personality" by S. Epstein. In R. C. Curtis (Ed.), *The relational self: Theoretical convergences in psychoanalysis and social psychology.* New York: Guilford Press. Adapted with permission.

not likely the case because having had emotionally significant past experience with mathematics problems is almost certain to implicate the experiential system. If such experiences have been associated with previous failure and unpleasant emotions, they will interfere with rational processing, and processing in the experiential mode may then be more influential than is processing in the rational mode. On the other hand, if past experience with mathematics is associated with past success and pleasant emotions, the experiential system is likely to be involved in a facilitative manner.

Although all behavior can be assumed to be influenced by a combination of experiential and rational processing, the balance between these two modes of processing will vary with both the nature of the situation and the person. All other things being equal, mathematics problems can be expected to elicit a greater degree of rational, relative to experiential, processing than interpersonal situations. Moreover, some people across situations can be expected to be more rational, relative to experiential, than are others (Epstein, Pacini, Denes-Raj, & Heier, 1996). Given the loosely structured, associative nature of dreams, it is evident that they are influenced to a greater extent by experiential processing than is waking behavior. Given, also, that some dreams are more logically structured than others, it is evident that rational processing must be involved in dreams to different degrees. In summary, dreams, like waking behavior, are regarded as a product of experiential and rational processing, although much more strongly weighted in the experiential direction. They also vary in the relative degree of contribution of the two processing modes.

The question may be raised as to what the relation is between the Freudian unconscious and the unconscious proposed in CEST with respect to their roles in dreams. According to CEST, the operation of the primary process as conceived in psychoanalysis corresponds to the operation of the experiential system in an altered state of consciousness that occurs during sleep. In this respect, it is noteworthy that as can be seen in Table 3.1, the experiential system is assumed to operate primarily by representing events imagistically, by relating events associatively, and by integrating information in the form of narratives. All of these are fundamental characteristics of the dream, and all are consistent with Freud's conception of primary process. In waking life, the experiential system operates in a coherent, adaptive manner because the higher regions of the brain are fully functioning and the person is primarily focused in a purposeful manner on external stimuli. In sleep, the higher brain centers are not fully functioning (Breger, 1967), and the person is unconcerned about adapting to external stimuli. The result is that attention is not focused on specific external events, and the person has only disconnected inner stimuli to which to respond. Responding in its narrative, integrative manner, the experiential system does the best it can to weave the diverse mental contents that happen to be present in dream working memory into some kind of coherent story. The result is that, although much dream content is nonsensical, it may nevertheless contain interesting and revealing elements and associations between elements, and depending on an appropriate combination of experiential and rational processing, it may even produce creative solutions to problems that have eluded the efforts of more analytic reasoning. The incoherence observed in reports of dreams is no doubt an underestimate of the actual incoherence in the dream itself because the rational-processing contribution to the report of the dream in the awake state can be assumed to be greater than its contribution in the sleep state.

CEST accepts Freud's views about the importance of displacement, condensation, symbolic representation, and association in dream representations. As will be seen, these concepts are well illustrated in the sample of dreams included in this chapter. However, CEST rejects Freud's assumptions that wish fulfillment is the motivation underlying all dreams, that taboo thoughts and impulses are the source of all adult dreams, that the only reason displacement occurs is to protect the ego from unacceptable thoughts, and that negative affect is the sole threat to maintaining the state of relaxation necessary for sleep.

The view in CEST about narrative processing goes a step further than simply noting that it occurs in dreams, because it assumes that the normal operation of the experiential system is to integrate information by constructing narratives in pictorial form. This suggests that the experiential system, during sleep, has the task of integrating all mental representations in dream working memory into some kind of story. Because the elements in dream working memory are often present for a variety of unrelated reasons, weaving them into a coherent narrative is often an impossible task. The dream (or more precisely, the experiential system operating on the elements in dream working memory) simply does the best job it can. Depending on the coherence of the elements in dream working memory, and the degree of contribution of the rational system relative to that of the experiential system, which is assumed to be influenced by depth and stage of sleep, the dream narrative will be more or less coherent.

What kinds of mental content are most likely to gain access to dream working memory? In order for sleep to be maintained, the potential elements for incorporation in dream working memory have to be at an appropriate level of excitation. If they are insufficiently arousing, the potential daytime candidates for inclusion in the dream will not attract sufficient attention to pass the threshold for access to dream working memory. If they are excessively arousing, they will awaken the dreamer, as is illustrated in anxiety dreams. Alternatively, they can gain expression in a less arousing form, such as when they are displaced, which will be discussed in a subsequent section. If they are somewhat stimulating, but lack the personal significance that would make them excessively arousing, they can be included in the dream directly, without displacement. This is illustrated in cases of surprising, incidental stimuli that have no particular personal significance. For example, one of my dreams included a car that attracted my attention the day before the dream because its floor seemed too high.

In summary, it is assumed that with the exception of anxiety dreams, which Freud considered to be an example of a failure in the dream work, in order to be included in a dream mental representations have to fall within an appropriate range of excitation. This assumption has important implications for understanding one of the reasons why displacement is nearly ubiquitously present in dreams, a topic to which I turn next.

Memories or thoughts that produce strong excitation are rarely represented directly in dreams because they are too arousing for sleep to be maintained. Their direct expression is normally inhibited, and only their displaced representations gain expression. Because a gradient of stimulus generalization (Dollard & Miller, 1950) is associated with every stimulus, it follows that, at some level of displacement, there must be an appropriate degree of excitation for the incorporation of a mental representation in a dream without jeopardizing sleep. The greater the cortical arousal produced by a thought or image, the greater must be its displacement for it to gain access to dream working memory. Does this mean that direct representations of highly stimulating experiences should never occur in dreams? Not necessarily. There are at least two exceptions. One is the occurrence of dreams in which the experience of a trauma is recapitulated and the dreamer awakens terrified (Grinker & Spiegel, 1945). The excitation associated with a dream element in such a case is so intense that inhibition is insufficient, and the memory of the distressing event is directly reproduced. The second exception is that a direct representation of a threatening event may occur after a sufficient passage of time, when the anxiety associated with the event has sufficiently abated. Analogous to gradients of stimulus generalization, in which decreasing excitation occurs as a function of increasing stimulus dissimilarity, are gradients of decreasing excitation as a function of increasing time. An example of this is provided by Freud's (1900/1965) report of a dream about failing an examination long after the issue was no longer of concern.

A second reason for the ubiquity of displacement in dreams is the associative nature of the experiential system. Consistent with Freud's concept of condensation, it is assumed that the likelihood of inclusion of any thought in one form or another in dream content is a function of the combined influence of all associations to the thought. Thus, the excitation produced by an indirect representation may be at a more appropriate level than a direct representation for inclusion in a dream. Expressed otherwise, the confluence of more than one association to an event results in a compromise, as manifested in the form of a displaced representation, that may give it an excitatory strength that provides it with greater accessibility to dream working memory than a direct representation.

A third condition that contributes to the prevalence of displacement in the dream is the existence of prototypical, well-rehearsed representations that have particularly low thresholds for inclusion in dream working memory. For one individual, feelings of being overwhelmed may be represented typically by dreams of tidal waves, whereas for another they may be represented by an inability to initiate movement. Such prototypical representations are more likely than direct representations to appear in dreams, not necessarily because they are less arousing, but because they are particularly strong representations of a specific state. Thus, when any situation occurs that evokes that state, there is a high likelihood that it will be represented in the dream by its prototypical representation.

It is assumed in CEST that most concerns expressed in dreams are similar to those in the waking state. A notable exception is that unconscious mental content that is inaccessible during the day may be accessible in dreams. No unique significance is accorded in CEST to wish fulfillment as the source of dreams. Rather, dream content is viewed as mainly reflecting current mental states. Thus, fear fulfillment is likely to be as prevalent in dreams as is wish fulfillment. Also, the reflection of a state of frustration in dream content is likely to be more prevalent than the depiction of the gratification of the frustrated desire because the former is more likely to occupy thoughts than the latter, which, of course, is adaptive. It follows that when a person has an anxiety dream that is associated with a motive or wish, it does not necessarily mean, as Freud assumed, that the anxiety was produced by guilt over the anticipated fulfillment of an unacceptable wish. More likely, it reflects the state of distress that is a consequence of the frustration.

From the assumption that dreams are, in the main, continuations of everyday thinking, it can be expected that most dreams do not have deep, unconscious meaning, but simply reflect everyday concerns expressed in the language of the dream (for similar views, see Domhoff, 1996; Fisher & Greenberg, 1996; Singer, 1997). Given the prevalence of displacement in dreams, it follows that dream content represents events in displaced form not only when they are guilt arousing, but for other reasons such as those already discussed.

A source of complication in dream interpretation is that dreams often contain mental representations from a variety of sources, some completely trivial and others of great personal significance. This can lead to misinterpretation of dreams, in which excessive significance is attributed to the trivial items. The complication is that some events that appear trivial at the manifest level in dreams may be demonstrated through free association to have deep, personal significance at the latent level. Nevertheless, it is important to recognize that there is considerable danger of overinterpretation, and that most trivial events at the manifest level, as will be illustrated, are of no personal significance and simply indicate the routine operation of the principles of association, displacement, condensation, and narrative integration.

As already noted, the concerns expressed in dreams, although often the same as those in everyday life, differ in one important respect, namely dreams draw more heavily on unconscious thoughts. As a broad inhibitory state (as indicated by the reduction in sensitivity to external stimuli), the state of sleep disinhibits more focused inhibitions (Pavlov, 1923/1928).

Thus, thoughts that are inaccessible in the waking state due to repression may gain expression in dreams. Other thoughts that are not inhibited, but were simply not the focus of attention in waking life (the nonrepressed unconscious) can also gain expression in dreams. Thus, dreams can be expected to reflect a combination of trivial and significant conscious and unconscious concerns all combined in a confusing narrative organization.

Dream content is often represented in the form of metaphors that are difficult to interpret because only one side of the metaphorical equation is presented. That is, the referent that elucidates the metaphor is omitted. For example, when a poet says the eyes of his beloved are beautiful limpid pools, there is no doubt about the meaning of the limpid pools. However, if two beautiful, clear pools appear in a dream, it is far from evident what they represent, and the inclusion of incidental, unrelated material in the narrative further obscures the meaning of a particular dream element. Should the dreamer freely associate to the pools in an attempt to decipher their meaning, it could lead in many different directions, which may or may not include the correct source of the metaphor, and even if it were included, how can the interpreter of dreams determine that this and not some other interpretation is the correct one? The possibility for arriving at false interpretations through free association is therefore considerable, which is not to deny that whatever associations are made can reveal personally significant material. Singer (1997) emphasizes this by comparing dream associations to Rorschach responses.

THE EMPIRICAL INVESTIGATION OF TRANSPARENT DREAMS

For the past 10 years, I have kept records of my dreams for the purpose of learning about the principles by which dreams represent events. To this end, I recorded only dreams and dream fragments whose meaning seemed clear to me, and that I thought would be viewed that way by any reasonable person who did not have a strong investment in a particular theory. I tried to adopt an attitude of being as open minded as possible, and simply to follow wherever the dreams would lead. Having deciphered the meaning of a dream to the satisfaction of my reasonable-person criterion, I raised the question of how the meaning could be represented more directly in the dream, and what it revealed about the principles of dream representation that it was not more directly represented. I can best convey the procedure with an example. On one occasion, I was pressing a deadline for an article I had been invited to write. On the night of the dream, I went to bed feeling frustrated because I had written far too much, having gone off on tangents that wasted a great deal of time and effort. That night I had the following dream: I was running to catch a flight to a psychological convention, where I was scheduled to give an invited address. I was unable to run very fast because I was burdened with a lot of baggage. If I were to have any chance of making the flight, I would have to jettison some of my luggage, which I proceeded to do, but not without some reluctance. I was still uncertain about whether I would make the flight. At this point I awoke. I made a point of remaining in bed for a while, letting my thoughts wander. They soon turned to concern about the article I was writing. I found myself reproaching myself for the excess writing I had done, assessing what remained to be done, and feeling concerned about exceeding the deadline.

I recorded this dream because its meaning seemed clear to me, and I thought any reasonable person would agree with my interpretation that the dream reflected my concern about meeting a deadline, and that the excessive baggage corresponded to my excessive writing. I then raised the question of how the dream could have represented the situation more directly. The answer is that it could have depicted me anxiously typing away, glancing at my watch in desperation, and being surrounded by a mound of discarded pages. This led to the question of what could be learned about the principles of dream representation from the manner in which the dream deviated from such a direct representation.

In response to this question, I discovered the following answer: Dreams characteristically represent events in a displaced form, and they do this for more general reasons than the avoidance of unacceptable thoughts, as had been proposed by Freud. What remained to be determined is the particular form that the displacement took. Why did the dream select the specific metaphors of running to catch a flight and of carrying excess baggage rather than some other metaphors? To answer this question, I searched for clues in the events of the recent past and anticipated future. This procedure led nowhere, because I had no scheduled flight, and I could not recall any recent incidents or thoughts concerning baggage. I next freely associated to airplane flights and to baggage, and again came up with nothing. I finally decided that the most reasonable explanation for the selection of the metaphor of being frustrated at the thought of missing a flight is that a failure to meet airline schedules is one of the more common themes in my anxiety dreams. This theme seems to be a prototypical representation of frustration in my dreams. It thus has a very low threshold for access to dream working memory when I experience any kind of frustration. It will be recalled that, according to CEST, schemata in the experiential system are mainly generalizations from emotionally significant experiences. In this respect, it is noteworthy that some of my most acute anxiety about deadlines has involved flights, so such a representation should qualify for inclusion in the experiential system as a prototype for concern about meeting deadlines. That is, it is a metaphor with a very low threshold for inclusion in dream working memory following any relevant frustrating experience.

I formulated the following hypotheses using the process of interpreting dreams, as just described, and the principles of experiential processing outlined in CEST (see Table 3.1):

1. Dreams occur in the form of narratives that attempt to integrate dream representations in working memory from a variety of unrelated sources, only some of which may be personally significant.

2. Displacement commonly occurs in dreams, not only to avoid awareness of taboo thoughts, but for other reasons as well, including the regulation of cortical arousal (displaced, less-arousing representations are expressed, whereas highly arousing representations are inhibited), the influence of multiple associations resulting in compromises or condensation, the existence of prototypical representations with low thresholds for access to working memory, and the influence of narrative construction.

3. Many dreams are simply an extension of waking thought, and are not necessarily motivated by unconscious conflict or wish fulfillment.

4. People have prototypical representations of emotionally significant events in their experiential systems that have low thresholds for retrieval into dream working memory following the occurrence of any relevant cues in the environment or in thought.

5. The function of dreams is not, as is believed by many students of the dream, to assimilate during sleep experiences which could not be assimilated during the day. Rather, the dream simply reflects a person's thoughts under the altered state of consciousness that is sleep. This is not to deny that dreams, through disinhibition, can reveal important information that is otherwise inaccessible.

Following are examples of the dreams that I recorded and of how I interpreted them in a way that gave rise to hypotheses one through five. Because the dreams are typical representations of many other dreams in my sample, and the hypotheses were formed early in the interpretive process, some claim can be made for verification of the hypotheses. However, I do not wish to imply that I regard the research as an example of objective and rigorous scientific procedure. It can best be regarded as exploratory research that is more useful in the hypothesis-generating than in the verifying stage of research. The procedure I employed could have been influenced by subjectivity in the selection of the dreams, and despite my best intentions, in their interpretation as well.

Some aspects of the research are more objective than others and can lead to reasonably sound, albeit limited conclusions. For example, at a descriptive level, it can be demonstrated that certain dream phenomena occur at least some of the time, and therefore have to be taken into account in any theory about the nature of dream representations. Thus, it is clear that the dreams to be described provide evidence that dreams take the form of narratives. These narratives integrate disparate material. Displacement, condensation, and association influence dream content, and, most important, displacement frequently occurs for reasons other than the avoidance of distressing thoughts, which has profound implications for dream theory.

In the final analysis, it is, of course, up to the reader to judge whether the interpretations that I found highly compelling appear to be equally so, and whether they meet the reasonable, unbiased-person criterion.

A Prototypical Anxiety Dream. I am at a bus station in Switzerland. A clerk asks to see my documents before allowing me to board the bus. After inspecting the documents, she asks whether I made arrangements in Switzerland or in the United States. I am confused and anxious because I don't remember. I am also concerned about delaying the people behind me. I make a guess. She accepts what I say, and processes my papers. I wonder if I will get in trouble later if my guess is incorrect. She gives me a very large boarding pass with a conspicuous yellow and red design on it.

After awakening, I let my mind wander without attempting to direct it. My thoughts turn to having misplaced a folder with my notes about Jung in it. I have not been able to find the notes after having used them recently for a lecture to my personality class. I need the notes for a book I am writing with a colleague to whom I had promised to give them after my lecture. I feel badly that the absence of the notes is preventing her from working on the book. With this thought, the meaning of the dream becomes apparent. The real-life frustration, which was the result of my carelessness or mindlessness, is represented in the dream by my frustration at not being able to recall the arrangements for my tickets, also an indication of mindlessness. The question remains as to why the displacement. Why did the dream not show me looking for a folder with "Jung" written on it? Surely such a representation is within the capacity of the dream. Is the displacement in the dream protecting me from unacceptable thoughts, as Freudian theory would suggest? I doubt that a reasonable case can be made for this interpretation because there is no reason to believe that the representation in the dream of being mindless about misplacing notes about Jung would be more distressing to me than the representation of being mindless about the travel arrangements in Switzerland. In fact, if anything, I suspect it would be the other way around because the problem with the travel arrangements involves a more threatening situation. A more reasonable explanation is that mindlessness about travel arrangements is, for me, a prototypical representation of mindlessness, and therefore has a particularly low threshold for inclusion in dream working memory.

Why did the dream–narrative take place in Switzerland, and not in the United States or some other country? Because Jung was Swiss, the association of Switzerland could easily have been activated by the thought of Jung. Thus, one dream representation apparently has the ability to activate other dream representations in dream working memory through association. Another reason that Switzerland may have been incorporated in the dream is that a few days before the dream, I thought about planning a trip to Switzerland. The recency of a thought, holding all other factors constant, can be expected to be directly related to its availability in dream working memory. Thus, for more than one reason, Switzerland had occurred in my thoughts, and therefore was available for incorporation in dream working memory.

Why the strange red and yellow design on the boarding pass? The day before the dream, the colleague to whom I wanted to give the notes about Jung showed me a brightly colored red and yellow crayon drawing that her younger daughter had made. The drawing attracted my attention because of the bright colors, and it was associated with the issue of mindlessness through its connection with the person my mindlessness had inconvenienced. Thus, there were two reasons for the red and yellow drawing to be represented in the dream.

In conclusion, this dream provides an example of fear fulfillment, and also illustrates how incidental observations of no great personal significance, such as the red and yellow drawing, are incorporated in a dream together with more emotionally significant material, such as my concern about my mindlessness. It demonstrates how the dream combines disparate mental representations in dream working memory into a somewhat cohesive narrative. Given the material it had to work with, the dream actually performed quite well in this respect.

Is there any basis for assuming there is a latent meaning to the dream that my interpretation overlooked? I can see no basis for such a conclusion. Certainly, such a situation is possible. However, the fact that such an hypothesis is untestable, because free association to anything can lead to deeper personal concerns, makes it of questionable scientific value.

Does the dream provide any evidence that dreams assimilate material that was unassimilated during the day? Rather than providing a solution to my mindlessness, the dream simply portrayed it. Did the dream serve some other constructive purpose, such as to remind me to be more mindful? To benefit from such a purpose, I would have had to remember the dream, and it must be considered that most dreams are not remembered. Moreover, even had I remembered it, I might have simply dismissed it if I were not recording my dreams.

Alternatively, the fact that it was an anxiety dream that awakened me suggests that I might well have attended to it. Moreover, representing my mindlessness in the form of a prototype that was more threatening than a direct representation might have made it a particularly good reminder to me to be more mindful in the future. Thus, certain anxiety dreams may serve a useful function by drawing attention to a source of concern. This, of course, is similar to what occurs in waking life, and simply extends it to the dream, with the modification that the anxiety is intensified and presented in the form of a prototypical personal representation of anxiety. Note that such an interpretation is based on the assumption that a displaced representation can be more arousing than a direct representation. When this occurs, rather than protecting sleep, the displacement can awaken the dreamer. This suggests that, given significant threats, the alerting function of dream representations may take precedence over the sleep-protecting function, and that displacements can serve either function. In any event, it is not necessary to conclude that this dream is doing anything more than reflecting a current state of mind by representing a specific experience in the form of a prototypical metaphor. That people can make constructive use of such representations by attending to them, interpreting them, and resolving to do something about them is one thing. That this dream, independent of what use is consciously made of it, is accomplishing something worthwhile is another.

The Dream of the Dead Guppy. In this dream fragment, I had a very clear image of a dead guppy floating in a fishbowl. At first I thought there were no other fish, but then I observed two dead fish on the bottom of the bowl. I later thought that there also might be one living fish.

Letting my thoughts wander, I remembered that on the day preceding the dream I had noticed a fishbowl on the shelf in my workshop when I was looking for something else. I wondered why I had bothered saving it because I had no use for it. This was a slightly surprising event, and as I have observed on other occasions, such surprising, innocuous events frequently crop up in dreams. The next thought that came to mind was about a recent meal my wife and I had eaten in a Chinese restaurant. The scallop dish we ordered had very few scallops in it. After I complained to the waiter, he returned the dish with about two more scallops cut into small pieces to make them look like more. I felt frustrated and cheated, although the rest of the meal was acceptable.

Assuming that the guppies in the dream are a displaced representation of the scallops in the meal, the questions arise as to why the displacement occurred at all, and why it took the form of guppies rather than of some fish more similar to scallops, such as shrimp or oysters? The answer is suggested by Freud's concept of condensation, the convergence of multiple associations on a common symbol. First, the fishbowl was more strongly associated with guppies than with shrimp or oysters because guppies, not shrimps or oysters, are kept in fishbowls. Second, before going to bed I had watched a TV program in which there was a news item about air pollution. My association to air pollution was of once having killed all but one of the fish in my aquarium, which included guppies, by polluting the air in which the aquarium was kept. I did this by sanding and varnishing furniture in the same room as the fish. This suggests that the image of the dead fish in the tank was determined by the condensation of the following memories from real life experiences: the frustrating incident with the scallops the day before the dream, the surprising observation of the fishbowl the day before the dream, the news item about pollution the day before the dream, and the association to pollution of having killed my fish. What we learn from this dream fragment is that even in the case of innocuous situations, dream representations may be displaced, that the relation of dream representations to real life experiences may occur through associative connections, and that dream representations may be determined by a confluence of associations. (i.e., by condensation).

A Dream That Appears to Have a Sense of Humor. I dreamt that I was at an expensive restaurant. I asked the waiter why there were no prices on the menu. He said it was a very expensive restaurant, and that if you had to know the prices, you did not belong there. I tried to select something very modest. I picked a salad that came with a side order of fried brains. The bill came to $69.00. I asked the waiter why it was so expensive. He said the salad was $4.00 and the brains were $65.00.

The day before the dream I was preparing a lecture to which the entire faculty at my university and the public was invited. The occasion was that I was being honored for my research and scholarly achievements. I was surprised to receive that degree of recognition because I did not feel I was in the same league as others who had previously received it. While working on the lecture, I received a call from a colleague who said he had discovered a wonderful spot for trout fishing, and he invited me to go fly-fishing with him that evening. I would have loved to, but I declined because I had to work on the lecture. I thought it was a mixed blessing to have achieved some measure of success. It occurred to me that if I were even more successful, it would mean a change in lifestyle that would not necessarily be a happier one.

After awakening from the dream, I could initially make no sense of it. I then let my mind drift. It turned to the invitation to go fishing, and I recalled my thought about it being a mixed blessing. I burst into laughter as a thought came to mind that made the meaning of the dream apparent. The thought was, "It is too costly to have brains!"

This dream is interesting because of its creative use of metaphors. The very expensive restaurant that is beyond my means represents the thought that the honor bestowed on me is more than I deserve. The use of the brain metaphor appears to be a particularly clever joke. Does this indicate that the dream functioned at a relatively high level of intellectual complexity, including having a sense of humor? Possibly, as this dream might have been influenced by a relatively high degree of rational processing. Alternatively, it is not necessary to assume that the humor was intended by the dream. A simpler explanation is that the humor was simply a fortuitous consequence of the association between the price of a meal and the price of success.

The question remains as to why the price of success was represented by the price of a meal, rather than more directly. A reasonable possibility is that the lecture was associated with a meal because there was an honorary dinner before the lecture. Also, I had been concerned at the time about improving my diet by eating foods low in fat and cholesterol. This explains why I ordered a salad in the dream. The brains were too expensive in more than one way because not only did they cost a great deal in the dream, but they are extremely high in cholesterol. Thus the symbols appear to be over determined, and once again we see the operation of condensation.

A Dream That Appears to Teach a Lesson. In this dream, I enter a stone building that contains a variety of men's urinals. I go to one that piques my interest because it is strange, consisting of a rectangular concrete platform on which several people stand and urinate at the same time. Around its periphery water flows in a channel into which people are expected to urinate. When I urinate in the stream, some of the liquid sprays back in my face. I realize I should have urinated in the direction of the current, not against it.

The evening before I went to bed I watched a television drama. The hero was upset because the authorities at the boys' school at which he teaches were about to accept a gift of a statue from a rich alumnus. The school desperately needed a new gymnasium, and our hero believes the benefactor should be requested to change his gift to a contribution toward a new gymnasium. A colleague whom the hero dislikes tells him that it would be better to accept the gift of the statue gracefully rather than risk alienating the benefactor, who might later be induced to contribute to the gymnasium. Our hero later expresses his indignation at this suggestion to his wife, a warm, understanding woman with a great deal of practical intelligence. To his surprise, she finds considerable merit in his colleague's advice.

When I awoke from the dream, I desperately had to urinate, hence the urination theme in the dream. After urinating, I returned to bed and let my thoughts wander. They immediately turned to the television drama, and it occurred to me that I am similar to the figure in the dream with respect to unrealistically holding to my ideals when it is evident that it will accomplish nothing but alienate others. With that thought, the meaning of the dream became apparent, as attested to by the immediately following thought, "There are times when one should go with the flow, rather than oppose it." I also remembered that a number of years ago I had been surprised to see just such a urinal in France.

This dream illustrates an interesting use of a metaphor and the integration of thoughts related by association, but conceptually unrelated, into a coherent narrative. Given the mental representation of the need to urinate, the thought about the unfavorable consequences of behaving in a contrary and idealistic manner, and the dream's attempt to form a coherent narrative, the solution that the dream arrived at is impressive because it succeeded in integrating a variety of disparate elements in a cohesive manner. But why, more specifically, was a metaphor selected for representing going against the flow based on a long-term memory of a urinal in France? Why did the dream not more directly show me swimming against a current? This can be explained by the condensation of the need to urinate, the association to this of the urinal in France, and the thought that it is unwise to be rigidly idealistic. The inclusion of the urinal in dream working memory provided a way of integrating all of these elements into a relatively cohesive narrative. This dream illustrates well the principles of association, displacement, condensation, and narrative integration.

Considering that the dream conveyed an important lesson in a clever and creative manner, does this mean that the dream was adaptive in the sense of purposefully accomplishing something of adaptive value? Although this is possible, a simpler explanation is that the dream simply presented thoughts and perceptions in a form modified by the principles of dream representation, namely association, displacement, condensation, and narrative integration. From this perspective, nothing would be gained from the dream in the absence of recalling and interpreting it in the waking state.

The Dream of the Royal Carpet. This is one of the few dreams I have had in vivid color. In the dream, I am walking on a country path with another man. Magically, the path is all white, as if there is snow on it, but it is fall, not winter. Both of us are at first puzzled. I soon realize that the path is covered with a blanket of tiny white flowers that have just sprung up. Suddenly the path changes to purple. The other person says it is magic. I reply that it is not magic at all, but that the path is now covered with royal purple flowers in place of the white flowers.

The day before the dream I had remarked to my wife as we walked on a trail in the woods that the fallen leaves were like a beautiful carpet. Before going to sleep that night I had read an article by an eminent social–cognitive psychologist who discussed his research demonstrations of the irrationality of people's thinking. I thought that the researcher had, in effect, tricked the participants by providing them with misleading information, and that their only mistake was in assuming the examiner had given them information that was useful rather than deceptive. In discussing the research with my wife, I referred to it as a magician's trick, and I said I might write an article discussing it in just those terms. At the same time I was pleased that my own research involved no deception or trickery.

Another relevant incident occurred 2 days before the dream. A German professor visited me and said he had a grant to visit the most distinguished personality psychologists in the United States. He told me how much he admired my research and how honored he felt meeting me. I felt that he was treating me as if I were a far more famous psychologist than I am.

Immediately upon awakening, the meaning of the dream became apparent. The trick of the social psychologist was represented by the magic flowers blooming out of season. Most important, unlike my visitor, I was not fooled by the magic display, but had a natural explanation for the phenomenon. The royal purple flowers represented the visiting professor treating me like royalty.

Assuming my interpretation is correct, what is to be learned from the dream not having represented the situation more directly, such as by showing a scene in which I detect the deception in a colleague's research and another scene in which I am admired by a visiting professor? Surely, if the dream had a message to convey, such direct representations would be preferable to displaced ones. Why, then, the displacement? In this case, there is nothing in a direct message that would either be so guilt arousing or so positively exciting as to rouse me from sleep. A more reasonable explanation is that the displacement was produced by the influence of multiple associations, the net effect of which was to produce a compromise, an outcome of condensation.

If a task of dreams is to integrate all the elements in dream working memory into as coherent a narrative as possible, it follows that there should be a tendency to select those representations for inclusion in a dream that are most amenable to integration, as was illustrated in the previous dream. That is, holding all other factors constant, including the influence of all activated associations, the integrative function of the dream can be expected to influence the selection of whatever representations gain access to dream working memory. Expressed otherwise, elements to be included in dream working memory are selected, in part, according to their fit in the context of the emerging dream narrative. This can help account for why a royal purple carpet appeared in the dream. Such a magical appearance following the previous magical appearance of the white carpet helped to integrate all the dream representations into a coherent and inclusive narrative. What is not clear is the extent to which such an integrative process is a consequence of processing in the experiential mode, and the extent to which it involves a contribution by the rational mode. According to CEST, the experiential mode itself has an integrative function, although to a lesser extent than the rational mode.

In this dream, the elements in real life that appeared in displaced form in the dream were the observation of a carpet of colored leaves on the forest floor the day before, the visit of an admiring foreign professor, and my pride in my ability to detect the deception in someone's research. The dream representations included the discovery of a magic trick and a forest path in royal purple. How are these disparate elements to be integrated into a cohesive story? The dream did a masterful and creative job of accomplishing this by its use of metaphors, much as a poet might proceed. The only difference is that poets normally include the referents of their metaphors, such as by stating, "and a path of purple flowers—a royal carpet spread at the feet of a king—suddenly appeared before him."

An Example of One Dream Elucidating Another. I dreamt that I had a pet sheep that was deliberately provoking a dog in a meadow. I tried to get the sheep to stop, but it ignored me because it enjoyed demonstrating its dexterity in avoiding the lunges of the dog. It was disconcertingly casual about the whole matter, as if what it did was so easy that it did not have to concentrate. It was completely unaware of another dog that was sitting on the sideline and observing what was going on. The sheep backed right into the other dog, who grabbed it by its hindquarters. I yelled at the dog, and thought of pulling it off, but realized that if I did, it would attack me. The dog finally let go, but in doing so it raked the hindquarters of the sheep. I thought the sheep would bleed to death, or at the very least, would be unable to walk, and that I should take it to a veterinarian immediately. Surprisingly, it walked off as if unhurt, but I still thought I should take it to a veterinarian.

At first, I could make no sense of the dream. My only relevant association was to the sheep at a farm that I pass every day on the way to my office. Last year, two dogs got into the compound and seriously injured several sheep. As I was trying to make other associations, another dream that had occurred before the one about the sheep came to mind and clarified the dream about the sheep. In the first dream, I am a young man (rather than the professor emeritus that I actually am) who is a passenger in a car being driven by an older man. We are on a multiple-lane highway with fast-moving traffic. Suddenly the car swerves out of control and goes up an embankment and onto railroad tracks. I urge the driver to get back on the road quickly, before a train comes. Getting on the highway is dangerous, because the traffic is moving very fast. I extend my arm outside of the window signaling that we wish to pull out, and one of the cars slows and lets us get safely back on the highway.

The day preceding the night of the dream, I had to slam on the brakes because I had casually looked away from the road, and when I looked back there was a stationary car a short distance in front of me. I had been following the car at a safe distance and at a steady speed for more than a mile when it suddenly stopped because the driver had to wait for an opportunity to make a left turn. I was lucky that I was barely able to stop in time. I was considerably shaken by this incident and realized that I should be more attentive in the future. The thought occurred to me that I may be getting less alert as I get older, and that it was therefore particularly important to concentrate on being alert.

The first dream clarified the meaning of the second dream by drawing my attention to the importance of being alert. The sequence of dreams raises the question of why there was greater displacement in the second dream than in the first. This supports the view that the function of displacement is not limited to protecting the dreamer from awareness of distressing thoughts because if that were the case, it would make no sense for the dream to first present its message fairly directly, and then after giving away its secret, disguise its message in a subsequent dream.

The question remains as to why the issue of alertness was represented in the second dream by a sheep that was too casual. In the incident 2 years ago, when the sheep were attacked by the dogs, the safety of the sheep was not jeopardized by their carelessness but by events beyond their control. I usually notice the sheep when I pass them on the way to my office, and when I do it brings to mind the attack by the dogs. The dream apparently combined this thought with the accident I had barely avoided.

Also of interest is the displacement in the first dream, in which the driver who is responsible for the accident is an older man, and I am a younger man, who not only is not responsible for the near accident, but who is the one who corrects the situation. This appears to be an example of wish fulfillment. The displacement of the responsibility for losing control of the automobile to someone other than me may have served to reduce arousal, thereby preserving sleep, which would be consistent with the observation that, in other dreams in which I have been responsible for an unfavorable outcome, I was awakened by the dream. On the other hand, despite greater displacement in the form of a careless sheep, I was awakened by the second dream. This, of course, may be because there was a strongly negative outcome in the second dream that was avoided in the first one. In any event, the pair of dreams provides additional evidence for the ubiquity of displacement in dream representations, and indicates that displacement occurs for reasons other than to protect the dreamer from taboo thoughts. The two dreams also indicate how one dream can elucidate the meaning of another. The first dream also provides some verification of the meaning of the less obvious symbols in the second dream. The pair of dreams, with their evident concerns about age, death, and competition with a younger person, support the view that dreams often reflect realistic, everyday concerns; and do not necessarily reflect deeply repressed, unacceptable thoughts and impulses. That they represent concerns in symbolic form, such as a speeding car representing life speeding by, and an error-prone youthful driver representing the fallibility of youth, provides further evidence that displacement and symbolic representation occur routinely in the dream, and not solely for the purpose of disguising unacceptable thoughts.

Lessons From a Repetitive, Traumatic Dream. Some years ago my younger daughter, who was 12 years old at the time, asked me if it is true that psychologists can interpret dreams. She said she wanted to understand the meaning of a dream she had the night before. She then added that she had been having very similar frightening dreams for as long as she can remember. In these dreams, she is desperately trying to catch up to some people who are ahead of her, and she is afraid that something terrible will happen before she gets there. Sometimes she is on a bicycle and sometimes she is running, and she always wakes up in terror. In the dream last night she was on a frozen wasteland trying to catch up to some older children who were far ahead of her. She was gradually catching up when she heard the howling of wolves in the distance. The howling grew louder and she was afraid the wolves would catch her before she reached the others. Suddenly a crevasse appeared, and she could advance no further. She woke up in terror with the thought that the wolves were closing in.

I told her that together we would try to understand what the dream meant. I asked her if she had any idea why she had the dream last night, and if any particular experience or observation could have triggered it. She said she had seen a scary television program before going to bed that night. The plot concerned a group of people who were lost in a barren wasteland of ice in the arctic, and it was uncertain if they would make it to safety. I asked her to report whatever thoughts or images came to mind when I gave her a word or image to consider. I started with the word "wolf," which she said reminded her of our German shepherd, a dog of which she was very fond. This went no place, so I asked her to report what else came to mind about wolf. After a moment, she said she had a ridiculous thought that was not worth reporting. I asked her to report it anyway, and she said she thought of a family by the name of "Wolf." She added that this was the family who had lived in a house near us when I was a visiting professor one summer at the University of Washington in Seattle. She said there were two girls in the family who were about the same ages as she and her older sister. The Wolfs' house was on a hill that overlooked their beach on Lake Washington. The older girls would roll down the hill and stop just before they reached the water. They then would tease the younger girls, daring them to do the same. The younger girls would do it, she said, but they were afraid and didn't like it. Suddenly, she looked startled, and said, "Oh, my goodness, I just had the strangest memory. I remember the time when I was a little kid and went sledding in my flying saucer, and smashed my head against a tree and nearly got killed. I had completely forgotten about it, but the memory is very clear now."

The incident that my daughter referred to occurred when she was 4 years old. We live on a hill overlooking a pond. On the day before the traumatic incident she had been sliding down the hill on her flying saucer. The snow was new fallen and soft, so the flying saucer did not go very fast, and she could easily maneuver it around the large oaks that grew on the hillside. Later in the day the temperature rose and the snow softened. That night it turned cold again, and on the next day there was an icy crust on the snow. My older daughter and her friend were walking by the pond at the bottom of the hill. It occurred to my younger daughter, who was at the top of the hill, that she could quickly catch up to them by going down the hill on her flying saucer. The saucer immediately gathered great speed, spun out of control, and sent her crashing head first into a large oak tree. Fortunately, she received only a glancing blow, or she would not have survived. The blow opened a large gash on her forehead from which blood gushed profusely, covering her eyes so she could not see. I was not home at the time, but fortunately a friend was visiting my wife, so she was able to drive to the hospital while my wife held our daughter on her lap and tried to comfort her. On the way, the child kept asking for reassurance that she was not going to die. She received 20 stitches that closed the wound so well that it healed with only the slightest hint of a scar. In time, the incident was forgotten, and my daughter made no mention of her frightening dreams until the incident I reported. Of particular interest, after recovery of the memory of the traumatic incident, the dream disappeared.

What lessons does this dream have to teach? Not surprisingly, my daughter had been sensitized to the event that almost killed her and that was the source of the dream. Normally, such a sensitivity is indicated by the intrusion of thoughts about the accident and by anxiety whenever reminders of the event are encountered. This, of course, is usually adaptive, because it alerts the person to possible recurrences of the dangerous event as well as to the occurrence of similar events. Assuming there are no recurrences, the sensitivity gradually diminishes, which is also adaptive. If the threats are great enough, as in the traumatic neurosis, the sensitivities are also exhibited in dreams. In my daughter's case, the sensitivity that was no longer manifested in her waking life continued to be exhibited in her dreams. How is this to be explained? One possibility is that the pain of the memory in real life made her avoid fully facing it, which is the condition necessary for assimilating the experience (Epstein, 1983). More specifically, she shut off the normal process of assimilation, which requires remembering the threatening event and understanding its significance within a broader context of meaning, such as realizing at the experiential, schematic level that although the world is more threatening than had previously been recognized, it is, nevertheless, a reasonably safe place in which to exist and to find happiness (Epstein, 1991; Janoff-Bulman, 1992; McCann & Pearlman, 1990).

The avoidance of the memory of the trauma in my daughter's conscious thinking did not extend to the memory of the incident in her unconscious (experiential) mind, so it kept reappearing in her dreams following exposure to relevant cues. In all likelihood, the very avoidance of the memory in her conscious thinking prevented her from assimilating the experience, which resulted in its maintenance in her unconscious thinking and therefore in her dreams. To the extent this explanation is correct, it follows that repetitious dreams often reflect unfinished business. Note that this does not necessarily imply that dreams play a constructive role in completing the unfinished business. If they did, the dreams would have long since disappeared. What was necessary to assimilate the experience and lay it finally to rest was to have the threatening event reassessed in a manner that reduced the threat by viewing it from a new and broader perspective. Once the situation was consciously identified, it became apparent that the recurrence of the threatening event was not a realistic concern. Thus, a recurrent anxiety dream suggests a failure of the dream to resolve a problem. It is important to note, in this respect, that the assimilation that took place with respect to my daughter's dream required conscious awareness of the dream, and did not occur simply as a result of the dream itself.

GENERAL DISCUSSION

Before proceeding, it will be helpful to provide a brief summary of the theory of dream representations I am proposing. The dream theory is an outgrowth of cognitive–experiential self-theory (CEST). According to CEST, there are two fundamental processing systems, the experiential system and the rational system, that operate in parallel and are interactive.

The experiential system is an automatic, preconscious, primarily imagistic, concrete, holistic, associative system, whiich integrates information through the construction of narratives. The rational system is a deliberative, primarily conscious system that operates according to a person's understanding of the rules of logic. The systems are assumed to contribute to behavior along a continuum from completely experiential to completely rational processing, with almost all behavior falling between the extremes.

In the waking state, the experiential system functions as a learning system. During the altered state of consciousness that is sleep, the experiential system, in the absence of external stimuli on which to focus (Domhoff, 1996; Fisher & Greenberg, 1996; Singer, 1997), operates using inner stimuli consisting of memories, thoughts, images, and feelings. These are often stimulated by the events of the day. In this mode of operation, lacking an external focus of attention, the experiential system is broadly associative and operates using whatever elements are in dream working memory by attempting to integrate them within a narrative framework. The narratives are often bizarre because the elements are frequently conceptually unrelated, consisting of a conglomeration of conscious and unconscious trivial and significant thoughts and images in any combination and at various levels of displacement. These elements gained access to dream working memory because they were at an appropriate level of excitation, as they were the strongest representatives of multiple associations, because of their coherence with a developing narrative, or because of some combination of these factors. Dream constructions, like waking information processing, vary along a continuum of degree of experiential, relative to rational, processing. However, in dreams, compared to waking mental activity, there is a considerable shift toward experiential processing, with variation around the mean of that shift. Although dreams involve a far greater degree of experiential processing than waking-state information processing, they cannot be regarded as a pure state of experiential processing. This is true because dreams vary in degree of coherence and organization, which suggests a contribution by the rational system.

The dreams that were presented provided examples of the following principles of dream representation: association, condensation, displacement, symbolic representation, and narrative integration. All of these elements are consistent with Freud's dream theory. What is not consistent with his theory is that many of the dreams were simply extensions of everyday waking thought, rather than disguised expressions of inhibited thoughts, and therefore of unconscious conflict. Thus, displacement occurred for reasons other than the avoidance of awareness of unacceptable thoughts. This suggests that Freud was an excellent observer of the dream process, but that his theorizing about dreams was incorrect.

There are at least three reasons why Freud may have overemphasized the role of unconscious conflict in dreams. Probably the most important is the prevalence of displacement in dreams. Freud made the reasonable assumption that displacement occurs because direct representations of the dreamer's unconscious thoughts were unacceptable to the ego, and therefore, if directly expressed would be distressing to the point that they would disrupt sleep, which is protected by dreaming. The near ubiquity of displacement in dreams led Freud to infer the widespread occurrence of unconscious conflict as the source of dreams. A second reason why Freud may have overestimated the prevalence of unconscious conflict in dreams is that he exclusively studied the dreams of neurotic individuals, including himself (Jones, 1953). A third reason is that Freud's interest in dream interpretation was to uncover the unconscious conflicts of his patients for therapeutic purposes. Thus, he was motivated to find unconscious conflict in the dreams of his clients, and his method of free association all but guaranteed that he would find what he sought. The result was that Freud never suspected that displacement could occur for reasons other than the avoidance of taboo thoughts, a topic to which I turn next.

Reasons for the Ubiquity of Displacement in Dreams

Perhaps the most interesting and surprising observation with respect to the dreams that were presented is the degree to which displacement was present. Displacement occurred for trivial events as well as for more personally significant ones. Of particular interest, it occurred in situations where it seemed to serve no purpose because the message it disguised was acceptable, and for that matter was not always new. The explanation for the widespread occurrence of displacement suggested by CEST is, as previously noted, that it occurs for four reasons: the regulation of cortical arousal (of which avoidance of taboo thoughts is a subset), the net influence of all activated associations, the availability of prototypical representations with low thresholds for access to working memory, and the fit (or coherence) of a particular representation within the context of a dream narrative. According to the first reason, when a thought or image is cortically arousing to the point that the state of relaxation necessary for maintaining sleep is jeopardized, displacement to a related representation that is less arousing occurs. The result is the inhibition of the most strongly arousing representations and the appearance in dream working memory of less arousing displaced representations. It should be noted that this explanation not only accounts for the kinds of distress produced by the unacceptable thoughts that Freud emphasized, but also considers all other sources of excitation, both positive and negative, conscious and unconscious. Supportive of this hypothesis is the absence of displacement in traumatic dreams that reproduce the experience of a traumatic event and awaken the dreamer in a state of terror (Grinker & Spiegel, 1945).

The second reason that displacement occurs is because of the combined influence in dream working memory of all activated associations, resulting in compromises. It was assumed, consistent with the concept of condensation, that each association to an event exerts a pressure for representation in dream working memory, and that it is the net effect from all such associations that determines the symbolic representation that appears in a dream. In several of the dreams that were reported, the influence of combined associative connections on dream representations was apparent. Moreover, it can reasonably be assumed that if single associations influence dream representations, multiple associations can do the same, thereby producing compromises, or condensations.

The third reason that displacement occurs is because prototypical representations have low thresholds for access to dream working memory. Such prototypes are interesting because they indicate that the experiential system, possibly with some contribution by the rational system, operates by deriving generalizations that it represents concretely, not infrequently in the form of metaphors. Once a metaphor is formed and repeatedly activated, it tends to become more accessible to dream working memory than both the direct and otherwise displaced representation of the instigating experience. That this occurs despite the anxiety that may accompany some metaphorical representations, which may be much greater than would be produced by a direct representation of the precipitating event, suggests that the alerting function of the experiential system in anxiety dreams often takes precedence over its sleep-maintaining function.

The fourth reason for displacement is the tendency for dreams to integrate dream representations within the framework of narratives. It will be recalled that, according to CEST, it is by means of narrative constructions that the experiential system integrates discrete elements of experience into meaningful wholes, often with means-end implications that provide lessons in living. This is readily observed in the Bible, the most widely read book in Western society, which presents lessons in living by means of parables rather than by intellectual discourse. According to CEST, dream content is influenced by the tendency of the experiential system to integrate individual concrete representations in stories, but not necessarily for the purpose of providing lessons in living. Instead, representations are integrated simply because it is the nature of the experiential system to combine individual items in narratives. That is, narrative integration is simply the way the experiential system operates, as contrasted with the abstract, analytical thinking of the rational system. As noted previously, the dream does the best it can to integrate the conceptually unrelated elements in dream working memory into some kind of coherent story, but it usually is able to succeed only in a limited way because of the conceptually discrepant elements it must integrate. Nevertheless, the striving for some kind of coherence in formulating narratives exerts an influence on the manner in which specific experiences are represented in dreams. All other things being equal, those representations are favored that are most compatible with the overall dream narrative. This effect contributes to displaced rather than direct representations because a specific direct representation may fit less well with the overall narrative than does a displaced representative.

Does Dreaming, In and of Itself, Accomplish Anything?

A common view among students of the dream is that dreams serve constructive functions, such as providing creative solutions to problems or assimilating the unassimilated events of the day, and relatedly, that dreaming is necessary for maintaining mental well-being (Breger, 1967). So far as I can determine, there is no evidence that dreaming, in and of itself, accomplishes anything worthwhile, which is not to deny that dreaming can be put to useful ends.

According to Koestler (1964), in his book *The Act of Creation*, creative solutions to important problems often occur in the absence of deliberate conscious effort, suggesting that the solutions occurred as the result of the operation of unconscious processes. He reports that often a person has worked hard at preparing the way for a solution to a problem, reaches an impasse, and then, during an incubation period in which deliberate effort is suspended, the solution suddenly appears. It should be considered that, although the outcome of such unconscious processing may be revealed in a dream, this does not necessarily mean that the dream played a role in the solution to the problem. The dream may simply be reflecting a solution previously unconsciously reached, much as it reflects past thoughts and events in everyday life without causing them.

Many examples suggest that the dream is not essential for unconscious processes to provide creative solutions to important problems. Both Einstein (cited in Ghiselin, 1952) and Galton (cited in Penrose, 1989) reported that they thought in nonverbal ways, suggesting a contribution by the experiential system in solving problems in physics and mathematics. After arriving at intuitive solutions, they had to engage in a laborious procedure of finding words to communicate their insights to others. That there is no evidence that dreaming, per se, provides creative solutions to problems does not, of course, rule out the possibility that it does. The consideration that dream content varies according to a range of combinations of experiential and rational processing makes it plausible that dreams, under certain circumstances, can make creative contributions.

Although the question of whether unidentified dreams can contribute to creative solutions to problems cannot be answered at this time, there can be no doubt but that consciously identified dreams can be. As a result of their loosely associative nature, they can, at the very least, accidentally establish new and interesting connections among mental elements, which when identified, can be capitalized on by the conscious, rational mind. In a way, this is like saying that dreams sometimes get the right answer for the wrong reason, which is not to deny the possibility that they sometimes may get the right answer for the right (i.e., the intended) reason. This issue requires much more research attention than it has received.

Do dreams serve the constructive function of assimilating information that could not be assimilated during the day? This interesting hypothesis lacks empirical support. It is evident from repetitive dreams, such as the one by my daughter, that dreams may reflect a failure in assimilation. Moreover, the repetition itself suggests attempts by the unconscious mind to assimilate the material, but there is no reason to believe that simply repeating a displaced or direct representation of unassimilated material in a dream resolves anything. Resolution occurred in the case of my daughter's dream only after it had been interpreted by the conscious mind. It would be wonderful, indeed, if dreams routinely assimilated otherwise unassimilable experiences. Dreaming then would be highly therapeutic, people would resolve their deepest conflicts automatically, and there would be little need for psychotherapists. Unfortunately, this does not appear to be the case.

The view that dreaming is necessary for maintaining physical and mental well-being is consistent with the assumption that dreams allow otherwise unassimilable experiences to be assimilated, thereby reducing stress. The view was also suggested by early research about brain activity during sleep, which demonstrated that deprivation of the sleep phase of rapid eye movement (REM) sleep, the phase in which most dreaming occurs, was associated with distress and other symptoms (see review in Van De Castle, 1971). However, later research has not been consistent with the earlier findings. Moreover, even if REM sleep were unequivocally demonstrated to be necessary for well-being, this would not necessarily mean that dreaming is necessary, because it may be that aspects of the REM phase other than the dreaming that occurs in it are what is important.

In summary, at this stage of our knowledge about dreams, the simplest explanation of what dreams accomplish is that, in and of themselves, they accomplish nothing other than to reflect what is occurring in a person's mind. Yet the possibility remains that they do more, and this possibility is supported by the consideration that dreams occur over a range of involvement of rational relative to experiential processing. Moreover, even if dreams accomplished nothing of value in and of themselves, if properly utilized, they can be a useful source of information about unconscious motives, conflicts, and concerns when recalled and interpreted in the conscious state. Dream content can also be used as a kind of Rorschach test (Singer, 1997), which I believe is the way it was unintentionally used in the past. Apart from whether interpretations of dreams are factually correct (i.e., reveal the true meaning of dream symbols) people's free associations to dream symbols can be revealing just as people's associations can be to inkblots. However, there is an obvious danger in such a procedure because it encourages subjective biases to enter both into the dreamer's associations and the interpreter's interpretations, which can lead to false verification of the investigator's hypotheses. There can be little doubt that such biases have exerted an important influence on previous dream theories that have relied on uncontrolled free association to dreams examined in an unconstrained manner.

ACKNOWLEDGMENTS

Preparation of this article and the research reported in it were supported by National Institute of Mental Health Research Grant MH01293 to S. Epstein.

I wish to acknowledge the contribution of Jefferson A. Singer, who served as action editor on this manuscript. His astute questions led me to reconsider the role of the rational system in the dream process and its implications for creative solutions to problems, among other important issues.

REFERENCES

Breger, L. (1967). Function of dreams. *Journal of Abnormal Psychology Monograph, 72,* 1–28.

Dollard, J., & Miller, N. E. (1950). *Personality and psychotherapy.* New York: McGraw-Hill.

Domhoff, G. (1996). *Finding meaning in dreams.* New York: Plenum.

Epstein, S. (1983). Natural healing processes of the mind: II. Graded stress inoculation as an inherent coping mechanism. In D. Meichenbaum & M. Jaremko (Eds.), *Stress prevention and management: A cognitive-behavioral approach* (pp. 39–66). New York: Plenum.

Epstein, S. (1991). The self-concept, the traumatic neurosis, and the structure of personality. In D. Ozer, J. M. Healy, Jr., & A. J. Stewart (Eds.), *Perspectives in personality* (Vol. 3A, pp. 63–98). London: Jessica Kingsley.

Epstein, S. (1994). Integration of the cognitive and the psychodynamic unconscious. *American Psychologist, 49,* 709–724.

Epstein, S., Pacini, R., Denes-Raj, V., & Heier, H. (1996). Individual differences in intuitive–experiential and analytical rational thinking styles. *Journal of Personality and Social Psychology, 71,* 390–405.

Fisher, S., & Greenberg, R. (1996). *Freud scientifically appraised.* New York: Wiley.

Freud, S. (1965). *The interpretation of dreams.* (J. Strachey, Trans.). New York: Avon Books. (Original work published 1900)

Ghiselin, B. (1952). *The creative process.* Berkeley: University of California Press.

Grinker, R. R., & Spiegel, J. P. (1945). *Men under stress.* Philadelphia: Blakiston.

Janoff-Bulman, R. (1992). *Shattered assumptions.* New York: The Free Press.

Jones, E. (1953). *The life and work of Sigmund Freud,* Vol. 1. New York: Basic Books.

Kihlstrom, J. F. (1987). The cognitive unconscious. *Science, 237,* 1145–1152.

Koestler, A. (1964). *The act of creation.* New York: Macmillan.

McCann, I. L., & Pearlman, L. A. (1990). *Psychological trauma and the adult survivor: Theory, therapy, and transformation.* New York: Brunner/Mazel.

Pavlov, I. P. (1928). *Conditioned reflexes.* (W. H. Gantt, Trans.). New York: Liveright Corp. (Original work published 1923)

Penrose, R. (1989). *The emperor's new mind.* Oxford: Oxford University Press.

Reber, A. S. (1993). *Implicit learning and tacit knowledge.* New York: Oxford University Press.

Schachter, D. L. (1987). Implicity memory: History and current status. *Journal of Experimental Psychology: Learning, Memory, and Cognition, 13,* 501–518.

Singer, J. L. (1997). *Daydreams, the stream of consciousness and self-representations.* Unpublished manuscript.

Van De Castle, R. L. (1971). *The psychology of dreaming.* New York: General Learning Press.

Independent Emotions and Consciousness: Self-Consciousness and Dependent Emotions

Carroll E. Izard
Brian P. Ackerman
David Schultz
University of Delaware

Almost a quarter century ago, Singer (1973) drew connections between make-believe play in young children and the later development of day-dreaming, fantasy life, and introversion. Singer also described the processes in consciousness that characterize this dimension of personality. He described one of the aspects of introversion as taking pleasure in self-awareness and another aspect as fear of social situations. Implicit in this theorizing are connections between emotions, self-consciousness, and personality. This was well before research from three- and five-factor models of personality provided strong empirical support for the existence of extroversion–introversion as a stable trait of the individual.

These thoughts contained a nascent theoretical framework that Singer later made explicit. He defined his position in terms of a cognitive-affective approach, and he applied the approach to the study of imagination, consciousness, personality, and psychotherapy. Because he is a scientist and a clinician, Singer brought extraordinary insights to the understanding of these phenomena.

Singer was influenced by Tomkins' (1962, 1979) description of ideo-affective organizations and scripts, as is our own conception of affective–cognitive structures and emotion–cognition relations. In our differential emotions theory (Ackerman, Abe, & Izard, 1998; Izard, 1977), affective–cognitive structures and schemas define the principal contents of consciousness and reflect the organization of emotions in personality and psychopathology.

The idea of affective–cognitive structures represents our common ground with Tomkins and Singer, and it is a pivotal construct in this chapter.

In this chapter, we present our view of the relation of emotions to consciousness and their role in framing perception, attention, learning, and memory. Next, we discuss the development of affective–cognitive structures as the source of emotion knowledge and emotion knowledge as the basis of empathy, prosocial behavior, and social competence. Finally, we discuss self-consciousness as a factor in the cognitively dependent emotion systems, and self-consciousness and the self-concept as factors in self-enhancement and dysadaptive behavior.

EMOTIONS AND CONSCIOUSNESS

We define emotions in terms of neural, behavioral–expressive, and experiential components, and we describe the latter in terms of motivational feeling states and action tendencies (Izard, 1993). In our framework, emotions are by definition a source of awareness. Although we are unaware of many important cognitive processes such as those involved in implicit perception, learning, and memory, we are always aware of emotion feelings.

An emotion feeling can exist without being in focal awareness, as is often the case when the emotion of interest drives creative activities. In a child's consciousness, awareness of the interest and joy that motivate his or her make-believe play takes a back seat to imaginary friends. Furthermore, emotion feelings can exist in consciousness without being accessible through language. This is always the case when emotions are activated in prelingual infants, and it is often the case in repressors and people suffering from alexithymia and other conditions characterized by dissociative processes (Bonanno & Singer, 1990). In some patients with facial agnosia, the presentation of the face of a loved one may elicit physiological arousal (increased skin conductance) but not face recognition or verbal report of emotion feelings (Tranel & Damasio, 1985). Of course, in conditions like alexithymia, a complex set of factors, not merely language accessibility, determines the dissociation of feeling and the ability to label and describe feeling.

Even dissociated emotion feelings are part of the contents of consciousness, and they influence cognition and behavior. Their lack of connection to language and reason does not strip them of their motivational properties. We propose that dissociated and unarticulated emotion-feeling states are the basis of what has been termed unconscious motivation, a position that seems consistent with Singer's (1985) interpretation of Freudian psychoanalytic theory. Some investigators of emotion–cognition relations have argued that emotion is always present in consciousness, always coloring appraisal and putting a value on everything we perceive (Johnson & Weisz, 1994; Pratto, 1994). In the next section, we review studies that demonstrate the effects of emotions on perceptual and cognitive processes.

EMOTIONS AND COGNITION

Neurological Substrates

Within the past 15 years, advances in neuroscience have allowed us to understand more fully some of the neural pathways by which the emotions influence cognition. The amygdala is now seen as an important center for the processing of a stimulus' emotional significance, at least in terms of threat. This processing can occur through subcortical or corticolimbic pathways (see LeDoux, 1989). Projections from the amygdala include destinations in the sensory cortex, association cortex, hippocampus, and the brainstem and forebrain cholinergic systems. The amygdala's emotional computation (LeDoux, 1989) concerning a stimulus can potentially influence, among other things, conceptual information processing, complex pattern recognition, and cortical arousal and vigilance. Given the expansiveness of the amygdala's projections, LeDoux (1994) suggests that the possibilities for the emotions' modification of cognitions are "enormous" (p. 222).

Attention

The emotions influence cognitive activity profoundly through their channeling of attention. By directing attentional processes, the emotions affect learning and memory. The fearful person appraises the world through tunnel vision. The joyful or happy person sees the world through rose-colored glasses, and the interested person is the one who concentrates on the matter at hand.

Empirical evidence for emotional influences on attention is most abundant for anxiety. Many view a primary function of anxiety to be the detection of threat (e.g., Eysenck, 1992; cf. McNally, 1996). Several different research methodologies have successfully detected this effect of anxiety. For example, compared to less anxious people, highly anxious people are found to: (a) detect an angry face amongst many happy faces more quickly (Byrne & Eysenck, 1995), (b) respond more quickly to probes occupying a position previously occupied by a threatening stimulus, compared to probes following a nonthreatening stimulus (Broadbent & Broadbent, 1988; Fox, 1993), and (c) get stuck on the content of what threatening words represent and are slower to label the color in which such words are presented (Mathews & MacLeod, 1985). These and other findings concerning other emotions provide ample support for Buck's (1986) proposition that, "in an important sense, feeling determines what we know" (p. 363).

Learning and Memory

Bower (1994) suggested that when an aversive event occurs to an organism, information is required to remedy the current situation, and to ensure that the situation does not recur. A person remedies a situation and prevents its recurrence by linking important aspects of the incident together (i.e., learning). The perception of personally relevant aspects of a situation is facilitated by attentional biases. In an important sense, therefore, emotional activity drives adaptive learning.

The effects of emotions on attentional biases occur not only in perception but also in working memory. Events of greater emotional intensity are more likely to be rehearsed (i.e., processed) in one's mind for hours or days after the experience, contributing to the personal significance of the event (cf. Christianson, 1992). This rehearsal may initially serve the function of examining associations between different stimuli within the situation, but then may also serve the function of strengthening the associations made in one's memory, heightening accessibility of the event memory to consciousness for the future. Extremely intensive emotional experiences may motivate maladaptive rehearsal and reliving of the experience, as seen in people with posttraumatic stress disorder.

Greater rehearsal of emotionally intensive experiences increases one's subsequent ability to retrieve memories of these experiences. In particular, the more emotional an experience, the easier it is to retrieve its memory into consciousness. The common example of this concerns *flashbulb memories*, in which people often can remember the context in which they heard about an event associated with strong emotions, such as President Kennedy's assassination or the bombing of Baghdad. A more subtle example, though, is seen in the finding that people who keep a diary and rate the emotional intensity of different events show better recall for those events with higher ratings of emotional intensity (Bower, 1994). Memory recall is also facilitated somewhat by congruity between one's emotional state at the time of recall and one's emotional state when the event was stored in memory (Blaney, 1986; Bower, 1992). This effect seems to be stronger for positive than for negative emotions (Matt, Vázquez, & Campbell, 1992; J. A. Singer & Salovey, 1988; Teasdale & Fogarty, 1979). In response to the consistency of findings on mood-dependent memory, Isen (1984) suggested that "material in memory must be encoded according to how that material makes one feel" (p. 218). Although this idea needs a stronger empirical foundation, it seems clear that in an important way emotional experience guides ongoing learning and memory.

Processing

A phenomenon related to attentional biases, learning, and memory is the processing of sensory material. Emotional states are found to have profound effects on the efficacy of an individual's cognitive processing. The work of Isen and her colleagues demonstrates these influences, especially with regard to positive affect and problem solving. The induction of even a mild positive affect (e.g., by being given a small bag of hard candy with pretty bows on the wrappings, by watching a few minutes of television bloopers) promotes creativity, efficiency, and thoroughness in problem solving. For example, positive mood induction motivates identifying a particular person (e.g., a bartender) with a weakly but plausibly related category (e.g., nurturant) to a significantly greater degree than does a more neutral affect induction (Isen & Daubman, 1984). Two qualifications are noteworthy concerning this finding. First, this effect is found if the category is positively perceived (e.g., nurturant people) but not when it is negatively perceived (e.g., emotionally unstable people) (Isen, Niedenthal, & Cantor, 1992). Second, positive mood induction enhances not only the ability to perceive relatedness between objects but also differences between objects (Isen, Daubman, & Nowicki, 1987). These findings suggest that in certain contexts, positive affect promotes greater elaboration of stimulus information (Isen, 1994).

Empirical results relating to the effects of negative emotions on cognitive processing are consistent with Bower's (1994) idea that these emotions function to facilitate adaptive learning. For example, negative mood induction: (a) heightens critical appraisal of a persuasive argument (Bless, Bohner, Schwarz, & Strack, 1990), and (b) binds a person to be consistent with prior decisions when making social judgments (Fiedler, Asbeck, & Nickel, 1991).

Finally, brief and even subliminal exposures to affectively biased stimuli affect subsequent person perception and interpersonal behavior in a way congruent with the bias (cf. Forgas & Bower, 1987; Tobias, Kihlstrom, & Schachter, 1992). For example, compared to control children, children induced into a negative mood and then exposed to interadult anger make more negative appraisals of the situation and have greater expectations of distress and lesser expectations of happiness for future interactions between the adults (Davies & Cummings, 1995). The implication of this and other findings is that emotional arousal and tone have a profound effect on the initial construction and appraisal of interpersonal events.

The initial effects of emotion on perception and memory become enduring influences when experiences link emotions and cognition to form affective–cognitive structures.

AFFECTIVE–COGNITIVE STRUCTURES, EMOTION KNOWLEDGE, AND SOCIAL BEHAVIOR

Taking a developmental perspective, differential emotions theory (DET) assumes the primacy of emotions and the relative independence of the emotions and cognitive systems. Hence, we assume that the major work in mental development consists of forming connections between emotions and cognition (Ackerman et al., 1998; Izard, 1994). For example, we focus not on developmental changes in emotions and cognitive abilities, but on the development of affective–cognitive structures and emotion knowledge. The construct of emotion knowledge organizes much of the recent developmentalist research about emotion–cognition relations. The construct of emotion knowledge, described in more detail in the following pages, concerns the individual's understanding of the various facets of emotion and emotion-cognition-behavior relations. It may be viewed as part of what Salovey and Mayer (1990) define as emotional intelligence, which also involves abilities that enable emotion regulation. A considerable body of evidence points to the potential importance of children's emotion knowledge for social adjustment (Denham, in press).

We have described nine facets of emotion knowledge (Schultz & Izard, 1997). These facets relate to emotion expression, emotion activation, emotion experience, and the understanding of intersystem relations or relations among emotion, cognition, and action.

Understanding Emotion Expression

Emotion-expression recognition is the most fundamental aspect of emotion knowledge. Evolutionary–genetic processes form the foundation for the recognition of emotion signals in patterns of facial movement. In primate research, Sackett (1966) has demonstrated that monkeys reared in social isolation respond differentially and appropriately to projected images of species-typical emotion expressions. Furthermore, Rolls (1986) has described the neuronal components involved in emotional and social responses to faces as a system that evolved for the rapid and reliable identification of signals that are fundamental to primate social life.

Only a few hours after birth, human infants show a preference for attending to the human face (Fantz, 1963) and some ability to mimic facial movements (Field & Walden, 1982; Meltzoff & Moore, 1992). In the first

6 months of life, infants respond differentially to mothers' simulated expressions of sadness and anger (Izard et al., 1995). By 7 months of age, infants can demonstrate the ability to recognize and categorize several emotion expressions (LaBarbera, Izard, Vietze, & Parisi, 1976; Nelson, 1987), and this ability improves during the next couple of months (Caron, Caron, & Myers, 1985).

Apparently, the ability to recognize discrete emotion expressions derives largely from our evolutionary–biological heritage and requires little in the way of specific experiences and learning. Cognitively, it requires only basic perceptual discriminations and the categorization of the physiognomic features in an emotion signal (facial expression). Thus, genetically driven abilities to recognize and categorize particular patterns of facial expressions guarantee that consciousness during social interactions will be frequently influenced by representations of emotion signals. The role of emotion information was vital in human evolution and remains critical in social adaptation. That we have an innate ability to recognize basic emotion signals does not preclude the role of learning and experience. It may be necessary to learn variations in expressions or expression-context relations brought about by culture-specific display rules or idiosyncrasies. Social learning enables us to distinguish the social smile used as a greeting and the genuine smile of joy.

Although recognition of the expressions of basic emotions emerges early and largely as a function of the maturation of the neural substrates and sensory organs of the perceptual system, emotion-expression labeling depends on cognitive development, particularly on verbal ability (Ackerman, Kogos, & Izard, 1996). Much that is relevant to individual and social functioning hinges on one's ability to label emotion signals of others (Bandura, 1986; Denham, 1998). Without the ability to decode the emotion information in emotion expressions in the social context, a person can neither respond appropriately to others' motivations and intentions nor appreciate social feedback relating to their behavior.

In summary, we hold that emotion–expression knowledge is an important source of early emotion information that gets linked to images and thoughts to form simple affective–cognitive structures. Much of the content of other facets of emotion knowledge derives from and builds upon these simple structures to form more complex affective–cognitive structures and higher order facets of emotion knowledge.

Understanding Emotion Experience

There are two levels of understanding emotion experience. The most rudimentary level is an appreciation of emotion as a motivational condition or quality of consciousness. This entails sensing that the activation of a particular emotion changes the quality of consciousness and tends to direct cognition and behavior along certain lines. In the normally developing individual, this level of understanding gradually merges with the ability to access emotion feeling through language. Language development, parenting practices, and socialization drive the increasing ability to label and articulate emotion experiences. The latter provides tools for regulating emotion experiences, and hence influences the quality of consciousness and social adaptation.

Without the ability to label internal signals, the individual is incapable of articulating emotion experiences and of dealing with them as affective–cognitive structures. A person senses and responds to the motivational power of the emotion feelings in consciousness but lacks the regulatory capacities that come with language and the linking of feelings and thoughts in affective–cognitive structures. Thus, emotion feelings that are not represented in consciousness as affective–cognitive structures are much more likely to run out of control and become maladaptive (cf. Tomkins, 1962).

Understanding Emotion Activation

Understanding of emotion activation derives from accurate appraisals of the personal significance of internal and contextual information (Lazarus, 1991). It also involves causal attributions based on assessment of the intentions of others and their ability to control their behavior (Roseman, 1991; Weiner, 1985). Toddlers have some understanding of the causes of their emotion feelings (Bretherton, Fritz, Zahn-Waxler, & Ridgeway, 1986), but their understanding is limited, as is their ability to articulate their perceptions. The development of the understanding of emotion activation is a function of both language development and socialization. In a sample of economically disadvantaged preschool children in a Head Start Program, 70%-90% correctly identified at least one activator (cause) of their experiences of joy, sadness, anger, and fear, but only 5% to 20% could identify three activators for each of these emotions. In a similar sample of first-grade children, 36% to 58% identified three activators of their experiences of these four emotions, indicating substantial growth in this facet of emotion knowledge between the ages of 5 and 7 years (Izard & Levinson, 1997; Kogos, Levinson, & Izard, 1997). Such growth in emotion knowledge results in part from cognitive and language development, and in part from parents' talking with children about their emotion feelings (Bretherton et al., 1986; Dunn, Bretherton, & Munn, 1987).

The other facet of understanding emotion activation is understanding of the causes of emotions in others. This facet of emotion knowledge has higher cognitive prerequisites because it requires all the abilities involved in understanding the causes of one's own emotions plus evaluation of cognitive and affective perspectives. Thus, the development of empathy should facilitate the growth of this understanding. Some signs of empathy, as well as providing indications of understanding of the causes of emotions in others, are present in rudimentary form in toddlers and preschool children (cf. Eisenberg et al., 1993) but probably continue to develop throughout the life span.

Understanding Intersystem Relations

The understanding of relations among the emotions, and cognitive and action systems develops as children learn the connections between specific emotions and particular thoughts, action tendencies, and actions. Basic to these developmental processes is a growing appreciation of the motivational properties of each of the discrete emotions, the effects of emotion feelings on self and others, and the effects of one's emotion expressions on others. It is the understanding of intersystem relations that enables understanding of display rules and dissimulation. For example, to understand dissimulation, one must understand that, in a particular emotion, cognition, action sequence, thoughts, feelings, and expressive behavior can operate as relatively independent modular systems.

In summary, we have argued that emotion knowledge—understanding of emotion expressions, emotion experiences, emotion activation, and relations among emotions, cognition, and action—is represented in consciousness primarily in the form of affective–cognitive structures. We have argued that affective–cognitive structures are vital to consciousness and are the building blocks of traits of personality. Absence of appropriate connections between our conscious experience of emotions and our thoughts and actions leads to maladaptive behavior.

It is easy to make a case for deficits in emotion knowledge as determinants of antisocial behavior. For example, emotion knowledge is clearly a prerequisite to empathy. Inability to detect and decode the emotion signals of another person precludes the possibility of responding with like emotion and assessing affective perspective. Inability to empathize with a person removes one of the barriers to aggressive behavior. A review of numerous studies about this topic revealed substantial evidence for at least a modest negative correlation of empathic responsiveness with antisocial behavior and interpersonal aggression (Miller & Eisenberg, 1988). Thus, the absence of vicariously experienced emotion in consciousness tends to increase the likelihood of undesirable social behavior.

SELF-CONSCIOUSNESS AND EMOTION EXPERIENCE

Affective–cognitive structures constitute a vital part of consciousness because they frame understanding of worldly events and motivate action tendencies. Affective–cognitive structures also constitute the stuff of self-consciousness because they mediate self-evaluations in the form of embarrassment, shame, guilt, and pride. The relation between self-concepts and self-conscious emotions is reciprocal. For instance, affective–cognitive structures represent attachment relations with parents (i.e., working models). These relations contribute to the child's earliest understanding of the enduring self (Cicchetti & Toth, 1994) and to the differentiation between self as an agent and knower and self as an object of evaluation. Self-evaluations, in turn, are expressed in discrete self-conscious emotions, which reflect and affect the self-concept. Embarrassment, shame, guilt, and pride derive from consciousness of self, but in turn constitute the affective qualia of self-consciousness and contribute variably to enduring feelings about the self-concept (e.g., self-esteem).

Self-Conscious Emotions

Self-conscious emotions and other basic emotions differ in their dependence on cognitive processes. Emotions like sadness, joy, anger, and fear represent independent emotions systems (Ackerman et al., 1998). Because they appear early in childhood, they do not depend on cognitive development or cognitive appraisal processes for activation, the experience of the emotion (i.e., feeling state) per se does not change with age, and the emotions are associated with unique and universal facial expressions. These independent systems recruit cognitive processes in the form of appraisals and causal attributions derived from representations of prior emotion experiences in memory. Eventually, the resulting affective–cognitive structures form enduring aspects of personality and the self-concept.

In contrast, self-conscious emotions, such as shame, guilt, and pride represent cognition-dependent emotions systems. Self-conscious emotions appear later in childhood, require cognitive operations involving perspective taking, appraisal, and attribution, and they require some knowledge of the standards and conventions governing social interactions. The experience of self-conscious emotions may change in depth of feeling and intensity with age, and these emotions are not associated with discrete and universal expressive behavior. These dependent emotion systems always reflect interactions of affective and cognitive processes, and self-conscious emotion experiences require a prior sense of self and an ability to distinguish between self and other.

Self-conscious emotion experiences have three general components. First, emotions such as shame, guilt, and pride usually are experienced within interpersonal contexts, and involve a sense of public scrutiny of self (real or imagined) and public comparison of self and other. The comparison is mediated by an understanding of normative standards for appropriate public behavior. These standards are socialized and internalized throughout childhood, and reflect both personal standards and conventional rules of social intercourse.

The second component is a self-referential evaluative process. The process constitutes a metaanalytic operation in which the self as an agent reviews the performance of self as an object. The operation usually involves: (a) an evaluation of performance versus internalized normative standards, (b) an attribution of personal responsibility for the performance, and (c) negatively or positively valenced affect associated with failure (shame, guilt) or success (pride), and finally (d) the affective experience of a self-conscious emotion often motivates some social action, though the action differs for particular emotions. Shame, for example, is associated with withdrawal from social relations, or if it turns to anger, a defensive lashing out and externalizing of self-blame. Shame is intensely focused on the social self, and the social image is at stake in shame-eliciting situations. Guilt, in contrast, is associated with behaviors that repair social relationships. Guilt relates more to the moral self with the conscience at stake in guilt-eliciting situations.

The third component describes the variable impact of self-conscious emotions on the self-concept. Self-conscious emotions focus on different aspects of self and behavioral performance, and the impact of the emotion experiences on enduring self-concepts varies accordingly. Shame, for instance, focuses on core properties of the self per se, and shame experiences can generalize into feelings of worthlessness and powerlessness. Thus, although shame can be a transient emotion that is elicited episodically, frequent shame experiences can affect self-conceptions generally, and self-esteem in particular. Guilt, in contrast, focuses on behavior, and guilt experiences have few necessary implications for enduring self-conceptions, given that the experiences are shame free. Feelings about self are shielded from guilt experiences, in particular, to the extent that transgressive behaviors are associated with atonement and reparation. Failures to atone, however, may induce shame. Embarrassment flows from the same well as shame, but is evoked by less serious social violations and really focuses on the situated or presented self rather than on core aspects of self. Shame and embarrassment may simply represent differences in affect intensity. Like guilt, experiences of embarrassment have few implications for enduring self-conceptions. We should note that self-conscious emotions often covary. For example, shame frequently accompanies guilt experiences.

Developmental Processes

Processes reflecting the articulation and transformation of affective–cognitive structures mediate the development of self-conscious emotions. Many recent studies (cf. Tangney & Fischer, 1996) have focused on developmental variations in the apparent experience and expression of shame, guilt, and pride. There is considerable debate about how these emotion experiences might look in toddlers and preschool children, who do not fully understand the verbal labels for the emotions. Indeed, debate remains even about the fundamental issue of whether children younger than 7 or 8 years of age have the capability of truly experiencing these self-conscious emotions. Theorists disagree, for instance, about the extent to which cognitive acquisitions, such as operational perspective taking and the experience of and ability to represent the self-concept, are necessary and sufficient or both for the experience of self-conscious emotions (cf. Barrett, 1996; Ferguson & Stegge, 1996; Lewis, 1991). In differential emotions theory (DET; Ackerman et al., 1998; Izard, 1991), the cognitive dependence of self-conscious emotions means that cognitive acquisitions are necessary, but not sufficient, for experiencing and articulating these affects.

Measurement is a central problem for inferences about the self-conscious emotions of younger children because the emotions are not associated with unique facial expressions or expressive behavior. Instead of relying on a discrete expression to infer emotion experience, then, researchers infer the experience by pairing adult-defined situational correlates of the experience with some child behavior that cues awareness of the situation. For example, Barrett, Zahn-Waxler, and Cole (1993) paired a situation in which a leg fell off a doll with differential responding by 2-year-olds in avoiding the situation (*avoiders*) or trying to repair the situation (*amenders*). Both kinds of behavior seem to signify awareness of a social transgression, and the behavioral differences suggest that children experience different underlying emotions: Avoidance may be shame related and amending behaviors suggest guilt. The inferential problems of these claims are endemic to many situations in which the experiencer cannot or will not validate the experience. For example, the children may have experienced some negative emotion other than shame or guilt, or might have experienced some inchoate and general negative feeling, or some process other than an emotion feeling state may have caused the behavior.

Despite measurement issues, our analysis of the components of selfconscious emotions and empirical research suggests that several developmental processes mediate the emergence of mature self-conscious emotions. The timing and nature of the emotions may differ somewhat for specific emotions, but in broad scope the processes apply generally to all self-conscious emotions. First, 2- and 3-year-olds seem to experience shamelike, guiltlike, and pridelike reactions to events such as toilet training accidents and successes and damage to household objects. These primitive reactions can be tied to other indexes of the emergence of self-consciousness, and this emergence constitutes the lower bound of readiness to experience self-conscious emotions in any form. Second, the affective–cognitive structures that mediate these emotions are transformed by cognitive acquisitions and emotion-related experiences in middle childhood (cf. Mascolo & Fischer, 1996). Increases in perspective-taking ability and separation of self and other, and increases in the ability to represent and evaluate self (i.e., metacognitive acquisitions) contribute to the cognitive side of the transformation. The experiential side includes socialization and interpersonal processes that facilitate appreciation of social rules and standards, and the associations of public successes and failures with affective processes.

Third, the transformative processes in later childhood reflect the emergence of causal attributes of personal responsibility and the emergence of more generalized self-evaluations (cf. Ferguson & Stegge, 1996). The primary appraisals of younger children focus on outcomes rather than on causes, and typically evoke emotions such as sadness and joy (Weiner, 1986). In contrast, the secondary appraisals of older children focus on causes and attributions of personal responsibility, and are more likely to evoke emotions like pride and guilt. Similarly, the emergence of general feelings about self and competence, as opposed to some specific aspect of self and performance, are necessary for intense feelings of shame. These developmental processes, lasting through late childhood, represent a progressive internalization and transformation of social rules and responsibility. Self-conscious emotions index this internalization because they both represent and enhance the personal significance of events.

Fourth, the relations between the experience of self-conscious emotions and the articulation and consolidation of the self-concept are reciprocal. The early appearance of shamelike, guiltlike, and pridelike reactions may require a primitive self-concept, but they also embody the self-concept and spur both recognition of self processes and development of self-focus.

Fifth, individual differences in the experience of self-conscious emotions also emerge early in childhood and become stable and consolidated with the late emergence of more mature forms of the emotions. Frequent and intense experiences of these emotions generate stable affective–cognitive structures that become a core aspect of a child's personality. Certainly, interpersonal relations in the family, discipline practices, and emotion socialization processes, in interaction with temperamental characteristics, have a great deal to do with children's experiences of self-conscious emotions (cf. Kochanska, 1995). Gender differences in these processes may contribute to differences in the experiences of self-conscious emotions for girls and boys and hence to differences in the vulnerability to internalizing problems (Zahn-Waxler, 1993; Zahn-Waxler, Cole, & Barrett, 1991). We next describe briefly some of the roles self-conscious emotions may play in the behavior of older children and adolescents.

Individual Differences and Psychopathology

For DET, discrete emotions motivate specific action tendencies that generally are adaptive. Shamefree guilt experiences, for example, motivate reparative behaviors and hence facilitate prosocial interactions. Emotion experiences are reciprocally related to representations of self-concepts, however, and it is likely that frequent and intense experiences of some self-conscious emotions, such as shame, may impair indexes of self-appreciation. Researchers have linked shame proneness, for example, to low self-esteem and to psychological symptoms of distress, including depression and anxiety (Tangney, Burggraf, & Wagner, 1995).

Similarly, the components of a hopeless or helpless attributional style, involving attributions of internal causality and stability and generality of negative events, play a role in shame experiences. There is a natural conjunction, then, between frequent failure experiences, frequent shame experiences, and a generalized sense of hopelessness or helplessness (cf. Thompson, 1989). Realization of a helpless style in response to life events may await consolidation of a generalized and stable sense of self and self-blame in early adolescence (Nolen-Hoeksema & Girgus, 1994), but the vulnerability for this style may come from earlier experiences of shame in childhood in response to perceived moral failures and social transgressions. Even earlier roots may be found in children's negative representations of self in attachment relations with parents and in self-directed and self-critical cognitions and emotions associated with negative interactions with parents about developmental tasks.

These links of shame-proneness with emerging psychopathology entail internalizing problems in children. Baumeister, Smart, and Boden (1996), however, have linked shame to externalizing problems as well, and to aggression in boys in particular. In this case, the root problem is not low self-esteem, but highly inflated self-esteem and favorable views of self that are relatively unstable. Because this self-appreciation is so unrealistically high, it is quite vulnerable to negative social feedback and disconfirming evidence. Such evidence threatens the generalized self-concept and provokes shame experiences. Shame, in turn, provokes anger and aggressive and ego-defensive lashing out against the threatening object or person.

Implications for Clinical Psychological Science

Several aspects of the emotion theory and research that we have described have implications for clinical psychological science and practice. First, exciting new findings identify the neural substrates of emotion, especially the structures and pathways involved in evaluating the emotional significance of events. For example, these data show that emotions can be activated through a thalamoamygdala pathway without involvement of the neocortex or higher order cognitive processes (LeDoux, Sakaguchi, & Reis, 1984). This may mean that clinicians will face the challenge of helping clients to deal with emotions they cannot readily label and articulate (LeDoux, 1996; cf. Bonanno and Singer, 1990).

Second, the evidence indicates that there are distinct neural pathways for each of the major aspects of emotion: emotion activation, emotion expression, and emotion feeling states (Damasio, 1994; LeDoux, 1996). An implication for psychotherapy is that components of emotion may become dissociated. The dissociation of expressions and feelings presents a difficult challenge for psychotherapy.

Third, the DET model of emotion activation describes both cognitive and noncognitive processes that activate emotions. Evidence for noncognitive emotion-activating systems suggests new concerns for cognitive and cognitive–behavioral psychotherapy.

Fourth, a growing body of evidence shows that emotions can have profound influences on perception, learning, and memory (e.g., see Niedenthal & Kitayama, 1994). A case can be made for the proposition that emotions drive cognition (Izard, 1993; Johnson & Weisz, 1994; Zajonc, 1980), and this suggests that cognitively based therapies should include techniques for inducing emotions and examining their linkages to thought and action (Greenberg & Safran, 1989; Izard, 1971, 1991). The controlled environment of psychotherapy should provide a stage for evaluating the effects of a particular emotion on perception and the construal of interpersonal communications and actions.

Fifth, research has now produced a considerable amount of information about the adaptive and functional properties of emotions. This includes knowledge of the distinct organizational and motivational characteristics of the basic emotions (Izard, 1991; Malatesta, 1990). This knowledge should directly inform the psychotherapist's effort to help clients regulate emotions and use emotions adaptively in coping with life's problems.

Sixth, emotion theory has described intersystem connections, the development of affective–cognitive structures, and the ways in which these structures persist to become building blocks of personality or psychopathology (Ackerman et al., 1998; Izard & Harris, 1995). Clinical psychology needs more research about the development of appropriate and inappropriate emotion–cognition connections. Such research should provide the science base for more effective psychotherapy and prevention programs.

Seventh, evidence indicates that children's understanding of emotions (emotion knowledge) predicts adaptive behavior (Denham, McKinley, Couchoud, & Holt, 1990; Garner, Jones, & Miner, 1994; Izard, 1971; Schultz & Izard, 1997). Gains from basic research about the development of emotion knowledge and emotion regulation should inform and strengthen efforts in clinics and schools to facilitate the development of social competence and the prevention of behavior problems (Goleman, 1995; Salovey & Mayer, 1990).

CONCLUSION

For DET, emotional development consists mainly of the development and transformation of affective–cognitive structures. Independent emotions like joy and sadness appear early in infancy, become linked to cognitive processes throughout childhood, and the resulting affective–cognitive structures form the stuff of consciousness. Cognition-dependent emotions appear later in childhood and reflect affective–cognitive structures linked to representations of self. Dependent emotions such as shame and guilt form the core of self-consciousness. These implicit connections among emotions, self-consciousness, and personality are core aspects of DET; and are also core aspects of Singer's seminal work about cognitive–affective processes in imagination, consciousness, and psychotherapy.

ACKNOWLEDGMENT

This work was supported by the William T. Grant Foundation Award #93-1548-93.

REFERENCES

Ackerman, B. P., Kogos, J. L., & Izard, C. E. (1996). *The relation between emotion knowledge and social variables for 4- and 5-year old children from low-income families.* Manuscript in preparation.

Ackerman, B. P., Abe, J. A., & Izard, C. E. (1998). Differential emotions theory and emotional development: Mindful of modularity. In M. Mascolo & S. Griffin (Eds.), *What develops in emotional development?* (pp. 85–106). New York: Plenum.

Bandura, A. (1986). *Social foundations of thought and action.* Englewood Cliffs, NJ: Prentice-Hall.

Barrett, K. C. (1996). A functionalist approach to shame and guilt. In J. P. Tangney & K. W. Fischer (Eds.), *Self-conscious emotions: The psychology of shame, guilt, embarrassment, and pride* (pp. 25–63). New York: Guilford.

Barrett, K. C., Zahn-Waxler, C., & Cole, P. M. (1993). Avoiders versus amenders: Implications for the investigation of guilt and shame during toddlerhood? *Cognition and Emotion, 7,* 481–505.

Baumeister, R. F., Smart, L., & Boden, J. M. (1996). Relation of threatened egotism to violence and aggression: The dark side of high self-esteem. *Psychological Review, 103,* 5–33.

Blaney, P. H. (1986). Affect and memory: A review. *Psychological Bulletin, 99,* 229–246.

Bless, H., Bohner, G., Schwarz, N., & Strack, F. (1990). Mood and persuasion: A cognitive response analysis. *Personality and Social Psychology Bulletin, 16,* 331–345.

Bonanno, G. A., & Singer, J. L. (1990). Repressive personality style: Theoretical and methodological implications for health and pathology. In J. L. Singer (Ed.), *Repression and dissociation* (pp. 435–470). Chicago: University of Chicago Press.

Bower, G. H. (1992). How might emotions affect memory? In S. A. Christianson (Ed.), *Handbook of emotion and memory* (pp. 3–31). Hillsdale, NJ: Lawrence Erlbaum Associates.

Bower, G. H. (1994). Some relations between emotions and memory. In P. Ekman & R. J. Davidson (Eds.), *The nature of emotion: Fundamental questions* (pp. 301–318). New York: Oxford University Press.

Bretherton, I., Fritz, J., Zahn-Waxler, C., & Ridgeway, D. (1986). Learning to talk about emotions: A functionalist perspective. *Child Development, 57,* 529–548.

Broadbent, D. E., & Broadbent, M. (1988). Anxiety and attentional bias: State and trait. *Cognition and Emotion, 2,* 165–183.

Buck, R. (1986). The psychology of emotion. In J. LeDoux & W. F. Hirst (Eds.), *Mind and brain: Dialogues in cognitive neuroscience* (pp. 275–300). Cambridge, England: Cambridge University Press.

Byrne, A., & Eysenck, M. W. (1995). Trait anxiety, anxious mood, and threat detection. *Cognition and Emotion, 9,* 549–562.

Caron, A. J., Caron, R. F., & Myers, R. S. (1985). Do infants see emotional expressions in static faces? *Child Development, 56,* 1552–1560.

Christianson, S. A. (1992). Emotional stress and eyewitness memory: A critical review. *Psychological Bulletin, 112,* 284–309.

Cicchetti, D., & Toth, S.L. (1994). *Disorders and dysfunctions of the self.* Rochester, NY: University of Rochester Press.

Damasio, A. R. (1994). *Descartes' error: Emotion, reason, and the human brain.* New York: Putnam.

Davies, P. T., & Cummings, E. M. (1995). Children's emotions as organizers of their reactions to interadult anger: A functionalist perspective. *Developmental Psychology, 31,* 677–684.

Denham, S. (1998). *Preschoolers' expression and understanding of emotion.* New York: Guilford.

Denham, S. A., McKinley, M., Couchoud, E. A., & Holt, R. (1990). Emotional and behavioral predictors of preschool peer ratings. *Journal of Child Psychology and Psychiatry, 32,* 595–608.

Dunn, J., Bretherton, I., & Munn, P. (1987). Conversations about feeling states between mothers and their children. *Developmental Psychology, 23,* 132–139.

Eisenberg, N., Fabes, R. A., Carlo, G., Speer, A. L., Switzer, G., Karbon, M., & Troyer, D. (1993). The relations of empathy-related emotions and maternal practices to children's comforting behavior. *Journal of Experimental Child Psychology, 55,* 131–150.

Eysenck, M. W. (1992). *Anxiety: The cognitive perspective.* Hove, UK: Lawrence Erlbaum Associates.

Fantz, R. L. (1963). Pattern vision in unborn infants. *Science, 140,* 296–297.

Ferguson, T. J., & Stegge, H. (1996). Emotional states and traits in children: The case of guilt and shame. In J. P. Tangney & K. W. Fischer (Eds.), *Self-conscious emotions: The psychology of shame, guilt, embarrassment, and pride* (pp. 174–197). New York: Guilford.

Fiedler, K., Asbeck, J., & Nickel, S. (1991). Mood and constructive memory effects on social judgment. *Cognition and Emotion, 5,* 363–378.

Field, T., & Walden, T. (1982). Perception and production of facial expressions in infancy and early childhood. In H. Reese & L. Lipsitt (Eds.), *Advances in child development and behavior* (Vol. 16, pp. 169–211). New York: Academic Press.

Forgas, J. P., & Bower, G. H. (1987). Mood effects on person-perception judgments. *Journal of Personality and Social Psychology, 53,* 53–60.

Fox, E. (1993). Allocation of visual attention and anxiety. *Cognition and Emotion, 7,* 207–215.

Garner, P. W., Jones, D. C., & Miner, J. L. (1994). Social competence among low-income preschoolers: Emotion socialization practices and social cognitive correlates. *Child Development, 65,* 622–637.

Goleman, D. (1995). *Emotional intelligence.* New York: Bantam.

Greenberg, L. S., & Safran, J. D. (1989). Emotions in psychotherapy. *American Psychologist, 44,* 19–29.

Isen, A. M. (1984). Toward understanding the role of affect in cognition. In R. Wyer & T. Srull (Eds.), *Handbook of social cognition* (Vol. 3, pp. 179–236). Hillsdale, NJ: Lawrence Erlbaum Associates.

Isen, A. M. (1994). Positive affect and decision making. In M. Lewis & J. M. Haviland (Eds.) *Handbook of emotions* (pp. 261–277). New York: Guilford.

Isen, A. M., & Daubman, K. A. (1984). The influence of affect on categorization. *Journal of Personality and Social Psychology, 47,* 1206–1217.

Isen, A. M., Daubman, K. A., & Nowicki, G. P. (1987). Positive affect facilitates creative problem-solving. *Journal of Personality and Social Psychology, 52,* 1122–1131.

Isen, A. M., Niedenthal, P., & Cantor, N. (1992). An influence of positive affect on social categorization. *Motivation and Emotion, 16,* 65–78.

Izard, C. E. (1971). *The face of emotion.* New York: Appleton-Century-Crofts.

Izard, C. E. (1977). *Human emotions.* New York: Plenum.

Izard, C. E. (1991). Perspectives on emotions in psychotherapy. In J. D. Safran & L. S. Greenberg (Eds.), *Emotion, psychotherapy, and change* (pp. 280–289). New York: Guilford.

Izard, C. E. (1993). Four systems for emotion activation: Cognitive and noncognitive processes. *Psychological Review, 100,* 68–90.

Izard, C. E. (1994). Cognition is one of four types of emotion activating systems. In P. Ekman & R. Davidson (Eds.), *The Nature of Emotion: Fundamental Questions* (pp. 203–207). New York: Oxford University Press.

Izard, C. E., Fantauzzo, C. A., Castle, J. M., Haynes, O. M., Rayias, M. F., & Putnam, P. H. (1995). The ontogeny and significance of infants' facial expressions in the first nine months of life. *Developmental Psychology, 31,* 997–1013.

Izard, C. E., & Harris, P. (1995). Emotional development and developmental psychopathology. In D. Cicchetti & D. J. Cohen (Eds.), *Manual of Developmental Psychopathology: Vol. 1. Theory and methods* (pp. 467–503). New York: Wiley.

Izard, C. E., & Levinson, K. L. (1997). *Emotional memories of economically disadvantaged children: Relations to discrete emotions and aggressive behavior.* Unpublished manuscript, University of Delaware, Newark, DE.

Johnson, M. K., & Weisz, C. (1994). Comments on unconscious processing. In P. M. Niedenthal & S. Kitayama (Eds.), *The heart's eye: Emotional influences in perception and attention* (pp. 145–164). San Diego, CA: Academic Press.

Kochanska, G. (1995). Children's temperament, mothers' discipline, and security of attachment: Multiple pathways to emerging internalization. *Child Development, 66,* 597–615.

Kogos, J. L., Levinson, K. L., & Izard, C. E. (1997, April). *Antecedents and behavioral correlates of children's self-reported anger.* Poster session presented at the biennial meeting of the Society for Research in Child Development, Washington, DC.

LaBarbera, J. D., Izard, C. E., Vietze, P., & Parisi, S. A. (1976). Four- and six-month-old infants' visual responses to joy, anger, and neutral expression. *Child Development, 47,* 535–538.

Lazarus, R. S. (1991). *Emotion and adaptation.* New York: Oxford University Press.

LeDoux, J. E. (1989). Cognitive-emotional interactions in the brain. *Cognition and Emotion, 3,* 267–189.

LeDoux, J. E. (1994). Cognitive-emotional interactions in the brain. In P. Ekman & R. J. Davidson (Eds.), *The nature of emotions: Fundamental questions* (pp. 216–223). New York: Oxford University Press.

LeDoux, J. E. (1996). *The emotional brain: The mysterious underpinnings of emotional life.* New York: Simon & Schuster.

LeDoux, J. E., Sakaguchi, A., & Reis, D. J. (1984). Subcortical efferent projections of the medial geniculate nucleus mediate emotional responses. *Journal of Neuroscience, 4,* 683–698.

Lewis, M. (1991). Self-conscious emotions and the development of self. In T. Shapiro & R. Emde (Eds.), New perspectives on affect and emotion in psychoanalysis. *Journal of the American Psychoanalytic Association (Suppl.), 39,* 45–73.

Malatesta, C. Z. (1990). The role of emotions in the development and organization of personality. In R. A. Thompson (Ed.), *Nebraska Symposium on Motivation: Vol. 36. Socioemotional development: Current theory and research in motivation* (pp. 1–56). Lincoln: University of Nebraska Press.

Mascolo, M. F., & Fischer, K. W. (1996). Developmental transformations in appraisals for pride, shame, and guilt. In J. P. Tangney & K. W. Fischer (Eds.), *Self-conscious emotions: The psychology of shame, guilt, embarrassment, and pride* (pp. 64–113). New York: Guilford.

Mathews, A., & MacLeod, C. (1985). Selective processing of threat cues in anxiety states. *Behavior Research and Therapy, 23,* 563–569.

Matt, G. E., Vázquez, C., & Campbell, W. K. (1992). Mood-congruent recall of affectively toned stimuli: A meta-analytic review. *Clinical Psychology Review, 12,* 227–255.

McNally, R. J. (1996). Cognitive bias in the anxiety disorders. In D. A. Hope (Ed.), *Nebraska Symposium on Motivation: Vol. 43. Perspectives in anxiety, panic, and fear* (pp. 211–250). Lincoln: University of Nebraska Press.

Meltzoff, A. N. & Moore, K. M. (1992). Early imitation within a functional framework: The importance of person identity, movement, and development. *Infant Behavior and Development, 15,* 479–505.

Miller, P. A., & Eisenberg, N. (1988). The relation of empathy to aggressive and externalizing/antisocial behavior. *Psychological Bulletin, 103,* 324–344.

Nelson, C. A. (1987). The recognition of facial expression in the first two years of life: Mechanisms of development. *Developmental Psychology, 58,* 889–909.

Niedenthal, P. M., & Kitayama, S. (Eds.). (1994). *The heart's eye: Emotional influences in perception and attention.* San Diego, CA: Academic Press.

Nolen-Hoeksema, S. & Girgus, J. S. (1994). The emergence of gender differences in depression during adolescence. *Psychological Bulletin, 115,* 424–443.

Pratto, F. (1994). Consciousness and automatic evaluation. In P. M. Niedenthal & S. Kitayama (Eds.), *The heart's eye: Emotional influences in perception and attention* (pp. 115–143). San Diego, CA: Academic Press.

Rolls, E. T. (1986). Neural substrates systems involved in emotion in primates. In R. Plutchik & H. Kellerman (Eds.), *Emotion: Theory, research, and experience: Vol. 3. Biological foundations of emotion* (pp. 125–143). San Diego, CA: Academic Press.

Roseman, I. J. (1991). Appraisal determinants of discrete emotions. *Cognition and Emotion, 5,* 161–200.

Sackett, G. (1966). Monkeys reared in isolation with pictures as visual input: Evidence for an innate releasing mechanism. *Science, 154,* 1468–1473.

Salovey, P., & Mayer, J. D. (1990). Emotional intelligence. *Imagination, Cognition, and Personality, 9,* 185–211.

Schultz, D., & Izard, C. E. (1997, April). *Young children's emotion knowledge and social development.* Poster session presented at the biennial meeting of the Society for Research in Child Development, Washington, DC.

Singer, J. A., & Salovey, P. (1988). Mood and memory: Evaluating the network theory of affect. *Clinical Psychology Review, 8,* 211–251.

Singer, J. L. (1973). *The child's world of make-believe: Experimental studies of imaginative play.* New York: Academic Press.

Singer, J. L. (1985). Transference and the human condition: A cognitive-affective perspective. *Psychoanalytic Psychology, 2,* 189–219.

Tangney, J. P., Burggraf, S. A., & Wagner, P. E. (1995). Shame-proneness, guilt-proneness, and psychological symptoms. In J. P. Tangney & K. W. Fischer (Eds.), *Self-conscious emotions: The psychology of shame, guilt, embarrassment, and pride* (pp. 343–367). New York: Guilford.

Tangney, J. P., & Fischer, K. W. (Eds.). (1996). *Self-conscious emotions: The psychology of shame, guilt, embarrassment, and pride.* NY: Guilford.

Teasdale, J. D., & Fogarty, S. J. (1979). Differential effects of induced mood on retrieval of pleasant and unpleasant events from episodic memory. *Journal of Abnormal Psychology, 88,* 248–257.

Thompson, R. A. (1989). Causal attributions and children's emotional understanding. In C. Saarni & P. L. Harris (Eds.), *Children's understanding of emotion* (pp. 117–150). New York: Cambridge University Press.

Tobias, A. A., Kihlstrom, J. F., & Schachter, D. L. (1992). Emotion and implicit memory. In S. A. Christianson (Ed.), *The handbook of emotion and memory* (pp. 67–92). Hillsdale, NJ: Lawrence Erlbaum Associates.

Tomkins, S. S. (1962). *Affect, imagery, consciousness: Vol. 1. The positive affects.* New York: Springer.

Tomkins, S. S. (1979). Script theory: Differential magnification of affects. In R. A. Dienstbier (Ed.), *Nebraska symposium on motivation: Vol. 26. Current theories and research in motivation.* (pp. 201–236). Lincoln: University of Nebraska Press.

Tranel, D., & Damasio, A. R. (1985). Knowledge without awareness: An autonomic index of facial recognition by prosopagnosics. *Science, 228,* 1453–1454.

Weiner, B. (1985). An attributional theory of achievement motivation and emotion. *Psychological Review, 92,* 548–573.

Zahn-Waxler, C. (1993). Warriors and worriers: Gender and psychopathology. *Development and Psychopathology, 5,* 79–90.

Zahn-Waxler, C., Cole, P., & Barrett, K. C. (1991). Guilt and empathy: Sex differences and implications for the development of depression. In K. Dodge & J. Garber (Eds.), *The development of emotion regulation and dysregulation* (pp. 243–272). New York: Cambridge University Press.

Zajonc, R. B. (1980). Feeling and thinking: Preferences need no inferences. *American Psychologist, 35,* 151–175.

Streams of Thought About the Self and Significant Others: Transference as the Construction of Interpersonal Meaning

Noah S. Glassman
Susan M. Andersen
New York University

Self-reflection and reflection about others have implications for people's interpretations of the social environment, and are fundamental to understanding each person as an idiosyncratic, social, and psychological organism. Although social psychology has tracked important processes concerning general principles of social thought, feelings, and behavior, it has not focused on individual private experience. Moreover, while personality psychology has helped elucidate nomothetic individual differences, as well as the structure of personality in taxonomic terms, it has also tended to neglect the study of individual experience. There have been infrequent attempts to integrate extant literatures into a coherent body of knowledge, and to identify and examine fruitful areas of empirical investigation concerning subjective experience. Singer, however, has contributed to the fields of clinical, personality, and even social psychology by having the courage and tenacity to choose as his life's work the problems of consciousness and private experience. He has substantially increased knowledge about essential questions that have been considered intractable. With an appreciation for theory and research, he has focused on the ways people consciously construct knowledge about the self and others, and on how such knowledge structures influence the sense made of the social environment. Literatures in these areas owe a debt to Singer's work.

Singer has had a probing curiosity about the interplay between internal, ongoing mental processes and "real" stimuli in the social environment in terms of how internal representations can combine with reality to shape subjective experience of the social world (e.g., Singer, 1975, 1984, 1985,

1988a; Singer & Bonanno, 1990; Singer & Salovey, 1991). Singer has noted that people attend not only to aspects of the environment, but also to their own continuous internal stream of thought and associations. Moreover, the interplay between these two sources of mental stimulation is determined, in part, by individual differences in the nature of the stream of consciousness. The imaginal processes of some individuals, for example, are characterized by a guilty–dysphoric daydreaming style with fantasies of hostility or failure, while others may experience a disorganized, distractible stream of consciousness with a poor ability to focus on extended fantasy. Still other individuals appear to have a positive-constructive inner life characterized by elaborate, playful, and wishful fantasy activity (e.g., Singer, 1993; Singer & Antrobus, 1972; Singer & Bonanno, 1990; Singer & Kolligian, 1987; see also Giambra, 1974; Golding & Singer, 1983; Huba, Segal, & Singer, 1977; Segal, Huba, & Singer, 1980).

One's style of daydreaming, and the contents of one's stream of associations, Singer argues, are likely to be influenced by stimulus events in the external world as well as by one's experiential history, including longstanding, unresolved interpersonal conflicts (Klos & Singer, 1981). These life experiences may lead to the development of frequently thought about social constructs in memory such as schemas, scripts, and prototypes, which readily come to mind for use in interpretation and association (e.g., Singer, 1988a; Singer & Kolligian, 1987). Singer has posited that "our life task involves an endless effort at organizing experiences and matching them to available schema" (Singer, 1975, p. 728; see also Pope & Singer, 1978). His cognitive–affective reinterpretation of transference (Singer, 1985, 1988a; Singer & Salovey, 1991; J. A. Singer & J. L. Singer, 1994; see also Freud, 1912/1958) reflects his interests in the interplay between inner experience and the environment in information-processing models, and has informed our own experimental research about social–cognitive processes in transference (e.g., Andersen & Glassman, 1996). Transference, in our model, is essentially the process by which past experiences, wishes, fantasies, and expectations emerge in a current relationship with a new person—not only a therapist, but anyone. We have demonstrated that transference occurs and suggest that it constitutes a basic meaning-making process. Importantly, Singer was among the first to argue that this kind of theoretical position might be fruitful for research progress because of the special methodological and empirical grounding of information-processing models.

Singer's research and theorizing have influenced and inspired our work in other ways as well. His work about the nature of self-reflection has also influenced our research concerning the construction of self-knowledge using one's own stream of private experiences, in contrast to public behaviors, as the basis for inferences about the self (Andersen, 1984; Andersen & Ross, 1984). More recently, we examined how such experiences—internal, covert, private experiences—are reflected in mental representations of self and significant others (e.g., Andersen, Glassman, & Gold, 1998), which is relevant to both our social–cognitive model of transference and to future directions in our research about transference (see Chen & Andersen, in press).

From our point of view, Singer's body of work alerted psychology to the importance of the systematic study of *inner life*—beyond observable behavioral responses (Singer, 1975)—long before most other researchers were concerned with the matter; this work paved the way for careful, controlled examination of private versus public aspects of self- and other representations, as well as of transference. In terms of the latter, his emphasis on the link between cognition and the transference process highlighted the notion that previous knowledge structures influence the meaning ascribed to new interpersonal situations. In our experimental social–cognitive research, we have now demonstrated exactly this—based on the activation and application of significant–other representations to newly encountered individuals (Andersen & Baum, 1994; Andersen & Cole, 1990; Andersen, Glassman, Chen, & Cole, 1995; Andersen, Reznik, & Manzella, 1996; Hinkley & Andersen, 1996).

Thus, our work dovetails Singer's longstanding intellectual and scholarly concerns. We have examined the process of transference, as well as privileged knowledge about the self and others. Singer's work has addressed some of these matters, although usually by assessing nomothetic individual differences in the nature of consciousness. By contrast, we have defined and examined the experience of self and others in *idiographic* terms in all of our work (see Allport, 1937; Kelly, 1955). That is, our aim has been to assess idiosyncratic knowledge representation in memory, and to track its influence on aspects of experience, such as affect and motivation, in interpersonal relations. Moreover, our conceptualization of transference in everyday social encounters emphasizes the notion that transference is not limited to psychotherapy, and is therefore pervasive in the patterns of interpersonal expectancies and responses of interest to personality theorists. In particular, our work provides one way of addressing the kinds of patterns of responding that define personality (Mischel & Shoda, 1995; Sullivan, 1953; see also Hinkley & Andersen, 1996). That is, one way to conceptualize personality is in terms of chronic tendencies to have particular relationships based on the activation and application of significant-other representations and other relevant relationship knowledge stored in memory (such as the relational schema, e.g., Baldwin, 1992).

In this chapter, we describe our social–cognitive model of transference and experimental evidence supporting it—in tribute to the theoretical inspiration provided by Singer's work. In particular, we present not only cognitive findings, but also affective and motivational findings that emerge in transference. We also highlight evidence demonstrating changes in self-experience, that is, in the "working self-concept" (e.g., Markus & Wurf, 1987) in transference, which supports the notion that patterns of change relevant to personality occur in the transference process. Defining transference in terms of basic social–cognitive principles has also allowed us to experimentally demonstrate nonconscious processes in transference. Importantly, Singer's contributions inform consideration of both conscious and nonconscious processes, and in this sense provide yet another avenue of connection between our work and his. Although our research about transference does not focus on the psychotherapy hour (cf., Luborsky & Crits-Christoph, 1990; see also Gill, 1982; Horowitz et al., 1991), we discuss how the activation and application of representations of significant others may become maladaptive and hence a focus of psychotherapy.

Finally, on the heels of our discussion of transference, we also describe the content and structure of self- and other-representations in memory, highlighting research which explores what is covert and private in knowledge about the self, significant others, and nonsignificant others, versus what is relatively overt and behavioral. Understanding the nature of these mental representations in memory is important in understanding how they operate in social relations.

EXPERIMENTAL RESEARCH ON TRANSFERENCE

Personality and clinical theorists have long proposed that past experiences with important individuals re-emerge in current interpersonal relations (e.g., Bowlby, 1969; Fairbairn, 1952; Freud, 1912/1958; Horney, 1939; Sullivan, 1953). Psychodynamic psychotherapy, for instance, typically focuses on early experiences with significant others and their likely impact on relations with the therapist, as well as with others outside of the therapy context, in the clinical concept of transference (e.g., Ehrenreich, 1989; Freud, 1912/1958; Greenson, 1965; Horowitz, 1991; Luborsky & Crits-Christoph, 1990; Sullivan, 1953). Transference is readily conceptualized from an information-processing perspective, as proposed by Singer (1985, 1988a) in his influential reinterpretation of traditional psychodynamic views of transference in terms of mental operations (see also Andersen & Glassman, 1996; Wachtel, 1981; Westen, 1988). Indeed, schema-focused models of cognitive therapy have begun to consider transference, both in and outside of the treatment relationship, in terms of relationship schemas (e.g., Young, 1990; see also Safran, 1990a, 1990b; Safran & Segal, 1990).

Singer's perspective highlights the notion that previously formed knowledge structures can influence processes of attention and encoding in social perception; in other words, people enter social situations with certain expectancies based on their past interpersonal histories (e.g., Klos & Singer, 1981). Moreover, in Singer's conception, transference is "an inherent feature of the human search for organization and integration of novelty and ambiguity" (Singer, 1988a, p. 187), such that levels of emotional arousal may be influenced by the various knowledge structures available and accessible for processing new information. We agree entirely with these assumptions and argue that transference may be conceptualized as part of a basic meaning-making process for coming to understand the interpersonal world (see also Andersen, Reznik, & Chen, 1997). This meaning-making process reflects the interaction of stimuli in the social environment and previously acquired knowledge structures used to interpret ongoing experience, as Singer suggests. Such knowledge structures may take the form of scripts, schemas, or prototypes encompassing the self, others, and social situations (Singer, 1985, 1988a; Singer & Kolligian, 1987; Singer & Salovey, 1991; J. A. Singer & J. L. Singer, 1994; see Cantor & Mischel, 1979; Carlson, 1981; Carlson & Carlson, 1984; Markus, 1977; Schank & Abelson, 1977; Tomkins, 1979). In our social–cognitive experimental research, we have begun to elucidate the cognitive structures and processes of transference in social perception and social relations.

Extending Singer's thinking, our social–cognitive model of transference specifies that the basic social–cognitive process of transference is the activation and application of mental representations of significant others (Andersen & Glassman, 1996). Harry Stack Sullivan's (1940, 1953) concept of parataxic distortion is a form of transference that is roughly consistent with our mental-representation model because it is based on "personifications" of the self and significant others, as well as "dynamisms" or dynamics involving the relational experience of the self with the other (Greenberg & Mitchell, 1983; Mullahy, 1970; see also Hinkley & Andersen, 1996; Ogilvie & Ashmore, 1991). Although Sullivan did not propose mental structures, per se, personifications and dynamisms can readily be considered in terms of a mental-representational model. In conceptualizing significant-other personifications as mental representations, we allow the content of significant-other representations to vary freely and subjectively across individual participants. Hence, the content of what is transferred in transference—the content of significant-other representations—is idiographic. The process of transference, on the other hand, is *nomothetic*, common across persons, and generalizable.

We conceptualize transference in terms of social construct theory (e.g., Higgins, 1989, 1996; Higgins & King, 1981). Significant-other representations are "proper" constructs (as in a proper name)—in contrast to social categories (Higgins & King, 1981)—and likewise are specific exemplars of individual persons (Smith & Zarate, 1990, 1992; see also Cantor & Mischel, 1979; Higgins & Bargh, 1987). As such, significant-other representations are used extensively as the basis for responding to new individuals (Andersen & Baum, 1994; Andersen et al., 1996). We measure the activation and application of significant-other representations to new persons largely in terms of representation-consistent inferences (Andersen & Cole, 1990; see also Bargh, Bond, Lombardi, & Tota, 1986; Higgins, Rholes, & Jones, 1977; Sedikides & Skowronski, 1991; Srull & Wyer, 1979), although we also assess evaluation, affect, motivation, and expectancy (Andersen et al., 1996). Because of the formation of a variety of important person representations throughout life—not only those of parents or primary caregivers developed in childhood—transference can involve a host of significant-other representations that can be applied in everyday circumstances to new individuals.[1]

Singer's work about recasting transference in cognitive–affective terms helped set the stage for carefully controlled experimental demonstrations of our social–cognitive model of transference. Research in this area is important not only because it verifies the long-assumed psychodynamic concept of transference, but also because examining transference in terms of linkages between the self and significant-other representations in memory constitutes, in essence, an operational definition for aspects of contemporary object-relations theories (see also Baldwin, 1992; Singer & Salovey, 1991; J. A. Singer & J. L. Singer, 1994; Westen, 1991; for overviews of object relations theories, see Greenberg & Mitchell, 1983; Guntrip, 1971).

---

[1]It is probably worth noting explicitly that one need not subscribe to classical psychoanalytic assumptions about psychosexual conflict in early relations (e.g., Freud, 1912/1958) to be interested in the process of transference, nor must one subscribe to the notion that transference occurs primarily on the basis of early parental representations. One need not even have a special interest in its use as a tool in psychotherapy. Indeed, we posit that transference occurs based on a mental representation of any important person in an individual's life (e.g., a spouse, an ex-spouse, a best friend, a sibling, a mother, father, uncle, influential mentor), that it occurs in everyday life and not uniquely in therapy, and that the content of what is transferred is idiographic and based on the real interpersonal experiences with a significant other (see Horney, 1939; Sullivan, 1953; Wachtel, 1981). This conceptualization, because it is supported by experimental evidence, involves simple social–cognitive assumptions, and yet is quite relevant to transference that pertains to the clinical enterprise (Andersen & Berk, 1998).

Demonstrating Basic Transference Phenomena

Our experimental research about transference enables us to test causality using participants' idiosyncratic, private understandings of their particular significant others. Idiographically generated attributes of a participant's significant other were used to construct descriptions of a target designed to trigger transference responses in a standard experimental paradigm. By using this combined idiographic–nomothetic methodology, we are able to draw nomothetic conclusions about the basic processes that underlie transference, while using idiographic stimulus materials that index the subjective meanings that participants give to their own significant others.

In our typical experimental paradigm, as outlined in Fig. 5.1, participants generated various descriptors (e.g., about a significant other) in a preliminary session. In a separate experimental session, typically 2 weeks later, participants learned about a new person (or persons), and then completed a memory test, often along with other measures as well. Recognition-memory confidence (described further), among other indices, reflects use of the representation to interpret the new person. Moreover, schema-triggered evaluation, affect, and motivation, based on the activation of a significant-other representation and its application to a newly encountered person, were also assessed (Andersen & Baum, 1994; Andersen et al., 1996).

Representation-Consistent Memory and Inference. Our experimental work has demonstrated that significant-other representations have greater inferential power than other types of social constructs in terms of filling in gaps in knowledge about new individuals (see Brooks, 1987; Gilovich, 1981). When participants learned about fictional characters and later were tested for their recognition memory, they showed more representation-consistent memory confidence when the character had some featural overlap with their own significant-other representation than with various control representations. That is, participants showed greater confidence for remembering representation-consistent information that went beyond what they learned about a new individual when that person resembled the participants' significant other versus a nonsignificant other (Andersen et al., 1995; Andersen & Cole, 1990), stereotype (Andersen & Cole, 1990; Chen, Andersen, & Hinkley, 1998), or someone else's (a yoked participant's) significant other (Andersen & Baum, 1994; Andersen et al., 1995, 1996; Chen et al., 1998; Hinkley & Andersen, 1996). Thus, participants use significant-other representations to go beyond the information given (Bruner, 1957) about a new person. The activation and application of a mental representation of a significant other to a new individual appears

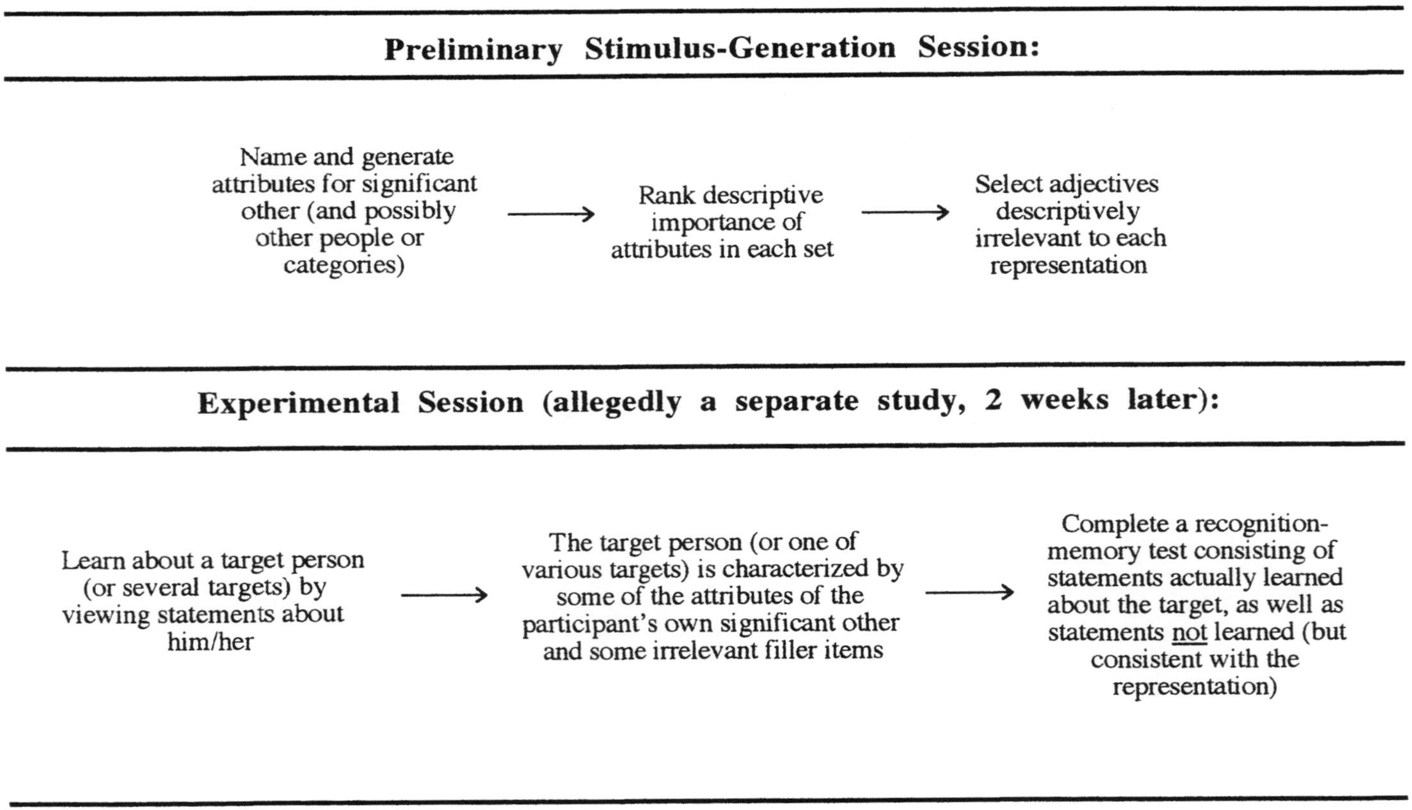

Preliminary Stimulus-Generation Session:

Name and generate attributes for significant other (and possibly other people or categories) $\longrightarrow$ Rank descriptive importance of attributes in each set $\longrightarrow$ Select adjectives descriptively irrelevant to each representation

Experimental Session (allegedly a separate study, 2 weeks later):

Learn about a target person (or several targets) by viewing statements about him/her $\longrightarrow$ The target person (or one of various targets) is characterized by some of the attributes of the participant's own significant other and some irrelevant filler items $\longrightarrow$ Complete a recognition-memory test consisting of statements actually learned about the target, as well as statements not learned (but consistent with the representation)

FIG. 5.1. The basic transference paradigm.

to constitute the basic mechanism of transference, and this process may be more ubiquitous in social perception than stereotyping or other kinds of social-construct-based processing.

Because significant others are frequently thought about, highly familiar, and highly important, representations of significant others should be chronically accessible, meaning that they should have a special readiness to be activated and applied (Bargh et al., 1986; Higgins, 1996a; Higgins & Brendl, 1995; Higgins & King, 1981). Indeed, recent research has shown exactly this; a significant-other representation can be activated and applied to a new individual even when the representation is not primed before the participant encounters the target (Andersen et al., 1995, Study 1). Moreover, significant-other representations are so readily accessed and applied that no featural overlap with the target is necessary for memory-based inferences to occur. That is, significant-other representations may be applied to others virtually willy-nilly, without triggering cues in the new person. On the other hand, significant-other-based memory is greater when relevant triggering cues are present in the target than when they are not (Andersen et al., 1995, Study 2), suggesting that although significant-other representations are chronically accessible, transient sources of activation combine additively with this chronicity to increase the likelihood of their use (see also Bargh et al., 1986). This reflects two distinct sources of the transference experience, one based on prior usage and one's own chronic tendencies, and the other based on stimulus-person-based context effects.

Schema-Triggered Affect and Motivation. In a linked-network model of social schemata, schemas are thought to have affective tags indicating positive or negative evaluations that extend beyond the feature-by-feature valence (Fiske & Pavelchak, 1986). That is, social categories have summary evaluations that may become linked to people who are categorized in these terms. Research has shown that when an affect-laden social category, such as a stereotype, is activated, the affective tag linked to the category is also activated, and the target person is categorized and evaluated accordingly.

Recent work has also examined schema-triggered affect based on the single exemplar of a significant other (Andersen et al., 1996; Andersen & Baum, 1994). When participants learn about a new individual who resembles their own, rather than someone else's, positively or negatively toned significant other, they are not only more likely to demonstrate representation-consistent memory based on the representation, but they are also more likely to make representation-consistent evaluations of the new person. That is, upon meeting a new individual who activates a positive or negative significant-other representation—by bearing some minimal resemblance to the representation—one may come to like or dislike the person in a representation-consistent manner. Hence, schema-triggered evaluation of the new person occurs in transference.

Indeed, data relevant to eliciting transient affect in transference, based on the activation of a positively versus negatively toned significant-other representation, have also been reported. When participants learn about a new individual who resembles their own significant other (either positively or negatively toned), rather than someone else's, they are somewhat more likely to experience representation-consistent transient affect in terms of self-reported mood (Andersen & Baum, 1994). In more recent work (Andersen et al., 1996), participants' facial responses were covertly videotaped at the moment information about a new target person was encountered. Trained judges then rated participants' facial expressions in terms of pleasantness. These ratings showed that representation-consistent facial affect was elicited at encoding in the context of transference—in a manner driven by the overall tone of the representation, not by the objective evaluative loading of the individual features presented about the target person. Thus, affective experiences appear to be elicited in the transference process as schema-triggered facial affect.

If affective information stored with significant-other representations can be activated along with the representation, then motivational constructs also associated with the representation should also be capable of activation. In this context, we conceptualize motivation as the psychological needs or goals that individuals pursue in their interpersonal behaviors with the other, rather than in terms of traditional drive-reduction models (cf. Koestner & McClelland, 1990). Although the influence of motivational sets or goals on social cognition and interaction has received much attention (see Srull & Wyer, 1986), relatively little had been known, until recently, about the extent to which cognitive processes (e.g., schema activation), triggered by stimuli in the environment, lead to the activation of associated motives and goals (see Bargh, 1990, 1997).

In the "auto-motive" model (Bargh, 1990), goals and motives are "represented in the mind in the same fashion as are social constructs," and have mental links with "the representations of the social situations in which those motives have been frequently pursued in the past," resulting in activation "whenever the relevant triggering situational features are present in the environment" (p. 100). Recent work, in fact, has demonstrated the direct activation of goals or motives (such as achievement and affiliation motives), via priming stimuli in the environment, and has done so by assessing the extent to which participants engaged in behaviors consistent with the goals that were primed (Bargh & Gollwitzer, 1994; Chartrand & Bargh, 1996).

In the context of transference and significant-other representations, we posit a relatively indirect route for the triggering of such goals. That is, in keeping with our proposed basic mechanism for transference, encountering a new individual who resembles a significant other should activate the significant-other representation as well as the motives or goals typically operative when one is with the significant other. Recent data suggest that this pattern of findings does indeed occur in the extent to which a participant wants to emotionally approach or avoid a new target individual (Andersen et al., 1996). Based on the overall positivity or negativity of the significant-other representation activated by the target, participants reported wanting to seek more or less emotional closeness with the target in a representation-consistent manner. No such effect occurred when the new target person did not resemble participants' own significant other. Hence, motivational states associated with a significant-other representation can be activated when the representation itself is activated by triggering stimuli (i.e., features) in the target person.

Transference as Personality: Changes in the Working Self-Concept

Given our argument that transference is a normal process of constructing interpersonal meaning, it is possible to consider defining *personality* as the chronic tendency to have particular interpersonal relationships influenced by idiosyncratic experiences with significant others (Hinkley & Andersen, 1996). Hence, the private personality—Singer's (1984) longstanding interest—can be conceptualized in terms of one's idiosyncratic transference patterns based on idiographic significant-other representations, which in turn have developed out of one's personal history of actual and interpreted experiences with these significant others. Transference can reflect individual differences in representation-based appraisals of interpersonal situations, conceptualized from an idiographic point of view.

Conceptualizing personality and transference in terms of chronic interpersonal patterns requires an understanding of the nature of the associative linkages between self- and significant-other representations in memory, and the specific consequences of significant-other activation for how one thinks, feels, and acts, as well as for how one defines the self (Hinkley & Andersen, 1996). That is, the activation and application of a significant-other representation in transference should lead to relevant changes in the working self-concept (e.g., Markus & Nurius, 1986; Markus & Wurf, 1987), because the contents of active memory with regard to the self should change on the basis of significant-other activation. Thus, those aspects of self that are experienced when one is with the significant other become activated (Ogilvie & Ashmore, 1991).

A whole host of possible self-representations may coexit for any given person, and these may be differentially active as a function of particular environmental circumstances (e.g., Higgins, 1987, 1989; Linville & Carlston, 1994; Markus, 1983; Markus & Nurius, 1986). This notion is in contrast to an assumption of one singular self-representation that is either active or inactive at any given time as a whole (see Higgins & Bargh, 1987; Higgins, VanHook, & Dorfman, 1988; Segal, Hood, Shaw, & Higgins, 1988). Hence, the social–cognitive model of transference assumes that there are various aspects of self linked with each significant other in memory. The model predicts that significant-other resemblance in a target individual should activate the significant-other representation, and thereby infuse the working self-concept with the subset of self-information pertaining to the self when with this significant other (Hinkley & Andersen, 1996). The overall affective tone of the significant-other representation should also be linked to self-definition when with the significant other, and hence, related changes in self-evaluation should occur in transference.

In a study investigating these hypotheses (Hinkley & Andersen, 1996), participants in a pretest session described themselves *as they are now*—essentially stream of consciousness about the self at that moment in terms of sentence completions—and then classified each sentence completion as either positive or negative. Afterward, participants generated descriptive sentence completions to characterize a positively toned significant other and a negatively toned significant other, respectively. They then completed a description of the self while with each of these significant others. In the experimental session, 2 weeks later, participants learned about a new target person who resembled either their own or someone else's (a yoked participant's) positively or negatively toned significant other, with the target description containing an equal number of positive and negative descriptors. After learning about the new target person, participants described themselves as they are now (the working self-concept), and classified the valence of each descriptor listed. As in other work, participants also completed a recognition-memory test.

Participants demonstrated greater representation-consistent memory confidence when the target resembled their own significant others, rather than a yoked participant's, across both positively and negatively toned significant others, verifying the occurrence of transference. Moreover, changes in the working self-concept occurred in the direction of the self, when with the significant other—as assessed by overlap between the participant's working self-concept in the experiment and the self-with-significant-other descriptors provided at pretest (using a measure adapted from Prentice, 1990). That is, when the target person resembled the participant's own, versus someone else's significant other, across both positively and negatively toned significant others, the working self-concept shifted toward the way the self is experienced when with the significant other. These data clearly suggest that linkages between the self and significant-other representations are traversed when the significant-other representation is activated, resulting in predictable changes in the content of the working self-concept.

Changes in self-evaluation also emerged in transference. The perceived valence of the self-features listed in the experimental session became more positive when the target resembled the participant's own positive versus negative significant other—an effect that did not occur when the target resembled a yoked participant's significant other. Hence, not only does the self-concept change in predicted ways in transference, but the self-evaluation reflected in aspects of these self-concept changes reflects the overall tone of the significant-other representation.

The notion that changes in the self-concept occur as a result of the activation of a significant-other representation in transference is in keeping with Sullivan's (1953) assertion that individuals may have as many personalities as they do relationships with important others. That is, one's experience of the self varies as a function of the relationship one has with particular others, and these differing expectations of self can be triggered by attributes of a newly encountered person. Our data support this assumption and are also largely consistent with models that posit the emergence of different aspects of personality in different situations (e.g., Mischel & Shoda, 1995). In our view, one way of defining the variability and continuity of personality is in terms of chronically accessible significant-other representations that have a special readiness to be activated and used, and which are likely to be triggered in relevant interpersonal situations (see also Andersen et al., 1997; Higgins, 1990; Sedikides & Ostrom, 1988).

The experimental literature about transference described thus far has involved the activation of a significant-other representation via consciously perceived triggering cues in the target person, and has emphasized changes in one's conscious experience of the self. We argue, nonetheless, that transference is likely to have nonconscious bases. That is, a significant-other representation may become activated without awareness on the basis of attributes in a new person that the perceiver is processing nonconsciously (Glassman & Andersen, 1998). Developments in the study of nonconscious processes in social cognition have made it possible to examine hypotheses concerned with the nonconscious triggering of transference—hypotheses which also reflect Singer's concerns with nonconscious processing and schema use.

Nonconscious Processes and Their Relevance to Transference

Singer has noted that ". . . unconscious processes reflect well-established or overlearned constructs, schemas, or metacognitions . . ." (Singer & Bonanno, 1990, p. 423). Moreover, he has asserted that "one of the major challenges to personality psychology posed by anecdotal reports and psychoanalytic theorizing deals with the extent to which major schemas about the self (and significant others) become so automatic that they remain largely outside the individual's consciousness" (Singer & Kolligian, 1987, p. 558; see also Singer & Salovey, 1991). Implicit in these statements is the notion that knowledge structures about important others may become triggered without awareness and may be brought to bear on interpretations of interpersonal situations. That is, the activation of a significant-other representation should occur nonconsciously.

Research has indeed shown that associative processes can be influenced by stimuli perceived without awareness (e.g. Bargh & Pietromonaco, 1982; Marcel, 1983; see also Bornstein & Pittman, 1992; although see Holender, 1986). In particular, nonconscious influences can affect social perception by inducing biased interpretations of relatively ambiguous behavior in a new person (e.g., Bargh et al., 1986; Bargh & Pietromonaco, 1982; Devine, 1989). Both the chronic accessibility of a given social construct and the extent to which the construct received transient activation, even if subliminally, contribute to its readiness for use in nonconscious processing (e.g., Bargh, 1989; Bargh et al., 1986; Higgins, 1989, 1996a; see also Andersen et al., 1995; Higgins & Brendl, 1995). Hence, significant-other representations, as chronically accessible social constructs, should be capable of activation outside of awareness.

The social–cognitive model of transference and psychodynamic perspectives assume that transference can be nonconscious in several ways. For example, the contents of what is transferred may not be available to consciousness, or the activation of transference may occur outside of awareness (Kihlstrom, 1987; Luborsky, Crits-Christoph, Friedman, Mark, & Schaffler, 1991; Singer & Salovey, 1991). That is, the relevant triggering cues that activated the significant-other representation may be nonconscious (for definitions of awareness, see also Bargh, 1994; Uleman, 1987).[2]

---

[2]This research does not investigate the possibility that some of the actual contents of significant-other representations are unconscious, in the Freudian sense (i.e., completely unavailable for conscious retrieval; see also Singer & Salovey, 1991). Information-processing models do, however, provide for this possibility. Memory structures can be classified as *declarative knowledge* (i.e., factual information), or *procedural knowledge* (i.e., rules, strategies, or skills that operate on declarative knowledge; e.g., Cantor & Kihlstrom, 1986; Kihlstrom, 1987; Smith, 1994); the latter is unavailable to consciousness (e.g., Lewicki, 1986; Lewicki & Hill, 1987). The current study, by exploring the subliminal activation of significant-other representations, may tap this type of procedural knowledge in the form of similarity-based activation of a significant-other representation. That is, people by and large may be unaware of the processes involved in activating declarative knowledge structures like significant-other representations. We assume, however, that people have access to the content of their declarative knowledge structures, at least enough to describe their significant others, even though parts of such declarative structures may not be fully conscious (Kihlstrom, 1987; Greenwald, 1992). Thus, although some aspects of significant-other representations may be relatively unconscious, this remains to be explored empirically, and is not the focus of the present research.

No empirical evidence we know of has examined the nonconscious nature of transference at any level. We examined the nonconscious activation of transference by manipulating the presence of subliminal triggering cues (Glassman & Andersen, 1998).

Nonconscious Processing in Social Cognition. Nonconscious process-ing, defined in terms of subliminal perception, has had a controversial history in the cognitive- and social-psychological literatures (e.g., Bowers, 1984; Greenwald, 1992; Greenwald & Banaji, 1995; Holender, 1986; Kihlstrom, Barnhardt, & Tataryn, 1992). A growing body of evidence, however, suggests that subliminally presented stimuli can influence lexical decision tasks (Marcel, 1983; Blair & Banaji, 1996; Greenwald, Klinger, & Schuh, 1995), self-evaluation (Baldwin, Carrell, & Lopez, 1990), impressions and recall of target persons (Bargh et al., 1986; Devine, 1989; Erdley & D'Agostino, 1988; Lewicki, 1986; Macrae, Bodenhausen, & Milne, 1995), and even social behavior (e.g., Bargh & Gollwitzer, 1994; Neuberg, 1988).

Ensuring activation without awareness requires not only rapid stimulus presentation combined with pattern masking, but also requires stimulus presentation in parafoveal vision, where diminished visual acuity further decreases the likelihood of conscious perception (Holender, 1986; Rayner, 1978). The utility of such a methodology has been demonstrated in sublimi-nal-priming research about the basis of trait dimensions, stereotypes, and goal constructs (Bargh et al., 1986; Chartrand & Bargh, 1996; Devine, 1989). Although subliminal methodologies may seem disconnected from any normal experience, there are analogies to subliminal activation in real life (cf. Bargh, 1992). For instance, the most important attribute or feature that triggers transference may not be one we know we have seen, possibly because attention was elsewhere at the time, or because the feature was exhibited or expressed by a target person too briefly to reach awareness. The subliminal method provides one of the only ways to ensure that the activation process is literally taking place without the participant's knowl-edge. Moreover, in terms of automaticity (see Bargh, 1989, 1994), subliminal priming procedures involve not only the efficiency element of automaticity, but the lack-of-awareness and lack-of-control elements with respect to the initial phases of activation and use.

Activating Transference Without Awareness. In a study designed to investigate nonconscious activation of transference on the basis of subliminally perceived significant-other attributes, participants named a significant other and completed sentences to describe him or her (Glassman & Andersen, 1998). To elicit self-generated stimuli for a no-representation control condition (cf. Greenwald, 1981; Greenwald & Banaji, 1989), we also asked participants to complete one sentence to describe each of several people who together did not constitute any particular category or mental representation.

One week later, participants arrived for an allegedly separate study. They were led to believe that they would play a computer game with another person—who was seated at a computer terminal elsewhere in the building—and who would send them self-descriptive statements via computer link. While participants received some supraliminal messages (i.e., in their awareness) that were irrelevant to the study, they were also exposed to subliminal presentations (i.e., pattern-masked sentence predicates exposed for approximately 86 milliseconds in parafoveal vision, modeled after Bargh et al., 1986). That is, in a between-subjects design, participants were subliminally exposed either to their own significant-other descriptors, to their own no-representation descriptors, or to a yoked participant's significant-other descriptors. After completing the computer game, participants gave their impression of their game partners by rating the descriptiveness of several statements. Participants who received subliminal presentations related to their own significant other were asked to assess their partner using descriptors of the same significant other that either were or were not subliminally presented. When participants were exposed subliminally to a yoked participant's significant-other features, they were also asked to assess their partner using their own significant other features, even though their significant-other representation should not have been triggered in this condition. Participants in the no-representation condition, by contrast, were exposed subliminally to their own no-representations features and were later asked to assess their partner using these features. Following these experimental procedures, participants completed a stimulus-identification task that served as a subliminality check. They were presented again with the subliminal exposures from the computer game and were asked to guess which of three answer choices had been shown. Participants' mean proportion of correct responses on the stimulus-identification task were not reliably greater than chance-level performance, indicating that the presentations were exposed at a level beneath the threshold of awareness.

Importantly, the primary results of this research indicated that participants were more likely to infer that the target person possessed extra representation-consistent descriptors—beyond those encountered subliminally—when the target subliminally resembled their own significant other than when the target resembled the control conditions. Hence, the data clearly demonstrate that significant-other representations can be activated without awareness, and that transference can be triggered nonconsciously on the basis of subliminally presented significant-other descriptors. The emergence of transference in social relations can have a nonconscious basis, because the triggering cues that activated the significant-other representation were processed outside of awareness. Thus, as Singer (e.g., 1988a) proposed, previously developed knowledge structures, such as the representations formed of significant others, may have a special readiness to be activated nonconsciously because these representations have been overlearned or rehearsed repeatedly (see also Meichenbaum & Gilmore, 1984) That is, the contents of these representations and their associates frequently come to mind and are therefore chronically accessible (Andersen et al., 1995), such that unconsciously perceived cues can trigger the use of these representations in social perception and transference.

TRANSFERENCE AND THE STREAM OF CONSCIOUSNESS: RESEARCH AND CLINICAL IMPLICATIONS

In our social–cognitive model of transference, a significant-other representation is a storehouse of information in memory about the significant other's attributes, behaviors, beliefs, feelings, and so on, generalized across numerous autobiographical experiences with the significant other. Importantly, the representation is linked with the self so that the interpersonal dynamics between self and other, or object relations, are stored in the associative linkages, or as part of the representation itself. These linkages have been demonstrated in our experimental research in numerous ways, including the emergence of significant-other-related affect, motivations for emotional intimacy, expectancies about acceptance or rejection in relation to a new person who triggers the significant-other representation, and in the shifting of one's experience of the self toward the experiences the self has when with the significant other (Andersen et al., 1996; Hinkley & Andersen, 1996). Hence, aspects of object relations emerge in relation to a new individual in transference, supporting the implication of Singer's work.

In addition, our social–cognitive model can readily account for the unconscious nature of object relations in transference. Transference can be initiated outside of consciousness on the basis of unconsciously perceived cues in a new person. Because the associative linkages between significant-other representations and the self—in terms of affect, goals, and expectancies—are likely to be stored as procedural knowledge unavailable to consciousness (e.g., Kihlstrom, 1987), as opposed to declarative knowledge amenable to conscious retrieval (see Footnote 2,) the relational dynamics stored in these linkages are likely to be unconscious as well. Indeed, these relational dynamics should be elicited when nonconscious activation of the significant-other representation occurs—an hypothesis that has yet to be empirically examined, but is readily testable using our idiographic–nomothetic experimental methods.

Singer's reinterpretation of transference has led to fruitful theorizing and research about transference-based constructions of subjective meaning in interpersonal contexts, and has helped to bring object relations theory closer to the domain of scientific psychology. Many complex empirical questions about transference remain, of course, especially those involving how the transference phenomenon becomes maladaptive. Furthermore, individual differences in people's experiences of their own stream of consciousness may have implications for what they typically transfer and experience in transference. We next briefly address issues pertinent to these questions.

Maladaptive Transference Patterns: Process Versus Content?

Experimental research supports the simple notion that transference is a normal process that occurs in populations outside of the treatment context. It follows from basic rules of information processing that operate in relation to any social construct, and it appears to be a basic way in which people make sense of new individuals they encounter (Singer & Salovey, 1991; J. A. Singer & J. L. Singer, 1994). However, transference does undoubtedly become maladaptive for certain individuals or under certain circumstances, and when it does, its problematic nature may largely be due to the content of the significant-other representation activated and applied (Andersen & Berk, 1998). For example, transference may become problematic when a new person activates a painfully toned significant-other representation associated with frustrated feelings of longing and a sense of despair or perhaps dread. Activation of such a representation could lead to self-defeating responses in interpersonal relations. Of course, it is also possible that the process of transference might become maladaptive if the inappropriateness of significant-other activation and application is extreme or overly rigid, or if the capacity to self-correct is minimal or absent (Andersen & Berk, 1998).

Awareness of One's Private Experience and Taking Control of Transference

Indeed, individual differences in one's ability to control or interrupt transference when it is problematic may be directly related to one's awareness of, and ability to control, one's own flow of associations, and may therefore be informed by Singer's work in these areas (e.g., Bonanno & Singer, 1993; Singer & Pope, 1978). That is, becoming aware of transference-based responses, and being alert to the possibility that particular triggering cues might lead to transference, may be useful interventions in transferential reactions. No doubt, an ability to attend to the ongoing stream of associations, images, feelings, and sensations that are elicited in interpersonal situations may also be required. For instance, when interacting with a new person, attentiveness to the occurrence of thoughts related to a particular significant other, or to the emergence of emotions, desires, or fears typically experienced when with the significant other, may be essential to disrupting transference. Certain individuals may be sensitive enough to their inner experience, or may be able to learn in psychotherapy to focus on the internal flow of associations, so that the emergence of transference-based responses in the stream of consciousness, as well as in behavior, is noticed and subsequently "corrected." Other individuals, by contrast, may have a more defensive style in relation to their inner experience, such as an avoidant style of information processing, and their awareness and capacity to learn to intercede in their own transference responses may be more limited. Repressors, for example, typically turn their foci away from what goes on internally (e.g., Bonanno, David, Singer, & Schwartz, 1991; Bonanno & Singer, 1990; Singer, 1990; see also Singer, 1988b), and may be especially likely to engage in transference without awareness. They may have particular trouble with catching themselves in the throes of transferential reactions or with learning to short-circuit their transference responses.

Questions also arise as to the most efficacious ways of taking conscious control over transference and interrupting it. For example, a thorough assessment of a client's potentially problematic significant-other representations—which, perhaps, have become apparent from the transference responses that have emerged in the client's current relationships and in the therapy relationship or both—could help identify particular significant-other attributes that are especially likely to serve as triggering cues for the transference process (Andersen & Berk, 1998). Fostering awareness of these cues, and attentiveness to their presence in interactions with new individuals could help the client to process information about new people in a more careful, piecemeal manner that might help prevent transference from occurring.

Alternatively, for some clients, because piecemeal processing of social stimuli in this manner may be too demanding of cognitive resources, identification of transference-based reactions—that is, feelings, thoughts, impulses, and behaviors—may be easier, and may be an important initial step in coping with maladaptive transference patterns. Once the transference-induced reactions have reached awareness, the client may then be able to engage in some form of compensatory processing. An awareness of the reactions in and of themselves may be sufficient to allow the client a moment of "freedom of movement" (e.g., Mahoney, 1974) in choosing how to respond to the transference-inducing new person. Additionally, questions remain as to what point in the transference process people are best able to exert control: at the point of encoding information about a new person and an interpersonal situation (so as to prevent inappropriate encoding and inference), or after significant-other activation but before aspects of the self have been activated, or after the whole activation process and initial responses have occurred (so that they can be recognized and corrected). Individual differences in access to and attentiveness to internal, subjective aspects of experience are likely to influence which types of transference interventions will work best for a given client (see also Singer, 1988a). More thoughtful, systematic examination of these issues is necessary.

PRIVATE EXPERIENCE IN MENTAL
REPRESENTATIONS OF SELF AND OTHERS

Beyond our work about transference and the experience of the self in transference contexts, another line of our research addresses people's inner lives in a different way, and hence dovetails Singer's innovative focus on subjective experience. Singer's theorizing and empirical work on the contents and flow of private experience has helped to bring consciousness and its measurement to the fore in psychology by addressing the internal workings of the mind (e.g., Singer, 1975; Singer & Antrobus, 1972; Singer & McCraven, 1961; Singer & Schonbar, 1961). Although, there are inherent difficulties in any systematic, scientific study of the mind, as Singer readily acknowledges, he has argued forcefully for the importance of empirical research as a means of examining the inner life of the individual person. He has argued that the individual's quality of *me-ness* or inner life, has not often been captured by empirical research because of psychology's emphasis on observable behaviors, resulting in the tendency to ignore the content and meaning of the individual's inner life. Singer and his colleagues have persuasively suggested that people are more than just their overt responses to particular tasks, and in fact, that people's covert, ongoing thoughts tend to stray quite a bit from the tasks set to them by experimenters (e.g., during signal detection; Algom & Singer, 1984; Antrobus, Coleman, & Singer, 1967; Antrobus, Singer, Goldstein, & Fortgang, 1970), implying that there is more subjectivity in experience than is seen in measures of overt task performance alone. Task-unrelated thoughts and images occur for most people more than half the time, regardless of the frequency of the external task-relevant signals, and even when participants are performing with high rates of signal detection (see Singer, 1993).

Moreover, Singer and his colleagues have argued that it is possible to assess the content and style of people's ongoing thoughts and images to show individual differences in the self-report of the flow of consciousness (e.g., Singer & Antrobus, 1972; Huba et al., 1977; Segal et al., 1980). Conducted largely in nomothetic terms, so as to generalize across participants, this work suggests that people can report their daydreams and show considerable variation in their imaginal processes. Thus, Singer helped to open the world of private experience to psychological research, showing that the flow of consciousness may provide fertile ground for experimental investigation. This work set the stage for later research examining how people make use of their ongoing internal experiences—that is, their covert experiences, such as internal thoughts, feelings, wishes, dreads—in constructing self-knowledge and knowledge about others (e.g., Andersen, 1984).

Self Reflection: Moving Beyond Self-Perception Theory

We extended self-perception theory (Bem, 1972), which defines self-perception in strictly behavioral terms, by demonstrating that, while overt behavior obviously does play a role in self-perception, just as it does in social perception, covert experience is also used as a basis of self-inference. People not only make inferences about themselves based on observations of their own behavior (when their internal states are weak or ambiguous and no situational causes are salient, e.g., Enzle, 1980; Jones, 1990; Jones & Davis, 1965; Olson, 1990), they make self-inferences on the basis of private experiences as well (Andersen, Lazowski, & Donisi, 1986; Andersen & Williams, 1985; for related discussions, see Gouaux, 1971; Levine, Wyer, & Schwarz, 1994). Other research suggests that people often base judgments on whatever affect they happen to be experiencing at the moment, at the exact time of the judgment (Clore, Schwarz, & Conway, 1994; Forgas, 1992; Johnson & Tversky, 1983; Levine et al, 1994; Schwarz, 1990), even when making judgments about the self (Levine et al., 1994). Hence, people use their "feelings as information" for making subsequent self-relevant judgments (Schwarz, 1990).

These data suggest a reframing of self-perception theory away from its strict behaviorist assumptions to a more contemporary cognitive (or cognitive–behavioral) perspective in which both internal states and overt behaviors may serve as the bases of self-inference (Andersen, Glassman, & Gold, 1998; see also Andersen, 1984; Andersen & Ross, 1984; Nisbett & Ross, 1980; Regan & Totten, 1975; Storms, 1973). Such a reframing is consistent with revisions of classical behaviorism that permit internal states to function as measured behaviors in terms of what is learned and stored in memory (Bandura, 1977; Mischel, 1973). Of course, other processes of self-inference undoubtedly exist as well, but the simple notion that internal states are crucial in the construction of self-knowledge is now quite widely agreed upon (although for discussions of cultural differences, see Andersen, 1987; Markus & Kitayama, 1991).

Indeed, some research has highlighted the greater importance of thoughts and feelings in self-inference relative to behaviors. One study showed that disclosing covert thoughts and feelings in a clinical interview, in contrast to disclosing overt behavioral responses (i.e., what one does), led naive listeners to believe that the disclosures about inner experience were more diagnostic of what the speaker was really like—which was in agreement with the speaker's view (Andersen, 1984). Other research demonstrated that when a person's own cognitive–affective reactions are made salient to him or her, using an experimental manipulation, these covert reactions are likely to influence the person's self-concept more than are overt behaviors when made similarly salient (Andersen et al., 1986; Andersen & Williams, 1985; on self-change in experiments, see Jones, 1990; Markus & Nurius, 1986). Such self-inference changes are best conceptualized as a change in the working self-concept (Markus & Nurius, 1986; Markus & Wurf, 1987), rather than as a change in stable self-concept features. Nonetheless, the data demonstrate that private experiences influence self-knowledge activation and use, and that internal experiences may be more likely to be the basis of self-inferences than overt behaviors. These findings clearly build on Singer's contributions to our understanding of private experiences in terms of nomothetic definitions of self-reflection, and make use of idiographic procedures in combination with nomothetic ones.

Although special emphasis is given to internal states in perceiving the self, and sometimes others as well (see also Johnson, 1987; Johnson, Struthers, & Bradlee, 1988), little work has explored how and why it is that the covert, internal states of others are sometimes given weight in perceiving them. Our current work extended our research to explore differences in the content, structure, and processing of self- and other representations based on intractable self–other perspective differences as well as on the emotional and motivational significance of the other (Andersen et al., 1998).

Knowledge About Others and Their Private Experiences

Differences in perspective between the self and others are important in how representations of self and others are structured in memory (Jones, 1979; Jones & Nisbett, 1972; Nisbett & Ross, 1980; Prentice, 1990). One's own private experiences are privileged relative to those of all other people because one experiences these covert states directly. Another person's internal, private experiences, by contrast, are experienced less directly than one's own, if at all, suggesting a difference in the perceptual modalities though which these experiences are encoded and represented in memory (on modality and mental representation, see Carlston, 1992). One's own private experiences occur internally, whereas those of another person are experienced or inferred from nonverbal cues or from verbal comments. Indeed, if the perceiver is not motivated to work to fill in the blanks about the other's internal states, it is likely that little will be known or inferred about these states beyond trait inferences characterizing behavior (e.g., Winter & Uleman, 1984).

In addition to differences in how the private domain is experienced about the self versus other, there are also differences in how the overt, public domain is experienced. The observable behaviors of other people are highly visually salient in comparison to one's own behavior (Gilbert & Jones, 1986; Heider, 1958; Jones & Nisbett, 1972; Kelly, 1967; Lord, 1980, 1987; Nisbett & Ross, 1980; Ross & Nisbett, 1991; see also Higgins, 1996a). That is, from a perceiver's standpoint, the public behavior of the other stands out relative to the other's internal experiences. Work about imagined visual scenes and their role in memory supports this notion (Lord, 1980, 1987). Such scenes are less effective as encoding devices when the person observed in the scene is the self rather than another person. It is difficult to observe, even in fantasy, one's own overt behaviors in memorable images because one does not typically see oneself in this way; hence, the process is unfamiliar. Imagining another person's overt responses, however, is relatively easy because this is how one always sees the other. Thus, self–other differences in perspective are basic in construal (e.g. Nisbett & Ross, 1980), and are crucial in the literature about actor–observer differences in attribution (e.g., Regan & Totten, 1975; Storms, 1973).

Concrete differences in visual perspective may have implications for the nature of the mental representations that people form of the self and of others. The representational consequences of self–other perspective differences, however, should be attenuated as the emotional and motivational significance of the other increases. That is, one's motivation to know the other's internal life may help to overcome, to some extent, basic perspective differences (Andersen et al., 1998) in terms of the type of information represented about the other in memory.

Perspective Differences Versus Emotional–Motivational Importance of the Other

When the other person being perceived is emotionally and motivationally significant to the perceiver, there are reasons why internal, covert experiences are important to know, or to believe one knows. A significant other is, by definition, an individual who is highly important in one's life and upon whom one's own outcomes depend—especially one's emotional outcomes (e.g., Andersen & Glassman, 1996; Andersen et al., 1997; Bowlby, 1969; Greenberg & Mitchell, 1983; Higgins, 1996b; Higgins, Loeb, & Moretti, 1995; Maccoby & Martin, 1983; Sullivan, 1953). In particular, the other person's ups and downs and his or her apparent acceptance or rejection of the self are all crucial because the motivation to be close to the significant other—to feel tenderness, warmth, or attachment in relation to him or her—is so basic to human nature. Indeed, the motivation to be close to and intimate with a significant other has been shown to be associated with information represented about significant others in memory, and has consequences for the type of knowledge activated and used in transference (Andersen et al., 1996). Moreover, the self is likely to be defined and experienced in part in relation to significant others (e.g., Aron, Aron, Tudor, & Nelson, 1991; Baldwin, 1992; Hinkley & Andersen, 1996; Markus & Cross, 1990), thus making the process of coming to know a significant other's covert, internal experiences potentially important in identity definition, as well as in transference responses. The emotional–motivational significance of the other person may thus provoke one to think especially carefully about him or her, in a manner more similar to how one thinks about the self, and this may include an extensive "filling in the blanks" about the thoughts and feelings of this person (Chen & Andersen, in press).

In particular, knowledge of a significant other's internal states may be highly relevant and important to the self because of the self-regulatory function of the significant other; that is, his or her expectations, preferences, and standards may have implications for affect and self-experience (e.g., Higgins, 1987, 1996b; Higgins, Roney, Crowe, & Hymes, 1994; Strauman & Higgins, 1987). Nonsignificant persons, on the other hand, have little motivational or self-regulatory importance, and hence knowing their overt public aspects—without inferring elaborate covert, internal states—may be sufficient in constructing knowledge about them. Thus, overt, behavioral aspects of nonsignificant persons may be emphasized more in representing them in memory than are internal states, whereas covert states may be given higher priority for significant others.

Of course, the desire to know the more private aspects of one's significant other is likely to derive not only from outcome contingencies with these others, but also from feelings of caring or empathy (see Ickes, 1996; Kestenbaum, Faber, & Sroufe, 1989; Mehrabian, Young, & Sato, 1988). Overall, the motivation to be close to and accepted by significant others may distinguish significant others from other less significant people. Of course, these factors distinguish positive significant others from negative, aversive significant others as well (Andersen et al., 1996).

The emotional–motivational significance of particular persons is thus likely to influence the way information about the other is attended to, encoded, retrieved, and used in social–cognitive processing. Although we cannot literally know the internal states of significant others in exactly the way that we experience our own, the private aspects of significant others should be represented in memory in a manner more similar to how privileged self-information is represented than to how such private information is represented about nonsignificant others because our desire and need to know significant others should influence the extent of inferences made about their internal states.

In recent work (Andersen et al., 1998), we used idiographic–nomothetic procedures to examine the structural properties of the covert versus overt aspects of representations of self, significant others, and nonsignificant others. We asked participants to complete sentences about both covert and overt aspects of the self, a significant other, and a nonsignificant other (e.g., "feels inadequate" is an example of a covert aspect listed, and "turns red when angry" is an example of an overt aspect). Free-retrieval latencies were assessed throughout the listings, and participants were asked to rate the relative descriptiveness of each of these idiographically generated sentence completions. Based on the dual assumptions of self–other differences in perspective and of emotional–motivational differences in the significance of particular others, we predicted self–other differences in the representation of covert and overt aspects of each person, as well as a tendency for significant-other representations to be more similar to the self than to representations of nonsignificant persons. The results demonstrated that self-representations are characterized by more covert than overt information in terms of the number of sentences participants completed to describe each aspect of the self. Moreover, private aspects of the self are more distinctive in memory than are the public aspects, in that participants rated overt information about the self as being more descriptive of covert aspects of the self than they rated covert information as being descriptive of overt aspects. This kind of rating asymmetry suggests that the covert aspects of self serve as a cognitive reference point and stand out in memory in relation to overt aspects (see Andersen & Cole, 1990; Andersen & Klatzky, 1987; Hampson, John, & Goldberg, 1986; Higgins & King, 1981; Holyoak & Gordon, 1983; Houston, Sherman, & Baker, 1989; Srull & Gaelick, 1983; Tversky, 1977). Importantly, although these structural patterns are less evident for representations of significant others, as was predicted on the basis of self–other perspective differences, significant others were, in fact, characterized to a greater extent than were nonsignificant others by distinctive covert information relative to overt information—as predicted on the basis of the emotional–motivational importance of significant others.

Interestingly, the free-retrieval latencies showed that overt aspects of both significant others and nonsignificant others are highly cognitively accessible relative to covert aspects—a finding that did not hold for the self. This highlights basic visual-perspective differences between self and other. Hence, in terms of cognitive accessibility, little evidence for differences in representations of others is apparent on the basis of emotional–motivational significance. Overall, the results demonstrate that even though people cannot have direct access to the private experiences of someone else, they do a fair amount of inferring or imagining the inner life of the other when the other is significant—presumably because of the emotional and motivational importance of this individual. This is reflected in the prevalence of relatively distinctive covert-experience information in representations of significant others versus in those of nonsignificant others. People are motivated to know (or to feel that they know) the internal states of their significant others, perhaps because their own emotional states are dependent on the inner life of the significant others, and because they want to be empathic with these important others. However, these global differences in information availability (see Higgins, 1989) and distinctiveness did not completely override self–other differences, as reflected in the cognitive accessibility of covert and overt experiences.

Our findings about internal sources of self-knowledge are supported by research about the expression and experience of emotion (Johnson, 1987), which has shown that people believe they overtly express relatively little of their own experienced emotion, and thus have considerable unexpressed affect. Importantly, familiar others are also seen as having a secret self in this way, whereas unfamiliar others are not. The differential availability of one's own thoughts and feelings relative to the thoughts and feelings of any other person, including a significant other, appears crucial (Johnson et al., 1988) in the extent to which covert experiential knowledge, in contrast to overt "expressive" knowledge, is part of estimations of people's feelings. Other research has also shown that people do in fact list more covert, private reactions to describe the self than to describe others, and that these descriptions include many behaviors about both self and other (McGuire & McGuire, 1986; Prentice, 1990; see also Fiske & Cox, 1979). More specifically, people list a preponderance of privileged information for the self (32.7%) and do this less so for others (12.5%), even for others who are highly familiar (16.7%; Prentice, 1990). Furthermore, people characterize themselves more by privileged information than by interpersonal information (9.1%) or physical descriptors (8.0%). Indeed, people characterize their significant others more by interpersonal information (20.6%) than they characterize themselves in these terms. Differences in privileged and interpersonal information thus appear to distinguish representations of self and other, as supported by our more recent findings (Andersen et al., 1998).

We argue that the heightened familiarity of significant others relative to nonsignificant others cannot directly account for the greater extent of covert experiences in significant-other representations. Rather, we suggest that what is significant about a significant other is one's need to know this individual "inside and out," which derives from the fundamental need to be connected with particular others. Thus, one is motivated to make inferences about the significant other's inner world, beyond observing overt responses in a passive manner and simply accumulating trait inferences based on frequent exposure to the individual and his or her behavior.

Imaginal Processes: Implications for the Nature of Self- and Other-Knowledge

Singer's work about imaginal processes has demonstrated individual differences in daydreaming styles (Singer & Antrobus, 1972; see also Giambra, 1974; Huba et al., 1977; Segal & Singer, 1976), and provides grist for speculation about our findings on the nature of covert and overt aspects of self- and other representations. Individual differences in one's attention to private aspects of experience may be relevant to differences in one's tendency to store such information about the self. For instance, individuals with a positive-constructive daydreaming style who have an accepting attitude toward a rich inner world may have special access to their own highly distinctive private experiences. On the other hand, individuals with a poor ability to focus on imaginal processes and who give little attention to their ongoing consciousness are likely to experience only fleeting private thoughts and feelings, and hence may not be likely to emphasize such subjective experiences in self-perception (see also Cheek & Briggs, 1982; Fenigstein, 1987). Of course, individuals with a repressive personality style (e.g., Bonanno, David, Singer, & Schwartz, 1991; Bonanno & Singer, 1990; Singer, 1990; see also Singer, 1988b) are likely to try to avoid many aspects of their inner experiences, and therefore may not be able to report on much of their covert reactions. Moreover, imaginal-process differences may determine the emphasis on private versus public information about other persons, including significant others. Individuals with a positive-constructive daydreaming style may be better able to construct the inner world of another person, when motivated to do so, relative to individuals who attend less to their own flow of daydreams.

In addition, individuals with a guilty-dysphoric pattern in their daydreaming styles—a type of daydreamer also identified by Singer—tend to have private experiences that parallel their levels of depression (e.g., Giambra & Traynor, 1978; Golding & Singer, 1983; Starker & Singer, 1975), in terms of self-critical fantasies with themes of failure and hopelessness (for more about hopelessness, see, e.g., Andersen, 1990; Andersen & Schwartz, 1992; Andersen, Spielman, & Bargh, 1992). Based on considerable evidence, we know that the private thoughts and feelings of depressive individuals are likely to have a more negative tone than those of nondepressives, which is reflected in self-representations (e.g., Bargh & Tota, 1988). One implication of such findings is that when self-representations are "projected" onto other individuals (e.g., Fong & Markus, 1982; Holmes, 1968; Markus, Smith, & Moreland, 1985), it is possible that depressive individuals may be especially likely to imagine the private experiences of their significant others to have a similarly negative tone (although see Blatt, 1990). However, it is also conceivable that parallels between depressive mood and a guilty-dysphoric daydreaming style may lead one to judge the inner world of others to be more carefree and positive than one's own, especially if it is the self-schema, and not the schemas of all others, that is negatively toned in depression (see Bargh & Tota, 1988.) The question of what role significant others play in depression, as represented in the memory in relation to the self-representation, remains provocative and largely open to empirical investigation.

In summary, research is needed about the extent to which different daydreaming styles, and other styles of attention to covert experience, may be reflected in the mental representations formed of self and others. Indeed, the nature and content of these representations have implications for knowledge activation and application in making sense of the interpersonal world, either when the self-representation is projected onto another individual, or when a significant-other representation is "displaced" onto a new person in transference.

SUMMARY

Singer's innovative work about the flow of ongoing thought, individual differences in private experience, and the construction of meaning from the interplay of chronic knowledge structures and stimuli in the social environment has laid the foundation for our theoretical and empirical work about the nature of representations of self and others, and about transference as a basic social–cognitive process. Singer has helped to broaden the focus of personality and clinical psychology to address some of the most essential aspects of what it means to be human: the stream of consciousness in subjective experience. Furthermore, he has helped to bring the long-standing psychodynamic notion of transference into the domain of contemporary psychology (J. A. Singer & J. L. Singer, 1994) by recognizing it as a social–cognitive phenomenon.

We agree with Singer's perspective that transference is a basic means of understanding others and of constructing subjective interpersonal meaning. Moreover, we argue that research supporting the social–cognitive model of transference has demonstrated that transference is, indeed, a normal process that operates by means of basic social–cognitive principles in everyday social relations. Our data indicate that people give idiosyncratic meaning to the attributes and responses of others on the basis of the activation and application of a significant-other representation, and this process has consequences for affect, motivation, and how the self is experienced. Furthermore, in keeping with Singer's (1989) reinterpretation of countertransference, it follows that therapists have their own interpersonal histories. They bring these to their understandings of current interactions, implying that they undoubtedly engage in their own transference processes (or countertransference) in their dealings with clients— and that this occurs as a normal social–cognitive process. In conclusion, we believe that the body of research generated by the social–cognitive model of transference, as well as that about self- and social inference processes, has built upon and extended Singer's foundation. One consequence of this work has been to normalize transference and object relations processes in ways that permit research that will further our understanding of important clinical phenomenon by clarifying both the normal processes and content from which psychopathology and suffering may deviate.

ACKNOWLEDGMENTS

Preparation of this manuscript was supported by a National Research Service Award from the National Institute of Mental Health (F32-MH11293) to the first author, and by a grant from the National Institute of Mental Health (R01-MH48789) to the second.

REFERENCES

Algom, D., & Singer, J. L. (1984). Interpersonal influences on task-irrelevant thought and imagery in a signal detection experiment. *Imagination, Cognition, and Personality, 4,* 69–83.

Allport, G. (1937). *Personality: A psychology interpretation.* New York: Holt, Rinehart & Winston.

Andersen, S. M. (1984). Self-knowledge and social inference: II. The diagnositicity of cognitive/affective and behavioral data. *Journal of Personality and Social Psychology, 46,* 294–307.

Andersen, S. M. (1987). The role of cultural assumptions in self-concept development. In K. Yardley & T. Honess (Eds.), *Self and identity: Psychological perspectives* (pp. 231–246). New York: Wiley.

Andersen, S. M. (1990). The inevitability of future suffering: The role of depressive predictive certainty in depression. *Social Cognition, 8,* 203–228.

Andersen, S. M., & Baum, A. (1994). Transference in interpersonal relations: Inferences and affect based on significant-other representations. *Journal of Personality, 62,* 459–498.

Andersen, S. M., & Berk, M. S. (1998). Transference in everyday experience: Implications of experimental research for relevant clinical phenomena. *Review of General Psychology, 2,* 81–120.

Andersen, S. M., & Cole, S. W. (1990). "Do I know you?": The role of significant others in general social perception. *Journal of Personality and Social Psychology, 59,* 383–399.

Andersen, S. M., & Glassman, N. S. (1996). Responding to significant others when they are not there: Effects on interpersonal inference, motivation, and affect. In R. M. Sorrentino & E. T. Higgins (Eds.), *Handbook of motivation and cognition* (Vol. 3, pp. 262–321). New York: Guilford.

Andersen, S. M., Glassman, N. S., Chen, S., & Cole, S. W. (1995). Transference in social perception: The role of chronic accessibility in significant-other representations. *Journal of Personality and Social Psychology, 69,* 41–57.

Andersen, S. M., Glassman, N. S., & Gold, D. (1998). Mental representations of self, significant others, and nonsignificant others: Structure and processing of private and public aspects. *Journal of Personality and Social Psychology.*

Andersen, S. M., & Klatzky, R. L. (1987). Traits and social stereotypes: Levels of categorization in person perception. *Journal of Personality and Social Psychology, 53,* 235–246.

Andersen, S. M., Lazowski, L. E., & Donisi, M. (1986). Salience and self-inference: The role of biased recollections in self-inference processes. *Social Cognition, 4,* 75–95.

Andersen, S. M., Reznik, I., & Chen, S. (1997). The self in relation to others: Cognitive and motivational underpinnings. In J. G. Snodgrass & R. L. Thompson (Eds.), *The self across psychology: Self-recognition, self awareness, and the self-concept* (pp. 233–275). New York: New York Academy of Science.

Andersen, S. M., Reznik, I., & Manzella, L. M. (1996). Eliciting facial affect, motivation, and expectancies in transference: Significant-other representations in social relations. *Journal of Personality and Social Psychology, 71,* 1108–1129.

Andersen, S. M., & Ross, L. (1984). Self-knowledge and social inference: I. The impact of cognitive/affective and behavioral data. *Journal of Personality and Social Psychology, 46,* 280–293.

Andersen, S. M., & Schwartz, A. H. (1992). Intolerance of ambiguity and depression: A cognitive vulnerability factor linked to hopelessness. *Social Cognition, 10,* 271–298.

Andersen, S. M., Spielman, L. A., & Bargh, J. A. (1992). Future-event schemas and certainty about the future: Automaticity in depressives' future-event predictions. *Journal of Personality and Social Psychology, 63,* 711–723.

Andersen, S. M., & Williams, M. (1985). Cognitive/affective reaction in the improvement of self-esteem: When thoughts and feelings make a difference. *Journal of Personality and Social Psychology, 49,* 1086–1097.

Antrobus, J. S., Coleman, R., & Singer, J. L. (1967). Signal detection performance by subjects differing in predisposition to daydreaming. *Journal of Consulting Psychology, 31,* 487–491.

Antrobus, J. S., Singer, J. L., Goldstein, S., & Fortgang, M. (1970). Mindwandering and cognitive structure. *Transactions of the New York Academy of Science* (Series II), *32,* 242–252.

Aron, A., Aron, E. N., Tudor, M., & Nelson, G. (1991). Close relationships as including other in the self. *Journal of Personality and Social Psychology, 60,* 241–253.

Baldwin, M. W. (1992). Relational schemas and the processing of information. *Psychological Bulletin, 112,* 461–484.

Baldwin, M. W., Carrell, S. E., & Lopez, D. F. (1990). Priming relationship schemas: My advisor and the Pope are watching me from the back of my mind. *Journal of Experimental Social Psychology, 26,* 435–454.

Bandura, A. (1977). Self-efficacy: Toward a unifying theory of behavioral change. *Psychological Review, 84*, 191–215.

Bargh, J. A. (1989). Conditional automaticity: Varieties of automatic influence in social perception and cognition. In J. S. Uleman & J. A. Bargh (Eds.), *Unintended thought* (pp. 3–51). New York: Guilford.

Bargh, J. A. (1990). Auto-motives: Preconscious determinants of social interaction. In E. T. Higgins & R. M. Sorrentino (Eds.), *Handbook of motivation and cognition: Foundations of social behavior* (Vol. 2, pp. 93–130). New York: Guilford.

Bargh, J. A. (1992). Does subliminality matter to social psychology?: Awareness of the stimulus versus awareness of its influence. In R. F. Bornstein & T. S. Pittman (Eds.), *Perception without awareness* (pp. 236–255). New York: Guilford.

Bargh, J. A. (1994). The four horsemen of automaticity: Awareness, intention, efficiency, and control in social cognition. In R. S. Wyer, Jr., & T. K. Srull (Eds.), *Handbook of social cognition* (Vol. 1, pp. 1–40). Hillsdale, NJ: Lawrence Erlbaum Associates.

Bargh, J. A. (1997). The automaticity of everyday life. In R. S. Wyer, Jr. (Ed.), *Advances in social cognition* (Vol. 10, pp. 1–48). Mahwah, NJ: Lawrence Erlbaum Associates.

Bargh, J. A., Bond, R. N., Lombardi, W. L., & Tota, M. E. (1986). The additive nature of chronic and temporary sources of construct accessibility. *Journal of Personality and Social Psychology, 50*, 869–878.

Bargh, J. A., & Gollwitzer, P. M. (1994). Environmental control of goal-directed action: Automatic and strategic contingencies between situations and behavior. *Nebraska Symposium on Motivation, 41*, 71–124.

Bargh, J. A., & Pietromonaco, P. (1982). Automatic information processing and social perception: The influence of trait information presented outside of conscious awareness on impression formation. *Journal of Personality and Social Psychology, 43*, 437–449.

Bargh, J. A., & Tota, M. E. (1988). Context-dependent automatic processing in depression: Accessibility of negative constructs with regard to self but not others. *Journal of Personality and Social Psychology, 54*, 925–939.

Bem, D. J. (1972). Self-perception theory. In L. Berkowitz (Ed.), *Advances in experimental social psychology* (Vol. 6, pp. 1–62). New York: Academic Press.

Blair, I. V., & Banaji, M. R. (1996). Automatic and controlled processes in stereotype priming. *Journal of Personality and Social Psychology, 70*, 1142–1163.

Blatt, S. J. (1990). Interpersonal relatedness and self-definition: Two personality configurations and their implications for psychopathology and psychotherapy. In J. L. Singer (Ed.), *Repression and dissociation: Implications for personality theory, psychopathology, and health.* Chicago, IL: University of Chicago Press.

Bonanno, G. A., David, P. J., Singer, J. L., & Schwartz, G. E. (1991). The repressor personality and avoidant information processing: A dichotic listening study. *Journal of Research in Personality, 25*, 386–401.

Bonanno, G. A., & Singer, J. L. (1990). Repressive personality style. Theoretical and methodological implications for health and pathology. In J. L. Singer (Ed.), *Repression and dissociation: Implications for personality theory, psychopathology, and health* (pp. 435–470). Chicago: University of Chicago Press.

Bonanno, G. A., & Singer, J. L. (1993). Controlling one's stream of thought through perceptual and reflective processing. In D. M. Wegner & J. W. Pennebaker (Eds.), *Handbook of mental control* (pp. 149–170). Englewood Cliffs, NJ: Prentice-Hall.

Bornstein, R. F., & Pittman, T. S. (Eds.). (1992). *Perception without awareness.* New York: Guilford.

Bowers, K. S. (1984). On being unconsciously influenced and informed. In K. S. Bowers & D. Miechenbaum (Eds.), *The unconscious reconsidered* (pp. 227–272). New York: Wiley.

Bowlby, J. (1969). *Attachment and loss: Vol. 1. Attachment.* New York: Basic Books.

Brewer, M. B., Dull, V., & Lui, L. (1981). Perceptions of the elderly: Stereotypes as prototypes. *Journal of Personality and Social Psychology, 41,* 656–670.

Brooks, L. R. (1987). Decentralized control of categorization: The role of prior processing episodes. In U. Neisser (Ed.), *Categories reconsidered: The ecological and intellectual bases of categories* (pp. 141–174). Cambridge, England: Cambridge University Press.

Bruner, J. S. (1957). Going beyond the information given. In H. E. Gruber, K. R. Hammond, & R. Jessor, *Contemporary approaches to cognition* (pp. 41–69). Cambridge, MA: Harvard University Press.

Cantor, N., & Mischel, W. (1977). Traits as prototypes: Effects on recognition memory. *Journal of Personality and Social Psychology, 35,* 38–48.

Cantor, N., & Mischel, W. (1979). Prototypes in person perception. In L. Berkowitz (Ed.), *Advances in experimental social psychology* (Vol. 12, pp. 3–52). New York: Academic Press.

Carlson, R. (1981). Studies in script theory: I. Adult analogues of a childhood nuclear scene. *Journal of Personality and Social Psychology, 40,* 501–510.

Carlson, L., & Carlson, R. (1984). Affect and psychological magnification: Derivations from Tomkin's script theory. *Journal of Personality, 52,* 36–45.

Carlston, D. E. (1992). Impression formation and the modular mind: The associated systems theory. In L. Martin & A. Tesser (Eds.), *Construction of social judgment* (pp. 301–341). Hillsdale, NJ: Lawrence Erlbaum Associates.

Chartrand, T. L., & Bargh, J. A. (1996). Automatic activation of impression formation and memorization goals: Nonconscious goal priming reproduces effects of explicit task instructions. *Journal of Personality and Social Psychology, 71,* 464–478.

Cheek, J. M., & Briggs, S. R. (1982). Self-consciousness and aspects of identity. *Journal of Research in Personality, 16,* 401–408.

Chen, S., & Andersen, S. M. (in press). Relationships from the past in the present: Significant-other representations and transference in interpersonal life. *Advances in Social Cognition.*

Chen, S., Andersen, S. M., & Hinkley, K. (1998). *Stimulus applicability and significant-other activation: Beyond similarity-based categorization.* Unpublished manuscript, New York University.

Clore, G. L., Schwarz, N., & Conway, M. (1994). Affective causes and consequences of social information processing. In R. S. Wyer & T. K. Srull (Eds.), *Handbook of social cognition: Vol. 1. Basic processes* (2nd ed., pp. 323–418). Hillsdale, NJ: Lawrence Erlbaum Associates.

Devine, P. G. (1989). Stereotypes and prejudice: Their automatic and controlled components. *Journal of Personality and Social Psychology, 56,* 5–18.

Ehrenreich, J. H. (1989). Transference: One concept or many? *The Psychoanalytic Review, 76,* 37–65.

Enzle, M. (1980). Self-perception of emotion. In D. M. Wegner & R. R. Vallacher (Eds.), *The self in social psychology.* (pp. 55–79). New York: Oxford University Press.

Erdley, C. A., & D'Agostino, P. R. (1988). Cognitive and affective components of automatic priming effects. *Journal of Personality and Social Psychology, 54,* 741–747.

Fairbairn, W. R. D. (1952). *An object-relations theory of the personality.* New York: Basic Books.

Fenigstein, A. (1987). On the nature of public and private self-consciousness. *Journal of Personality, 55,* 543–554.

Fiske, S. T., & Cox, M. G. (1979). Person concepts: The effect of target familiarity and descriptive purpose on the process of describing others. *Journal of Personality, 47,* 136–161.

Fiske, S. T., & Pavelchak, M. (1986). Category-based versus piecemeal-based affective responses: Developments in schema-triggered affect. In R. M. Sorrentino & E. T. Higgins (Eds.), *Handbook of motivation and cognition* (pp. 167–203). New York: Guilford.

Fong, G. T., & Markus, H. (1982). Self-schemas and judgments about others. *Social Cognition, 1,* 191–205.

Forgas, J. P. (1992). Affect in social judgments and decisions: A multi-process model. In M. P. Zanna (Ed.), *Advances in Experimental Social Psychology* (Vol. 25, pp. 227–275). San Diego, CA: Academic Press.

Freud, S. (1958). The dynamics of transference. In J. Strachey (Ed. and Trans.), *The standard edition of the complete psychological works of Sigmund Freud* (Vol. 12, pp. 99–108). London: Hogarth. (Original work published 1912)

Giambra, L. M. (1974). Daydreaming across the life span: Late adolescent to senior citizen. *International Journal of Aging and Human Development, 8*, 197–228.

Giambra, L. M., & Traynor, T. D. (1978). Depression and daydreaming: An analysis based on self-ratings. *Journal of Clinical Psychology, 34*, 14–25.

Gilbert, D. T., & Jones, E. E. (1986). Perceiver-induced constraint: Interpretations of self-generated reality. *Journal of Personality and Social Psychology, 50*, 269–280.

Gill, M. M. (1982). *Analysis of transference: Vol. 1. Theory and technique.* New York: International Universities Press.

Gilovich, T. (1981). Seeing the past in the present: The effect of associations to familiar events on judgments and decisions. *Journal of Personality and Social Psychology, 40*, 797–808.

Glassman, N. S., & Andersen, S. M. (1998). *Activating transference without consciousness: Using significant-other representations to go beyond the subliminally given information.* Unpublished manuscript, New York University.

Golding, J. M., & Singer, J. L. (1983). Patterns of inner experience: Daydreaming styles, depressive moods, and sex roles. *Journal of Personality and Social Psychology, 45*, 663–675.

Gouaux, C. (1971). Induced affective states and interpersonal attraction. *Journal of Personality and Social Psychology, 20*, 37–43.

Greenberg, J. R., & Mitchell, S. A. (1983). *Object relations in psychoanalytic theory.* Cambridge, MA: Harvard University Press.

Greenson, R. R. (1965). The working alliance and the transference neurosis. *Psychoanalytic Quarterly, 34*, 155–181.

Greenwald, A. G. (1981). Self and memory. In G. H. Bower (Ed.), *Psychology of learning and motivation* (Vol. 15, pp. 201–236). New York: Academic Press.

Greenwald, A. G. (1992). New look 3: Unconscious cognition reclaimed. *American Psychologist, 47*, 766–779.

Greenwald, A. G., & Banaji, M. R. (1989). The self as a memory system: Powerful, but ordinary. *Journal of Personality and Social Psychology, 57*, 41–54.

Greenwald, A. G., & Banaji, M. R. (1995). Implicit social cognition: Attitudes, self-esteem, and stereotypes. *Psychological Review, 102*, 4–27.

Greenwald, A. G., Klinger, M. R., & Schuh, E. S. (1995). Activation by marginally perceptible ("subliminal") stimuli: Dissociation of unconscious from conscious cognition. *Journal of Experimental Psychology: General, 124*, 22–42.

Guntrip, H. (1971). *Psychoanalytic theory, therapy, and the self.* New York: Basic Books.

Hampson, S. E., John, O. P., & Goldberg, L. R. (1986). Category breadth and hierarchical structure in personality: Studies of asymmetries in judgments of trait implications. *Journal of Personality and Social Psychology, 51*, 37–54.

Heider, F. (1958). *The psychology of interpersonal relations.* New York: Wiley.

Higgins, E. T. (1987). Self discrepancy: A theory relating self and affect. *Psychological Review, 94*, 319–340.

Higgins, E. T. (1989). Knowledge accessibility and activation: Subjectivity and suffering from unconscious sources. In J. S. Uleman & J. A. Bargh (Eds.), *Unintended thought* (pp. 75–123). New York: Guilford.

Higgins, E. T. (1990). Personality, social psychology, and person-situation relations: Standards and knowledge activation as a common language. In L. A. Pervin (Ed.), *Handbook of personality* (pp. 301–338). New York: Guilford Press.

Higgins, E. T. (1996a). Knowledge: Accessibility, applicability, and salience. In E. T. Higgins & A. W. Kruglanski (Eds.), *Social psychology: Handbook of basic principles* (pp. 133–168). New York: Guilford.

Higgins, E. T. (1996b). Ideals, oughts, and regulatory focus: Affect and motivation from distinct pains and pleasures. In P. M. Gollwitzer & J. A. Bargh (Eds.), *The psychology of action* (pp. 91–114). New York: Guilford.

Higgins, E. T., & Bargh, J. A. (1987). Social cognition and social perception. In M. R. Rosenzweig & L. W. Porter (Eds.), *Annual Review of Psychology* (Vol. 38, pp. 369–425). Palo Alto, CA: Annual Reviews.

Higgins, E. T., & Brendl, C. M. (1995). Accessibility and applicability: Some "activation rules" influencing judgment. *Journal of Experimental Social Psychology, 31*, 218–243.

Higgins, E. T., & King, G. (1981). Accessibility of social constructs: Information processing consequences of individual and contextual variability. In N. Cantor & J. F. Kihlstrom (Eds.), *Personality, cognition and social interaction* (pp. 69–121). Hillsdale, NJ: Lawrence Erlbaum Associates.

Higgins, E. T., Loeb, I., & Moretti, M. (1995). Self-discrepancies and developmental shifts in vulnerability: Life transitions in the regulatory significance of others. In D. Cicchetti & S. L. Toth (Eds.), *Emotion, cognition, and representation: Rochester symposium on developmental psychopathology* (Vol. 6, pp. 191–230). Rochester, NY: University of Rochester.

Higgins, E. T., Rholes, W. S., & Jones, C. R. (1977). Category accessibility and impression formation. *Journal of Experimental Social Psychology, 13*, 141–154.

Higgins, E. T., Roney, C. J. R., Crowe, E., & Hymes, C. (1994). Ideal versus ought predilections for approach and avoidance: Distinct self-regulatory systems. *Journal of Personality and Social Psychology, 66*, 276–286.

Higgins, E. T., VanHook, E., & Dorfman, D. (1988). Do self-attributes form a cognitive structure? *Social Cognition, 6*, 177–207.

Hinkley, K., & Andersen, S. M. (1996). The working self-concept in transference: Significant-other activation and self change. *Journal of Personality and Social Psychology, 71*, 1279–1295.

Holender, D. (1986). Semantic activation without conscious identification in dichotic listening, parafoveal vision, and visual masking: A survey and appraisal. *Behavioral and Brain Sciences, 9*, 1–23.

Holmes, D. S. (1968). Projection as a defense mechanism. *Psychological Bulletin, 69*, 248–268.

Holyoak, K. J., & Gordon, P. C. (1983). Social reference points. *Journal of Personality and Social Psychology, 44*, 881–887.

Horney, K. (1939). *New ways in psychoanalysis.* New York: Norton.

Horowitz, M. J. (1991). Person schemas. In M. J. Horowitz (Ed.), *Person schemas and maladaptive interpersonal patterns* (pp. 13–31). Chicago: University of Chicago Press.

Horowitz, M. J., Merluzzi, T. V., Ewert, M., Ghannam, J. H., Hartley, D., & Stinson, C. H. (1991). Role-relationship models configuration (RRMC). In M. J. Horowitz (Ed.), *Person schemas and maladaptive interpersonal patterns* (pp. 115–154). Chicago: University of Chicago Press.

Houston, D. A., Sherman, S. J., & Baker, S. M. (1989). The influence of unique features and direction of comparison preferences. *Journal of Experimental Social Psychology, 25*, 121–141.

Huba, G. J., Segal, B., & Singer, J. L. (1977). The consistency of daydreaming styles across samples of college male and female drug and alcohol users. *Journal of Abnormal Psychology, 86*, 99–102.

Ickes, W. (1996). *Empathic accuracy.* New York: Guilford.

Johnson, E. J., & Tversky, A. (1983). Affect, generalization, and the perception of risk. *Journal of Personality and Social Psychology, 45*, 20–31.

Johnson, J. T. (1987). The heart on the sleeve and the secret self: Estimations of hidden emotions in self and acquaintances. *Journal of Personality, 55*, 563–582.

Johnson, J. T., Struthers, N. J., & Bradlee, P. (1988). Social Knowledge and the "secret self": The mediating effect of data base size on judgments of emotionality in the self and others. *Social Cognition, 6*, 319–344.

Jones, E. E. (1979). The rocky road from acts to dispositions. *American Psychologist, 34*, 107–117.

Jones, E. E. (1990). Constrained behavior and self-concept change. In J. M. Olson & M. P. Zanna (Eds.), *Self-inference processes: The Ontario Symposium* (Vol. 6, pp. 69–86). Hillsdale, NJ: Lawrence Erlbaum Associates.

Jones, E. E., & Davis, K. E. (1965). From acts to dispositions. In L. Berkowitz (Ed.), *Advances in experimental social psychology* (Vol. 2, pp. 220–266). New York: Academic Press.

Jones, E. E., & Nisbett, R. E. (1972). The actor and the observer: Divergent perceptions of the causes of behavior. In E. E. Jones et. al. (Eds.), *Attribution: Perceiving the causes of behavior* (pp. 79–94). Morristown, NJ: General Learning Press.

Kelley, H. H. (1967). Attribution theory in social psychology. In D. Levine (Ed.), *Nebraska Symposium on Motivation* (Vol. 15, pp. 192–240). Lincoln: University of Nebraska Press.

Kelly, G. A. (1955). *The psychology of personal constructs.* New York: Norton.

Kestenbaum, R., Faber, E. A., Sroufe, L. A. (1989). Individual differences in empathy among preschoolers: Relation to attachment history. In N. Eisenberg (Ed.), *Empathy and its development: New directions in child development* (Vol. 44, pp. 51–64). New York: Cambridge University Press.

Kihlstrom, J. F. (1987). The cognitive unconscious. *Science, 237*, 1445–1452.

Kihlstrom, J. F., Barnhardt, T. M., & Tataryn, D. J. (1992). The psychological unconscious: Found, lost, and regained. *American Psychologist, 47*, 788–791.

Klos, D. S., & Singer, J. L. (1981). Determinants of the adolescent's ongoing thought following simulated parental confrontation. *Journal of Personality and Social Psychology, 41*, 975–987.

Koestner, R., & McClelland, D. C. (1990). Perspectives on competence motivation. In L. A. Pervin (Ed.), *Handbook of personality: Theory and research* (pp. 527–548). New York: Guilford.

Levine, S. R., Wyer, R. S., Schwarz, N. (1994). Are you what you feel? The affective and cognitive determinants of self-judgments. *European Journal of Social Psychology, 24*, 63–77.

Lewicki, P. (1986). *Nonconscious social information processing.* San Diego, CA: Academic Press.

Lewicki, P., & Hill, T. (1987). Unconscious processes as explanations of behavior in cognitive, personality, and social psychology. *Personality and Social Psychology Bulletin, 13*, 355–362.

Linville, P. W., & Carlston, D. E. (1994). Social cognition of the self. In P. G. Devine, D. C. Hamilton, & T. M. Ostrom (Eds.), *Social cognition: Impact on Social Psychology* (pp. 143–193). New York: Academic Press.

Lord, C. G. (1980). Schemas and images as memory aids: Two modes of processing social information. *Journal of Personality and Social Psychology, 38*, 257–269.

Lord, C. G. (1987). Imagining self and others: Reply to Brown, Keenan, & Potts. *Journal of Personality and Social Psychology, 53*, 445–450.

Luborsky, L., & Crits-Christoph, P. (1990). *Understanding transference: The CCRT method.* New York: Basic Books.

Luborsky, L., Crits-Christoph, P., Friedman, S. H., Mark, D., & Schaffler, P. (1991). Freud's transference template compared with the core conflictual relationship theme (CCRT): Illustrations by the two specimen cases. In M. J. Horowitz (Ed.), *Person schemas and maladaptive interpersonal patterns* (pp. 167–195). Chicago: University of Chicago Press.

Maccoby, E. E., & Martin, J. A. (1983). Socialization in the context of the family: Parent-child interaction. In P. H. Mussen (Ed.), *Handbook of child psychology: Volume 4. Socialization, personality, and social development* (pp. 1–101). New York: Wiley.

Macrae, C. N., Bodenhausen, G. V., & Milne, A. B. (1995). The dissection of selection in person perception: Inhibitory processes in social stereotyping. *Journal of Personality and Social Psychology, 69*, 397–407.

Mahoney, M. J. (1974). *Cognition and behavior modification.* Cambridge, MA: Ballinger.

Marcel, A. J. (1983). Conscious and unconscious perception: Experiments on visual masking and word recognition. *Cognitive Psychology, 15*, 197–237.

Markus, H. (1977). Self-schemata and processing information about the self. *Journal of Personality and Social Psychology, 35*, 63–78.

Markus, H. (1983). Self-knowledge: An expanded view. *Journal of Personality, 51*, 543–656.

Markus, H., & Cross, S. (1990). The interpersonal self. In L. A. Pervin (Ed.), *Handbook of personality* (pp. 576–608). New York: Guilford.

Markus, H., & Kitayama, S. (1991). Culture and the self: Implications for cognition, emotion, and motivation. *Psychological Review, 98*, 224–253.

Markus, H., & Nurius, P. (1986). Possible selves. *American Psychologist, 41*, 954–969.

Markus, H., Smith, J., & Moreland, R. L. (1985). Role of the self-concept in the social perception of others. *Journal of Personality and Social Psychology, 49*, 1494–1512.

Markus, H., & Wurf, E. (1987). The dynamic self-concept: A social psychological perspective. *Annual Review of Psychology, 38*, 299–337.

McGuire, W. J., & McGuire, C. V. (1986). Differences in conceptualizing self versus other people as manifested in contrasting verb types used in natural speech. *Journal of Personality and Social Psychology, 51*, 1135–1143.

Mehrabian, A., Young, A. L., & Sato, S. (1988). Emotional empathy and associated individual differences. *Current Psychology: Research and Reviews, 7*, 221–240.

Meichenbaum, D., & Gilmore, J. B. (1984). The nature of unconscious processes: A cognitive-behavioral perspective. In K. Bowers & D. Meichenbaum (Eds.), *The unconscious reconsidered*. New York: Wiley.

Mischel, W. (1973). Toward a cognitive social learning reconceptualization of personality. *Psychological Review, 80*, 252–283.

Mischel, W., & Shoda, Y. (1995). A cognitive-affective system theory of personality: Reconceptualizing situations, dispositions, dynamics, and invariance in personality structure. *Psychological Review, 102*, 246–268.

Mullahy, P. (1970). *Psychoanalysis and interpersonal psychiatry: The contributions of Harry Stack Sullivan*. New York: Science House.

Murray, S. L., & Holmes, J. G. (1993). Seeing virtues in faults: Negativity and the transformation of interpersonal narratives in close relationships. *Journal of Personality and Social Psychology, 65*, 707–722.

Neuberg, S. L. (1988). Behavioral implications of information presented outside of conscious awareness: The effect of subliminal presentation of trait information on behavior in the prisoner's dilemma game. *Social Cognition, 6*, 207–230.

Nisbett, R. E., & Ross, L. (1980). *Human inference: Strategies and shortcomings of social judgment*. Englewood Cliffs, NJ: Prentice-Hall.

Ogilvie, D. M., & Ashmore, R. D. (1991). Self-with-other representations as a unit of analysis in self-concept research. In R. C. Curtis (Ed.), *The relational self: Theoretical convergences in psychoanalysis and social psychology*. New York: Guilford.

Olson, J. M. (1990). Self-inference processes in emotion. In J. M. Olson & M. P. Zanna (Eds.), *Self-inference processes: The Ontario Symposium* (Vol. 6, pp. 17–42). Hillsdale, NJ: Lawrence Erlbaum Associates.

Pope, K. S., & Singer, J. L. (1978). Regulation of the stream of consciousness: Toward a theory of ongoing thought. In G. E. Schwartz & D. Shapiro (Eds.), *Consciousness and self-regulation* (Vol. 2). New York: Plenum.

Prentice, D. A. (1990). Familiarity and differences in self- and other-representations. *Journal of Personality and Social Psychology, 59*, 369–383.

Rayner, K. (1978). Foveal and parafoveal cues in reading. In J. Requin (Ed.), *Attention and performance* (Vol. 7, pp. 149–161). Hillsdale, NJ: Lawrence Erlbaum Associates.

Regan, D. T., & Totten, J. (1975). Empathy and attribution: Turning observers into actors. *Journal of Personality and Social Psychology, 59*, 369–383.

Ross, L., & Nisbett, R. (1991). *The person and the situation: Perspectives of social psychology*. New York: McGraw-Hill.

Safran, J. D. (1990a). Toward a refinement of cognitive therapy in light of interpersonal theory: I. Theory. *Clinical Psychology Review, 10,* 87–105.

Safran, J. D. (1990b). Toward a refinement of cognitive therapy in light of interpersonal theory: II. Practice. *Clinical Psychology Review, 10,* 87–105.

Safran, J. D., & Segal, Z. V. (1990). *Interpersonal processes in cognitive therapy.* New York: Basic Books.

Schank, R. C., & Abelson, R. P. (1977). *Scripts, plans, goals, and understanding: An inquiry into human knowledge structures.* Hillsdale, NJ: Lawrence Erlbaum Associates.

Schwarz, N. (1990). Feelings as information: Informational and motivational functions of affective states. In E. T. Higgins & R. M. Sorrentino (Eds.), *Handbook of motivation and cognition* (Vol. 2, pp. 527–561). New York: Guilford.

Sedikides, C., & Ostrom, T. M. (1988). Are person categories used when organizing information about unfamiliar sets of persons? *Social Cognition, 8,* 229–240.

Sedikides, C., & Skowronski, J. J. (1991). The law of cognitive structure activation. *Psychological Inquiry, 2,* 169–184.

Segal, B., Huba, G. J., & Singer, J. L. (1980). *Drugs, daydreaming, and personality: A study of college youth.* Hillsdale, NJ: Lawrence Erlbaum Associates.

Segal, B., & Singer, J. L. (1976). Daydreaming, drug and alcohol use in college students: A factor analytic study. *Addictive Behaviors, 1,* 227–235.

Segal, Z. V., Hood, J. E., Shaw, B. F., & Higgins, E. T. (1988). A structural analysis of the self-schema construct in major depression. *Cognitive Therapy and Research, 12,* 471–485.

Singer, J. A., & Singer, J. L. (1994). Social-cognitive and narrative perspectives on transference. In J. M. Masling & R. F. Bornstein (Eds.), *Empirical perspectives on object relations theory* (pp. 157–193). Washington, DC: American Psychological Association.

Singer, J. L. (1975). Navigating the stream of consciousness: Research in daydreaming and related inner experience. *American Psychologist, 30,* 727–738.

Singer, J. L. (1984). The private personality. *Personality and Social Psychology Bulletin, 10,* 7–30.

Singer, J. L. (1985). Transference and the human condition: A cognitive-affective perspective. *Psychoanalytic Psychology, 2,* 189–219.

Singer, J. L. (1988a). Reinterpreting the transference. In D. C. Turk & P. Salovey (Eds.), *Reasoning, inference, and judgment in clinical psychology* (pp. 182–205). New York: The Free Press.

Singer, J. L. (1988b). Sampling ongoing consciousness and emotional experience: Implications for health. In M. J. Horowitz (Ed.), *Psychodynamics and cognition* (pp. 297–346). Chicago, IL: University of Chicago Press.

Singer, J. L. (1989). Countertransference and cognition: Studying the psychotherapist's distortions as consequences of normal information processing. *Psychotherapy, 26,* 344–355.

Singer, J. L. (Ed.). (1990). *Repression and dissociation.* Chicago: University of Chicago Press.

Singer, J. L. (1993). Experimental studies of ongoing conscious experience. In G. R. Bock & J. Marsh (Eds.), *Experimental and theoretical studies of consciousness* (Ciba Foundation Symposium 174; pp. 100–122). Chichester, England: Wiley.

Singer, J. L., & Antrobus, J. S. (1972). Daydreaming, imaginal processes, and personality: A normative study. In P. W. Sheehan (Ed.), *The function and nature of imagery* (pp. 175–202). New York: Academic Press.

Singer, J. L., & Bonanno, G. (1990). Personality and private experience: Individual variations in consciousness and in attention to subjective phenomena. In L. A. Pervin (Ed.), *Handbook of personality: Theory and research* (pp. 419–444). New York: Guilford.

Singer, J. L., & Kolligian, Jr., J. (1987). Personality: Developments in the study of private experience. In M. R. Rosenzweig & L. W. Porter (Eds.), *Annual Review of Psychology, 38,* 533–574.

Singer, J. L., & McCraven, V. (1961). Some characteristics of adult daydreaming. *Journal of Psychology, 51*, 151–164.

Singer, J. L., & Pope, K. S. (1978). The use of imagery and fantasy techniques in psychotherapy. In J. L. Singer & K. S. Pope (Eds.), *The power of imagination: New methods in psychotherapy* (pp. 3–34). New York: Plenum.

Singer, J. L., & Salovey, P. (1991). Organized knowledge structures and personality: Person schemas, self-schemas, prototypes, and scripts. In M. J. Horowitz (Ed.), *Person schemas and maladaptive interpersonal patterns* (pp. 33–79). Chicago: University of Chicago Press.

Singer, J. L., & Schonbar, R. (1961). Correlates of daydreaming: A dimension of self-awareness. *Journal of Consulting Psychology, 25*, 1–6.

Smith, E. R. (1994). Procedural knowledge and processing strategies in social cognition. In R. S. Wyer, Jr., & T. K. Srull (Eds.), *Handbook of social cognition* (Vol. 1, pp. 95–151). Hillsdale, NJ: Lawrence Erlbaum Associates.

Smith, E. R., & Zarate, M. A. (1990). Exemplar and prototype use in social categorization. *Social Cognition, 8*, 243–262.

Smith, E. R., & Zarate, M. A. (1992). Exemplar-based model of social judgment. *Psychological Review, 99*, 3–21.

Srull, T. K., & Gaelick, L. (1983). General principles and individual differences in the self as a habitual reference point: An examination of self-other judgments of similarity. *Social Cognition, 2*, 108–121.

Srull, T. K., & Wyer, R. S., Jr. (1979). The role of category accessibility in the interpretation of information about persons: Some determinants and implications. *Journal of Personality and Social Psychology, 37*, 1660–1672.

Srull, T. K., & Wyer, R. S., Jr. (1986). The role of chronic and temporary goals in social information processing. In R. M. Sorrentino & E. T. Higgins (Eds.), *Handbook of motivation and cognition: Foundations of social behavior* (Vol. 1, pp. 503–549). New York: Guilford.

Starker, S., & Singer, J. L. (1975). Daydreaming and symptom patterns of psychiatric patients: A factor analytic study. *Journal of Abnormal Psychology, 84*, 567–570.

Storms, M. D. (1973). Videotape and the attribution process: Revising actors' and observers' points of view. *Journal of Personality and Social Psychology, 27*, 165–175.

Strauman, T. J., & Higgins, E. T. (1987). Automatic activation of self-discrepancies and emotional syndromes: When cognitive structures influence affect. *Journal of Personality and Social Psychology, 53*, 1004–1014.

Sullivan, H. S. (1940). *Conceptions of modern psychiatry.* New York: Norton.

Sullivan, H. S. (1953). *The interpersonal theory of psychiatry.* New York: Norton.

Tomkins, S. S. (1979). Script theory: Differential magnification of affects. In H. E. Howe, Jr. & R. A. Dienstbier (Eds.), *Nebraska Symposium on Motivation* (Vol. 26, pp. 201–236). Lincoln: University of Nebraska Press.

Tversky, A. (1977). Features of similarity. *Psychological Review, 84*, 327–352.

Uleman, J. S. (1987). Consciousness and control: The case of spontaneous trait inferences. *Personality and Social Psychology Bulletin, 13*, 337–354.

Wachtel, P. L. (1981). Transference, schema, and assimilation: The relationship of Piaget to the psychoanalytic theory of transference. *Annual of Psychoanalysis, 8*, 59–76.

Westen, D. (1988). Transference and information processing. *Clinical Psychology Review, 8*, 161–179.

Westen, D. (1991). Social cognition and object relations. *Psychological Bulletin, 109*, 429–455.

Winter, L., & Uleman, J. S. (1984). When are social judgments made? Evidence for the spontaneousness of trait inferences. *Journal of Personality and Social Psychology, 47*, 237–252.

Young, J. E. (1990). *Cognitive therapy for personality disorders: A schema-focused approach.* Sarasota, FL: Professional Resource Exchange.

II

COGNITION AND PERSONALITY

6

A Framework for the Study of Individual Differences in Personality Formations

John D. Mayer
University of New Hampshire

Years ago, B. F. Skinner (1956/1968, p. 29) wrote, ". . . control your conditions and you will see order," a command that echoed with each orderly prediction he made. How does a personality psychologist control conditions so as to improve prediction? Skinner would encourage us to control external influences. An alternative approach, but of potentially equal promise, is to control internal conditions: personality. Controlling internal conditions is plainly not what Skinner had in mind. To Skinner, observable behavior was all important and most things mental, and hence unobservable, were part of a black box to be ignored. Aside from Skinner's objections, controlling the internal conditions of personality may seem impractical simply because personality parts exist that cannot be readily manipulated by the experimentalist: life history, intelligence, models of the future, and so forth.

Although direct manipulation of personality's internal conditions is often impossible, other means of control can be exercised. Given that personalities naturally vary, those variations can be identified and controlled either quasi-experimentally or statistically. Individual differences researchers study such variation. Quasi-experimental research involves assigning people to groups based on their similar internal conditions, and then comparing the groups regarding other internal or external characteristics. Statistical control involves measuring a naturally varying internal condition and then using it to predict internal or external outcomes. In either case, understanding the person's internal conditions yields better prediction than knowing nothing. Personality psychologists thus rewrote Skinner's command as, "Know your internal personalities and you will see order."

Knowing internal personalities is plainly a broad agenda for the field, and it is difficult to carry out because of the fractured nature of personality psychology today. The field of personality is balkanized both into various theories, such as Freud's, Jung's, and Bandura's, and also into various research areas such as repression, traits, and person perception (Mayer, 1998). Research about individual differences is balkanized along with the rest of the field. For example, many individual differences concern variations in traits such as intelligence, extroversion, and the like, which are studied by trait researchers. Individual differences exist in many other parts of personality as well, including in fantasies, consciousness, and unconsciousness (J. L. Singer, 1975, 1984, 1990; J. L. Singer & Bonanno, 1990). These latter differences are often studied by psychodynamically oriented experimental psychologists. Creating a unified framework for studying individual differences—traits, dynamics, and others—could improve how we know internal personalities.

This chapter presents a framework for organizing and classifying types of individual differences. The framework first identifies formations (or forms) in personality. I use the term *formation* (or *form*) to refer to any component, organization, or development inside the personality that accounts for an individual difference. The term *formative type*, is also used to refer to any personality possessing the given formation. The formative type describes only that limited and defined aspect of personality that accounts for a given individual difference; it is different from a *personality type*, which attempts to characterize the whole person.[1]

The framework developed is part of a systems approach to organizing the discipline of personality. The specific systems framework from which it draws is one of several new approaches proposed to better organize personality psychology (e.g., Mayer, 1995a, 1998; McAdams, 1996; J. A. Singer, 1995). The systems framework divides personality studies into four central topics: (a) *identification*, which defines and locates personality, (b) personality *components*, which studies its parts, (c) the *organization* of those components, and (d) *development*, how personality changes over time. Table 6.1 provides a summary of this systems framework. There, the four system topics are arranged across the top of the table. Underneath

---

[1]The whole person is unlikely to be readily categorized because it is so complex. Rather, as Allport (1937) has noted, ". . . a [personality] typology is always a device for exalting its author's special interest. . . . Every typology is based on the abstraction of some segment from the total personality, and the forcing of this segment to unnatural prominence" (p. 196).

TABLE 6.1
Introductory Overview of the System-Topics Framework

The Four System-Topics

	I. Identification	*II. Components*	*III. Organization*	*IV. Development*
Coverage of the Topic	The system is identified amidst its neighboring systems such as biology and the family. In so doing, personality is defined.	The personality system is divided into its component parts and the concept of a component is defined. Next, the major classes of personality components are discussed.	The major components within personality and systems external to personality are organized together.	The manner in which the personality components and their organization develop over time is examined.
Purpose of Coverage	The identification of personality locates the system, and by so doing, begins to define the importance of the subject, and establishes a foundation for the remaining topics.	From the beginning of the century, much confusion has centered around the proper units of study in personality psychology. This topic's purpose is to identify the major parts of personality and to classify, systematize, and regularize them as much as is possible.	Once personality's components are identified, the exposition turns to how they are organized together, both structurally (already covered, to some extent, in locating personality) and dynamically (i.e., how one component influences another).	When personality's components, structures, and dynamics are first established in infancy they begin to develop toward adulthood and maturity. The developmental topic describes the progression of these changes in the personality.

each topic is a brief description of parts of the field it organizes, and the central purpose for which the topic is included in the field.

After this introduction, the chapter's second section, A Relational System for Personality Formations, examines several different types of formations. These formative types run parallel to the last three of four categories of the systems framework (components, organization, development). That is, the classification system orders formations according to their complexity from single-component formations, to organizational forms, to developmental forms. The chapter's third, and final section describes advances in prediction that may be obtained by recognizing distinct classes of formations. It also addresses the question of which formations are the most important to study.

A RELATIONAL FRAMEWORK FOR PERSONALITY FORMATIONS

Component Formations

The simplest formations correspond to single parts of personality. Thus, an extroversion formation might correspond to a high level of extroversion, or a sex-drive formation might correspond to a high level of sexual drive. A brief survey of personality components, therefore, can help illustrate these formations. If formations all corresponded to individual components, there would be no value to a language of formations. The formation becomes of value when examining more complex combinations of components. The present discussion of formations lays the basis for a discussion of those more powerful, complex formations also to be described in this chapter.

Single-Component Formations and the Commonly Used Units in Personality

Roughly 400 parts of personality are commonly discussed in personality textbooks today; such units can be divided into 4 main types and 21 subtypes that are employed across all theoretical perspectives within personality psychology (Mayer, 1995a). The four broader classes of components are enablers, establishments, themes, and agencies. Underlying these psychological components are networks of neurons, cells specialized in information processing and computation. A molecular-molar continuum is often used to discriminate smaller (molecular) from larger (molar) objects of study in the sciences. At the molecular level, near personality, neurons communicate with one another in part through electrochemical signals, termed action potentials, that are transmitted along thin, tubal extensions of the cell body, termed axons (Eccles, 1973). These action potentials terminate at the cell synapses, where they release chemical packets that travel to the receptor areas of neighboring neurons (Bloom, Lazerson, & Hofstadter, 1988). The electrochemical conductivity of a given neuron and its neighboring neurons constitute an important aspect of biological brain activity.

Enablers and Enabler Based-Formations. If we switch the level of analysis from the neuron's biological activity to the more molar level of information it conveys, then we are speaking psychologically. It is at this psychological level of description that we can best understand the smallest mechanisms of personality, the enablers. Collectively, the enablers form the underlying building blocks of personality, closest to the biological level relative to other personality units, and carrying out the basic functions that enable the personality system to operate (see Mayer, Chabot, & Carlsmith, 1997, for a more detailed exposition). Enablers can be divided into four subtypes. The first, *conative subtype*, translate bodily requirements into basic motivations such as hunger pangs or sexual yearnings. The second, *affective enablers*, construct basic, unlearned emotional responses such as delight or distress in response to bodily or basic social events. The third, *cognitive enablers*, make possible the acquisition, retention, and abstraction of knowledge. These cognitive enablers are independent of the acquired knowledge itself. That is, long-term memory is the enabler; knowledge structures stored within long-term memory, however, are defined as more complex structures, called *establishments* (see next section). The fourth, *consciousness enablers*, permit awareness and its perturbations, and include such elements as the stream of consciousness.

Because enablers are mechanisms close to the neurological level, and relatively molecular in relation to the rest of personality, they are incorporated quickly within the higher parts of personality. This creates a challenge to disentangle their operation from more complex mental structures. To accomplish this, enablers typically are studied comparatively in animal species with limited learning capacity, or they are studied developmentally in human infants and children before a great deal of brain maturation and learning has taken place.

In theory, there exist as many different enabler-based formations as there are enablers. Examples would include high sex-drive formations (conative enablers), depressive formations (affective enablers), and high-capacity short-term memory formations (cognitive enablers).

Enablers, the Molecular-Molar Continuum, and Establishments. The transition from the neurological to the enabler level involved moving along the molecular–molar continuum from biological signals to psychological processes. The enablers can be seen relative to their biological underpinnings in Fig. 6.1. Figure 6.1 is arranged so that the vertical dimension represents the molecular–molar dimension, running from the biological–molecular beneath, to the sociological–molar above. Internal personality is represented as a box in the center of the diagram. On the floor of the personality cube the four types of enablers are arranged. Each enabler is surrounded by a different visual pattern representing its unique mode of processing. Enablers represent the most molecular of the units commonly discussed within personality psychology.

The figure's second dimension runs horizontally so as to separate that which is internal to personality, including the enablers, from that which is external to personality, such as its behavioral interactions with a given situation. The depth of the figure is provided by a third dimension, an organismic-constructed dimension, that separates components that are most enmeshed within the organism (front portion of figure), such as conative enablers (e.g., hunger urges), from those components, such as cognitive enablers (e.g., reasoning; back portion of figure), that are able to operate more flexibly beyond the realm of the individual organism, that is, that operate to acquire and reason with socially and culturally relevant information. Three more molar classes of personality components exist relative to enablers: establishments, themes, and agencies. If we move another step along the continuum we arrive at the level of personality establishments.

Establishments. *Establishments* are mental contents that are so named because they are established by the individual through learning. Establishments are content focused and typically model some portion of the self, the world, or the self-in-the-world. Models of the self include states and traits. Models of the world include knowledge of such subjects as arithmetic, dancing, and dinosaurs. Models of the self-in-the-world include models of interactions with others, such as the forms of attachment that work best for oneself. Along the molecular–molar continuum, larger units of analysis typically incorporate smaller units in their function. The establishments incorporate the lower level enablers in their function. For instance, the self-concept establishment incorporates motivational urges, emotional reactions, and cognitive processing of the self.

Diagrammatically, the establishments exist above the enablers on the molecular–molar continuum, as is shown in Fig. 6.2. There, the three subtypes of self, world, and self-in-world establishments extend from the front to the rear of the figure. Models of the self are to the left because they are more internal; models of the world are to the right because they are more external. Each establishment class has arranged, around its sides, all four visual patterns associated with the four lower level enablers

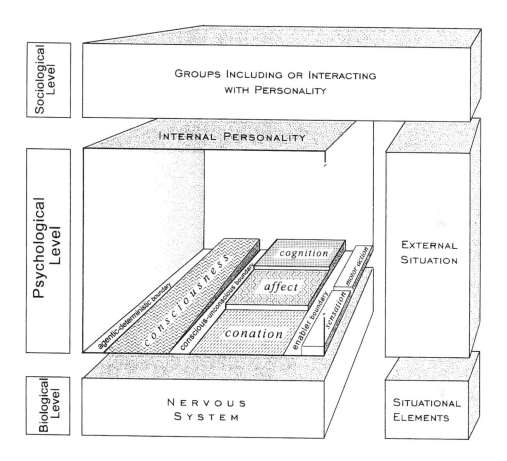

FIG. 6.1. The personality system is represented in three dimensions. The vertical, molecular–molar dimension, separates personality (middle) from the more molecular nervous system (below) and from the more molar groups (above). The horizontal, internal–external dimension separates those systems internal to personality (left) from those external in the situation (right). The third dimension, depth, separates those components of personality most enmeshed with the organism (in front) from those most independent (in back). The floor of the cube marked personality has arranged upon it the four classes of enablers, as well as the sensory and motor systems that regulate communication between the interior and exterior of personality.

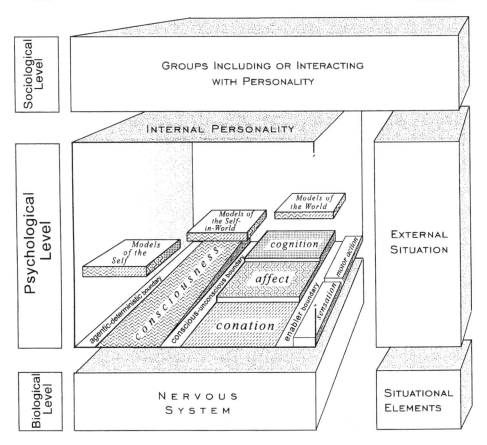

FIG. 6.2. The same as Figure 1 except that the three classes of establishments are added, above the enabler level.

functions, because the establishments incorporate the enabler's function in their construction. All parts of personality are viewed as potentially connected, and dynamic causality potentially occurs in all directions.

Considerable research has been devoted to the relatively midlevel establishments. For example, models of significant other people are frequently examined experimentally according to how they are learned, remembered, and according to their accuracy (Andersen & Cole, 1990; Mayer, Rapp, & Williams, 1993; J. A. Singer & Salovey, 1993; J. L. Singer & Salovey, 1991). Dynamics among such components are also studied. For example, a discrepancy between one's actual and ideal selves may lead to humility or to depression (Dewey, 1887/1967, p. 254; Freud, 1923/1960, p. 27; Higgins, 1987, p. 322). Formations based on establishments include formed perceptions (models) of others as all caring or all dangerous, as well as to formed interests in dancing or in dinosaurs.

Themes. Another step along the molecular–molar continuum yields the third sort of personality component—the *theme*. This component involves features of enablers and establishments that are interwoven to form a coherent program of action. For example, the theme of extroversion combines both an enabler-level need for stimulation, with an establishment-level knowledge of how to throw a party and how to tell stories. Thus, extroversion is motivated sociability arising from features of both enabler needs and establishment models (as well as from other features). Themes are particularly useful for study because they can translate into important behavior patterns external to the person. As another example, intelligence employs cognitive enablers that carry out rapid, complex mental transformations. These cognitive enablers establish, and then interact with, highly accurate and sophisticated world models. Classes of themes are represented on a still-higher plane of the model, as illustrated by Fig. 6.3.

Themes are perhaps the most researched units in contemporary psychology (themes are used here interchangeably with traits).[2] Large numbers of studies examine the themes of intelligence, self-consciousness, authoritarianism, ego strength, Machiavellianism, and many more. In addition, considerable effort has been expended to identify important groups of themes such as the Big Five (e.g., Goldberg, 1993), which include extroversion–introversion, emotionality–stability, agreeableness–disagreeableness, conscientiousness–carelessness, and openness–closedness. Other groups of themes include the Big Seven (e.g., Almagor, Tellegen, & Waller, 1995), and the Big Two (Eysenck, 1990; Eysenck & Eysenck, 1968). Formations denote particular levels of traits, such as a high degree of extroversion or a small amount of disagreeableness.

Agencies. The fourth and final type of personality component is the *agency*, which is a composite of enablers, establishments, and themes. The agency incorporates large portions of personality function, but without the complex integration of the whole personality. For example, Freud's id agency combines enabler-based sexual and aggressive drives with established sexual and aggressive fantasies; and with narcissistic, self-centered themes. The id, in other words, lacks the integrated sophistication of the whole. It lacks the capacity for rational thought, effective behavior, or moral reflection. For these, it requires interaction with other agencies such as the ego and the superego. A single example of an agency, James' (1925/1892, pp. 195–196) "self-as-knower" agency, is shown amidst the rest of personality in Fig. 6.3 (top left). The *self-as-knower* agency is the part of the self that thinks about the rest of personality—an identity consciousness. It is similar

---

[2]More technically, themes are defined as the internal manifestations of traits (Mayer, 1995b).

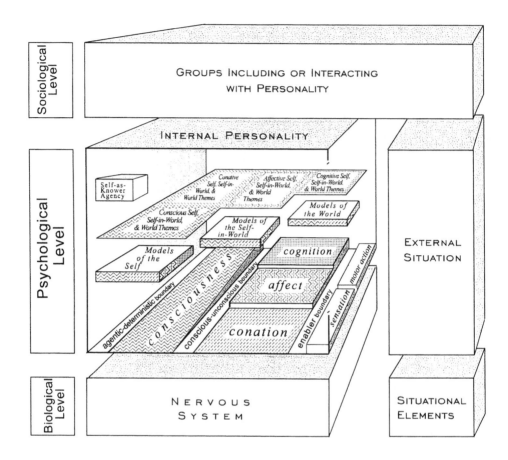

FIG. 6.3. The complete personality system is represented in three dimensions. The vertical, molecular–molar dimension, separates the more molecular enablers (floor of personality cube) from the establishments (second level), themes (third level), and one example of an agency (fourth level). The horizontal, internal–external dimension separates those systems most internal to personality such as consciousness, the self, conscious themes, and the self-as-knower dimension (left) from those components more external in orientation such as conation, affect, and cognition, models of the world, and cognitive themes (right). The third dimension, depth, separates those components of personality most enmeshed with the organism such as conation (in front) from those most independent such as cognition (in back). The three dimensions also position the systems surrounding personality, such as the nervous system, external situation, and larger groups.

to Freud's ego, though narrower in scope (closer perhaps to Jung's conscious ego).

Agencies are often so large and poorly defined that they are difficult to research, but exceptions exist. For example, Loevinger (1976) studies the ego according to its life-span development, charting its growth across levels of ego development (for a different but related approach, see Block, 1981). Thus, a formation involving the ego might be *ego strength*, that is, the ego's general capacity to engage effectively with the inner and outer worlds.

Personality as a Single Unit. Actually, one can proceed along the molecular–molar continuum again to a still more molar, fifth type of unit: the whole personality. For example, von Bertalanffy, the founder of General Systems Theory, approached personality as a single unit. He described how personality (and other systems) might be considered according to its "wholeness" (von Bertalanffy, 1967, p. 64). This search for the whole unit, though, seemed to ignore important articulations within the system. In one instance, von Bertalanffy stated that personality possessed ". . . no sharp borderline between bodily function, unconscious and the conscious mind. In the last resort, they may be the very same thing" (p. 100). To gloss over such distinctions makes the further analysis of personality almost impossible: The mixing together of, say, the bodily function with the unconscious, seems to lose the personality amidst the organism.

Perhaps it is unrealistic to expect a biologist such as von Bertalanffy to understand exactly what is needed within the discipline of personality psychology. Even Andras Angyal, a systems theorist schooled in personality, was often plagued by abstraction and generality. Like Bertalanffy, Angyal deliberately blurred the distinction between the organism and its environment (Angyal, 1941, Chapter IV). Hall and Lindzey (1957) regard Angyal as sometimes becoming "lost in the whole universe" (p. 333; this line was deleted in their 1978 edition). Perhaps Allport (1937) can claim the final word on treating the whole personality as a unit. Such holistic conceptions, he wrote:

> . . . do little more than assert personality to be an "Indivisible Whole," "a total integrated pattern of behavior," . . . Personality . . . is like a symphony. Granted; but does not the comprehension of symphonic unity come only through an understanding of the articulate weaving of motifs, movements, bridge-passages, modulations, contrasts, and codas? Nothing but empty and vague adjectives can be used to characterize the work as a whole. If a totality is not articulated, it is likely to be an incomprehensible blur; it can then be extolled, but not understood." (p. 343)

From Single- to Multiple-Component Formations. Formations of single components account for the simplest types of individual differences. Formations that combine components yield more sophisticated and interesting differences, and those will be discussed. Before proceeding, however, it is worth noting that Allport (1937) was once hopeful that certain single components could be used to describe a personality's important features. He proposed the existence of a *radix* (Latin for root) to designate fundamental units from which he believed others grew—even components that existed in apparent opposition to one another. He illustrated the concept with the case of D:

> This man, a teacher, seemed one moment meticulous in his behavior, the next, careless and even slovenly . . . But by looking further into the case . . . it appears that D is always orderly in respect to his personal possessions, and always disorderly in respect to other people's. . . Pursuing the case still further, even these opposites are reconciled through their relation to a single essential quality of self-centeredness peculiar to D. This root quality "explains" the inconsistency in his expressive traits. (p. 357)

Allport recognized, however, that only unusual cases of personality could be reduced so conveniently. At least five or six components seemed necessary to him to adequately describe the individual. Sets of interorganized, multiple components, account for the more important formations. We turn to those multicomponent formations next.

Multicomponent Formations

Table 6.2 describes several types of multicomponent formations. The simplest multicomponent formation (column 2) is a *list formation*: it lists components that are most pronounced in an individual, drawn from those components commonly present to some degree in all people (Allport, 1937). A list formations' components are often independent of or uncorrelated with one another. A good example of such a list formation would be one based on an individual's subscale profile on Cattell's 16PF (Cattell, Cattell, & Cattell, 1993). The 16PF is a personality test that measures 16 independent personality factors with the factors lettered from A forward. The 16 scales are derived from factor analysis. For example, the first three scales include: (a) affectothymia versus sizothymia, (b) intelligence, and (c) ego strength versus emotionality. A person could be high on all the scales, high on some, or high on none. A list formation, in this case, simply lists the individual's characteristics, as indicated by the scale profile. Thus, a person high on scale A, or low on B and high on C, would be high on affectothymia, that is, "good-natured, easy-going . . . [and] attentive to people . . . ," low on intelligence, and high on ego strength (Cattell, 1965, p. 66). Predictions from a given formation are made by adding together its units in a weighted combination; the statistical emphasis, like the

TABLE 6.2
Common Features Underlying Component, Organizational, and Developmental Sets

Nature of Comparison	Component Form	Organizational Form (Structural)	Organizational Form (Dynamic)	Developmental Form
Purpose of component set	To efficiently describe the nature of a person's components by measuring multiple units at once.	To describe personality structure; that is to describe the static arrangement of personality components relative to one another.	To describe important features of personality dynamics.	To describe something of a person's development in a particular area of personality.
Type of component employed	*Common components*: Components that are shared in common by all members of the population.	*Common or arranged components*: Common components chosen because they can be arranged in a meaningful pattern.	*Selected or idiographic components*: A subset of common components that are particularly relevant to a single individual, or a subclass of individuals.	*Selected or time-elapsed units*: A subset of common components or a single component's development is charted according to multiple examples of that unit over time (e.g., ego at age 5, ego at age 10, etc.).
Relation among components	*Independence among components*: Selection of components treats them individually and separately from one another.	*Structurally interrelated*: Components are arranged according to their structural (e.g., correlational–empirical or conceptual) relationships.	*Mutually, substantively, interconnected*: Components are related to one another according to the influence they exert over one another, and the outcomes of their interactions.	*Causal, sequenced development*: The components develop from one to the other, or the components represent the potential changes in a single component over time.

(Continued)

TABLE 6.2
(Continued)

Nature of Comparison	Component Form	Organizational Form (Structural)	Organizational Form (Dynamic)	Developmental Form
Customary statistical treatment	*Independent or additive treatment*: Components may be examined individually, or in some cases added together.	*Weighted or clustered additive treatments*: Components within a given structure (e.g., a factor or dimension) are weighted and added, or just added.	*Synergistic, taxonic*: New compound components may be formed from the presence of critical combinations of individual units; alternatively, samples may be divided according to the presence of absence of a given component combination.	*Cumulative achievement*: The individual is described according to the most developmentally advanced version of the component that can be found; presence of a developmentally advanced component typically assumes presence of the components that have come before.
Level of description	*Simple description or profile*: The individual is profiled across the components studied.	*Simple description or profile*: Same as under "Component Form," but the components are placed in relation to one another.	*Dynamics or types*: The individual is described as possessing certain configurations, forms, or dynamics, or as belonging to a particular class, type, or taxon.	*Developmental attainment or type*: The individual is described according to the degree of development he or she has undergone, or the developmental type he or she is.
Subtypes and examples	MMPI; Cattell's 16PF (when scales are interpreted individually, that is, excluding profile interpretations); Q-Sorts.	Big Five and their subcomponents; Eysenck's Big Two and their subcomponents.	Allport's idiographic types; Weinberger et al.'s repressive coping.	Freud's anal personality; Loevinger's ego development.

conceptual one, is on the components' independent contributions rather than on their interactions. This perspective is illustrated by Cattell's (1965) description of how to predict tennis playing from the 16PF's first three traits:

> Obviously, general intelligence, B, will enter into success because intelligent planning is necessary in match tennis. Possibly also trait A will produce effects because the easy-going affectothymes will not follow up with the tenacity and precision of the sizothymes. Finally, ego strength, C, will also play a part because a low C person, who loses his temper easily or easily becomes discouraged, will not use his abilities to best advantage.
>
> Presumably, by adding each person's scores on these three traits (A and C negatively) we should obtain a first approximation to the relative goodness of each. . . . (p. 78)

Cattell's discussion captures the elementalist aspects of the list formation very well.

List formations with slightly higher levels of coherence also occur. For example, the MMPI includes nine clinical scales, each reflecting one of Kraepelin's influential diagnostic categories of mental illness: hypochondria, depression, hysteria, paranoia, and so on through manic depression (Hathaway & McKinley, 1943). Although the test's subscales cohere in the sense that they represent a diagnostic system, the individual scales were developed absent from any theory of personality organization or development. The scale's original approach, consequently, represented a component list, but specifically of pathology-related characteristics.

When a person is assessed according to most component sets, it is in relation to other people. So, if a person is labelled high on Cattell's dimension of sizothymia or on the MMPI's scale of hysteria, it means he or she scored higher than most other individuals. This is an interpersonal comparison. An alternative list formation exists in which common traits are ranked according to their prominence within the individual—an intrapersonal comparison (sometimes termed *ipsative*). For example, in Block's (1978) Q-sort approach, the person (or a rater) arranges 100 defining statements (e.g., "likes to be alone") according to its applicability in relation to the person. The components are sorted into 10 categories according to their applicability to an individual or a type of personality. Average Q sorts are then sometimes calculated for a group. For example, a group of young men low in both masculinity and socialization (as measured by the California Personality Inventory) is described in terms such as "tends to feel guilty," "seeks reassurance from others," and "is self pitying," because those are high relative to other characteristics within the same individual (Block & Ozer, 1982, p. 1175).

Organizational Forms

Whereas the list formations discussed contain components that operate independently of one another, organizational forms contain components that interrelate with one another. Table 6.2 divides organizational forms into two types: structural formations and dynamic formations.

Structural Forms. The term *structural* refers to a static arrangement of parts within the system-topics framework. One structural relation in particular is the relation between a so-called supercomponent to its subordinate parts. A *supercomponent* (or superfactor) is a superordinate variable that can be divided into smaller, highly intercorrelated variables. For example, the supercomponent extroversion can be divided into three highly correlated but distinct components of impulsivity, sociability, and sensation seeking. *Structural formations* are basically list formations of supercomponents. These structural formations are of specific interest because each larger variable is divisible into many subvariables, and this makes structural forms efficient descriptions of many different parts of personality. For example, a formation consisting of high extroversion and high emotional stability—two superfactors studied by Eysenck—describes many subvariables as well. On the one hand, the extroversion indicates impulsivity, sociability, and sensation seeking; on the other hand, the emotional stability indicates positive mood, stable mood, and nonreactive emotionality. Thus, the advantage of structural forms to list forms is that they convey information about the individual more efficiently. Comparing formations of Eysenck's two superfactors to Cattell's 16PF suggests that Eysenck's formations quickly summarize many of Cattell's measures. Emotional stability indicates the presence of Cattell's affectothymia (i.e., good-naturedness) as well as Cattellian surgency (i.e., cheerfulness).

Dynamic Formations. In the system-topics framework, the term *dynamics* refers to causes, and *dynamic forms* involve units that are mutually causal—that is, that exert influences on one another to bring about something unique within the personality.

Idiographic Dynamic Sets. Recall Allport's concept of the radix—a root component that explains many of the further components of an individual's personality. In Allport's aforementioned case of D., selfishness was the root characteristic that brought about both D.'s care for his own possessions, and his careless disregard for others' possessions. From a dynamic perspective, the selfishness maximized D's care of his own belongings while minimizing his care for the belongings of others.

Such dynamic forms are not necessarily present in other personalities; they may be of little relevance in describing most personalities (see Winter, 1996, pp. 409–422, for a review; and Baumeister & Tice, 1988; Bem & Allen, 1974, for research treatments). Dynamic forms share in common:

1. that some units will be important only within some individuals (this contrasts with the common or universal units of the component and structural sets),

2. that certain forms are particularly interesting because they involve important causal interactions among the parts (this contrasts to the relative independence of components in component formations, or their hierarchical relations in structural forms), and

3. that personalities possessing a given form may be radically different from those that don't possess it. Allport sometimes argued that certain dynamics would be unique to a single person, and argued that idiographic research should be focused on individuals. Today, however, dynamics are generally studied as the property of small groups of people, so that what is learned within one individual can be generalized to others in the group.

A good example of a dynamic formation studied today is repressive coping style (Weinberger, 1990; Weinberger, Schwartz, & Davidson, 1979). *Repressive coping* involves the competition between social approval seeking, on the one hand, and emotional awareness, on the other. The people around us generally encourage us to be happy, merry, and joyful; to please those others, most of us will cover up negative feelings from time to time. Repressive copers deny any negative feelings so consistently that they lose track of them all together. For example, studies indicate that repressive copers react to threat at a physiological level (e.g., with EEG and heart rate alterations) but verbally deny any negative feelings.

Dynamic formations often incorporate aspects of structural formations. For example, the supercomponent negative affectivity includes anxiety as a subcomponent. When Weinberger et al. (1979) introduced the concept of repressive coping, it pertained only to the denial of anxiety. Soon after, however, Weinberger substituted negative affect for anxiety, which broadened the dynamic formation.

As already noted, a given dynamic is meaningful only in some personality structures—that is, the dynamic is not common to everyone. In contrast, traits such as extroversion or emotional stability are often viewed as nearly common to everyone (but see Baumeister & Tice, 1988). Because dynamics are present in only some people, they encourage a switch to a typological perspective more so than do component or structural forms. For example, although repressive coping can be considered a dynamic form within the person, a person also may be referred to as a repressive coper. The presence of the repressive formation renders the person different, in some sense, from others. In fact, the dynamic-focused researcher frequently shifts back and forth between describing a person as possessing a dynamic pattern, and describing the person as being a type.[3] Empirically, a person is assigned to the type through the use of cutpoints on the relevant measured dimensions. Weinberger and Schwartz (1990) note:

> Investigating how intersections of dimensions jointly influence individuals' personality structures requires a shift from a variable-centered perspective to a person-centered, typological one . . . The focus moves from correlations between isolated dimensions to patterns of characteristics of types of people. Across the sciences, categorical representations tend to be more efficacious than dimensional ones when one is interested in entities that differ on a large number of attributes. . . . (p. 384)

Finally, it is worth noting that there exists a mathematically strong form of typologies in which there is a discontinuity in measurement between a given type and other types. Meehl (1992, p. 121) describes this as a mathematical discontinuity between taxons (i.e., categories), and likens cutting categories at that discontinuity as akin to Plato's admonition to "carve nature at its joints" (cited in Meehl, 1992, p. 121). Meehl's MAXCOV procedure and similar alternatives may be used for hypothesis testing in this area.

Developmental Formations

The final group of forms are the developmental ones. *Developmental forms* are composed of components that emerge together at a single point in time. Developmental forms may represent the remnant of a phase of development, or represent the individual's current overall maturational level.

Developmental Forms as Remnants or Residues of Important Developmental Change

Developmental forms sometimes arise as a consequence of a particularly powerful or influential developmental event. According to Freud, exces-

---

[3]Or, as Allport (1937, p. 295) put it, "A man can be said to have a trait; but he cannot be said to have a type. Rather he fits a type." Thus, the trait is something inside the individual, whereas the person is something inside a typological category. This may be less of a difference than it seems because, after all, it is the trait (or other component) inside that determines the typological category into which the person may fit. Thus, although it is convenient to say that a person is a genius, it is almost as easy to say that the person possesses genius-level intelligence or genius-level attributes. The shift to discussing types, therefore, often may be a matter of convenience.

sively tolerant or severe bowel training in the second to third year of life gives rise to the obsessive (or anal) developmental form. During the period of bowel training, the child struggles with the parents over control of his or her bowel movements (see Sears, 1951, pp. 24–25, on anal eroticism). This struggle for control, involving a contest of wills between the child and caretaker(s), becomes a model of the individual's need for control; as such, it generalizes to other lifespheres potentially including the control of time, money, promptness, and conscientiousness. Sometimes, specific developmental subtypes may arise (Pollak, 1979). For example, the anal retentive form involves orderliness, parsimony, and obstinance:

> . . . orderliness refers to both exceptional bodily cleanliness and a high degree of reliability and conscientiousness in the performance of all actions, however inconsequential. Parsimony involves frugality and, in the extreme, stinginess and avarice, whereas obstinacy involves strong tendencies to be negativistic, defiant, and even hostile in relation to authority figures. (p. 226)

Individuals possessing such developmental forms are described as dogged, persistent, stubborn, and potentially defiant. They are demanding, prefer to do things their own ways, and resent interference. They feel harassed, in part because they are perfectionistic, and for that reason they are always busy but are never finished. They live by routine and are easily upset when the routine is changed; they are meticulous organizers, indexers, and planners. Finally, they hate to waste money or time (e.g., Shapiro, 1965). Note that such developmental formations touch on recognizable human characteristics with a greater depth than even the dynamic formation just encountered.

Hierarchical Sets

A developmental form often indicates an individual's level of current developmental functioning in one sphere or another. The obsessive formation just described can be thought of as indicating a person's developmental level in regard to control (although Freud viewed it as concerning psychosexual development). Most developmental formations also represent a position along a specific developmental sequence. The anal personality is part of a psychological sequence that includes the oral, phallic, and genital personalities. Similarly, Loevinger (1976) has developed a hierarchy of ego states. People progress through 10 stages of ego development from the presocial to the integrated. Empirically, these levels are measured according to a judge's evaluations of sentence completion responses (on the Washington University Sentence Completion Test for Ego Development, or WUSCTED).

A sense of Loevinger's hierarchy can be gained by considering its last four stages, which describe, first, a conscientious ego characterized by the use of self-evaluated standards and self-criticism. When confronted with "If I can't get what I want," a conscientious-level person might say, "I try to forget about it." As the ego enters the next, individualistic stage, it distinguishes between its own style of conscientiousness and the potentially alternative but equally conscientious styles of others. In the next, autonomous stage, the ego develops a heightened awareness of its own conflicting inner needs, and copes with those conflicts. Finally, the integrated ego not only recognizes and copes with conflicts, but is able to reconcile inner conflicts and to renounce the unattainable (Loevinger, 1976, pp. 24–25). When confronted with "If I can't get what I want," the integrated-ego person might say, "I realize that, for much of my life, I have gotten the most important things I have hoped for; although I have had disappointments, they have often made me more appreciative of what I have . . ." (pp. 237–240). A person's score is at the highest level he or she manifests.

Summary

This concludes the review of several classes of personality formations. As can be seen, they range from least to most theoretically integrated, where component forms involve the least theory, and dynamic and developmental forms involve the most.

The Concept of Internal Formations Generalized to External Formations

The chapter has focused exclusively on internal formations. Personality was modeled earlier in terms of its molecular–molar, internal–external, and organismic-constructed dimensions (for example, see Fig. 6.4). In this model, the internal personality system (middle left) is surrounded by various external environments: below personality is a molecular, biological environment; to the right is an external, situational environment; and above personality is an incorporative environment. Just as internal formations arise from internal components, external formations arise from external components. The same is true of organizational and developmental forms. That is, the classes of internal personality formations correspond to classes of external formations across the external environments.

The correspondences among internal and external classes of formations are illustrated in Table 6.3. For example, internal component formations include sensation seeking and Machiavellianism (Table 6.3, row 1, column 1). These correspond to a class of biological formations that includes

TABLE 6.3
Internal and External Formations Compared

Personality Formations and (Uncorrelated) Examples of Parallel Formations in Neighboring Systems*

Class of Formation	Internal Personality	Biology	Situational	Incorporative
Component	Sensation seeker, Machiavellian.	Good heart, red hair.	Owns risky investments, frequently talks to others.	**Member** of the PTA, Book-of-the-month club.
Structural	Extrovert, emotional.	Good cardiovascular system, relatively weak skeletal–muscular system.	Is married, works as a sales-person.	New Rochelle school system resident, received BS., MS. in education.
Dynamic	Represses negative affect, balances masculine and feminine qualities.	Exercises regularly to alleviate back trouble.	Balances work with parenthood.	Balances family of origin with in-laws.
Developmental	Parental, generative stage of growth; issues around esteem needs.	Physical development consonant with middle adulthood.	Is generally treated with respect of middle adulthood; underaccomplished relative to work.	Now taking leadership in family matters. In the co-hort group of those born in the 1960s. Various successions of member-ships (e.g., from high school clubs to present organizations).

*No implication is intended that the specific internal or external formations in a given row are correlated or predictive of one another; all that is intended is to highlight formations with similar scope in neighboring systems.

strong hearts and red hair (column 2). Note that this correspondence between internal and external classes of formations is based on the fact that components can be identified in each; there is no implication of correlation between them. The same class of component formations can be found in the situational environment, which includes social-conversational forms and book-reading forms (column 3). In the incorporative environment are component forms that include PTA and Democratic Party membership. Similarly, recall that the class of internal dynamic formations (row 2) includes repressive coping. That class of internal dynamic formations is parallel to the class of biological dynamics that includes clogged arteries placing more strain on the heart, as well as to the class of situational dynamics that includes driving while eating, and to the class of incorporative formations that includes balancing one's family-of-origin membership and one's family-by-marriage membership. Similar parallels can be found for developmental formations (row 3).

External formations are of crucial importance because a central aim of personality psychology is to predict from the internal personality to the external environment. Moreover, it is possible that such prediction can be enhanced if one knows the type of formations one is predicting between.

DISCUSSION

What does all this discussion of forms—both internal and external—achieve? Why are personality psychologists constantly drawn to this problem? At the beginning of this chapter, I suggested that one motto for personality psychologists is, "Know your internal personalities and you will see order." To know internal personalities requires an understanding of the broad range of formations that may be found in such personalities. One purpose of the present framework was to provide an overview and organization of those formations. A second purpose is to improve personality prediction by illustrating that different personality forms may require different types of prediction. A third and final purpose of the framework is to facilitate the choice of which formations are most important to investigate.

Improving Categorization

The present system is the first comprehensive classification system for individual differences that has been recently proposed. Before the present system, the most common approach to differential psychology was to proceed from individual differences, to typologies, to group differences.

To the extent that such approaches distinguished among individual differences at all, they typically involved a crude dichotomy between abilities and personality variables (e.g., Anastasi & Foley, 1949). Outside of a differential psychology framework, personality differences were primarily associated with trait psychology, either as a theory (e.g., Allport, 1937; Cattell, 1965), or as a research area (Cattell, 1965; Eysenck, 1990; Goldberg, 1993). This identification of individual differences with traits meant that nontrait individual differences were dealt with separately. For example, dynamic formations such as repressive coping were typically split off from trait treatments, and if they were covered at all, were covered in research about unconsciousness (e.g., J. L. Singer, 1990). Developmental formations, similarly, were handled in theory books covered by Freud and Erikson, or were not covered at all.

The organizing principle of the present classification system is to show how simpler formations, based solely on one or two components, can be compared with progressively more complex formations based both on dynamics and on development. Recognition of this continuum makes it possible to bring together individual differences in themes and other components, along with individual differences in dynamics and in development. This creates a single coherent perspective about the various structures potentially arising within personality rather than isolating them by theory or by research area. These individual-differences concepts are integrated with one another, and are best examined together.

Another advantage of the present work is its close linkage to the systems framework. The systems framework is a natural outgrowth of many integrating movements in personality since the beginning of the century (Mayer, 1998). Its inclusive and impartial nature, and its independence from any specific research program or theoretical agenda, make it of general utility to the field. Perhaps most importantly, the systems framework is now by far the most carefully developed new framework for personality psychology, with organized classification systems for components, dynamics, organization, data, and now, for individual differences (Mayer, 1993–94, 1995a, 1995b, 1998; Mayer, Chabot, & Carlsmith, 1997).

A system that can convincingly and coherently express the contents of a discipline can strengthen that discipline. A framework is an outline, really, of all the contents of the field. If the outline is good, then the contents of the field can be more powerfully expressed, thereby attracting better students, better justifying and explaining the field's purpose to other scientists, and better explaining it to others who are interested in the field's findings. Of course, such a clear presentation should also provide insights as to how scientific work in the area can be enhanced. Some meaningful scientific advances may be gleaned from the present classification system.

Improving Predictions

A classification's categories keep its members in orderly interposition and distinguish among members, which are different in important ways. The more distinct the categories are, the more powerful the classification system is (other things being equal). In the present system, component, organizational, and developmental forms are recognizably distinct from one another. This continuum from component to developmental form can be characterized in several ways: from simple to complex, from molecular to molar, from isolated to grouped, and in possession of independent versus coordinated elements. The different formative classes are not only descriptively distinct, but may also be distinct in the predictions they make about personality.

Consider the atomistic, independent end of this continuum, characterized by component forms. The component forms are composed of elements (if more than one) that are largely independent of each other. For example, the component form of sensation-seeking has little influence on anything else in personality. It exists atomistically, independently, and by itself (or at least its relations to the rest of personality are left unspecified). The very atomistic, isolated nature of the component form means that only rather simple predictions can be made from it. Because no interacting elements are specified, it never turns on or off, it is never contingent (cf. Mischel, 1990). Its influence (i.e., the need for stimulation) affects the individual consistently throughout the day, week, and year.

Now consider the molar, grouped, coordinated end of the continuum characterized by the developmental form. In these forms, elements work together at a high level of interdependence, combining memories of personal history, cognitive and affective integration, and converging and diverging thematic courses of action. The influence of the developmental form is strategic, capable of responding and of withholding responses planfully. As a consequence, such forms manifest themselves flexibly and in an overall sophisticated fashion.

Component and developmental forms represent two quite different influences on the systematic functioning of personality. Component forms exert a relatively simple, consistent influence on the personality system. Developmental forms exert a highly flexible, intermittent, planful influence on the personality system. Moreover, at any time, these two types of forms (and forms intermediate on the continuum) coexist in personality. For example, component forms may operate independently, but also in parallel with more sophisticated forms: Thus, the sensation-seeking form might coexist with a high ego-integration level. The search for novel experiences would not necessarily interfere with the operation of a highly integrated ego that manifested considerable wisdom. Alternatively, the integrated ego might allow for sensation seeking, indulging it in all but the most dangerous contexts, and exercising any damage control necessary so that the sensation-seeking can be satisfied in a rewarding fashion. Of course, the integrated ego might also operate in conflict with the sensation seeking, attempting unsuccessfully to prevent its expression. That sensation-seeking form, however, might be so uncontrollable that its manifestations simply cannot be prevented; on the other hand, it cannot overturn the more sophisticated ego formation.

The different classes of forms also yield different predictions regarding personality. For example, because component functions are relatively simple, consistent, elemental variables, they are likely to have small but consistent influences on a large number of external component formations. Sensation seeking might be related—in very small ways—to hundreds of situational variables, from wearing slightly flashier clothing than the norm, to reading slightly more sexual books, to choices of more violent or risque movies, to eating spicier meals, or to holding riskier investments. Because component forms are embedded amidst more complex forms, any one of these relationships can be turned off or disappear. The sensation seeker's desire for spicier foods might be turned off by stomach ailments. His or her enjoyment of violent movies might be turned off by ethical scruples. Nonetheless, it should be operative in more domains than not. As a consequence, component formations should correlate with the sum of many small potentially related external criteria. Thus, in one study from our laboratory, we correlated another component form, need for solitude (Burger, 1995), with a list of activities related to solitude. These included, "I ate my lunch alone every day last week," and "In the past two weeks, I rented a movie by myself and watched it alone," and found a correlation ($r = .38$, $p < .01$) between internal preferences and external activities (Chabot, Dearing, Mangan, Smirles, & Mayer, 1998).

The predictions of component forms are simple, consistent, and broad; the predictions for developmental forms, however, are unlikely to be this way. For example, a high level of ego development means that a person has been able to integrate a number of divergent trends in his or her life, among other things. This person's ability to integrate different desires, feelings, and thoughts internally would suggest that he or she is also more ready to integrate different people living with one another in families, or working with one another in organizations. As a consequence, a person with high ego development, may, (other things being equal) be more highly regarded and depended upon within a family. In addition, such an individual might attain a higher level of managerial responsibility in certain well-run organizations. It is also apparent, however, that such an ego integration may be fairly independent of particular books read, particular movies seen, and so forth, for the simple reason that most environments don't afford expression to such high-level integration.

For that reason, we need to create new criterion variables external to personality that are of a complexity and sophistication comparable to our internal developmental (or dynamic) forms. We need to find the external formations that correspond to the internal ones we wish to elucidate. Although this is not an easy task, it is by no means impossible. Let me describe, for example, my concept of an external developmental form. My concept of such a form is that it reflects a developmental sequence or record of experiences the individual has undergone. A person might check off going on a date, getting engaged, getting married, or celebrating a fifth wedding anniversary, and this would tell us something about the individual's development. This would probably be different from the person who goes on a date, lives with another, breaks up, dates again, and lives together with someone else. A board game exists—the Game of Life (Milton Bradley, 1991)—in which the players run cars around the board along developmental paths, deciding (or having decided for them) along the way whether or not they receive a college education, get married, have children, adopt, engage in community service, and so forth. This board game provides the elements of a simple but elegant blueprint for the sorts of external formations we need to compose to study internal formations such as ego strength. As personality psychologists, we should pay particular attention to how personality relates to the game of life.

Our parents and grandparents used to tell us that certain experiences allow a person to grow, and that a person who has gone through them is different than before. The individual who has overcome an illness, fought in a war, and raised a child is different from the individual who has not. And the way that individual has gone about coping with the experience also distinguishes him or her. The individual who has overcome a serious illness but remains a shut in afterward, rarely venturing out and frequently requesting others' help, is different from the individual who has overcome the illness and goes on to volunteer at hospital programs to assist others facing the same disease. The individual who survives a war but then votes, agitates, or prepares for more war is different from the one who works, instead, for peace.

Choosing Formations for Study

Scientific Considerations

What about the selection of the most productive or important formations to study? The number of possible internal and external personality formations is essentially astronomical. (Just consider that they can be constructed from components drawn 1, 2, 3, or more at a time, from hundreds of different personality components). This variety should not surprise us: Dahlstrom (cited in Buss & Craik, 1985) once noted:

> The fact that the known species in either zoology or botony numbers in the millions serves to shame the pretenses of any behavioral typologist who seeks to employ at most a dozen 'species' of personality organization to account for human behavioral diversity. (p. 945)

Still, it raises the question of which personality formations are most important to study.

It would be nice if all the formations could be reduced, somehow, to three or four groups so that we could assign people to those simple groups, and could always refer to a person as being a Type 1, 2, 3 or 4. As soon as we said Type 4, we could tailor our predictions accordingly. Such attempts have been made. For example, one system that dates back to Hippocrates divided people into sanguines, cholerics, phlegmatics, and melancholics. This was based on observational classification, which can be quite accurate (e.g., Mayer & Bower, 1986). As Eysenck has pointed out, those four categories closely correspond to variations in two central dimensions of personality: variations in Extroversion–Introversion and Stability–Emotionality. Thus, sanguines were stable extroverts (calm and outgoing), cholerics were emotional extroverts (distressed and outgoing), phlegmatics were stable introverts (calm and withdrawn), and melancholics were emotional introverts (distressed and withdrawn).

Are those the right four categories for classifying everyone? Big Five researchers want to add three more dimensions to Eysenck's two: Agreeableness–Disagreeableness, Conscientiousness–Carelessness, and Openness–Closedness. This would yield $2 \times 2 \times 2 \times 2 \times 2 = 32$ categories. From a convenience standpoint we might want only, say, four categories, evenly dispersed in the population so that we could find them readily, and set up so as to maximize the statistical power of our tests. Also, we would want the groups to be sufficiently different, across a range of attributes, to warrant their division. It is unlikely that we will arrive at any single four-fold division upon which we might all agree. One more viable alternative, incidentally, would be to work simultaneously with different sets of four.

Need and Value-Based Approaches

The criteria for the most important formations to study will probably emerge from outside of science, from the wellspring of human needs and values. Personality psychology will, as will engineering, biotechnology, and other applied fields, be directed by human needs and values—both individual and societal. Such needs include the search for happiness in the internal environment. They also include, externally, good health in the biological environment, good interpersonal relations and effective skills in the situational environment, and good group memberships and good intergroup relations in the incorporative environment. There is nothing wrong with taking direction from these needs and values as long as scientists make clear that they are foregoing their scientific roles in such an instance, and are speaking as individuals (or as members of a political party, or religion, or some other group). Speaking as an individual, it seems to me that one of the best ways we have of choosing formations may be according to such criteria outside of science.

For example, a small class of internal formations exist, closely related to consciousness and to the conscious self, that are valued intrinsically. That is, they are valued whether or not they are ever discerned beyond the individual's most private concerns, and whether or not they ever influence anything external to the individual's private thoughts. Two individuals could behave in the same way, with one very happy, content, and loving on the inside; the other, miserable, self-hating, and spiteful, but successfully disguising it so that others simply cannot perceive it. Although their behavior is the same how different it feels on the inside! Certainly we would prefer to be that person who is happy rather than unhappy. Comfort within our singular human consciousness is an end in itself. It is for this reason, certainly, that Singer encouraged us to study the private personality, its stream of consciousness, its accompanying daydreams, repressions, fantasies, and the like (J. L. Singer, 1975, 1984, 1990). The formations involved with better internal experience are understudied at present, but will form a centerpiece to the study of personality.

Just as much as internal consciousness can be valued intrinsically, much the same point can be made for good health in the biological realm, good behavior in the situational realm, and good memberships in the incorporative realm. Indeed, assuming that internal personality and its neighboring biological, situational, and incorporative systems interact, we must move beyond the evaluation of consciousness by itself, to further consider it in relation to its external environments. This takes us to the prediction from internal to external formations, and vice versa. Formations exist along a continuum of complexity, from the component based to the developmentally based. Although personality and its neighbors can be described and valued individually, they can also be viewed as complex, interacting systems. It returns us, once again, to the personologist's job to predict from internal to external formations and back again. The classification provided here may help that pursuit by letting us know our internal personalities—and find order.

POSTSCRIPT

Almost everyday I worked on this chapter, I was reminded of Singer's contributions to the field of personality psychology: both to the field's specific workings and to its larger outlines. Singer was, and remains, one of the pioneer clinician researchers. Throughout my career, I have felt personally encouraged and renewed by his thoughtful integration of the most sophisticated clinical concepts with the most sophisticated research ideas. I hope this systems perspective about personality formations captures some of that sophisticated thinking. The development of this system owes something to his consistent exhortations to remember the importance of internal feelings and thoughts. More directly, Singer was willing to publish the first article about the systems framework in 1993–1994. The present article, fairly broad though it is, is insufficient to illustrate all the areas in which Singer's work has informed my own; to go further, however, would require another article, so I must finish.[4] Before I do, I also wish to express my warm thanks to my esteemed colleague Jefferson Singer, and to my esteemed colleague and veteran collaborator, Peter Salovey, who together kindly honored me with the opportunity to honor, in turn, Jerome Singer.

REFERENCES

Allport, G. (1937). *Personality: A psychological interpretation.* New York: Henry Holt & Company.

Almagor, M., Tellegen, A., & Waller, N. G. (1995). The Big Seven model: A cross-cultural replication and further exploration of the basic dimensions of natural language trait descriptors. *Journal of Personality and Social Psychology, 69*, 300–307.

Anastasi, A., & Foley, J. P., Jr. (1949). *Differential psychology.* New York: Macmillan.

Andersen, S. M., & Cole, S. W. (1990). "Do I know you?": The role of significant others in general social perception. *Journal of Personality and Social Psychology, 59*, 384–389.

Angyal, A. (1941). *Foundations for a science of personality.* New York: The Commonwealth Fund.

Baumeister, R. F., & Tice, D. M. (1988). Metatraits. *Journal of Personality, 56*, 571–598.

Bem, D. J., & Allen, A. (1974). On predicting some of the people some of the time: The search for cross-situational consistencies in behavior. *Psychological Review, 81*, 506–520.

Block, J. (1978). *The Q-sort method in personality assessment and psychiatric research.* Palo Alto, CA: Consulting Psychologists Press.

Block, (1981). Some enduring and consequential structures of personality. In A. I. Rabin, J. Aronoff, A. M. Barclay, & R. A. Zucker (Eds.), *Further explorations in personality* (pp. 27–43). New York: Wiley.

---

[4]I can't help but mention somewhere that the Singer family lived across the small town of Ardsley, NY, from the Mayer family when I was growing up, and I occasionally played with the Singer boys during that time; I believe we may have traded stamps from our respective collections. There must have been something about Ardsley (pop: 2,000) that encouraged an interest in the mind, for in addition to the psychology contingent, there are now quite a few psychiatrists hailing from there, including Paul Summergrad, Director of the Psychiatry Network for the Partners Healthcare System (founded by Massachusetts General Hospital and other hospitals, Boston, Massachusetts), and Peter Kramer, whose book *Listening to Prozac*, was responsible for popularizing the drug.

Block, J., & Ozer, D. J. (1982). Two types of psychologists: Remarks on the Mendelsohn, Weiss, & Feimer contribution. *Journal of Personality and Social Psychology, 42,* 1171–1181.

Bloom, F. E., Lazerson, A., & Hofstadter, L. (1988). *Brain, mind, and behavior* (2nd ed.). New York: Freeman.

Burger, J. M. (1995). Individual differences in preference for solitude. *Journal of Research in Personality, 29,* 85–108.

Buss, D. M., & Craik, K. H. (1985). Why *not* measure that trait? Alternative criteria for identifying important dispositions. *Journal of Personality and Social Psychology, 48,* 934–946.

Cattell, R. B. (1965). *The scientific analysis of personality.* Chicago: Aldine-Atherton.

Cattell, R. B., Cattell, A. K., & Cattell, H. E. (1993). *Sixteen Personality Factor Questionnaire* (5th ed.). Champaign, IL: Institute for Personality and Ability Testing.

Chabot, H., Dearing, E., Mangan, M., Smirles, K. A., & Mayer, J. D. (1998). *Does the outside look like the inside? A correlational study of external and internal personality factors.* Unpublished manuscript.

Dewey, J. (1967). Psychology. In *John Dewey: The early works, 1882–1898, Vol 2: 1887.* Carbondale, IL: Southern Illinois University Press. (Original work published 1887)

Eccles, J. (1973). *The understanding of the brain.* New York: McGraw-Hill.

Eysenck, H. J. (1990). Biological dimensions of personality. In L. A. Pervin (Ed.), *Handbook of personality: Theory and research* (pp. 244–276). New York: Guilford.

Eysenck, H. J., & Eysenck, S. B. G. (1968). *Manual for the Eysenck Personality Inventory.* San Diego, CA: Educational and Industrial Testing Service.

Freud, S. (1960). *The ego and the id.* (J. Strachey, Ed.). New York: Norton. (Original work published 1923)

Goldberg, L. R. (1993). The structure of phenotypic personality traits. *American Psychologist, 48,* 26–34.

Hall, C. S., & Lindzey, G. (1957). *Theories of personality.* New York: Wiley.

Hathaway, S. R., & McKinley, J. C. (1943). *The Minnesota Multiphasic Personality Inventory* (rev. ed.). Minneapolis: University of Minnesota Press.

Higgins, E. T. (1987). Self-discrepancy: A theory relating self and affect. *Psychological Bulletin, 94,* 319–340.

James, W. (1925). *Psychology: briefer course.* New York: Henry Holt & Company. (Original work published 1892)

Loevinger, J. (1976). *Ego development.* San Francisco: Jossey-Bass.

Marcus, H., & Nurius, P. (1986). Possible selves. *American Psychologist, 41,* 954–969.

Mayer, J. D. (1993–94). A System-Topics Framework for the study of personality. *Imagination, Cognition, and Personality, 13,* 99–123.

Mayer, J. D. (1995a). The System-Topics Framework and the structural arrangement of systems within and around personality. *Journal of Personality, 63,* 459–493.

Mayer, J. D. (1995b). A framework for the classification of personality components. *Journal of Personality, 63,* 819–878.

Mayer, J. D. (1998). A systems framework for the field of personality psychology. *Psychological Inquiry, 9,* 118–114.

Mayer, J. D., & Bower, G. H. (1986). Learning and memory for personality prototypes. *Journal of Personality and Social Psychology, 51,* 473–492.

Mayer, J. D. Chabot, H. F., & Carlsmith, K. (1997). Conation, affect, and cognition in personality. In G. Matthews (Ed.), *Cognitive science perspectives on personality and emotion.* New York: Elsevier.

Mayer, J. D., Rapp, H. C., & Williams, L. (1993). Individual differences in behavioral prediction: The acquisition of personal-action schemata. *Personality and Social Psychology Bulletin, 19,* 443–451.

McAdams, D. P. (1996). Personality, modernity, and the storied self: A contemporary framework for studying persons. *Psychological Inquiry, 7,* 295–321.

Meehl, P. (1992). Factors and taxa, traits and types, differences of degree and differences of kind. *Journal of Personality, 60,* 117–174.

Milton Bradley (1991). *The game of LIFE.* Springfield, MA: Milton Bradley.

Mischel, W. (1990). Personality dispositions revisited and revised: A view after three decades. In L. A. Pervin (Ed.), *Handbook of personality theory and research* (pp. 111–134). New York: Guilford.

Pollak, J. M. (1979). Obsessive-compulsive personality: A review. *Psychological Bulletin, 86,* 225–241.

Sears, R. R. (1951). *Survey of objective studies of psychoanalytic concepts.* New York: Social Science Research Council.

Shapiro, D. (1965). *Neurotic styles.* New York: Basic Books.

Skinner, B. F. (1968). A case history in scientific method. In A. C. Catania (Eds.), *Contemporary research in operant behavior* (pp. 27–39). Glenview, IL: Scott Foresman. (Original work published 1956)

Singer, J. A. (1995). Seeing one's self: Locating narrative memory in a framework of personality. *Journal of Personality, 63,* 429–457.

Singer, J. A., & Salovey, P. (1993). *The remembered self: Emotion and memory in personality.* New York: The Free Press.

Singer, J. L. (1975). Navigating the stream of consciousness. *American Psychologist, 30,* 727–738.

Singer, J. L. (1984). The private personality. *Personality and social psychology bulletin, 10,* 7–30.

Singer, J. L. (1990). *Repression and dissociation: Implications for personality theory, psychopathology, and health.* Chicago, IL: University of Chicago Press.

Singer, J. L., & Bonanno, G. A. (1990). Personality and private experience: Individual variations in consciousness and in attention to subjective phenomena. In L. A. Pervin (Ed.), *Handbook of personality theory and research* (pp. 419–444). New York: Guilford.

Singer, J. L., & Salovey, P. (1991). Organized knowledge structures and personality: Person schemas, self-schemas, prototypes, and scripts. In M. J. Horowitz (Ed.), *Person schemas and maladaptive interpersonal patterns* (pp. 37–79). Chicago: University of Chicago Press.

von Bertalanffy, L. (1967). *Robots, men, and minds.* New York: Braziller.

Weinberger, D. A. (1990). The construct validity of the repressive coping style. In J. L. Singer (Ed.), *Repression and dissociation: Implications for personality theory, psychopathology, and health.* Chicago, IL: University of Chicago Press.

Weinberger, D. A., & Schwartz, G. E. (1990). Distress and restraint as superordinate dimensions of self-reported adjustment: A typological perspective. *Journal of Personality, 58,* 381–417.

Weinberger, D. A., Schwartz, G. E., & Davidson, R. J. (1979). Low-anxious, high-anxious, and repressive coping styles: Psychometric patterns and behavioral and physiological responses to stress. *Journal of Abnormal Psychology, 88,* 369–380.

Winter, D. G. (1996). *Personality: Analysis and interpretation of lives.* New York: McGraw-Hill.

7

Consciousness and Meaning

Shulamith Kreitler
Tel-Aviv University

The purpose of this chapter is to present a cognitive approach to consciousness rooted in a theory of meaning, and to describe some of its theoretical implications and empirical applications. Hence, the first part of the chapter deals with various aspects of the theory of meaning that have to be clarified before the new approach to consciousness can be presented in the second part of the chapter.

PROPERTIES OF CONSCIOUSNESS

It is most striking that while we cannot yet define consciousness we can characterize it in terms of different properties. For example, we know that consciousness applies to cognitive events and functions, including both contents and process, namely, to phenomena such as sensations, moods, emotions, and dreams (Flanagan, 1992, p. 109). Also, consciousness may vary in the amount of contents and processes to which it applies, ranging from a very few items to big sets. The limits of these are still being discussed (e.g., "limited capacity," "global access"; Baars & McGovern, 1996). Likewise, it may vary in duration, from milliseconds (the so-called flicker of consciousness) to long periods. As is commonly assumed, consciousness may vary in clarity, from very dim and barely perceptible to highly clear. Consciouness also may vary in the degree of awareness that characterizes it and suggests some kind of linking of the cognitive contents to the self (Nunn, 1996). Sometimes the self plays a prominent role as the agent of consciousness, the "I" who is conscious (as in ordinary consciousness) or as an observer (as in hypnosis); at other times the "I" may play the role of the object (as in some dreams) or may be hardly involved at all, or even non-existent. Another property of consciousness is its experiential quality, or what Tart (1978, p. 65) calls "the gestalt feel" of the whole state. Experiential quality could include, for example, a sense of ordinariness or of bizarreness or nonreality, of coherence or fragmentation, or of stability or flimsiness. Last but not least, consciousness may occur or be manifested in the form of different states, which are commonly assumed to range from ordinary consciousness to a variety of states grouped under the title altered states of consciousness (e.g., being drunk, drugged, or hypnotized), differing in mode of functioning and experiential quality.

CONSCIOUSNESS AND COGNITION

It is noteworthy that all the listed properties refer in some form to the relation of consciousness to cognition. The emerging impression that there is a special affinity between consciousness and cognition is fully borne out even by a cursory review of the literature dealing with consciousness. The prominent role that cognition fulfills in regard to consciousness is manifested in four major ways. First, cognition is presented as the object of consciousness, the substance with which consciousness deals, or to which it refers. Thus, James (1890/1950) claimed that consciousness refers to contents of primary memory (a kind of short-term working store) defining the psychological present; Flanagan (1992) specified that consciousness refers to mental events such as sensations, perceptions, moods, emotions, dreams, and intentional states; and Gillett (1995) described consciousness as an active structure dealing with (grasping and using) concepts.

Second, cognition is the antecedent, condition, or cause for consciousness; for example, high level processing in the domains of perception or language gives rise to consciousness (Churchland & Sejnowski, 1992; Mandler, 1984; Neisser, 1967).

Third, cognition is affected by consciousness. As may be expected, most of the evidence for these effects concerns altered states of consciousness. For example, ordinary consciousness with high clarity favorably affects learning new and complex material (Baars & McGovern, 1996, pp. 74–75; Hardcastle, 1995); imagining one is in dream consciousness promotes creative problem solving (Brodsky, Esquerre, & Jackson, 1990–91); being in a hypnotic state of consciousness intensifies the subject's imaginative processes (Barber, Spanos, & Chaves, 1974); and being in a wakeful, altered state of consciousness may change perception of reality and self and promote thinking about specific contents—absolute, universal, and religious themes (Kokoszka, 1992–93).

Fourth, cognition is the function of consciousness. A great many theories of consciousness emphasize that the function of consciousness is related to specific cognitive subsystems or operations, for example, the contents of short-term memory stores (Atkinson & Shiffrin, 1971), episodic memory (Tulving, 1983), the perceptual module (Marcel, 1983) or the language system (Dennett, 1969); or consists of performing specific cognitive tasks, such as controlling mental events (e.g., direct attention, trigger planning; Johnson-Laird, 1988; Umilta, 1988). Another function of consciousness could be to assign to the stimulus a particular quality, bring cognitive resources to bear on its processing, and link it to the self structure (Kihlstrom, 1993). Other cited functions of consciousness are to guarantee flow of information between different control systems of one activity and between these systems and the rest of the cognitive system (Shallice, 1988); to disseminate information widely throughout the cognitive system (Baars, 1988); to enable selection of information in the cognitive system (Sviderskaia, 1992); to apply reflexivity and represent specific contents (Frith, 1992); or construct coherent plausible world models from the current information (Foulkes, 1990). The most prominent emphasis on the functions of consciousness was presented by Baars (1988, chap. 10), who set up the following comprehensive list of functions of consciousness:

1. identifying: identifying inputs and evoking relevant contents for the input.
2. learning: representing and adapting (i.e., assimilating) new and significant events.
3. elaborating: editing the contents, correcting errors, repairing mistakes, and noting significant events.
4. recruiting: eliciting relevant contents for activating a goal.
5. prioritizing and access control: retrieving contents stored in memory and rendering it more or less readily available.
6. decision making: resolving some choice point by recruiting or eliciting or triggering contents or systems supporting one or another goal.
7. analogy-forming: searching for partial matches between new contents and stored ones, which is especially important in representing new information in the absence of close models for it.
8. meta-cognitive or self-monitoring function: reflecting upon and controlling our own functioning (e.g., through conscious imagery and inner speech, by labeling our own intentions, expectations, and

beliefs, or by comparing one's own performance to the set of criteria constituting the self-concept).

9. autoprogramming and self-maintenance: providing the self-system information to use in its task of maintaining stability in the face of changing conditions (for example, through the ability of the attentional systems to control access of contents).

Notably, all the listed functions are of a cognitive nature.

ASSUMPTIONS FOR A COGNITIVE THEORY OF CONSCIOUSNESS

The close interrelatedness of consciousness with cognitive processes and contents suggests that a theory of consciousness would probably be an essentially cognitive theory. In recent years there have been several serious attempts to propose a cognitive theory of consciousness (e.g., Baars, 1988; Johnson-Laird, 1988; Kihlstrom, 1993; Laughlin, McManus, & d'Aquili, 1992; Natsoulas, 1994; Velmans, 1996). However, so far these attempts do not seem to have led to a deeper and better understanding of consciousness. It is plausible that the reason for this is rooted in the assumptions underlying these previous attempts. The major assumptions, not all of which are explicit, seem to be the following:

1. There is a unitary dominant consciousness. Its nature is not defined precisely and seems to hover between an entity, a property, or a state. This one consciousness is modulated by the triarchic set of conscious–preconscious–unconscious (which denote essentially discrete values, but are often grasped as a continuum). The triarchic set is largely reducible to differences in clarity and awareness. Consciousness may assume different degrees of clarity and awareness, so that when endowed with the highest degrees it equals so-called ordinary consciousness, when endowed with lower degrees it equals preconsciousness, and when endowed with the lowest degrees it equals unconsciousness.

2. Altered states of consciousness are different variations of consciousness characterized by combinations of different values on clarity and awareness (e.g., high clarity and low awareness as in an hallucinogenic experience, low clarity and low awareness as in a psychotic state). All are considered to be on a lower level than ordinary consciousness.

3. Consciousness is distinct from cognition, which it may, however, affect.

4. Cognition is conceptualized basically in terms of standard functions, such as memory, attention, and problem solving, mostly overlooking other functions such as daydreaming or dreaming.

5. Changes in consciousness are mediated by agents external to consciousness, or for that matter, to cognition (e.g., physiological phenomena, drugs) and are not themselves cognitive.

These assumptions, which may be implicit, have resulted in conceptualizations of both cognition and consciousness, which are too narow and do not suffice for a comprehensive theory.

It is the purpose of this chapter to outline a blueprint for a new cognitive approach to consciousness, which is based on a different set of assumptions. The major assumptions are:

1. Consciousness and cognition are inextricably bound together. Though distinct, one cannot be described satisfactorily without the other.

2. Consciousness is a characterization of the cognitive system as a whole, not just a part of it. It expresses or manifests something that inheres in or depends on the totality of the cognitive system, and has both experiential and functional implications.

3. The cognitive system includes not only processes (e.g., abstracting, categorizing) as is commonly assumed, but also includes contents (e.g., memories, informations) which are involved in the performance of all cognitive functions, both the standard ones (e.g., memory, problem solving) as well as the not-yet-standard ones (e.g., dreaming).

4. Finally, cognition is basically a psychosemantic system; namely, it is a meaning-processing and meaning-processed system. In more specific terms, it is a system that produces, assigns, stores, retrieves, transforms, applies, and elaborates meaning. This assumption will become clearer after the next section that deals with defining meaning and illustrating its role in cognition.

MEANING AND COGNITION

Definition and Assessment of Meaning

The system of meaning was developed in order to enable the characterization and assessment of meanings. It was designed to be broader in coverage and to have better validity than the available measures of meaning (H. Kreitler & S. Kreitler, 1976, chap. 2). The major assumptions that underlie this system are first, that meaning is a complex phenomenon with a multiplicity of aspects, which implies that it cannot be wholly reflected in a measure assessing a single aspect such as actions (in line with the behaviorist tradition). Second, meaning is essentially communicable, because most of the meanings we know have been learned from or through others. Third, meaning can be expressed or communicated by verbal or nonverbal means. Fourth, there are two types or varieties of meaning—the general, interpersonally shared meaning, and the personal-subjective meaning. These assumptions underlie the methods for collecting and coding data in the domain of meaning that have led to a new definition of meaning and to the Meaning Test. Meaning communications in response to a great variety of verbal and nonverbal stimuli were obtained from thousands of subjects differing in age (2 years to more than 90 years), gender, cultural background, and education. On the basis of the empirical data and theoretical considerations, *meaning* was defined as a referent-centered pattern of meaning values. In this definition, referent is the input or the carrier of meaning, which can be anything including a word, an object, a situation, an event, or even a whole period; whereas meaning values are cognitive contents assigned to the referent for the purpose of expressing or communicating its meaning. For example, if the referent is "Table," responses such as "made of wood," "stands in a room," "I have one," or "a piece of furniture" are four different meaning values. The referent and the meaning value together form a meaning unit (e.g., table—a piece of furniture).

Five sets of variables were defined for characterizing the unit of meaning:

1. *Meaning Dimensions*, which characterize the contents of the meaning values from the viewpoint of the specific information communicated about the referent, such as the referent's sensory qualities (e.g., grass—green), feelings and emotions it evokes (e.g., storm—scary) or feels (e.g., I—love my sister), range of inclusion (e.g., body—the head, arms, torso and legs).

2. *Types of Relation*, which characterize the immediacy of the relation between the referent and the cognitive contents, for example, attributive (e.g., summer—warm), comparative (e.g., summer—warmer than spring), exemplifying instance (e.g., country—the United States).

3. *Forms of Relation*, which characterize how the relation between the referent and the cognitive contents is regulated, in terms of its validity (positive or negative; e.g., Yoga—is not a religion), quantification (absolute, partial; apple—sometimes red), and form (factual, desired or desirable; law—should be obeyed, money—I wish I had more).

4. *Referent Shifts*, which characterize the relation between the referent and the presented input, or—in a chain of responses to some input—the

relation between the referent and the previous one, for example, the referent may be identical to the input or to the previous referent, it may be its opposite, or a part of it, or even apparently unrelated to it (e.g., when the presented stimulus was "U.S." and the subject responded by saying "I love New York", the subject was responding to a part of the stimulus).

5. *Forms of Expression*, which characterize the forms of expression of the meaning units (e.g., verbal, denotation, graphic) and its directness (e.g., actual gesture or verbal description of gesture; S. Kreitler & H. Kreitler, 1990).

Together, the five sets of variables constitute the system of meaning (see Appendix for a full list). It will be noted that the list of variables is comprehensive in the sense that it includes many if not all the variables proposed by other investigators for the assessment of meaning such as the behaviorist emphasis on actions (e.g., Skinner, 1957) is represented by the meaning dimension actions (number 4); the so-called operational definition (Bridgeman, 1927) is represented by the meaning dimension manner of occurrence and operation (number 5); and the three dimensions of the semantic differential (Osgood, Suci, & Tannenbaum, 1957): Evaluations, Dynamism, and Potency are represented by the meaning dimensions judgments and evaluations (number 21) and state (number 11).

In assessing communications of meaning the material is first reduced to meaning units, and then each unit is coded on one meaning dimension, one type of relation, one form of relation, one referent shift, and one form of expression. For example, when the referent is "eyes" and the meaning value is "blue," the coding on meaning dimensions is sensory qualities, on types of relation—exemplifying-illustrative, on forms of relation—positive, on referent shifts—identical to input, and on forms of expression—verbal.

The Meaning Test was developed for assessing individuals' tendencies to use the different meaning variables. The test includes 11 standard stimuli (e.g., street, ocean) and requests the subject to communicate the interpersonally shared and personal meanings of these stimuli to someone who does not know the meanings, using any means of expression that seem adequate. Coding the responses in terms of the meaning variables yields the subject's meaning profile which summarizes the frequency with which the subject used each of the meaning variables in the test.

Role of Meaning Variables in Cognition

Studies showed that each meaning variable has characteristic manifestations in the different spheres of cognitive functioning. For example, comparing subjects who in the Meaning Test frequently use a meaning dimension like locational qualities with those who use it infrequently shows that the former more readily notice perceptual cues relevant for location, show better recall of items referring to location, score higher on tests that involve locational aspects (viz., the Spatial Orientation and Spatial Visualization tests of the Guilford-Zimmerman Aptitude Survey, Guilford & Zimmerman, 1981), have more associations referring to places, and are evaluated as navigating better and faster on foot in open spaces according to maps or instructions (Arnon & S. Kreitler, 1984; Haidu, 1991; S. Kreitler & H. Kreitler, 1985b).

Scores on single meaning variables and performance in cognitive tasks do not reflect, however, a one-to-one correspondence. Good performance on the Spatial Orientation test, for example, corresponds not only to a high score on the meaning dimension locational qualities, but to a whole pattern of scores on meaning variables, which includes locational qualities. Patterns of this kind (which often include high scores on some meaning variables and low scores on others) are identified by comparing the meaning profiles of subjects who do well on cognitive tasks of some specific kind with those who do poorly on them. Specific patterns of meaning variables—which could be called meaning profiles of tasks—were found to correspond to good performance on cognitive tasks that assess spatial navigation, curiosity, creativity, conservation, problem solving, planning, learning of reading, and reading comprehension (Haidu, 1991; H. Kreitler & S. Kreitler, 1990a; S. Kreitler & H. Kreitler, 1986d, 1987b, 1987c, 1989, 1994; S. Kreitler, Nussbaum, Cohen, & Shealtiel, in press; Lahav, 1982; Weissler, 1993). Such patterns reveal, as it were, the understructure of the cognitive processes involved in performing the cognitive act of, say, planning or solving a problem, thereby providing insight into the cognitive dynamics characteristic of the act. Furthermore, evidence is beginning to accumulate showing that meaning variables can be taught. The frequency with which they are used can be changed, and training individuals to employ the meaning variables corresponding to good performance on some tasks raises the performance level of those individuals on the specific tasks (e.g., S. Kreitler & H. Kreitler, in press-a).

When meaning variables are used for exploring the cognitive processes involved in specific cognitive tasks, they are grasped in a dynamic sense, whereby each meaning variable corresponds to some process (e.g., the meaning dimension range of inclusion—to analyzing into components, the comparative type of relation—to detecting similarity or difference). The meaning system can however be conceptualized also in a static sense, whereby each meaning variable corresponds to some specific domain of contents (e.g., the meaning dimension sensory qualities—to contents such as sensations of different kinds, the metaphoric type of relation—to metaphors). The contents may take the form of meaning values occurring singly (e.g., red, dangerous, to the right) or in combinations, such as images (e.g., a map), beliefs (e.g., First, one should open the box, then put in . . .), sentences, etc. The static, content-bound approach to the meaning system has been applied in analyzing literary texts, jokes, questions and answers, or meanings of similar terms in different cultures. Such analyses were very helpful in unravelling the underlying structures of a variety of cognitive products, identifying sources for effects such as funniness, or difficulties in understanding and communication, or features of individual styles (H. Kreitler & S. Kreitler, 1990b; S. Kreitler, Drechsler, & H. Kreitler, 1988; S. Kreitler & H. Kreitler, 1986a, 1986b, 1988).

It is evident that the dynamic and static conceptualizations of the meaning system complement each other. The dynamic conceptualization views the meaning variable primarily as a cognitive process underlying the elicitation or production of a specific kind of cognitive contents, whereas the static conceptualization views it primarily as a specific kind of cognitive contents (resulting from the elicitation of particular cognitive processes) which influence future cognitive processing. In many cases the dynamic aspect of the meaning variable may be viewed as the vector or motor of the cognitive act, and the static aspect may be viewed as providing the raw materials for the act (e.g., S. Kreitler & H. Kreitler, 1989); in other cases, the dynamic aspect provides the general direction and the static aspect, the specific implementation (e.g., S. Kreitler & H. Kreitler, 1987c). In some contexts (e.g., when problem solving is at issue) it makes more sense to focus on the semantic implications of particular meaning values or the dynamic impact of meaning dimensions like antecedents and causes, whereas in other contexts (e.g., when retrieval from memory is at issue) it makes more sense to focus on the available contents of meaning. In several cases both approaches were applied, as in the studies of the horizontal decalage or planning (S. Kreitler & H. Kreitler, 1987c, 1989).

Thus, horizontal decalage signifies the inconsistent performance of individuals in problems requiring the same cognitive processes. It constitutes a major problem for the Piagetian theory of cognitive development, which regards it as unpredictable and analogous to error variance. In a series of four studies, S. Kreitler and H. Kreitler (1989) demonstrated the double-pronged approach to horizontal decalage in conservation problems. The dynamic approach led to identifying the set of cognitive processes (assessed by meaning variables) involved in conservation (e.g., the comparative type of relation of difference, causes and antecedents, and categorization) so that those scoring high on these processes solved better the conservation problems. The content approach led to showing that subjects who mastered the specific contents involved in the problems (e.g., size or quantity) solved better conservation problems in these domains of contents. Applying both approaches accounted for most of the variance and showed that horizontal decalage is a highly predictable phenomenon.

CHARACTERISTIC FEATURES OF MEANING ASSIGNMENT

Both the dynamic and the static conceptualizations of the meaning system depend on the meaning assignment process. Therefore, in order to better understand the functions of the meaning system, it is necessary to dwell briefly on some of the major characteristics of the meaning assignment process.

First, the raw materials of meaning are *cognitive contents*, which emphasizes that meaning deals with representations of contents (e.g., actions, feelings, sensory qualities, and so on) rather than with actual actions, feelings, sensory qualities, and so on.

Second, the meaning assignment process functions with *regular cognitive contents*, that is, cognitive contents that may be involved in different cognitive functions (e.g., problem solving, concept formation), but in the course of meaning assignment assume functions that subserve the purpose of stating, manifesting, or expressing meaning.

Third, meanings are constantly formed and disbanded, which means that the main bulk of meanings are newly formed structures of meaning units, that do not seem to be stored for further use but disintegrate into meaning values or in rare cases into other or simpler meaning units.

Fourth, meaning assignment is a highly sensitive process that is shaped interactively in view of constraints of the input, the context, the prevailing organization of the whole meaning system and the tendencies of the individuals (S. Kreitler & H. Kreitler, 1985b).

Fifth, meaning assignment occurs in sets or patterns that are characterized by specific properties, in line with the overall nature of the pattern, which may correspond to a cognitive function, to the self concept, to a personality trait or to a particular feeling or emotion.

Functions of Meaning

The central role that meaning fulfills in regard to cognition has led to the conceptualization of cognition as a meaning-processing and meaning-processed system. This conceptualization expresses one of the basic functions of meaning, which is to provide the understructure and the raw materials for cognitive functioning. However, our studies revealed other basic functions of meaning, including a major one in the domain of personality. A body of research has shown that each of more than 150 personality traits was correlated with a specific set of meaning variables.

For example, the pattern of meaning variables corresponding to extraversion (as assessed by Eysenck's MPI) includes a positive correlation with the meaning dimension sensory qualities (e.g., form, sound, taste, smell) but is negative with internal sensations. This is confirmed by many studies indicating that extraverts focus on external stimuli but overlook, to the point of repression, internal physical experiences, which may be manifested in both their higher pain tolerance and only weak tendency for psychosomatic complaints. Also, the pattern includes positive correlations with the meaning dimensions actions and possessions (manifesting interest in the material realistic aspects), negative correlations with the dimensions consequences and results (reflecting risk proneness) and judgments and evaluations (manifesting disregard for rules and norms), positive correlations with the number of different referent shifts (reflecting tendencies for variability and low rigidity), and negative correlations with the type of relation of metaphors (reflecting poor internal fantasy life; for more detail see S. Kreitler & H. Kreitler, 1990, pp. 136–143).

Analyzing and examining the sets of meaning variables corresponding to different personality traits led to the conceptualization that a personality trait corresponds to a unique pattern of meaning variables that is characterized by specific qualities in terms of number of variables, proportion of representation of the different sets of meaning variables, and proportion of meaning variables related to the trait positively and negatively (S. Kreitler & H. Kreitler, 1990, 1997). Thus, a second function of the meaning system is to provide the cognitive foundations for personality traits.

Other studies showed the involvement of the meaning system in further domains, such as defense mechanisms (S. Kreitler & H. Kreitler, 1993a). Two of these deserve mentioning in the present context. Studies showed that the self-concepts of individuals consist of a set of meaning values related to specific meaning variables, that it shares specific meaning variables with those used in the conceptions the individual has of other persons, and that it is related to the individual's meaning profile and undergoes characteristic changes with age (S. Kreitler & H. Kreitler, 1987d, 1991). Thus, it seems that a third function of the meaning system is to provide the cognitive raw materials for the self-concept.

Finally, as may be expected, there is evidence that the meaning system is involved in emotions. A study focusing on anxiety showed a pattern of meaning variables corresponding to anxiety (on the basis of correlations between the individuals' meaning profiles and scores on seven anxiety scales), with specific features differing from those characterizing the patterns corresponding to personality traits (S. Kreitler & H. Kreitler, 1985a). Another study showed that a manipulation that consisted in changing (by means of a brief training procedure) the frequency of the use of the meaning variables in the pattern of anxiety produced predicted changes in the indivudals' state anxiety and in their performances on a logical problem-solving task (S. Kreitler & H. Kreitler, 1987a). These findings suggest that a fourth function of the meaning system is to provide the cognitive foundations for emotions, namely, the cognitive raw materials and processes that are involved in the elicitation, selection, and implementation of emotions.

In summary, four functions of the meaning system that have been identified concern providing the understructure or raw materials, or both, for cognitive functioning, personality traits, the self-concept, and emotions.

Major Properties of the Meaning System

In order to explore the interrelations of consciousness with meaning we will sum up the major properties of the meaning system as a whole:

1. Meaning is a system; that is, it has different constituent parts and they are interconnected to the point of affecting each other under specific conditions (e.g., when a chain of meaning units is produced in the act of meaning assignment to a specific input).

2. Meaning is a complex system, with a multiplicity of aspects and levels; that is, it includes five sets of different meaning variables, each of which includes both more general contents or labels (e.g., meaning dimension material) as well as more and more specific contents (e.g., organic and nonorganic materials; elements, compounds, and mixtures; rocks, sand, metals; iron, lead, glass).

3. Meaning is a self-embedded system; that is, each of its parts can serve as a focal point around which all the rest of the system is organized. The structure is self-enfolding. Thus, if the meaning dimension feelings and emotions becomes the focus, then all other meaning dimensions become subdimensions, as it were, expressing the functions, locational qualities, results, actions, and so on of the feelings and emotions dimension, while using the other sets of meaning variables (e.g., types of relation, forms of expression). For example, feelings and emotions function for self-preservation, or feelings and emotions are manifested in the body, or feelings and emotions cause changes in behavior, and so on. This characteristic implies first, that the meaning system has a flexible organization in the sense that it can assume different total organizations and is susceptible to a multiplicity of organizations defined by its different elements. Second, it implies that the meaning system can be accessed from each of its constituent elements.

4. Meaning is a regressive system; that is, its elements are defined in terms of its other elements. Thus, each meaning value or each meaning variable has a meaning which can be expressed in terms of the meaning system, whereby the meaning of these terms is also expressible in terms of the meaning system, and so on.

5. Meaning is a selective system; that is, it neither functions nor is it manifested in its totality under most circumstances, but it is subject to selection in line with certain principles or constraints. Some selective principles are more constant, such as culture, family background, personality dispositions and traits, or profession. These may be responsible for the salience and strength of some meaning variables and the weakness or infrequent use of others (e.g., S. Kreitler & H. Kreitler, 1988, 1990). Other selective principles are more transient and depend on the input to which meaning is assigned, and the context in which meaning assignment occurs (S. Kreitler & H. Kreitler, 1985b, 1993b).

6. Meaning is a developing system; that is, it is subject to development and enrichment through learning and its activation. Development consists in the acquisition of new constituents (viz., meaning variables), new connections among constituents, new organizations of the whole system, formation or learning of new schemes for meaning assignment, enlargement of the pool of meaning values that can be elicited by each meaning variable, enrichment of the meaning values that may be potentially assigned to different referents, etc.

7. Meaning is a *dynamic* system; that is, its special characteristics become manifest when the meaning assignment process is put into operation (see "Characteristic features of meaning assignment").

Two Classes of Changes in Cognition

The properties of the meaning system and the characteristics of meaning assignment have highlighted the dynamic nature of both cognition and meaning and their interrelations. Because we assume that consciousness is involved in this dynamic interface between cognition and meaning, the nature and motivation of the dynamics will be further explored.

There are different kinds of changes in cognition, which are mediated by the meaning system. There are two kinds of typical changes. The first kind are changes in meaning values within the same meaning variable, for example, in a meaning dimension, such as feeling and emotions, going from "fear" to "anger," or in a comparative type of relation, such as similarity going from "like a man" to "like a woman"; or in a referent-shift variable, such as superordinate referent going from "vertebrates" to "living things" (when the input was "bird"). The second kind are changes from one meaning variable to another in the same set of variables, for example, from the meaning dimension feelings and emotions to actions or from the attributive to the comparative type of relation, or from the verbal to the graphic form of expression.

Changes may vary in complexity. Relatively simple changes occur when the change is from one meaning value to one other meaning value, or from one meaning variable to another. More complex changes occur when more than one meaning value or more than one meaning variable is involved in the change (e.g., from two meaning variables that were focal to two or three others). More complex changes may be more comprehensive and bring about a broader range of effects.

Regardless of its complexity, each of the changes in itself may be small, medium, or large as assessed in terms of steps intervening between the point of origin and the endpoint in the framework of a structure in which the variables are embedded. For example, the meaning dimensions are ordered along the circumference of a circle with the properties of a circumplex, which may be described in terms of the two major axes recurring in most studies:

1. the approximately vertical axis of abstractness concreteness which is anchored, on the one hand, in the meaning dimension contextual allocation and, on the other hand, in the meaning dimension sensory qualities, and

2. the approximately horizontal axis of action emotion, which is anchored, on the one hand, in the meaning dimension action and potentialities for action reflecting predominantly external motor-type activities, and, on the other hand, in the meaning dimension feelings and emotions reflecting predominantly internal emotional experiences (S. Kreitler & H. Kreitler, 1990).

Changes of the described types may occur for two major reasons that define two classes of changes. One major reason for the changes originates in the cognitive system. It has to do with performing some externally presented task, such as solving a problem, making a decision, memorizing, retrieving from memory, or comprehending, or with some task arising from the needs of the cognitive system itself, such as organizing material or processing some information. Because the cognitive system interacts with other systems in and outside of the individual, the cognitive goals may arise in response to needs of other systems such as emotional needs, social needs, and personality dynamics. Thus, changes motivated by cognitive goals of this kind are a manifestation of the constant cognitive dynamics and are necessary for cognitive functioning. They are usually of short duration and are replaced by other changes, as dictated by the needs of attaining the specific cognitive goal salient at the time.

Another major reason for the changes originates in the meaning system. It has to do with the needs and dynamics of the meaning system, for example, reorganizing when a mass of new contents or meaning values has become available, or developing structural complexity, or matching new with old relationships, or complementing a rudimentary or fragmentary view of reality, etc. Such needs of the meaning system may arise in response to needs of other systems, for example, the emotional or the social. Changes motivated by the dynamics of the meaning system typically consist of placing one or more specific meaning variables or even one or more meaning values in the focal position and changing the whole structure of the meaning system accordingly (organizational transformation). Changes motivated by the meaning system include placing in a focal position (a) the meaning dimensions contextual allocation, results and consequences, and causes and antecedents which manifest the so-called abstract approach; (b) the meaning dimensions sensory qualities, size and dimensions, weight and mass, and perhaps also locational qualities—all of which manifest the so-called concrete approach or concrete thinking; or (c) the meaning dimension feelings and emotions, which would manifest the emotional approach. Likewise, we could refer to the evaluative–judgmental approach, when the meaning dimension judgments and evaluations is in the focal position, the actional approach when the meaning dimension actions and potentialities for actions is in the focal position, the comparative approach when one or more of the comparative types of relation is in the focal position, the disjunctive (or either/or) approach when the disjunctive form of relation is in the focal position, or the nonverbal approach when one of the nonverbal forms of expression (e.g., gestural, graphic) is in the focal approach. As a matter of fact, almost any of the meaning variables and quite a number of sets of meaning variables could serve as foci for the meaning system and could be the carriers of an organizational transformation. The account would not be complete without mentioning the possibility that even specific meaning values, such as danger or I love her–him or God could be placed in a focal position.

The organizational transformation brought about by the placement of different meaning constituents in a focal position includes changes in meaning variables that are manifested in changes in contents, in cognitive processes, and in the adjustment of the processes to the contents. More specifically, as a result of the transformation, certain types of contents or processes may become very salient, or hardly accessible (i.e., so-called unconscious), or frozen in a position of no change (e.g., perseveration on specific contents or processes), or uncontrollable (i.e., they may be manifested in forms that are not determined by ongoing activity in the cognitive system and may not participate in this activity), or determined by factors external to the cognitive system (e.g., as sometimes in hypnosis or after ingesting a specific drug). Further, the freedom with which cognitive processes may be applied to the different contents may be changed. For example, some processes may become bound more to some contents than are others (e.g., causality will become clearer in regard to contents that represent actions than those that represent emotions). Also the interconnectedness between processes as well as between contents may be transformed. For example, a cluster of processes based on the meaning dimensions feelings and emotions, cognitive qualities and judgments and evaluations may be formed so that they tend to be elicited together; or a cluster of contents such as dirt–disorder–immorality may be formed and then often arise together (e.g., S. Kreitler & H. Kreitler, 1990, pp. 216–218). (Other common clusters of contents could be street-danger-rape that could be involved in agoraphobia or person x-threat-defense that could be involved in paranoia). Alternately, some connections may become weaker and rarer. For example, the meaning variables possessions and belongingness and function, purpose and role may be dissociated so that acquisitiveness may proceed without concern for its functionality; or the meaning values I and different feelings and emotions may be dissociated, as, for example, in alexithymia.

The clusterings of meaning values may be reminiscent of affective sequences leading to scripts and sometimes even to ideological patterns of the personality that were described by Tomkins (1991). There are two main differences. First, clusterings in terms of meaning values are not necessarily affective in contents or origin; and second, when they are affective they do not serve the function primarily emphasized by Tomkins to promote the control of affects and their socialization, but may be the basis for psychopathological symptoms, personality dispositions, and ideologies.

The changes brought about by the placement of different meaning constituents in a focal position include changes in the nature, salience, and interconnectedness of contents and cognitive processes that affect cognitive functioning. The changes are not limited to the cognitive sphere. Because the meaning system is also involved in personality traits and in the self-concept and emotions (see discussion in section headed Functions of Meaning), it is likely that the organizational transformations of the meaning system affect these spheres too, directly or indirectly. Hence, one may expect the organizational transformations of the meaning system to be manifested in changes in cognitive functioning (e.g., changes in attention, memory, creativity, the difficulty of solving different types of problems, styles of decision making, fluency and flexibility of associations, etc.), in changes in the self-concept (e.g., thoughts about oneself, self-esteem, one's biographical narrative, the experiential atmosphere of the self, etc.), in changes in personality traits (e.g. changes in the strength and salience of different traits and other personality dispositions), and in changes in emotions (e.g., changes in the strength and salience of different emotions and moods). These changes may in turn bring about further changes in the affected domains as well as in other domains including overt behavior and physiological reactions. The nature and extent of the changes in all spheres, as well as the degree to which they are direct or mediated, depend to a large degree on the meaning constituents that have been the source of the organizational transformation.

In sum, two classes of changes in cognition have been described. One class is motivated by the dynamics of the cognitive system itself and is related to performing different cognitive tasks or attaining specific cognitive goals. The other class is motivated by the dynamics of the system of meaning and affects the first class of changes in the cognitive system itself.

To emphasize and further clarify the difference between the two classes of changes, it may be helpful to use an analogy from the arts. Accordingly, the changes in the meaning system itself resemble in several respects those attributed to mode in the arts. Thus, mode in literature (Cudden, 1992, p. 550) is described as similar to kind, form, and genre, and is associated with method, manner, and style, which involves choice of words, figures of speech, and other language devices as well as the shape of sentences and paragraphs. Indeed, the writer's choices are manifested in "every conceivable aspect of his language and the way in which he uses it" (Cudden, 1992, p. 922). Similarly, mode in music is dependent on scales or the arrangement of tones and semitones, and is associated with a particular melodic style or collection of musical motifs, cadences, etc. (Hiley, 1984). Four features characterize the definition of mode in both contexts: (a) mode is distinct from the contents of the art, so that the same contents can be expressed in different modes; (b) mode is distinct from the means of expression or channel of communication, for example tones or imagery, because there are different modes in the context of the same means of expression; (c) mode affects the operation or manifestations of the art in the most diverse forms, for example, it affects the selection of contents and their sequence, structure, form of expression, etc.; and (d) the effects of mode are pervasive (i.e., it may affect the cognitive, emotional, and even behavioral effects of a work of art). For these reasons, despite the nebulous character of the artistic definitions, mode seems to be a good analogy for the effects of organizational transformations in the meaning system (see the Personal and Interpersonal Modes of Meaning section).

It should be emphasized that mode as used here differs from common uses of the term in other contexts, where (in contrast to feature b, above) it is mostly defined in terms of means of expression, for example, Horowitz's (1970, pp. 69–82) three "modes of thought representation"— enactive, images and lexical (viz., actions, imagery, words), Bruner's (1964) three forms of representation—enactive, iconic, and symbolic, or Paivio's (1986) verbal and nonverbal dual coding systems.

BLUEPRINT FOR A MEANING-BASED COGNITIVE THEORY OF CONSCIOUSNESS

In a previous section (Assumptions for a Cognitive Theory of Consciousness) we stated four assumptions designed to serve as introductory background for the present blueprint. Two (c. & d.) referred to cognition, and two (a. & b.) to the relations between cognition and consciousnes. The clarification of the nature of meaning and the meaning-based nature of cognition (see Meaning and Cognition section), makes it possible to present some of the elements of a meaning-based cognitive theory of consciousness.

The two assumptions referring specifically to cognition and consciousness are that they are interconnected and that consciousness characterizes the whole of the cognitive system. To better understand the interconnectedness it is necessary to clarify the wholeness characteristic.

The statement that consciousness characterizes the whole of the cognitive system means that it is a function of, or depends on, something that affects the whole of the cognitive system. If cognition is a meaning-processing and meaning-processed system, the source or agent of the effect is to be sought in the meaning system. Hence, we view consciousness as a product of the meaning system. More specifically, consciousness is a product of the organizational transformations in the meaning system that affect the cognitive system (see section entitled Two Classes of Changes in Cognition). The reasons for this latter assumption are first, that the organizational transformations in the meaning system affect the cognitive system, but do not replace its intrinsically-motivated dynamics and functioning, and second, that the effects of the organizational transformations in the meaning system on the cognitive system concern the whole of the cognitive system.

Thus, we consider consciousness as reflecting a gestalt quality of the totality of the cognitive system and other systems in the individual (emotions, personality, self) dependent upon, and originating in, organizational transformations in the meaning system. Hence, consciousness refers to a total state of the individual that in principle encompasses, in addition to the cognitive system, also other systems affected directly by changes in the meaning system or in the cognitive system or both.

In principle, any organizational transformation in the meaning system may be considered as generating a consciousness. Thus, there are an infinite number of possible consciousnesses or states of consciousness. In practice, however, not all organizational transformations affect the cognitive system and other systems (personality, emotions, etc.) to the same extent. Sometimes the changes may be minimal, or hardly noticeable, so that they may pass unnoticed, or at best may be experienced or considered as fluctuations in the prevailing consciousness. In other cases the changes may be salient to the point of being dramatic, so much so that they are clearly experienced or considered as alterations in consciousness (viz., altered states of consciousness).

The extent of the changes may be associated with their duration, but does not depend on them. There may be dramatic changes in consciousness that may last milliseconds and yet be noticed, or sometimes even treasured for a lifetime. Other factors that may affect the extent of the changes are probably the number and nature of the meaning variables that are placed in the focal position in the meaning system bringing about the organizational transformation in the system, the salience of emotional reactions among the changes, and the difference between the resulting consciousness and the one habitual for the individual. Examples of organizational transformations that have been examined in detail are those focused on the personal or the interpersonal modes of meaning (see previous section entitled Personal and Interpersonal Modes of Meaning).

Some changes in consciousness become noticeable, not necessarily or only because of their extent, but because they are sanctioned by the culture to which the individual belongs, or are bound to a specific technique that is salient in a particular culture (Faber, 1981). Thus, people who have gone through the Zen experience became attuned through the training to perceive differences between four kinds of consciousness which are conceptualized as four stages: ego loss (koan), deep meditation (sunmay), hallucinatory phase (makyo), and enlightenment (satori or kensho; Johnston, 1971). For those who are not Zen conoisseurs, the distinctions are barely clear on the conceptual level, and less so on the experiential one. Likewise, the training of Yoga may focus on differentiation of states of consciousness that a regular untrained person from Western culture can hardly make sense of (e.g., *Dharna*—"an uninterrupted concentration to hold the mind on a fixed center (such as a thought, an object . . ." versus *Dhyan*—maintaining the former "but at a constant rate of flow"; Fischer, 1978, p. 42).

Thus, changes in consciousness seem to form a continuum, whereby some changes are prominent or noticeable or are considered important enough to be grasped as discrete consciousnesses (or states of consciousness), at least in the framework of some culture or for some individuals, whereas other changes are experienced merely as fluctuations or are hardly experienced at all.

Although each consciousness is a discrete state, there may be different degrees of similarity between consciousnesses, based on the extent and kind of changes generated by the organizational transformation. This may be the basis for groupings of consciousnesses into sets, as for example the so-called altered states of consciousness in Western culture or the states of hypoarousal and tranquillity in Eastern cultures (Fischer, 1978). The similarity of the different consciousnesses may also play a role in determining the degree to which one may recall or reconstruct contents or experiences of one consciousness when one is operating in the framework of another, and the ease with which one may shift from one consciousness to another spontaneously or at will (see Personal and Interpersonal Modes of Meaning).

Defining consciousness as reflecting the state of the cognitive system (and other systems) under the sway of a meaning-based organizational transformation resembles in some respects other definitions of altered states of consciousness described as "a given selection of potentials available" organized in a specific manner (Tart, 1978, p. 65) or as "a pattern of distributed activation and inhibition of selected portions of sensory, cognitive, and motor modules" (Antrobus, 1991). Definitions of this type emphasize the manifest effects of what we define in terms of the underlying organizational transformation in the meaning system. Further, in contrast to these definitions, which imply the existence of the consciousness (presumably denoting the ordinary consciousness of the normal adult in the Western culture of the 20th century), and so-called altered states of consciousness, the suggested meaning-based definition implies that there are an infinite number of potential consciousnesses and that all are evaluated as of equal potential importance and status. In principle, any one of them can become dominant for any duration and can come to characterize a given culture.

There are further implications stemming from the suggested definition. An important one concerns the familiar distinction between being conscious or unconscious. It seems that in many cases the construct consciousness and the descriptive adjective conscious have come erroneously to be used interchangeably. According to the definition suggested here, conscious–unconscious denotes poles or states along a dimension that can be used to describe the state of different contents and processes in each of the consciousnesses. Hence, unconsciousness is not a state of consciousness or an altered state of consciousness, but denotes a specific degree of availability or readiness for evocation and can be applied in regard to each consciousness. Different consciousnesses may differ from each other in exactly which contents or processes or both are unconscious, the duration of the unconsciousness, the ease with which the unconsciousness can be overcome or suspended, and the rules defining which material (contents or processes) is rendered unconscious. Thus, in so-called ordinary consciousness material is rendered unconscious if it contradicts the superego (Freudian conception) or the self-concept (self-psychology conception); in the hypnotic consciousness the defining rule is the order given by the hypnotist or the subject's own decision (according to different methods of hypnosis—by hypnotist or self-hypnosis); in meditation the rule is often a result of the technique that dictates focusing on one's internal world, thus shutting off or blocking perceptions from the external world, as was shown by Singer (1970).

Another important implication of the suggested definition is that consciousness depends on, and is characterized by, changes occurring in the cognitive system (through an organizational transformation in the meaning system), regardless of the nature of the agent or conditions that brought about the changes. Even when the changes are induced by conditions external to meaning and cognition, for example, behavioral, emotional, or physiological, the changes that form the basis for consciousness are those that occur in cognition.

Indeed, it would be possible to characterize a consciousness by the kind of changes that occur in cognition. For example, one could start with the list of basic cognitive functions profferred by Baars (1986–87, 1988; see Consciousness and Cognition) and examine which of the functions is being performed by a consciousness. The answer would differ for different consciousnesses. However, in order to use this as a criterion for characterizing consciousnesses and even comparing them, the list (which seems to have been based mainly on functions in ordinary consciousness) would have to be complemented by other basic functions (occurring perhaps more often in other consciousnesses), such as symbol formation (S. Kreitler, 1965), metaphorization, humor production, or artistic expression.

At this stage, our basic assumption about the interconnectedness of consciousness and cognition can be stated more specifically. Consciousness reflects the state of cognition as a whole, as determined by the prevalent organization of the meaning system. Hence, cognition—its existence and functioning—is a necessary condition for consciousness. On the other hand, consciousness is not a necessary condition for cognition. Cognition could function even if there were no consciousness at all. However, if we want to understand how cognition functions at a given time, it is necessary to consider what is the prevailing organization in the underlying meaning system. Considering this organization could clarify, for example, why at a certain point in time a certain individual did not solve given logical problems, or recalled a mass of emotionally-toned material, or shaped a most apt symbol for expressing his or her state of mind. Considering consciousness is often a convenient way to refer to the overall meaning-induced changes in cognition and other spheres (experiential, etc.) in the individual (see Personal and Interpersonal Modes of Meaning).

These interrelations between consciousness and cognition also suggest some hypotheses about developmental aspects of consciousness. It is obvious that consciousness requires, as a precondition, a meaning system that is sufficiently complex or rich in elements to enable organizational transformations of any momentum. Thus, the clarity of consciousnesses and their number increase when the complexity of the meaning system increases. Concomitantly, the manifestations of consciousness increase with the increase of effects in personality, emotions, the self-concept, and behavior—which in turn also depend on the level of complexity of these domains. Complexity of the meaning system and the other domains is a function of development, both ontogenetically and phylogenetically.

In conclusion, here are some of the more salient advantages of our suggested approach to consciousness. First, our approach provides a well-based theoretical groundwork for a cognitive theory of consciousness. Second, our approach takes into account diverse components of consciousness—primarily cognition, but also others, such as emotions, personality traits and dispositions, the self-concept, and even behaviors. Third, our approach enables dealing with an infinite number of consciousnesses, beyond the major types of ordinary and altered that have dominated the scene until now, and it considers them on an equal footing. Fourth, because we are dealing in each case with a different organization or patterning of the same elements in the meaning system, or by derivation—in the cognitive system—our approach provides a ready means for comparing different consciousnesses in terms of their underlying structure, organization, and operation, as well as in terms of their manifestations in the spheres of cognition, self, personality, and emotions. Fifth, in principle, our approach enables defining new consciousnesses by specifying which constituents are to be placed in a focal position in the meaning system, and which changes are to be introduced in the other parameters of the meaning system. In some science-fictional future such specifications could lead to conjuring up the specified consciousness as a virtual reality. Sixth, our approach enables changing consciousness by introducing specified changes in the meaning system by a method of induction that has already been applied in a number of studies (see Personal and Interpersonal Modes of Meaning).

In summary, because cognition, meaning, and consciousness are all tightly interwoven, it may be helpful to reiterate in more formal terms both the major distinctions between them and their interrelations. Thus, *meaning* is a system that deals with assigning meanings to inputs and other referents and creating meaning units of varying complexity (e.g., beliefs, images). In this way, meaning turns such meaning-assigned entities into raw materials adequate for use in and by cognition—as objects and elicitors and shapers of processes in cognition and other systems (mainly self, personality, and emotions). *Cognition* deals with meaning-assigned contents and meaning-elicited or meaning-shaped processes for ordering, categorizing, organizing, checking, storing, or transforming them and using them for solving problems in different domains (e.g., scientific, personal, financial) and of different levels of complexity. It thereby uses schemata, algorithms, different heuristics, rules, etc. *Consciousness* is a specific characteristic generated by an organizational transformation in the meaning system that affects the cognitive system as a whole and also the self, personality, and emotions. This definition of consciousness enables specifying conditions under which no changes in consciousness are to be observed: (a) when there was no change in the meaning system; (b) when the change in the meaning system was not a transformational organization but of a different kind; (c) when the change in the meaning system did not affect the whole of cognition but only specific parts in it; and (d) when the change in the meaning system did not affect other systems, primarily personality, self, and emotions. The list does not include the experiential aspect because it is not clear whether a particular experience is a necessary accompaniment or correlate of each consciousness at the time it occurs or later.

These conditions enable differentiating, at least on a preliminary basis, between states or shifts which are changes in consciousness and those which are not. For example, there are doubts concerning the set of dichotomies (e.g., intellectual vs. intuitive, convergent vs. divergent, objective vs. subjective), popularized in the 1970s by writers like Ornstein (1977) and Bogen (1975), and often associated with brain laterality or hemisphericity (Springer & Deutsch, 1989). Because it is unclear whether the cited changes involve the whole of cognition and whether they affect also the self, personality, and emotions (see c and d previously discussed), they do not seem to reflect differences in consciousness regardless of their origin. Similarly, Horowitz's "states of mind"—defined as recurrent patterns of emotional experience and verbal or nonverbal behavior, e.g., posture, facial expression (Horowitz, 1987, pp. 27–43)—do not seem to reflect consciousnesses because they do not involve changes in cognition or personality and are not meaning-generated. A closer approximation to consciousnesses is represented by Epstein's (1985) rational and experiential systems which involve comprehensive changes in cognition, personality and experiencing.

PERSONAL AND INTERPERSONAL MODES OF MEANING

For limitations of space we will illustrate our approach to consciousness by means of studies done only in one domain. We focused on two complementary organizational structurings of the meaning system: one is focused on the focal position of the interpersonally shared (or lexical) mode of meaning and the other is focused on the focal position of the personal (or subjective) mode of meaning. Both are defined in the meaning system in terms of types of relation (see Appendix). Thus, the interpersonally shared mode of meaning is defined by the two following types of relation:

1. the attributive, which relates the meaning value to the referent directly in a substantive (e.g., flower—in the garden) or actional way (e.g., dog—can bark);
2. the comparative, which relates the meaning value to the referent through the mediation of another referent, by way of similarity (e.g., sea—has the same color as the sky), difference (e.g., house—unlike a tent is built of wood or bricks), complementarity (e.g., wife—has a husband), and relationality (e.g., highway—broader than a path).

The personal mode of meaning is defined by the two following types of relation:

1. the exemplifying–illustrative, which relates the meaning value to the referent by way of an example, in the form of an instance (e.g., wisdom—Moses), an image portraying a situation (e.g., mother-hood—a woman holding a baby in her arms) or a scene with dynamic elements (e.g., aggression—an unemployed person comes to the government agency for employment, the clerk tells him that there is no work for him, the person feels warm anger rising in him, his fists clench, his vision becomes blurred, etc.).
2. the metaphoric–symbolic, which relates the meaning value to the referent in a mediated way using nonconventional contents, in the form of an interpretation (e.g., life—the unknown known), metaphor (an image related interpretatively to a more abstract referent, e.g., wisdom—cool water in the desert at noon), or symbol (a metaphoric image that resolves contrasting elements, e.g., love—a fire that produces and consumes).

The definition of the meaning modes in terms of the types of relation is based on the results of studies which showed that when individuals are requested specifically to communicate the interpersonally shared meanings of stimuli, they use predominantly (in over 75% of the cases) the attributive and comparative types of relation, whereas when they are requested specifically to communicate the personal meanings of stimuli they use predominantly, the exemplifying–illustrative and metaphoric types of relation (S. Kreitler, 1965). Further evidence supporting the definitions of the two meaning modes was derived from findings that metaphors, symbols, and concretizations abound in contexts and conditions promoting assignment of personal and subjective meanings such as psychotic states, schizophrenia, psychotherapy, sensory deprivation, daydreaming, night dreaming, and play (e.g., Arieti, 1974, 1976; S. Kreitler, 1965; Singer, 1974; Singer & Antrobus, 1972; Singer & Singer, 1990; Zuckerman, 1969). However, specific attributive (i.e., x is so or is not so, y does this and that) and comparative statements (underscoring identity, similarity, analogies, contrasts, or differences) abound in contexts emphasizing computation, quantitative thinking, assessment, logic, planning, social behavior, and goals, etc., all of which require and promote interpersonally shared lexical meanings (e.g., Labouvie-Vief, 1980; Sternberg & Wagner, 1986).

Following these definitions, we performed several studies to examine the effects of the use of the interpersonally shared and personal modes of meaning on cognitive functioning in different domains. Findings showed, for example, that the personal mode of meaning is used more often by art lovers describing objects of art, by individuals working on a task requiring creativity, by subjects who score high on anxiety or those in whom state anxiety has been elicited, and by schizophrenics (H. Kreitler & S. Kreitler, 1983, 1990a; S. Kreitler & H. Kreitler, 1985a, 1986c). However, the interpersonal mode of meaning was used more often by individuals performing well on solution of logical problems, planning, and mathematics (S. Kreitler & H. Kreitler, 1985a, 1987b).

These findings suggested the possibility that the interpersonally shared and personal modes of meaning represented two alternate organizational structures of the system of meaning, giving rise to two distinct consciousnesses. Accordingly, we expected the two consciousnesses to give rise to differences in constructions of reality, cognitive functioning, experiences, and emotional reactions, among other manifestations. For the purpose of examining this general hypothesis, an experimental method for the induction of modes of meaning was developed. It was designed to bring about the predominance of the interpersonally shared or personal modes of meaning in the subject's meaning assignment for a brief period of time. This was brought about by guiding the subject to respond in terms of the desired types of relation to a set of specific referents chosen as particularly evocative for the desired types of relation (e.g., plan or media for the interpersonal and mother or loneliness for the personal) and rewarding the correct responses (see description of method in S. Kreitler, H. Kreitler, & Wanounou, 1987–88).

When the subjects were under the impact of the induction of the mode of meaning, they were administered different tasks. Thus, under the impact of the induction of the interpersonally shared mode, schizophrenic subjects responded to the Rorschach much less pathologically than they otherwise did. For example, they had much higher reality testing, more emotional reactions, but fewer special phenomena such as contamination or confabulation. Similarly, normal subjects under the impact of the induction of personal meaning reacted with lower reality testing and more fantasy, metaphors, and symbols, as well as more original and pathological responses (S. Kreitler, H. Kreitler, & Wanounou, 1987–88). Another study with children showed that induction of the personal mode of meaning increased their creativity responses as compared to a control group that underwent no induction (Lahav, 1982). Again, normal adults under the impact of induction of personal meaning—as compared with their performance under the impact of interpersonally shared meaning induction—had higher scores on visual memory tasks, identifying embedded figures, and recalling faces; had higher scores on the creativity measures of fluency, flexibility, and originality; reported many more unusual and bizarre experiences; produced a greater number of associations; grasped texts more often in metaphoric terms; made more mistakes in judging the validity of syllogisms; and expressed stronger views against harming animals. Most importantly, they had higher scores on scales assessing emotions (negative as well as positive; S. Kreitler & H. Kreitler, in press-b).

Finally, a study that dealt with assessing completeness and ease of shifting between the personal and interpersonal modes when instructed by an experimenter to do so, showed individual differences in the ability to shift. Notably, schizophrenic participants performed the shifts with longer RTs and more errors than normal participants (S. Kreitler & H. Kreitler, in press-b).

The differences in performance under the impact of the two modes of meaning are so clear-cut that they suggest the advisability of administering different psychological tasks, including cognitive tasks and personality tests, under the two modes of meaning, or at least checking under which mode of meaning the subject was operating when completing the task. Specifying the mode of meaning when the task was performed may help in assessing more precisely the individual's ability or state. Further, when planning some psychological intervention it may be useful to consider the characteristics, potentialities, and limitations of the two modes of meaning so as to administer the specific intervention under the most propitious conditions for its functioning and effects. For example, it seems that interventions leaning heavily on the uses of imagery and sensory expression (e.g., art psychotherapy, various forms of healing) (Lusebrink, 1990; Singer, 1974) would benefit from being administered to individuals in whom the personal mode of meaning had been induced, whereas interventions making use of cognitive analyses and focused problem solving or training in thinking and decision making (e.g., Neimeyer, 1995; Vye, Delclos, Burns & Bransford, 1988) would benefit from being administered to individuals in whom the interpersonal mode of meaning had been induced.

In summary, the induction of modes of meaning brings about a great number of effects in cognitive functioning, viewing of reality, emotional responses, and even personality traits. Hence, it seems justified to consider the possibility that induction of modes of meaning corresponds to the evocation of a consciousness. The described method and experimental design could serve as a paradigm for further studies in which the effects of other organizational structures and transformations of meaning would be explored. The results could serve to expand our view of consciousness, our methodology for studying consciousness, and our ability to manipulate, shape, and experience consciousness.

APPENDIX

Major Variables of the Meaning System

I. *Meaning dimensions* (Dim)
1. Contextual allocation
2. Range of inclusion
   - 2a. Subclasses of referent
   - 2b. Parts of referent
3. Function, purpose, and role
4. Actions & potentialities for action
   - 4a. By referent
   - 4b. To/with referent
5. Manner of occurrence or operation
6. Causes and antecedents
7. Consequences and results
8. Domain of application
   - 8a. Referent as subject
   - 8b. Referent as object
9. Material
10. Structure
11. State & possible changes in state
12. Weight and mass
13. Size and dimensionality
14. Quantity and number
15. Locational qualities
16. Temporal qualities
17. Possessions (17a) & Belongingness (17b)
18. Development
19. Sensory Qualities
    - 19a. Of referent
    - 19b. By referent
20. Feelings & emotions
    - 20a. Evoked by referent
    - 20b. Felt by referent
21. Judgments and evaluations
    - 21a. About referent
    - 21b. By referent
22. Cognitive qualities
    - 22a. Evoked by referent
    - 22b. Of referent

II. *Types of relation* (TR)
1. Attributive
   - 1a. Qualities to substance
   - 1b. Actions to agent
2. Comparative
   - 2a. Similarity
   - 2b. Difference
   - 2c. Complementarity
   - 2d. Relationality
3. Exemplifying-illustrative
   - 3a. Exemplifying instance
   - 3b. Exemplifying situation
   - 3c. Exemplifying scene
4. Metaphoric-symbolic
   - 4a. Interpretation
   - 4b. Conventional metaphor
   - 4c. Original metaphor
   - 4d. Symbol

Modes of meaning
  Lexical Mode: Attributive + Comparative
  Personal Mode: Exemplifying–illustrative + Metaphoric-Symbolic

III. *Forms of relation* (FR)
1. Positive
2. Negative
3. Mixed positive & negative
4. Conjunctive
5. Disjunctive
6. Combined positive & negetive
7. Double negative
8. Obligatory
9. Question
10. Absolute, general
11. Desired

IV. *Shifts of referent* (SR)
1. Identical
2. Opposite
3. Partial
4. Modified
5. Previous meaning value
6. Associative
7. Unrelated
8. Grammat. variation
9. Linguistic label
10. Combined meaning values
11. Superordinate category
12. Synonym

V. *Forms of expression* (FE)
1. Verbal
  1a. Direct
  1b. Verbal description of explanation, interpretation
2. Graphic
  2a. Actual
  2b. Verbal description of drawing or painting
3. Movements, gestures, & facial expressions
  3a. Actual enactment
  3b. Verbal description of movements, gestures and facial expressions
4. Sounds and voices
  4a. Actual voicing
  4b. Verbal description of sounds and voices
5. Denotation of object or situation
  5a. Actual presentation
  5b. Verbal description of object or situation to be presented

REFERENCES

Antrobus, J. (1991). Dreaming: Cognitive processes during cortical activation and high afferent thresholds. *Psycholgical Review, 98*, 96–121.

Arieti, S. (1974). *Interpretation of schizophrenia* (2nd ed.). New York: Basic Books.

Arieti, S. (1976). *Creativity: The magic synthesis.* New York: Basic Books.

Arnon, R., & Kreitler, S. (1984). Effects of meaning training on overcoming functional fixedness. *Current Psychological Research and Reviews, 3*, 11–24.

Atkinson, R. C., & Shiffrin, R. M. (1971). The control of short-term memory. *Scientific American, 224*, 82–90.

Baars, B. J. (1986–1987). What is a theory of consciousness a theory of? The search for criterial constraints on theory. *Imagination, Cognition, and Personality, 6*, 3–23.

Baars, B. J. (1988). *A cognitive theory of consciousness*. Cambridge, MA: Cambridge University Press.

Baars, B. J., & McGovern, K. (1996). Cognitive views of consciousness: What are the facts? How can we explain them? In M. Velmans (Ed.), *The science of consciousness* (pp. 63–95). London: Routledge.

Barber, T. X., Spanos, N. P., & Chaves, J. F. (1974). *Hypnosis, imagination and human potentialities*. Elmsford, NY: Pergamon.

Bogen, J. E. (1975). The other side of the brain, VII: Some educational aspects of hemispheric specialization. *UCLA Educator, 17*, 24–32.

Bridgeman, P. W. (1927). *The logic of modern physics*. New York: Macmillan.

Brodsky, S. L., Esquerre, J., & Jackson, R. R. (1990–1991). Dream consciousness in problem solving. *Imagination, Cognition and Personality, 10*, 353–360.

Bruner, J. S. (1964). The course of cognitive growth. *American Psychologist, 19*, 1–15.

Churchland, P. S., & Sejnowski, T. J. (1992). *The computational brain*. Cambridge, MA: MIT Press.

Cuddon, J. A. (1992). *The Penguin dictionary of literary terms and literary theory* (3rd ed.). New York: Penguin.

Dennett, D. C. (1969). *Content and consciousness*. Boston: Routledge & Kegan Paul.

Epstein, S. (1985). The implications of cognitive-experiential self-theory for research in social psychology and personality. *Journal for the Theory of Social Behavior, 15*, 283–310.

Faber, M. D. (1981). *Culture and consciousness: The social meaning of altered awareness*. New York: Human Sciences.

Fischer, R. (1978). Cartography of conscious states: Integration of East and West. In A. A. Sugerman & R. E. Tarter (Eds.), *Expanding dimensions of consciousness* (pp. 24–57). New York: Springer.

Flanagan, O. (1992). *Consciousness reconsidered*. Cambridge, MA: MIT Press.

Foulkes, D. (1990). Dreaming and consciousness. *European Journal of Cognitive Psychology, 2*, 39–55.

Frith, C. D. (1992). Consciousness, information processing and the brain. *Journal of Psychopharmacology, 6*, 436–440.

Gillett, G. (1995). Consciousness, thought and neurological integrity. *Journal of Mind and Behavior, 16*, 215–233.

Guilford, J. P., & Zimmerman, W. S. (1981). *The Guilford-Zimmerman Aptitude Survey*. Beverly Hills, CA: Sheridan Psychological Services.

Haidu, G. G. (1991). *Improving the ability of navigating on foot in open space by means of the method of assessing meaning and training of meaning dimensions*. Unpublished master's thesis, Tel-Aviv University.

Hardcastle, V. G. (1995). A critique of information processing theories of consciousness. *Minds and Machines, 5*, 89–107.

Hiley, D. (1984). Mode. In D. Arnold (Ed.), *The new Oxford companion to music* (Vol. 2: k-z, pp. 1183–1189). Oxford, England: Oxford University Press.

Horowitz, M. J. (1970). *Image formation and cognition*. New York: Appleton-Century-Crofts.

Horowitz, M. J. (1987). *States of mind: Configurational analysis of individual psychology* (2nd ed.). New York: Plenum.

James, W. (1950). *The principles of psychology*. New York: Dover. (Original work published 1890)

Johnson-Laird, P. N. (1988). A computational analysis of consciousness. In A. J. Marcel & E. Bisiach (Eds.), *Consciousness in contemporary science* (pp. 357–368). Oxford, England: Clarendon.

Johnston, W. (1971). *The still point*. New York: Harper & Row.

Kihlstrom, J. F. (1993). The continuum of consciousness. *Consciousness and Cognition, 2*, 334–354.

Kokoszka, A. (1992–1993). Occurrence of altered states of consciousness among students: Profoundly and superficially altered states in wakefulness. *Imagination, Cognition, and Personality, 12,* 231–247.

Kreitler, H., & Kreitler, S. (1976). *Cognitive orientation and behavior.* New York: Springer.

Kreitler, H., & Kreitler, S. (1983). Artistic value judgments and the value of judging the arts. *Leonardo, 16,* 208–211.

Kreitler, H., & Kreitler, S. (1990a). The psychosemantic foundations of creativity. In K. J. Gilhooly, M. Keane, R. Logie, & G. Erdos (Eds.), *Lines of thought: Reflections on the psychology of thinking* (Vol. 2, pp. 191–201). Chichester, England: Wiley.

Kreitler, H., & Kreitler, S. (1990b). The psychosemantics of responses to questions. In K. J. Gilhooly, M. Keane, R. Logie, & G. Erdos (Eds.), *Lines of thought: Reflections on the psychology of thinking* (Vol. 1, pp. 15–28). Chichester, England: Wiley.

Kreitler, S. (1965). *Symbolschoepfung und Symbolerfassung: Eine experimentalpsychologische Studie* [Symbol formation and symbol perception: Experimental studies]. Munich-Basel: Reinhardt.

Kreitler, S., Drechsler, I., & Kreitler, H. (1988). How to kill jokes cognitively? The meaning structure of jokes. *Semiotica, 68,* 297–319.

Kreitler, S., & Kreitler, H. (1985a). The psychosemantic determinants of anxiety: A cognitive approach. In H. van der Ploeg, R. Schwarzer, & C. D. Spielberger (Eds.), *Advances in test anxiety research* (Vol. 4, pp. 117–135). Lisse, The Netherlands: Swets & Zeitlinger.

Kreitler, S., & Kreitler, H. (1985b). The psychosemantic foundations of comprehension. *Theoretical Linguistics, 12,* 185–195.

Kreitler, S., & Kreitler, H. (1986a). Individuality in planning: Meaning patterns of planning styles. *International Journal of Psychology, 21,* 565–587.

Kreitler, S., & Kreitler, H. (1986b). The psychosemantic structure of narrative. *Semiotica, 58,* 217–243.

Kreitler, S., & Kreitler, H. (1986c). Schizophrenic perception and its psychopathological implications. In U. Hentschel, G. Smith, & I. G. Draguns (Eds.), *The roots of perception* (pp. 301–330). Amsterdam, The Netherlands: North-Holland.

Kreitler, S., & Kreitler, H. (1986d). Types of curiosity behaviors and their cognitive determinants. *Archives of Psychology, 138,* 233–251.

Kreitler, S., & Kreitler, H. (1987a). Modifying anxiety by cognitive means. In R. Schwarzer, H. van der Ploeg, & C. D. Spielberger (Eds.), *Advances in test anxiety research* (Vol. 5, pp. 195–211). Lisse, The Netherlands: Swets & Zeitlinger.

Kreitler, S., & Kreitler, H. (1987b). The motivational and cognitive determinants of individual planning. *Genetic, Social and General Psychology Monographs, 113,* 81–107.

Kreitler, S., & Kreitler, H. (1987c). Plans and planning: Their motivational and cognitive antecedents. In S. L. Friedman, E. K. Scholnick, & R. R. Cocking (Eds.), *Blueprints for thinking: The role of planning in cognitive development* (pp. 110–178). New York: Cambridge University Press.

Kreitler, S., & Kreitler, H. (1987d). Psychosemantic aspects of the self. In T. M. Honess & K. M. Yardley (Eds.), *Self and identity: Individual change and development* (pp. 338–358). London: Routledge & Kegan Paul.

Kreitler, S., & Kreitler, H. (1988). Meanings, culture and communication. *Journal of Pragmatics, 12,* 135–152.

Kreitler, S., & Kreitler, H. (1989). Horizontal decalage: A problem and its resolution. *Cognitive Development, 4,* 89–119.

Kreitler, S., & Kreitler, H. (1990). *Cognitive foundations of personality traits.* New York: Plenum.

Kreitler, S., & Kreitler, H. (1991). The psychological profile of the health-oriented individual. *European Journal of Personality, 5,* 35–60.

Kreitler, S., & Kreitler, H. (1993a). The cognitive determinants of defense mechanisms. In U. Hentschel, G. Smith, W. Ehlers, & J. G. Draguns (Eds.), *The concept of defense mechanisms in contemporary psychology: Theoretical, research and clinical perspectives* (pp. 152–183). New York: Springer.

Kreitler, S., & Kreitler, H. (1993b). Meaning effects of context. *Discourse Processes, 16,* 423–449.

Kreitler, S., & Kreitler, H. (1994). Motivational and cognitive determinants of exploration. In H. Keller, H. Schneider, & B. Henderson (Eds.), *Curiosity and exploration* (pp. 259–284). New York: Springer.

Kreitler, S., & Kreitler, H. (1997). The paranoid person: Cognitive motivations and personality traits. *European Journal of Personality, 11,* 101–132.

Kreitler, S., & Kreitler, H. (in press-a). *Treatment-by-Meaning of retarded children.* New York: Plenum.

Kreitler, S., & Kreitler, H. (in press-b). *Modes of meaning.* New York: Plenum.

Kreitler, S., Kreitler, H., & Wanounou, V. (1987–1988). Cognitive modification of test performance in schizophrenics and normals. *Imagination, Cognition, and Personality, 7,* 227–249.

Kreitler, S., Nussbaum, S., Cohen, M., & Shealtiel, B. (in press). Cognitive determinants of reading comprehension: Assessment and intervention. *School Psychology.*

Labouvie-Vief, G. (1980). Beyond formal operations: Uses and limits of pure logic in life-span development. *Human Development, 23,* 141–161.

Lahav, R. (1982). *The effects of meaning training on creativity.* Unpublished master's thesis, Tel-Aviv University, Tel Aviv, Israel.

Laughlin, C. D., McManus, J., & d'Aquili, E. G. (1992). *Brain, symbol and experience: Towards a neurophenomenology of human consciousness.* New York: Columbia University Press.

Lusebrink, V. B. (1990). *Imagery and visual expression in therapy.* New York: Plenum.

Mandler, G. (1984). *Mind and body: Psychology of emotion and stress.* New York: Norton.

Marcel, A. (1983). Conscious and unconscious perception: An approach to the relations between phenomenal experience and perceptual processes. *Cognitive Psychology, 15,* 238–300.

Natsoulas, T. (1994). The concept of consciousness-sub-4: The reflective meaning. *Journal for the Theory of Social Behavior, 24,* 373–400.

Neimeyer, R. A. (1995). An appraisal of constructivist psychotherapies. In M. J. Mahoney (Ed.), *Cognitive and constructivist psychotherapies: Theory, research, and practice* (pp. 163–194). New York: Springer.

Neisser, U. (1967). *Cognitive psychology.* New York: Appleton-Century-Crofts.

Nunn, C. (1996). *Awareness: What it is, what it does.* London: Routledge & Kegan Paul.

Ornstein, P. (1977). *The psychology of consciousness.* New York: Harcourt Brace.

Osgood, C. E., Suci, G. J., & Tannenbaum, P. H. (1957). *The measurement of meaning.* Urbana: Illinois University Press.

Paivio, A. (1986). *Mental representations: A dual coding approach.* New York: Oxford University Press.

Shallice, T. R. (1988). Information processing models of consciousness: Possibilities and problems. In A. J. Marcel & E. Bisiach (Eds.), *Consciousness in contemporary science* (pp. 305–333). Oxford, England: Clarendon.

Singer, D. G., & Singer, J. L. (1990). *The house of make-believe.* Cambridge, MA: Harvard University Press.

Singer, J. L. (1970). Drives, affect and daydreams: The adaptive role of spontaneous imagery or stimulus-independent mentation. In J. S. Antrobus (Ed.), *Cognition and affect* (pp. 131–158). Boston: Little, Brown.

Singer, J. L. (1974). *Imagery and daydream methods in psychotherapy and behavior modification.* New York: Academic Press.

Singer, J. L., & Antrobus, J. S. (1972). Daydreaming, imaginal processes, and personality: A normative study. In P. W. Sheehan (Ed.), *The function and nature of imagery* (pp. 175–202). New York: Academic Press.

Skinner, B. F. (1957). *Verbal behavior*. New York: Appleton-Century-Crofts.

Springer, S. P., & Deutsch, G. (1989). *Left brain, right brain* (3rd ed.). San Francisco: Freeman.

Sternberg, R. J., & Wagner, R. K. (Eds.). (1986). *Practical intelligence: Nature and origins of competence in the everyday world*. Cambridge, MA: Cambridge University Press.

Sviderskaia, N. E. (1992). Consciousness and the selection of information. *Journal of the Russian and East European Psychology, 30*, 29–42.

Tart, C. T. (1978). Altered states of consciousness: Putting the pieces together. In A. A. Sugerman & R. E. Tarter (Eds.), *Expanding dimensions of consciousness* (pp. 58–78). New York: Springer.

Tomkins, S. S. (1991). The negative affects: Anger and fear (Vol. 3). In S. S. Tomkins (Ed.), *Affect, imagery, consciousness* (Part 2, pp. 109–561). New York: Springer.

Tulving, E. (1983). *Elements of episodic memory*. Oxford, England: Oxford University Press.

Umilta, C. (1988). The control operations of consciousness. In A. J. Marcel & E. Bisiach (Eds.), *Consciousness in contemporary science* (pp. 334–356). Oxford, England: Clarendon.

Velmans, M. (1996). What and where are conscious experiences? In M. Velmans (Ed.), *The science of consciousness* (pp. 181–196). London: Routledge.

Vye, N. J., Delclos, V. R., Burns, M. S., & Bransford, J. D. (1988). Teaching thinking and problem solving: Illustrations and issues. In R. J. Sternberg & E. E. Smith (Eds.), *The psychology of human thought* (pp. 337–365). New York: Cambridge University Press.

Weissler, K. (1993). *The cognitive determinants of learning to read in first and second graders*. Unpublished master's thesis, Tel-Aviv University, Tel Aviv, Israel.

Zuckerman, M. (1969). Hallucinations, reported sensations and images. In J. P. Zubek (Ed.), *Sensory deprivation: Fifteen years of research* (pp. 85–125). New York: Appleton-Century-Crofts.

8

Consciousness Makes a Difference

Seymour Feshbach
University of California, Los Angeles

The psychoanalytic focus on the role of unconscious processes in human behavior elicited a major debate among psychologists that still continues. Few question that there are motoric responses governed by automatic mechanisms of which the individual is unaware. Most psychologists would agree that there are conditioned responses which are also automatic, and that the individual may not be cognizant of the conditioned stimulus evoking the response. The experimental work about subception (Balay & Shevrin, 1988; Silverman, Ross, Adler, & Lustig, 1978) and about parallel processing (MacKay, 1987), with many other studies, provides strong evidence for the influence of environmental stimuli affecting cognitions and behavior of which the individual is unaware. Yet the debate persists.

The debate is about issues that are far more subtle and complex than the question of whether human behavior is influenced by unconscious factors. Questions arise as to the meaning of the term unconscious and the utility of various operations for distinguishing between conscious and unconscious influences. If an individual, initially unable to verbalize and seemingly unaware of a stimulus that influenced his or her behavior, is subsequently able to do so through reviewing the circumstances in which the behavior occurred, does that influence still qualify as unconscious? If a tachistoscopically presented stimulus elicits sexual associations, but the person can only correctly identify part of the stimulus, e.g. "pen" for the stimulus word "penis," can we assert that the sexual associations were unconsciously influenced? If an individual experiences an affect but mis-identifies it, e.g, labels a sexual feeling as anger, can one make reference to unconscious sexual impulses? In what sense can one perceive or ap-prehend a stimulus without being conscious of the stimulus? Does un-conscious cognition depend upon conscious cognition, or can they be dissociated from each other? Is it meaningful to distinguish between unconscious cognitions and impulses that have been repressed from other unconscious influences? What is the nature of empirical support for the construct of repression? These and related questions are addressed in detail in various articles (Greenwald & Banaji, 1995; Greenwald, Klinger, & Schuh, 1995) and edited volumes (Bornstein & Pittman, 1992; Singer, 1990; Uleman & Bargh, 1989).

In this chapter, I shall focus primarily, although not exclusively, on variations in awareness of emotions. I shall take the liberty of reviewing a number of previously published studies in which significant differences in cognitive and behavioral effects are found between situations in which there is more or less full awareness of an affective stimulus, versus situations of limited or lack of awareness of the stimulus. These studies demonstrate that constraints on awareness that are not instances of re-pression can, nevertheless, produce effects similar to those attributed to the activation of repressed affect, and conversely, awareness reduces these effects. In addition, the studies touch on such theoretical issues as whether the constraint must be a psychological defense and whether constraints on positive affects result in effects comparable to those found with nega-tive affects.

In most of these studies, factors are introduced to inhibit awareness. It may be that there are different effects associated with the kinds of variables that influence awareness: for example, anxiety and conflict, focusing on one aspect of a stimulus situation resulting in limited aware-ness of others, lack of rehearsal resulting in difficulty in retrieving a past interaction with a current stimulus, etc. I will have very little to say about such differences; my primary emphasis will be on the effects of factors such as guilt, anxiety, and social pressure that motivate the individual to deny or block from awareness feelings and motivations that have been evoked in a particular situation. A third critical element, in addition to activated emotions or motivations and inhibitory forces, is the nature of the relationship of the elicited emotions or motivations to the response requirements of the situation. These are not task-centered feelings or motives, but are instead irrelevant to, or may interfere with, the task at hand.

The focus of these studies is on variations in the degree of awareness, rather than on unconscious versus conscious influences. In addition to the operational difficulties entailed in determining whether an influence is unconscious, an unfortunate source of confusion has been the frequent use of the nominative case in reference to such influences, as in the unconscious. The use of the nominative implies that there is a structure or place in which unconsciousness resides. The psychoanalytic predilection to use nominatives such as the id or the superego where descriptors or adjectives would be more appropriate reinforced this confusion. Although Freud (1927) himself was guilty of nominative usage in regard to these constructs, he also recognized that the unconscious is not a place in the mind, but rather is an attribute of processes and behavior. That is, one may properly refer to unconscious mechanisms or unconscious influences, but not to an unconscious.

At the same time Freud made a sharp distinction between unconscious factors and factors accessible to consciousness of which the individual may be unaware. These latter factors Freud considered as largely falling within the province of the preconscious. The distinction between preconscious and unconscious influences has an operational referent in that access to stimuli within the former category presumably requires much less cognitive work than access to stimuli within the latter category. However, the use of categorical descriptions such as preconscious and unconscious can be misleading because it provides a qualitative distinction for what probably should be a quantitative distinction. The stimuli that influence one's behavior vary in the degree to which one has access to them. The critical question is the kind and degree of functional differences associated with variation in degree of conscious access to stimulus influences. The effects of stimuli that lie within the range of Freud's preconscious may well be similar, but are perhaps different in degree, to those considered to be truly unconscious.

The theoretical analysis guiding these studies is straightforward and simple, perhaps too much so. It is similar to the psychoanalytic view of the effects of repressed affects and drives on behavior, and how bringing repressed materials into consciousness modifies these effects. It differs from the classic psychoanalytic position in that repression and suppression are considered as having functionally similar consequences. In this respect, the approach is similar to that articulated by Erdelyi (1990). A basic assumption is that motives and feelings that have been aroused in a situation, although irrelevant to the task requirements, can influence the individual's cognitions and behavior, especially when the individual is not conscious of these feelings and motives. Because these affects or motives, of which the individual is unaware, are not germane to the task at hand, the resultant cognitions and behavior are likely to be distorted or inappropriate.

It makes little difference from this theoretical perspective whether the lack of awareness is a consequence of suppression or repression. The

suppressed or repressed affect, if evoked in a situation and not acknowledged by the individual, will tend to have a distorting influence on
judgments and behavior. This influence can be reduced through awareness and labeling of these feelings and motives, the task of bringing
repressed feelings and motives into consciousness is admittedly more
difficult than bringing suppressed feelings and motives into consciousness. In either case, awareness enables the individual to discriminate and
separate these affects and desires from task relevant stimuli so that judgments and behaviors are primarily influenced by task relevant stimuli
rather than by irrelevant affective stimuli. One theoretical difference between this approach and the psychoanalytic model, and possibly that of
Erdelyi (1990), is that the task irrelevant affect or drive need not be one
that elicits anxiety or guilt. Any motivational factor that fosters unaware-
ness of a feeling or desire that is elicited in a situation should facilitate
the influence of that feeling or desire on the individual's judgment and
behavior in that situation.

STUDY 1: EXPRESSION AND SUPPRESSION OF FEAR

The first study of the role of consciousness or awareness on behavior that
I shall review is concerned with the effects of affect arousal on perception
and social judgment (Feshbach & Singer, 1957). The particular affect in
question is fear. Fear was elicited through random electric shocks administered while individual male college students observed a film of a young
man's performance on a number of different tasks. The participants were
required to make judgements of the fearfulness of the stimulus person as
observed, and of his fearfulness and aggressiveness in other situations.
Some participants (fear-expression group) were encouraged to be aware
of and to express their feelings while others (fear-suppression group) were
encouraged not to think about and to forget their feelings, so as to make
more accurate judgments. A comparison group of participants who were
not shocked while observing the film (control group) was also included
in the study.

The differences between the experimental groups in their direct perceptions of the stimulus person were small but in the predicted direction.
The fear-suppression participants perceived the stimulus person as more
afraid than did either of the other groups, the difference between the
fear-suppression group and the control group was significant. The differences on the indirect judgements of fearfulness and aggressiveness in
other situations were more pronounced. The fear-expression participants
judged the stimulus person as significantly more fearful and more aggressive than the controls, while the fear-suppression group attributed

the most fearfulness and aggressiveness to the stimulus. The effects of fear suppression as compared to fear expression on these indirect judgments were more pronounced than the differences obtained in the direct perceptions. Thus, 60% of the participants who were encouraged to suppress their feelings, in contrast to 25% of the participants who were encouraged to express their feelings, judged the stimulus person as extremely fearful on at least one item of the fear judgment scale. Those in the fear-suppression group also believed the stimulus person to be more aggressive than did the fear-expression participants. While there was a tendency for the fear-expression group to have more elevated judgments of fearfulness and aggression than the controls, the more significant and larger effects were obtained as a result of the fear suppression instructions. It may be noted the obtained differences were specific to attributions of fearfulness and aggressiveness and were not found for judgments of other negative personality traits.

These findings bear some similarity to classic projection, but there are also important differences because the distortions of judgment of fearfulness and aggressiveness did not require the mechanism of repression. The experience of strong affect, in itself, was sufficient to influence the individual's perceptions and cognitions, a finding similar to those obtained in studies of the cognitive effects of mood (Bower, 1981). Most importantly, the suppression of acknowledgment of these feelings exaggerated the degree of perceptual and cognitive distortions.

Another difference between these findings and classic projection is the nature of the affect being projected. Classic projection entails socially unacceptable impulses. The affect of fear, while inhibited by the fear-suppression participants, would ordinarily not be included among these socially unacceptable impulses. However, the college students, all males, may have considered fear to be socially unacceptable in this experimental situation. In addition, because it is possible that aggression was also elicited in the fear-suppression group, and aggression would be considered a socially unacceptable impulse, the question remains of whether the suppression of socially acceptable impulses results in projection or in cognitive distortions. This issue is addressed more directly in the next study to be reviewed.

STUDY 2: SUPPRESSION OF POSITIVE AFFECT

The experimental paradigm employed in this second study (Feshbach, 1963) was similar to that utilized in the initial study, with the exception that the affect that was varied was happiness or joy rather than fear. Female college students were randomly assigned to a neutral control condition or to a success condition in which they were informed that their performance on a task was superior to that of 75% of college students, and they were also given a small financial reward. The subjects then met in a group and made individual judgments about the degree of happiness–sadness of facial stimuli. Prior to these judgments and placement in the group setting, half of the participants in the success condition were asked to suppress their feelings when interacting with others and not to indicate how well they had done on the task verbally or through nonverbal expressions such as a smile or wink.

In accordance with the experimental hypothesis, the success participants who were encouraged to suppress their feelings attributed significantly more happiness to the facial stimuli than did the controls and, most importantly, more than the success group who were not given suppression instructions. There may be some question as to the degree of awareness of affect in the suppression group because they were instructed not to communicate their feelings rather than, as in the prior study, not to think about their feelings. However, inhibiting the experience of affect is similar to limiting one's consciousness of affect, and appears to have similar functional consequences. Stimuli blocked from expression, like stimuli blocked from awareness, tend to have exaggerated effects on one's judgments.

STUDY 3: MODIFYING VERSUS INHIBITING AGGRESSION

The prior studies have addressed the influence of suppression and degree of awareness of the affects of fear and joy on social perception and social attributions. We turn now to the effects of suppression and reduced awareness of an affect and drive that psychodynamically oriented clinical theories view as often subject to repression and inhibition—namely, anger and aggressive impulses. We will be examining the effects of suppression and reduced awareness of these impulses on decisions and actions that have punitive consequences, in particular, decisions that entail the displacement of anger.

The primary dependent variable in this third study (Kaufmann & Feshbach, 1963) was the degree of punishment advocated for a juvenile delinquent. Prior to introducing the experimental variations, male and female college students, meeting in groups of three, were individually presented with a case history of a juvenile delinquent. They were subsequently divided into high- and low-punitive individuals on the basis of their agreement with the assertion that the delinquent "should be punished severely". In addition to indicating their degree of agreement with severity of punishment, the students also completed a form indicating their reasons for their recommendation. After collecting the completed forms, the experimenter distributed to each participant two similar forms which purportedly had been filled out by the other participants.

Variations in the content of these forms constituted one of the major independent variables. For participants in the neutral group, the "Don't know" alternative was checked for both forms. The reasons offered stated essentially that the writer had not quite made up his or her mind and would like more information before deciding. Participants randomly assigned to two other conditions—constructive alternative and aggression inhibition—received forms that were both checked indicating extreme disapproval of harsh punishment. The critical variation was the reasons offered for the disapproval.

Participants in the aggression-inhibition group received inhibitory appeals that stressed the negative and shameful consequences of aggressive behavior and of expressing one's anger (e.g., "It's a sin to raise your hands against your fellowman"—"We must learn to control our emotions"—"Getting mad at the world or at each other only gets us into trouble.") It was anticipated that when these participants were subsequently angered, they would displace their aggression in the form of advocacy of greater punishment for the juvenile delinquent despite exposure to a group norm expressing disapproval of severe punishment of the delinquent. The basis for this anticipated outcome is the general model that has guided these studies—namely, inhibiting affect and blocking affective cues from consciousness increases the likelihood of exaggerated influence of the affect upon ongoing cognitions and actions.

This proposition does not imply that restraining from acting on an aggressive impulse will increase the likelihood of displaced and irrational aggressive behaviors. The restraint may be mediated by conscious considerations of alternatives, including awareness of one's angry feelings, rather than by guilt or anxiety. The latter interfere with recognition of one's anger and with the conscious review of alternatives and their consequences. In contrast, awareness of one's angry feelings and the consideration of consequences for others and oneself should foster coping with anger without the need for displacement.

The constructive-alternative condition was included to obtain data bearing on this hypothesis. Participants in this condition read comments on the forms given them that essentially stated that rational, nonaggressive responses to provocation and instigation were more mature, as well as more profitable and creative means of coping with such situations, than retaliation and vengeance. The following excerpt from one of the experimental constructive communications illustrates the approach taken: "I cannot help thinking of the times when I have acted in a cruel and aggressive manner, merely in order to show that 'nobody can push me around'. Since then I have learned that repaying in kind benefits no one, neither the offender nor those who have been attacked. It takes more courage and maturity to transcend the offense and the provocation and react constructively and purposefully." It will be noted that this communication focuses on the aggressive act, and not on anger or the aggressive impulse.

Half of the neutral group—that is, those participants who had received the "Don't know" communications regarding severity of punishment for the delinquent, and both the constructive-alternative and aggression-inhibition groups were subjected to scathing, insulting remarks from an experimenter (Note: For various reasons, prior to the formation of human subjects' committees, we stopped using the insult procedure employed here and in the following study in our subsequent research. We also ceased using the administration of electric shock as a measure of aggression.) The case history of the delinquent was then readministered, followed by five items concerning recommendations for his disposition. These were then summed such that a higher score reflects the advocacy of more severe punishment.

The data for each of the experimental groups are presented in Table 8.1. The possible range of the mean punishment scores is from 5 to 25. The proportion of males and females in each experimental condition was similar, and because there were no significant gender differences on the dependent measures, the data for males and females were combined. As can be seen from Table 8.1, those participants who were initially low in degree of support for severe punishment for the delinquent maintain relatively low and similar punishment scores under the various experimental conditions. The punishment scores of those who initially supported severe punishment are, as to be anticipated, higher, and all of the experimental differences occur with this group. The first two columns— neutral and neutral insult reflect the effects of the insult treatment. The mean punishment score of the neutral-insult group is significantly higher than that of the neutral group, indicating that the anger evoked by the insult resulted in displaced aggression toward the delinquent.

TABLE 8.1
Mean Degree of Punishment Recommended for the Juvenile Delinquent as a Function of Initial Differences in Punitiveness, Insult, and Aggression Inhibition vs. Constructive Alternative Communication

	Neutral	Neutral Insult	Aggression Inhibition	Constructive Alternative
Initially High Punitive	17.6	20.1	19.2	17.1
Initially Low Punitive	14.5	14.8	13.3	13.6

In accord with theoretical expectation, the scores of the aggression-inhibition group were also significantly higher than those of the neutral group, providing evidence of displacement of aggression by this group. It is particularly noteworthy that this effect occurred despite the fact that the aggression-inhibition subjects had received communications expressing strong disagreement with the recommendation that the delinquent be severely punished. Any influence effects of these peer judgments were overridden by the displaced aggression resulting from the inhibition of aggressive affect produced by the guilt-eliciting communications.

The contrast between the mean delinquent punishment scores of the aggression-inhibition group and the constructive-alternative group is striking. The mean for the constructive-alternative group is significantly lower than that for the neutral-insult group, as well as the aggression-inhibition group, and is similar to that of the neutral-communication subjects who were not insulted. Thus, the constructive-alternative participants were able to cope with the insult without displacing aggression toward the delinquent. It may be noted that in response to questions concerning degree of agreement with their partners, the mean for the constructive-agreement group was exactly the same as that for the aggression-inhibition group, both expressing disagreement. However, the arguments proposed in the constructive-agreement communications were, nevertheless, effective, at least with regard to management of the insult and the resulting anger.

It is, of course, possible to argue that additional measures of aggression, both direct and indirect, might have provided evidence of inappropriate anger management by the constructive-agreement group. However, it would seem parsimonious to propose that the mechanism operating in this experiment is similar to that mediating the findings in the two prior studies. Reducing awareness of one's feelings increases the likelihood that these feelings will be expressed in an arbitrary and inappropriate manner.

STUDY 4: WITNESSING AGGRESSION: REINFORCEMENT WITHOUT AWARENESS

Each of the prior studies involved experimental efforts to inhibit and reduce awareness of affect. There is another element of awareness involved that was not addressed—namely, awareness of the connection between the affect and the judgment or behavior influenced by the affect. This element was undoubtedly of considerable importance in the last study. The relationship between punishment of a delinquent and expression of one's anger toward an experimenter is not an obvious one. Lack of awareness of a possible connection, and the lack of discrimination between the stimulus object instigating one's anger and the stimulus object to which one is currently reacting, is probably essential to the displacement of aggression.

More generally, being aware of one's feelings and desires, and being aware of the relevance of a particular act to one's feelings and desires, enables one to engage in sounder, more adaptive behaviors. This study demonstrates that the infliction of pain can be reinforcing when one is unaware of the connection between pain infliction and one's own feelings of anger. However, the point of this study is not to provide further evidence that learning or conditioning can take place without awareness. Rather, the principal objective of the study is to show that the absence of awareness of the connections between one's angry feelings, one's behavior, and the painful consequences of that behavior can result in aggressive behaviors that particular individuals would not carry out if they were aware of these connections.

To investigate the reinforcing function of the infliction of pain under conditions in which individuals were unaware of the relationship between their behavior and pain infliction, we made use of the verbal-conditioning paradigm (Krasner, 1958)). If the infliction of pain or suffering is reinforcing in the same manner as such stimuli as saying, "Mmmm-hmmm" and "Good," and is made contingent upon the use of a particular verbal response, then the frequency of these selected verbal responses should increase. The verbal-conditioning situation provides subjects with an opportunity to disclaim responsibility for, or even any knowledge of, having committed a hostile act. One can then hope to at least partially circumvent inhibitory tendencies associated with the expression of aggression.

Procedure

The experimental design consisted of randomly assigning participants to one of four experimental conditions generated by two independent variables: insult or noninsult, and the employment of shock or light, contingent upon the participant's use of particular pronouns in sentences made from prompt cards (Feshbach, Stiles, & Bitter, 1967). Two earlier studies without the light conditions yielded results similar to those to be reported here. The two light groups were added to control for the possibility that a conditioning effect might result from the interaction of provocation with any stimulus change, rather than from the interaction of provocation with witnessing the infliction of pain.

The participants in the study (35 female college students) were seen on two separate occasions. For the first session, they met in small groups and were administered an Aggression Anxiety (AA) Scale. This measure is designed to assess degree of conflict and anxiety over the expression of aggression. It correlates negatively with indices of aggressive behavior

(Feshbach & Singer, 1971) that assess direct, overt expressions of anger and aggression. The participants were then randomly assigned to one of the four experimental conditions with the restrictions imposed by equating scores on the AA scale.

At the second session, a male confederate, presumably another participant in the study, interacted in a rude, unfriendly manner with a female participant. The two then completed brief questionnaires eliciting their attitudes toward art, philosophy, and other areas, and in addition, were asked to provide their first impressions of the other subject's personality. The male confederate, who continued to behave rudely toward the female participant, left the area while the experimenter provided to the participant the confederate's first impression of her. These were either neutral (noninsult condition) or highly insulting (insult condition).

The female participant then entered an observation room through which she could see the confederate seated in front of a box of switches (with two wires attached to his hand in the shock condition). She was informed that the study was concerned with emotional tension in a stressful situation, and that the other participant (confederate) was trying to complete a circuit by flipping the correct sequence of switches. However, the task was very difficult because random variations were introduced into the sequence. Participants in the shock condition were then told that to make the task more stressful, the participant being observed would be receiving mild electric shocks. They were informed that these shocks would occur at random intervals and did not depend on his performance (the second part of the statement was true, but not the first). In the light condition, they were informed that the light behind the participant would flash at random intervals and had no relationship to his performance.

The participants' task was presumably to rate the confederate on his level of emotional tension during the course of his efforts to solve the circuit problem, and they were given rating sheets for this purpose. They were further instructed that to keep the ratings of emotional tension independent, they would be given an irrelevant task between each rating of emotional tension. That task would consist of constructing a sentence using the verb and one of the pronouns on a card presented to them. Each card contained one verb and the following six pronouns—I, we, they, he, she, and you.

For the first 15 trials, no conditioning was attempted in order to provide a base rate sample of the participant's pronoun usage. During the next 45 trials, participants in the shock condition observed the confederate sharply jerking his hand each time they constructed a sentence using the pronoun we or they. Participants in the light condition observed a bright light flashing when we or they was selected to construct the sentence.

After completion of the experiment, an elaborate interview was conducted to determine the participant's awareness of the contingency, and degree of anger, and suspiciousness as to whether the other participant was actually a real subject. The participant was then given a thorough explanation of the procedures and purpose of the experiment, and was requested not to reveal its nature to anyone. Because awareness is so critical to this study (and to this presentation), a few examples of the 14 questions asked in the interview are provided:

"What do you think of his impressions of your personality?"

"Some people, when they're in this situation, make little hypotheses about what we're trying to get at or what the purpose of the experiment is, and we'd be interested in anything that might have crossed your mind."

"How did you decide which pronouns to use?"

"Did you attempt to find any connection between what you were doing and the shocks (light)?"

No participant had full awareness of all of the elements of the study. Three participants, one in the insult-shock group and two in the noninsult shock group had some awareness of a contingency between their sentences and the shock. Exclusion of these individuals from the statistical analysis did not affect the significance of the relationships obtained.

Results

The changes in frequency of we and they responses between the last 15 and first 15 trials are presented in Table 8.2. The interaction between the insult versus noninsult and shock versus light conditions is statistically significant ($p < .05$). Almost all of these significant differences are due to changes in the frequency of the pronoun they. The data relating to changes in the frequency of they responses are presented in Table 8.3. The interaction term is again significant and the difference between the insult shock and noninsult shock groups is also significant.

TABLE 8.2
Mean Changes in Frequency of We Plus
They Responses From First to Last 15 Trials

	Insult Shock	Noninsult Shock	Insult Light	Noninsult Light
N	(12)	(11)	(4)	(8)
	1.08	−1.73	−1.25	.38

TABLE 8.3
Mean Changes in Frequency of *They*
Responses From First to Last 15 Trials

	Insult Shock	Noninsult Shock	Insult Light	Noninsult Light
N	(12)	(11)	(4)	(8)
	1.42	−1.18	−.75	.88

Thus far the results indicate that angered individuals will engage in behaviors that result in pain to the object of their anger, and that this process can take place without awareness of the relationship between their behavior and pain infliction. Of central interest is the behavior, under these conditions, of individuals who ordinarily experience anxiety when they feel aggressive and tend to inhibit the expression of aggression. To assess the influence of aggression-anxiety, participants were divided into high aggression anxious (high AA) and low aggression anxious (low AA) groups on the basis of a median split of their scores on the aggression-anxiety inventory. The individual change scores obtained by high and low AA scorers in the insult shock and noninsult shock condition are presented in Table 8.4.

It is apparent that the greatest increments in the usage of they were manifested by high AA participants when they were insulted, and observed the individual who had insulted them being shocked. The difference between the high AA insult shock and noninsult shock conditions is quite striking ($p < .004$; Mann-Whitney U test). Most impressively, the increments for the high AA insult shock participants are significantly

TABLE 8.4
Frequency Change Scores of *They* From First to Last 15 Trials
For Each Insult High and Low Aggression Anxiety Subject

	Insult Shock	Noninsult Shock
High	0	−2
Aggression	4	−1
Anxiety	1	−6
	3	1
	3	−1
	6	−1
Low	−3	−2
Aggression	−2	−3
Anxiety	1	−4
	1	3
	2	3
	1	

greater ($p < .05$) than those for the low AA insult shock participants; that is, high AA individuals who typically manifest less aggression than low AA individuals, in this situation manifested more aggression.

The absence of or limited degree of awareness is central to this finding. Ordinarily, high aggression-anxious individuals inhibit aggression. It appears that the high aggression-anxious individuals were able to engage in aggression when the circumstances for carrying out an aggressive act are indirect, such that the individual has no or only a vague awareness of any aggression and can disclaim responsibility for actions resulting in pain infliction. The high aggression-anxious subjects are not sadistic. Their use of verbal responses resulting in shock tended to decrease when they had not been insulted by the confederate. Anger arousal, in addition to limited awareness, was essential to their aggressive behavior.

We did not quantitatively assess the degree of affect arousal and affect recognition in the high aggression-anxious subjects. The focus of the manipulation of consciousness in this experiment was on the connections between an affect, a behavior, and the consequences of the behavior. Given that they characteristically express less direct aggression, it is likely that the high aggression-anxious individuals did not give full conscious recognition to the angry feelings elicited by the insulting, demeaning, and brusque behavior of the confederate. In any case, this experiment highlights the importance of awareness of the factors that influence a decision to arrive at the most appropriate, ego-syntonic choice.

STUDY 5 AND SOME SPECULATIVE COMMENTS: CONSCIOUSNESS AND DECISIONS BEARING ON WAR AND PEACE

The studies that have been reviewed here were concerned with the cognitive effects of degree of consciousness of different affects, and the behavioral effects of consciousness of the relationship between one's feelings and one's behavior. The studies were all experimental, and inferences from them are constrained by the experimental contexts and the measures employed. There would seem to be a very large gap that would have to be bridged to draw inferences from this research regarding issues of war and peace. Indeed there is a large gap. Nevertheless, I would like to conclude this presentation with a discussion of the importance of the role of consciousness in matters affecting national military and armament decisions.

A common feature of national military policies is differences among policymakers and their advisers as to the most judicious and effective policies to adopt. Debates between those who take more dovish and those who take more hawkish positions usually revolve around differences in assessments of the intentions of potential enemies, of their likely response to particular policies, and of differences in the predicted outcomes of particular actions—number of casualties if war takes place, probability of victory, and related parameters. Thus, those who supported nuclear disarmament treaties with the former Soviet Union argued that such a policy would be more likely to foster peace, while those who opposed the disarmament treaties argued that a strong and dominant nuclear arsenal was the best guarantor of peace. Similarly, policymakers in Israel differ sharply as to which policies are likely to foster the shared goal of peace and security.

What is striking about the differences among these policymakers in their evaluation of external threats and policy outcomes, and many other examples could be cited, is that they are being enunciated by individuals who are equally knowledgeable and intelligent, and who presumably share the same goal. There are many factors—political, personality, and socioeconomic that are contributing to these differences. Some of these factors are unverbalized and unconscious. In accordance with our overall thesis, that awareness of the factors that influence one's behavior increases the likelihood of more rational, adaptive judgments and actions, policymakers and their advisers need to strive to verbalize and make explicit these possible influences. Such an effort may help to reconcile differences. At the very least, the body politic will have a better understanding of the basis for different policy recommendations.

Social scientists, through research and advocacy, can contribute to the effort to illuminate unverbalized, relatively unconscious factors that affect policymaking. Some factors such as displaced anger may be specific to a particular situation and military policy decision. Others may be broader in scope. For example, views on nuclear armament policy have been shown to be related to values one places on children (Feshbach & Singer, 1986) and to values one places on life (White & Feshbach, 1987). Those who value children because they like them or feel they are important for family intimacy and maintenance tend to be for nuclear arms reduction. In contrast, those who value children instrumentally—because they carry on the family name, keep you company when you're old, contribute to family income, or serve as soldiers, tend to be for nuclear armament. Similar correlations can be anticipated with attitudes toward war inasmuch as there is a substantial correlation ($r = .61$) between attitudes toward nuclear armament and attitudes toward war (Feshbach, 1987). It should be noted that the finding that pro-nuclear-armament attitudes are positively correlated with more militant, hawkish attitudes towards war suggests that the goal of peace is not commonly shared, or that it is thought of differently by pronuclear disarmament and pro-nuclear-armament advocates. In regard to the values placed upon children, feelings about children may relate directly, or indirectly, through other values and ob-

jectives, to the military policies one supports. Policymakers need to make explicit the values and goals, other than military threat, which might conflict with the goal of peace and lead to military actions.

In brief, I am suggesting that unconscious factors may, in many circumstances, play a major role in attitudes and decisions bearing on war and peace. I am not suggesting that policymakers and their advisers be psychoanalyzed in order to bring these unconscious factors into awareness. However, to the extent that social scientists have clarified feelings and motives such as anger, superiority, and masculine assertion; and values such as importance placed on children, on human life, on democracy, on territory, and on national pride that may influence unwillingness or readiness to arm and engage in war, these feelings, motives, and values should be brought into consciousness and enter into the discussion of policies bearing on war and peace. Just as consciousness of the factors that influence our behavior is in the interest of individual mental health, such consciousness is in the interest of our society's health.

REFERENCES

Balay, J., & Shevrin, H. (1988). The subliminal psychodynamics activation method: A critical review. *American Psychologist, 43*, 161–174.

Bornstein, R. F., & Pittman, T. S. (1992). *Perception without awareness*. New York: Guilford.

Bower, G. H. (1981). Mood and memory. *American Psychologist, 36*, 129–148.

Erdelyi, M. H. (1990). Repression, reconstruction and defense: History and integration of the psychoanalytic and experimental frameworks. In J. L. Singer (Ed.), *Repression and dissociation: Implications for personality theory, psychopathology and health*. Chicago: University of Chicago Press.

Feshbach, S. (1963). The effects of emotional restraint upon the projection of positive affect. *Journal of Personality, 31*, 471–481.

Feshbach, S. (1987). Individual aggression, national attachment, and the search for peace: Psychological perspectives. *Aggressive Behavior, 13*, 315–325.

Feshbach, S., & Singer, R. D. (1957). Effects of fear arousal and suppression of fear upon social perception. *Journal of Abnormal and Social Psychology, 55*, 283–288.

Feshbach, S., & Singer, R. D. (1971). *Television and aggression*. San Francisco: Jossey-Bass.

Feshbach, S., & Singer, R. D. (1986, April). *Some values relevant to nuclear armament-disarmament attitudes*. Paper presented at the annual meeting of the Western Psychological Association, Seattle, WA.

Feshbach, S., Stiles, W. B., & Bitter, E. (1967). The reinforcing effect of witnessing aggression. *Journal of Experimental Research in Personality, 2*, 133–139.

Freud, S. (1927). *The ego and the id*. The International Psychoanalytic Library No. 12. London: Hogarth Press.

Greenwald, A. G., & Banaji, M. R. (1995). Implicit social cognition: Attitudes, self-esteem and stereotypes. *Psychological Review*, 102, 4–27.

Greenwald, A. G., Klinger, M. R., & Schuh, E. S. (1995). Activation by marginally perceptible (subliminal) stimuli: Dissociation of unconscious from conscious cognition. *Journal of Experimental Psychology, 124*, 22–42.

Kaufmann, H., & Feshbach, S. (1963). The influence of anti-aggressive communications upon the response to provocation. *Journal of Personality, 31*, 428–444.

Krasner, L. (1958). Studies of the conditioning of verbal behavior. *Psychological Bulletin, 55*, 148–170.

MacKay, D. G. (1987). *The organization of perception and action: A theory for language and other cognitive skills.* New York: Springer-Verlag.

Silverman, L. H., Ross, D., Adler, J., & Lustig, A. (1978). A simple research paradigm for demonstrating subliminal psychodynamic activation. *Journal of Abnormal Psychology, 87*, 341–357.

Singer, J. L. (1990). *Repression and dissociation: Implications for personality theory, psychopathology and health.* Chicago: University of Chicago Press.

Uleman, J. S., & Bargh, J. A. (1989). *Unintended thought.* New York: Guilford.

White, M. J., & Feshbach, S. (1987). Who in Middletown supports a nuclear freeze? *Political Psychology, 8*, 201–209.

Cognitive and Affective, Empirical and Clinical Aspects of Problems of Volition

Lawrence A. Pervin
Rutgers University

In this chapter I consider breakdowns in self-regulation, which I call problems of volition. I consider both clinical and empirical research, emphasize the importance of affect and motivation in personality functioning, and touch upon issues of consciousness, conflict, and defense. Not coincidentally, these are all topics that have been of concern to Singer and to which he has made major contributions (Singer, 1984, 1990; Singer & Bonanno, 1990).

SELF-REGULATION AND THE PROBLEM OF VOLITION

> If we compare the outward symptoms of perversity together, they fall into two groups, in one of which normal actions are impossible, and in the other abnormal ones are irrepressible. Briefly, we may call them respectively the obstructed and explosive will. (James, 1892, p. 436)

In the 1970s I was struggling with issues relevant to the person–situation controversy, seeking a way to understand both stability and change in individual behavior. I monitored daily behavior in participants and emphasized purposive behavior, leading to a theory of goals to account for what I called the stasis and flow of behavior (Pervin, 1983). I described goals in terms of their cognitive and affective components, with the affective component emphasized as central to their motivational power. This emphasis was influenced by Tomkins (1970), and some of my research about the role of affect in drug addiction (Pervin, 1988). Essentially, the theory of goals followed an expectancy-value approach to motivation. That is, it suggested that individuals choose the path of action that has the highest probability (*expectancy*) of attaining the most valued goal or goals (*value*). Shortly thereafter I became interested in what appeared to be violations of such a rational choice model of behavior. In further research, participants described ways of behaving that violated the model (e.g., being overcome with emotion despite every effort to control their emotions) and in my clinical practice I had a number of cases, to be presented herein, that involved patients struggling with behaviors they were unable to control. In other words, despite their judgment of what was best for them and their best intentions, they found themselves engaged in activities that were experienced as beyond their control that seemed to violate a rational choice model of psychological functioning.

It was these observations that led me to become interested in *problems of volition*, that is, the inability to do what one intends or wants to do and the inability to stop oneself from doing what one does not intend or want to do. A problem in volition involves a problem in the implementation of an intention. What I have in mind, for example, is the student or professor who cannot get down to studying or writing a paper, or the person who feels compelled to eat while trying to remain on a diet, or feels compelled to smoke, drink, gamble, steal, have sex, or take drugs. The former I call *problems of inhibition*, the latter *problems of addiction*. They are what James (1892) referred to as problems of obstructed will and explosive will.

The problem of will dates back at least as far as the Greek concern with *akrasia*, the weakness of will, and as noted, was of concern to James (1892). However, under the behaviorist influence, it ceased to be of concern to American psychologists. As the psychologist Meyer reported in 1933, "the 'will' has virtually passed out of our scientific psychology today; the 'emotion' is bound to do the same. In 1950, American psychologists will smile at both these terms as curiosities of the past" (p. 300). Clearly this psychologist was incorrect in his prediction concerning emotion and, I believe, has turned out to be incorrect in his prediction concerning issues of will and purposive behavior as well. At the same time, it is clear that in considering problems of volition, we are entering into a complex area filled with controversy and confusion. The question of a definition and proper understanding of intentional behavior is one that has troubled psychologists (Boden, 1972), philosophers (Anscombe, 1976; Dennett, 1987), and legal theorists for generations. In addition, it involves issues of consciousness: Do volitional and nonvolitional behaviors involve different states of consciousness? Do volitional and nonvolitional activities involve different cognitive processes (e.g., controlled and automatic processes)? Let me suggest that, as noted by Bargh (1989), we should be careful about assuming simple linkages among degrees of consciousness, type of information processing (e.g., automatic vs. controlled), and quality of regulation of behavior (e.g., voluntary vs. involuntary).

In this chapter I want to suggest that problems of volition are common and are of considerable theoretical importance. Before turning to a discussion of the phenomena and alternative explanations for them, let us consider four questions: How common are problems of volition? Why are they of theoretical interest? What are the relevances of cognitive and affective variables to problems of volition? Are different research traditions associated with different points of emphasis and different approaches toward understanding problems of volition?

How Common Are Problems of Volition?

Informal surveys and questionnaire studies suggest that almost every person has a problem of volition of one kind or another. That is, almost every person reports that some aspect of his or her functioning violates what is intended or desired.

Why Are Such Problems of Theoretical Interest?

I believe that problems in volition say something fundamental about what motivates people generally, and that they should not be treated as just mere aberrations. They speak to fundamental deficiencies in some of our current theoretical efforts to understand motivation and action. More generally, volition has been described by Baars (1993) as a foundation problem in psychology and by Gibson (1994) as a hallmark of being human and therefore part of the fundamental agenda for psychology.

What Is the Relation of Cognitive and Affective Variables to Problems of Volition?

Probably all important psychological processes involve elements of both cognition and affect. Thus, we should not be surprised to find both cognitive and affective processes relevant to problems of volition. However, just as the field of psychology has at times witnessed controversy concerning the relation between, and relative importance of, cognition and affect, so too we shall see that explanations of problems of volition vary in their emphases on relations between the two.

What Is the Relation Between Clinical
and Empirical Approaches to Problems of Volition?

Throughout the history of psychology three research traditions have been described—experimental, correlational, and clinical. Psychologists have contrasted pairs of these traditions, often proclaiming the virtues of one over the other (Bindra & Scheier, 1954; Cronbach, 1957; Dashiell, 1939; Hogan, 1982, Kimble, 1984). I have been struck with the tendency for the three traditions to be associated, not only with different methods of observation, but with attention to different kinds of phenomena and with different theoretical approaches as well. For example, in the personality area, it seems to me that the three research traditions are associated with different theoretical orientations (e.g., experimental—social cognitive theory, correlational—trait theory, clinical—psychodynamic theory) and their associated emphases on different phenomena (e.g., social cognitive theory—cognition, trait theory—aggregations of behavior and behavioral dispositions, psychodynamic theory—motivation).[1] It is my belief that each of the traditions has something to contribute to our understanding of problems of volition but that until now members of each tradition have tended to emphasize different observations and contributing factors. More specifically, I want to suggest that members of the correlational and experimental disciplines tend to focus on the healthier and more adaptive aspects of human functioning, those which are volitional and rational as opposed to those which are nonvolitional and seemingly irrational. Thereby, they tend to ignore some very important phenomena relevant to our understanding of basic aspects of motivation and personality functioning generally, the very phenomena that are of interest to the dynamically oriented clinician.

PROBLEMS OF VOLITION:
THE NATURE OF THE PHENOMENA

As indicated, my interest in problems of volition came from my clinical practice. At one point I was seeing a number of patients who were struggling with issues of volition, either unable to get themselves to do things or to stop themselves from doing things, struggling either with problems of inhibition or of addiction. Note that I use the term addiction rather than compulsion because of the more limited association of the latter with mechanical, ritualistic pieces of behavior. Although the term

---

[1]Note that these are tendencies rather than absolute relationships. One can find exceptions within each tradition, and even occasional illustrations of the use of multiple research methods, but I believe that overall these relationships hold.

addiction often is associated with a physiological basis and with withdrawal symptoms, many addictions lack such characteristics and yet retain the quality of craving and loss of sense of voluntary control which are characteristic of the phenomena of interest.[2] Illustrative problems of inhibition include a patient who struggled with the problem of procrastination and lateness and another patient who struggled with the problem of shyness. The first could not get himself to turn his work in on time, the second could not get himself to speak in social situations, although he could communicate well via e-mail—a modern day Cyrano de Bergerac. In therapy the first came late to almost every appointment and the second could not look at me while talking about sexual matters and could not say anything that might be construed as profane. What I want to emphasize is the tremendous struggle experienced by these individuals and the price paid by each because of the difficulty. Anyone who has talked with a student struggling with the problem of procrastination in studying for an exam or in writing a paper, a problem experienced by students with incredible frequency, knows at least to some extent how difficult such problems can be.

Illustrative problems of addiction include a patient who felt compelled to rent pornographic movies despite great shame associated with the activity, a patient who felt compelled to visit prostitutes despite the threat to his marriage and career, and a patient who spent hundreds of dollars calling telephone numbers through which sexual fantasies could be exchanged with an unknown person. Although these three cases involve sexual addictions, obviously such problems in volition are not limited to the sexual realm. People experience cravings for alcohol, nicotine, gambling, food, love, excitement, risk, etc. Regardless of the form of addiction, they typically follow a similar pattern consisting of a building up of tension and focusing of attention on the desired substance or experience, associated with a period of struggle over whether or not to succumb to the irresistible urge, and a satisfying of the craving, followed by some guilt and promises to give up the activity. Often there is some form of denial, either in terms of denial that the addiction exists at all or in terms of the belief that they do have control over the activity. There can exist, then, the seemingly strange combination of the experience of craving and irresistible urge, and the belief that self-control indeed exists.

It is important to emphasize that these are not just little vices that the individuals enjoy. Rather, they are activities filled with excitement, crav-

---

[2]This does not preclude the possibility that all forms of addiction, those associated with a chemical substance (e.g., nicotine, alcohol, cocaine, heroin) as well as those associated with activities (e.g., gambling, sex, shopping) have a common biological basis. Indeed, there is evidence that a common neural basis, located in the amygdala, exists for the craving associated with all addictions (Goleman, 1996, p. C1).

ing, guilt, and shame.[3] Typically, when they become public they lead to profound disruptions in relationships and often to the destruction of careers. Often they reveal a tremendous discrepancy between what Singer (1984) has called the public personality and the private personality. At the same time, it is important to emphasize that in a more modified form these conflicted cravings exist in many people. Thus, for example, it is not unusual for people to report having chocolate or ice cream cravings, to struggle with restraint of their appetites, or to struggle with the urge to "shop until I drop."

At one point I wondered if individuals might have only one or the other kind of problem of volition, inhibition or addiction, obstructed will or explosive will. However, individuals are quite capable of struggling with both. For example, one patient struggled with procrastination and the inability to complete necessary tasks—school papers, letters, the filing of health insurance forms, etc. She would experience tremendous anxiety about not taking care of things, berate herself for being so irresponsible, yet let weeks elapse before completing the task—if it was completed at all. At the same time, she was bulimic and felt compelled to eat foods that she knew were deleterious to her health. Gaining weight and eating certain foods were problematic for her heart condition, yet this was not enough to dissuade her from eating them, like the smoker who cannot quit smoking despite the destructive impact upon the lungs and heart. Vomiting was a way of undoing all of the destructive consequences of eating and there was the usual cycle of commitments to dieting, violation of the commitment through binging, followed by remorse and vomiting, to be followed by binging and the repeat of the cycle.

In these cases there is an intense struggle as the individuals attempt to do what they rationally feel is in their best interests. In each of these cases, rationality and will power are not adequate for the person to follow through on intention. Despite the best of intentions, the task does not get done or the abhorrent act is committed. It is not the case that the person lacks skill or will power. Most of these cases involve individuals who show great ability to tolerate delay of gratification and to regulate behavior in most areas of their lives.

---

[3]A dramatic illustration of such a mixture of emotions can be seen in the case of the mass murderer Danny Starrett (Naifeh & Smith, 1995). Starrett described the craving for the feeling of exhilaration dangerous acts gave him and the conflicting emotions associated with sexual activities: "The guilt I felt was tremendous but it was no match for the strange and wonderful feelings which overwhelmed my innocent mind (p. 88) . . . I cannot begin to describe the mixture of conflicting emotions which raged through my mind at the moment. I felt as if I were teetering on the edge of a precipice (p. 104) . . . I felt guilty and ashamed (p. 106)."

In describing these phenomena, I want to emphasize the tremendous turmoil experienced by the individuals and their subjective experience of lack of control. I do this because some individuals do not believe that they represent true problems of volition. That is, the suggestion has been made that, on a conscious or unconscious level, the individual is doing what he or she wants to do (Shapiro, 1996). I am reminded of a conversation I had with Baumeister, who has written extensively on related phenomena (Baumeister & Heatherton, 1996; Baumeister, Heatherton, & Tice, 1994). He insisted that such cases did not represent true problems of volition because the individuals could overcome their inhibitions or addictions if they truly wanted to. As proof, he suggested a test: If a gun was held to their heads, would they still have a problem of volition? At first I rejected the question as due to an inadequate appreciation of clinical phenomena on the part of one of those ivory tower academics, a social psychologist at that. However, upon further reflection I decided that Baumeister really did have an interesting point, even if I disagreed with his conclusion. It indeed is true that given a gun to the head, the individuals described could overcome their inhibitions and inhibit their addictive behavior. Thus, there is what might be called a gun to the head phenomenon. Given a deadline, most students stop procrastinating and get their papers in, and given sufficient negative consequences, most people are able to curb their addictions.

Consider, for example, the extreme case of the serial killer Ted Bundy. Bundy describes experiencing many of the characteristics associated with addictions: "That whole kind of consciousness was just totally dominant. I mean, the need, the thought, the feeling, the excitement . . . was absolutely paramount. Driving me. I mean, that was coming from some source within me, and yet it was not me. And it was very powerful, very strong, very erratic" (Nelson, 1994, p. 293). Yet, when asked if he could have stopped had a police officer been there, he replied: "Well, I would have . . . yes . . . and I would equate that to a predator having pulled down the prey, is approached by a bigger predator, and runs off. For its own survival. I don't know if that makes sense? The predatory instincts and the survival instincts are still intact" (pp. 294–295). Apparently in the gun to the head situation most people would be able to do what they otherwise seem unable to do, or to inhibit what they otherwise seem compelled to do. On the other hand, in their normal daily lives and in the absence of a force comparable to the gun to the head, they appear unable to act volitionally in an important aspect of their functioning.[4]

---

[4]As noted in an editor's comment by Jefferson Singer, individuals in treatment for addictions often report control over their urges or even freedom from cravings. However, once in their old environment, with its associated cues, or once experiencing a period of stress, the cravings return and relapse is common.

As I said, the phenomena are complex, controversial, and confusing. At the same time, given their frequency and theoretical significance, it is these phenomena that call for our understanding. If my assumption is correct that these represent extreme examples of basic motivational phenomena, then we have an opportunity to consider the fundamental question of how important motives are acquired and how they operate in our daily lives.

ALTERNATIVE EXPLANATIONS FOR PROBLEMS OF VOLITION

How are we to account for problems in volition, problems of inhibition and addiction, and problems of obstructed will and explosive will? Fortunately, commentaries on a recent target article about self-regulation failure by Baumeister and Heatherton (1996) give us the opportunity to consider alternative explanations of leading theorists in the field. In this article the authors suggest that self-regulation is a complex, multifaceted process that can break down in several ways. They emphasize two types of problems, *underregulation* (i.e., failure to exert self-control) due to deficient standards, inadequate monitoring, or inadequate strength to override the responses they wish to control, and *misregulation* (i.e., counterproductive control) due to false assumptions or misdirected efforts. Although no single cause is presented, the authors suggest that "the control of attention is central to self-regulation and loss of attentional control is a decisive precursor of many forms of self-regulation failure" (p. 13). They also reject a model of self-regulatory failure that emphasizes irresistible impulses because it is believed that people will control their behaviors if they have to do so. Although it is difficult to do justice to their view in just a few sentences, I believe it accurate to suggest that it primarily focuses on cognitive processes, particularly in so far as the emphasis is on attentional control. Twenty-one individuals commented on the target article. In general I believe that the following five categories of explanation do justice to the views presented. They also reflect both the different research traditions present in the field and the differing emphases on cognitive and affective variables.

Pavlovian Classical Conditioning

In his commentary Tomie (1996) emphasizes classical conditioning processes, in particular the negative automaintenance phenomenon. Tomie sees such phenomena as related to the problem of the misbehavior of organisms first reported by Breland and Breland (1961). The Brelands were interested in problems in training animals. For example, raccoons were trained to pick up wooden coins and deposit them through a slot into a metal box, then they were rewarded with food. Although things initially went well, with time the raccoons began to misbehave in terms of not letting go of the coins, frequently dipping them into the slot but then taking them out. In the end, instead of depositing the coins, the raccoons chewed, licked, scratched, rubbed, and washed the coins, despite the resulting delay or loss of the food rewards. In the related phenomenon of negative automaintenance, a small object that serves as a discriminative stimulus and is predictive of reward becomes overly valued. A requirement of negative automaintenance phenomena is that the discriminative stimulus or reward cue shares a common spatial locus with the object contacted or manipulated in performing the instrumental response, what is described as a spatial conjunction of cue and manipulandum (CAM). According to Tomie (1996):

> The behavior of animals described in reports of misbehavior and negative automaintenance are especially puzzling and perplexing because the responding is so clearly maladaptive and occurs persistently despite extended training with contingent reinforcement. Were the animal participants able to restrain responding, presumably they would do so, and the training would go according to plan. Rather, responding appears to be uncontrollable and unrestrainable, persistent, and perhaps even wholly refractory to instrumental contingency. Simply put, the animal participants appear unable to quit responding despite themselves. It is as though the making of the response is not subject to voluntary self-control and control of the performance resides outside the realm of the subject's prerogative. (p. 84)

Tomie (1995) has extended the model to an explanation of the rewarding properties of drug-taking implements in cases of drug addiction.

Although not emphasized by Tomie in his commentary, there are two other aspects of classical conditioning that may be relevant to problem of addiction. First, in the phenomenon of superconditioning, an appetitive–aversive interaction can lead to the enhancement of appetitive conditioning (Dickinson & Pearce, 1977). That is, rather than the association of a stimulus with an aversive value interfering with conditioning to the stimulus' appetitive value, in the case of superconditioning, the association of the stimulus with an opposite affective value actually increases conditioning. In summary, the association of a stimulus with negative affect serves to increase the appetitive value of the stimulus rather than to inhibit its appetitive value. In humans, the association of a stimulus or goal with negative affect (e.g., fear, guilt, shame) as well as with positive affect may serve to increase the appetitive value of the stimulus or goal. This may be due to the increased arousal associated with the negative affect or the anticipated reduction in negative affect associated with experiencing the appetitive value of the stimulus.

The second relevant aspect of classical conditioning has to do with generalization and resistance to extinction. According to Bouton (1994), "conditioning seems to generalize well across contexts, but the learning that occurs in extinction does not. Extinction seems especially dependent on the context for retrieval" (p. 51). That is, extinction tends to be specific to context and one cannot necessarily expect it to generalize to other contexts. For example, the addict who has recovered and gained control in one setting may be confronted with the problem of relapse in returning to settings in which the addiction was present, both because the old cues are being reinstated and because the extinction has not generalized to these settings.

Operant Conditioning

Ainslie (1992, 1996) and Logue (1995, 1996) both emphasize operant principles, specifically the discounting principle. According to them, self-control and impulsivity are types of choice behavior that are relevant to nonhumans as well as to humans, and in all cases follow operant principles. Thus, animals prefer larger to smaller rewards, and sooner to later rewards. Because organisms discount the value of later rewards, they disproportionately value imminent rewards. "The simplest explanation for why organisms fail to maximize their expected rewards would be that they discount the value of future rewards" (Ainslie, 1992, p. 56). "This book will contend that impulsiveness is caused by our tendency to discount, or value less, events that are delayed as compared with events that are immediate. A good grade received in 3 months is worth less to a student than is a good grade received immediately" (Logue, 1995, p. 4). Logue (1996) rejects a reliance on hypothetical constructs such as will or volition, emphasizing instead the role of the size of the rewards and the length of delay in all choice behavior (i.e., self-control and impulsiveness choice behavior). Among other alternatives, it is suggested that delay can be increased by making the delayed outcome larger or by decreasing the sensitivity to delay (e.g., by making the time pass more quickly). Included by Logue (1995) in her discussion of problems of self-control are overeating, anorexia, bulimia, drug abuse, gambling, and impulsive sexual behavior.

In common with Tomie, both Ainslie and Logue suggest that the same learning principles apply to all animals and are sufficient to account for cases of self-regulatory failure, at least those involving a failure in delay (i.e., what have been characterized as problems of addiction). There is an emphasis on laboratory research, particularly experimental research involving rodents and pigeons. Cognitive principles, or other principles specifically applicable to humans, are apparently viewed as unnecessary. Problems of self-regulatory failure involving inhibition are not discussed. The approaches differ, however, in focus and learning principles emphasized. Tomie's focus is on the acquisition of reward value by a stimulus (i.e., the CS) while for Ainslie and Logue it is on choices between rewards. In addition, Tomie emphasizes classical conditioning principles, while operant principles are emphasized by Ainslie and Logue. In fact, Ainslie (1992) specifically rejects the need for explanations based on classical conditioning, as well as explanations emphasizing automatic cognitive processes.

Traits

Currently the five-factor model is gaining popularity among trait theorists, to the extent that it is suggested that a consensus has emerged around the Big Five as the fundamental structural units of personality (Digman, 1990). I do not know of a proponent of this model specifically addressing the problem of self-regulatory failure but presumably there would be an emphasis on the traits of Neuroticism (N) and Conscientiousness (C). A few years ago an undergraduate student was interested in this issue and developed a Problems of Volition Questionnaire, scores on which were correlated with scores on N and C as measured both by the NEO-PI-R (Costa & McCrae, 1992) and the Goldberg (1992) adjective scales. Statistically significant correlations (.3 to .4) were found between all four scales and scores on the Problems of Volition Questionnaire. In other words, evidence was found of an association between problems of volition and the traits of Neuroticism and Conscientiousness, with individuals scoring high on problems of volition tending to score high on Neuroticism and low on Conscientiousness. These relationships held for both problems of inhibition and problems of addiction. However, it should be noted that much of these relationships may have to do with similarity of item content. That is, both the volition and trait questionnaires contain items referring to difficulties in doing what is intended or adjectives associated with the lack of such difficulties (e.g., conscientious, efficient, systematic).

A more cognitive trait explanation is offered by Kuhl (1996). Kuhl is one of the few personality psychologists to seriously address the problems under consideration: "Despite the many conceptual confusions and operational problems involved in this research, I am convinced that psychologists will never be able to explain complex phenomena of human behavior without concepts like volition, willpower, self-regulation, and self-control" (Kuhl, 1981, p. 161). He includes both problems of procrastination and problems in delay of gratification under the rubric of self-regulatory failure. Kuhl seeks to decompose self-regulation into its components, attentional control being included among them. In problems of self-regulatory failure there is a *state orientation* as opposed to an *action orientation* (Kuhl, 1992; Kuhl & Beckman, 1994). That is, in problems of volition the person focuses or ruminates about aversive events or states rather than focusing attention on goal-directed activity. It may be inappropriate to include Kuhl within the trait category because of his emphasis on cognitive processes as well as motivational and emotional processes, and because he describes his view as a personality systems interaction theory (Kuhl, 1996). At the same time, in contrast with social–cognitive views, he does speak of state orientation and action orientation as traits.

Cognitive Processes

A wide variety of theorists emphasize the importance of cognitive processes in self-regulatory failure. As noted, both Baumeister and Heatherton (1996) and Kuhl (1996) view the loss of attentional control as basic in many forms of self-regulatory failure. Generally an emphasis on cognitive processes takes two forms. First, there is an emphasis on automatic, routinized cognitive processes as opposed to controlled processes, the former characterized as fast, efficient, and effortless but also as inflexible, the latter characterized as slow, inefficient, and effortful but flexible (Baumeister & Heatherton, 1996; Berkowitz, 1996; Carver & Scheier, 1996). The former often are also seen as less conscious or more unconscious, although as noted previously, no absolute connection between automatic information processing and nonconsciousness can be made. At the same time, as Bargh (1989) notes, automatic cognitive processes have been associated with effects of which a person is unaware and effects that are unintentional, autonomous, and involuntary or uncontrollable. In many cases of self-regulatory failure, then, there is the need for cognitive processes to be brought under executive or supervisory control.[5]

Second, cognitive explanations of self-regulatory failure may focus on problems of attentional focus. In addition to the previous examples, Mischel (1990) emphasizes the importance of attentional focus in problems of delay of gratification. "Persons can sustain delay most effectively for the sake of preferred but delayed gratifications, if during the delay period they shift attention away from these gratifications, occupying themselves with cognitive distractions" (p. 122). According to Mischel, children competent in delay of gratification situations are able to shift from hot to cold cognitions. Bandura (1986) emphasizes as well the ability to focus attention on distal goals, or at least on proximal goals related to distal goals.

---

[5]Tiffany (1990) offers a cognitive model of drug urges and drug-use behavior that emphasizes the role of automatized action schemata. However, the model also emphasizes the role of classical conditioning and offers many useful references in this regard. In addition, as will be seen, the model recognizes the importance of both positive and negative affect in drug-taking behavior and relapse.

The emphasis on cognitive processes clearly is distinct from the three forms of explanation previously considered. First, it can be contrasted with the classical conditioning and operant conditioning explanations that focus on noncognitive processes common to all animals. The contrast is even greater when one considers the role of low self-efficacy beliefs and inadequate or excessive standards emphasized by social cognitive theorists such as Bandura (1986, 1989). Second, the problems of self-regulatory failure are viewed as context-specific rather than as generalized, trait-like qualities.

It seems to me that an emphasis on cognitive processes clearly is appropriate in terms of the phenomena being considered. That is, problems of volition clearly involve problems in attentional focus, either in terms of the person being unable to focus his or her attention on what he or she wants to achieve, as in problems of inhibition, or the person being unable to divert attention from what compels attention, as in problems of addiction. At the same time, four points are in order. First, the emphasis on attentional focus is more descriptive than explanatory. People experiencing problems of volition have difficulties with focusing their attention on what they seek to do, but that is the very nature of the problem rather than an explanation of the problem. Why is it so difficult to focus on the task in problems of avoidance and procrastination, and why is it so difficult to turn one's attention away from cravings or urges in problems of addiction? Second, purely cognitive explanations fail to take into consideration what Wegner (1992, 1994) describes as problems in the suppression of unwanted thoughts. Thus, Wegner suggests that efforts at attentional control (e.g., thought suppression) often have unintentional, undesired effects, namely the effects of making the thoughts to be controlled more frequent and arousing. In other words, the person struggling to keep his or her mind off what is craved may, by the very process of efforts at thought suppression, have the ironic effect of making thoughts of what is craved more frequent and even more exciting. Anyone who has attempted to stay on a diet by keeping his or her mind off of food, or to stay away from sexual activity by putting it out of mind, is familiar with what Wegner describes as the unintended effects of efforts at thought suppression.

Third, problems of volition, in particular problems of addiction, appear to be fundamentally different from the problem of delay of gratification, which often is used as illustrative of problems of this type. In the delay of gratification situation there is a choice between a smaller reward now and a larger reward later. In problems of volition there appears to be more of a conflict between reward and punishment. In the case of inhibition, there is the immediate reward of relief from doing an undesired, unpleasant task (e.g., study for an exam, write a paper, pay bills) and the reward of engaging in a more pleasurable activity (e.g., watch TV, party) as opposed to the distant anticipated punishment (e.g., more time pressure, poorer performance). The potential distant rewards of a high grade and pride in accomplishment seem improbable, if recognized at all. In the case of addiction, there is the perceived very large immediate reward (e.g., satisfy the cravings or urges) as opposed to the distant anticipated punishment (e.g., guilt, shame, legal punishment). In other words, rather than a choice between a small reward now and a large reward later, problems of volition seem to involve the choice of a reward now viewed as quite large in the case of addictions, despite the threat of punishment later. People with problems of volition appear to follow the principle of take the reward or pleasure now and worry about the future punishment later. Note that this is not necessarily what they would rationally say or state as their intention, but rather seems to fit their behavior, and at times even seems to fit their thought processes.

This brings us to the final point, which is that purely cognitive explanations tend to leave out the element of denial or self-deception. In emphasizing the immediate reward, individuals with problems of volition tend to minimize the risk of later punishment. They do this either by kidding themselves into believing that they have volitional control (e.g., "I'll get to work on studying tomorrow," "I'll stop drinking tomorrow," "I'll just gamble until I get even") or by self-deceptively minimizing the punishment (e.g., "No one will find out," "Because this is the last time, I will not need to feel guilty or ashamed"). Gilovich (1991), in a study of the thoughts of bettors during football games, describes how gamblers explain away their losses by making undoing statements, such as losses were due to bad luck or to a fluke.

I believe that at the root of the difficulties of purely cognitive explanations is the neglect of the role of affect, both in terms of the role of anxiety in problems of inhibition and also that of pleasure or positive arousal in the case of addictions. In addition, considerable research suggests that escape from negative affect plays an important role in addictive behavior (Brandon, 1994; Tiffany, 1990). In my own research about drug-taking behavior it was clear that addicts take drugs as a means of escape from negative affects such as anxiety and depression, and that they have preferred drugs of abuse in this regard (Pervin, 1988).

A Psychodynamic-Systems Explanation

I will now offer some tentative proposals for a psychodynamic-systems explanation for problems of volition. By a psychodynamic-systems view, I mean one that emphasizes the interplay among motives or forces, some of which may be conscious and others unconscious (Pervin, 1989b). Affect is viewed as the major basis for motives (Pervin, 1983; Tomkins, 1970). Finally, there is an emphasis on psychodynamic principles of conflict and defense. Although clearly related to psychoanalytic theory, the view does not include an emphasis on all of the elements of traditional Freudian psychoanalytic theory, nor is it limited to psychoanalytic principles. For example, it draws on learning theory and research, in particular on classical conditioning, and on recent research in neuroscience. However, as is true for psychoanalytic theory, it takes as its root the observations of clinical phenomena and emphasizes the interplay among motives in psychological functioning. In offering this explanation I will draw on the clinical phenomena previously described and the relevant experimental literature. Discussion will focus on two main points. First, problems of volition involve the interplay among multiple goals that are in conflict with one another. Second, the primary explanatory task is to account for the strong affect, negative in cases of inhibition and positive in the case of addiction, that is associated with goals involved in problems of volition.

I will give only brief consideration to problems of inhibition because it is the problems of addiction that I consider to be more challenging and of far greater theoretical interest. Why is it that a person is not able to implement a decision to pursue a goal—the problem of inhibition? In my experience all such problems of volition involve anxiety associated with pursuit of the intended goal and it is this anxiety that leads to procrastination and inhibition. To return to the two clinical cases discussed previously, the individuals find value in their intended goals, in the first case in completing work and in the second case in speaking with others. Also, they have the requisite skills, but in both cases there is considerable anxiety associated with potential failure in relation to pursuit of the goal. In both cases there has been past experience of a strict standard and harsh criticism for less than expected performance in related tasks.

In Bandura's terms, there are high standards and low self-efficacy beliefs. However, although accurate, an explanation strictly in terms of self-efficacy beliefs fails to do justice to the conflicting goals and the affects associated with them. As one considers individual cases in detail, one generally finds additional goals and conflicts. For example, the patient who could not turn work in on time also viewed this as an opportunity for rebellion and defiance against parents who insisted on his being on time, but who often kept him waiting. In addition, one can consider the affects involved with alternative activities. These too generally involve conflict, if for no other reason than that they are substitutes for doing what the person otherwise intends to do and feels he or she should do. Thus, for example, reading or watching television has positive affective value, but there is anxiety associated with not working on the paper. In the second case, communicating electronically has positive affective value and avoids the potential for exposure and humiliation that is possible in interpersonal communication. However, there also is negative affect associated with it because the sender is left lonely and with low self-esteem due to inability to participate in conversation with others.

In summary, what is being suggested is, that in problems of inhibition, there is anxiety associated with following through on intention. The problem is not that the goal (e.g., get the work done, be more sociable) lacks sufficient value, but rather that there is low expectancy for success, high negative affect associated with failure, and both positive affect and high probability of success associated with the pursuit of other activities. One might say, don't most of us experience some anxiety, perhaps a great deal of anxiety, in the pursuit of goals, in following through on intention? What is it, then, that differentiates the person with the problem of volition from the person without such a problem? Why is it that my friend ceases to write once he experiences anxiety, whereas I am able to get past my initial anxiety and procrastination and go on to write a paper?

This, of course, is always a difficult question, just as it is to account for why a single individual has the problem in one area but not another, or at one time but not another. My sense is that in all cases a balance of forces is involved. There is the benefit–cost analysis of following through on the intention as well as that of pursuing alternative activities. There is not only a perceived cost–benefit outcome associated with pursuing the intended goal, but also a perceived cost–benefit outcome associated with not pursuing the goal or with pursuing alternative goals. For some, the threat associated with not trying, with not writing the paper or turning the work in on time, is so great that it overrides that associated with potential failure—better to try and fail than to not try at all. What is being suggested, in other words, is that problems of inhibition have an apparently irrational aspect to them because they violate the intentions of the person. However, they do not violate an expectancy-value or subjective expected-utility model when the multiple goals and associated affects of the relevant activities are considered.

Do similar forces enter into cases of addiction? Do such problems of volition fit an expectancy-value model? What is it that gives the unintended act its compelling quality? What is suggested here is that these acts have a strong positive affect associated with them. In addition, two further factors contribute to their compelling quality. First, the association of tension in the form of anxiety or guilt increases arousal and thereby intensifies the positive affect associated with the activity. For example, in the patients described, there is positive affect associated with viewing the pornographic movies or meeting with prostitutes. The guilt and anxiety associated with these activities intensifies the associated arousal and anticipated pleasure. In addition, efforts to suppress the activity serve to intensify rather than to reduce the urge to engage in what is forbidden and unintended.

Two previously discussed processes are being suggested. First, positive affect associated with a goal is intensified by negative affect that also is associated with the goal. In other words, as in superconditioning, an amplification of positive affect rather than an interference with or diminution of positive affect takes place. In cases of addiction there is a strong positive value associated with the goal, probably established on the basis of classical conditioning. In addition, there is the association of negative affect (e.g., fear, guilt, shame) which serves to increase the appetitive value of the goal. The second process, described by Wegner (1992, 1994), involves the intensification of affective arousal by the effort to suppress thinking about or engaging in the activity. In other words, in attempting to suppress thoughts and cravings associated with addictions, individuals find themselves obsessing more about what is craved, and the urges become increasingly exciting and powerful. Tiffany (1990) also suggests that cognitive control processes, often stimulated by negative affect, may interfere with other control (nonautomatic) processes directed at the task of drug abstinence.

Why are such addictions so difficult to give up? Classical conditioning research may suggest some answers. Classically conditioned affective responses can be particularly difficult to extinguish because they are controlled by more automatic levels of information processing (Ohman & Soares, 1993). In addition, context can be particularly important. Bouton (1994) reports that, in what he calls the *renewal effect*, conditioning that occurs in one context, followed by extinction in a different context, need not result in extinction of the conditioning in the original context. Following extinction in the second context, a return to the original conditioning context can lead to a strong recovery even after prolonged extinction. This renewal effect can be caused by a difference in physical context or a change in state. Thus, fear conditioned in one state, and then extinguished in the context of alcohol or tranquilizers, can be renewed when there is a return to the alcohol-free or tranquilizer-free state. As noted earlier, conditioning appears to generalize across contexts, while extinction appears to be context specific. Such effects present obvious problems for efforts at therapeutic change. "Because extinction and counterconditioning are not necessarily the result of unlearning, there is always a potential for relapse that may come about after clinical treatment" (Bouton, 1994, p. 52).

SUMMARY AND CONCLUSIONS

In this chapter, I have attempted to do a number of things. First, I have suggested that problems of volition, what James called problems of obstructed will and explosive will, and what I have called problems of inhibition and addiction, are common and of considerable theoretical significance. In particular, I believe that problems of volition force us to address fundamental motivational issues concerning the acquisition of goals. Although goals have become a popular concept in the fields of personality and social psychology (Bargh & Gollwitzer, 1996; Pervin, 1989a), the issue of how goals or motives are acquired has remained largely neglected. Second, I have suggested that three disciplines exist in personality that are associated with different theoretical perspectives and research procedures. In terms of problems of volition, the clinical approach is associated with an emphasis on the experiences of individuals as they struggle with competing feelings, urges, cravings, and discrepancies between what they intend to do and what they find themselves doing. The correlational approach is associated with an emphasis on traits associated with problems of volition, specifically the traits of neuroticism and conscientiousness. The experimental approach is associated with an emphasis on classical and operant conditioning processes common to all animals. Following the cognitive revolution, this approach is associated with an emphasis on cognitive processes, in particular on problems of attentional focus and control. Although not an absolute linkage, I believe these are associations between research method and theoretical explanation that generally hold. Although additional factors can be described in relation to problems of volition, they cover the major explanations offered in terms of problems of addiction or self-regulatory failure.[6]

My own view is that the clinical approach offers insight into important aspects of human experience. The clinical approach, and associated clinical theories, most emphasize a dynamic perspective wherein complex behaviors are seen as resulting from the interplay among motives, some of which may be in conflict with one another and many of which are not available to conscious self-report. At the same time, clearly the psychodynamic-systems view presented draws from other approaches as well, in particular emphasizing basic principles of learning established through experimental procedures. In summary, my sense is that the phenomena being considered, like the vast majority of phenomena of interest to personality psychologists, require the insights offered by multiple approaches if we are to make any progress in scientific understanding. I view the clinical approach as central to bringing important phenomena to our attention, and as essential to keeping explanations relevant to phenomenological experience. I view the correlational approach as useful in establishing links between the phenomena of interest and basic per-

---

[6]Illustrative additional factors are the self-handicapping strategy described by Polivy (1996) and a genetically based reward-deficiency syndrome common to all addictions (Blum, Cull, Braverman, & Comings, 1996).

sonality units, in particular those for which there seem to be some genetic base. Finally, I view the experimental approach as central to establishing causal processes.

Problems of volition cannot escape the attention of anyone working with individuals with a broad array of psychological problems. From a psychodynamic-clinical perspective, problems of volition can be seen as involving the interplay among goals, in particular the interplay among goals in conflict with one another, goals that often are associated with strong affect. Although the emphasis on conflict is not unique to this perspective (e.g., Emmons, King, & Sheldon, 1993; Kuhl, 1992), it is fundamental to it.[7] From this perspective, problems of volition do not violate expectancy-value theory, but instead require an explication of why the relevant goals have the expectancies and values they do. In particular, what is needed is explication of why problems of inhibition are associated with insufficient expectancy or value to lead to the enactment of intention, and why problems of addiction are associated with such enormous value that action occurs despite intentions to the contrary.

The gun to the head phenomenon does not negate the importance of such affective, motivational variables. Rather, it emphasizes the importance of understanding the power of these variables. In other words, the gun to the head phenomenon does not mean that motive conflict is irrelevant or that there is not a problem of volition, but rather that the gun has created a sufficient shift in the balance of forces so that action in accord with intention is possible. And, while cognitive processes can be seen to play a major role in problems of volition, recognition of these processes should not preclude attention to the role of affects in the development and operation of powerful motives.

ACKNOWLEDGMENT

Portions of this chapter are adapted from Pervin (1991, 1996).

REFERENCES

Ainslie, G. (1992). *Picoeconomics*. New York: Cambridge University Press.
Ainslie, G. (1996). Studying self-regulation the hard way. *Psychological Inquiry, 7,* 16–20.

---

[7]Recent contributions to the goals literature emphasize the importance of approach and avoidance motives, both in terms of individual differences in focus and the balance between the two types of motives within each individual (Elliot & Sheldon, 1997; Elliot, Sheldon, & Church, 1997; Roney, Higgins, & Shah, 1995). Such research may be relevant to the proposed focus on the importance of conflicting motives in problems of volition.

Anscombe, G. E. M. (1976). *Intention.* Ithaca, NY: Cornell University Press.

Baars, B. J. (1993). Why volition is a foundation problem for psychology. *Consciousness and Cognition, 2,* 281–309.

Bandura, A. (1986). *Social foundations of thought and action: A social cognitive theory.* Englewood Cliffs, NJ: Prentice-Hall.

Bandura, A. (1989). Self-regulation of motivation and action through internal standards and goal systems. In L. A. Pervin (Ed.), *Goal concepts in personality and social psychology* (pp. 19–85). Hillsdale, NJ: Lawrence Erlbaum Associates.

Bandura, A. (1996). Failures in self-regulation: Energy depletion or selective disengagement. *Psychological Inquiry, 7,* 20–24.

Bargh, J. A. (1989). Conditional automaticity: Varieties of automatic influence in social perception and cognition. In J. S. Uleman & J. A. Bargh (Eds.), *Unintended thought* (pp. 3–51). New York: Guilford.

Bargh, J. A., & Gollwitzer, P. M. (Eds.). (1996). *The psychology of action.* New York: Guilford.

Baumeister, R. F., & Heatherton, T. F. (1996). Self-regulation failure: A review. *Psychological Inquiry, 7,* 1–15.

Baumeister, R. F., Heatherton, T. F., & Tice, D. M. (1994). *Losing control: How and why people fail at self-regulation.* San Diego, CA: Academic Press.

Berkowitz, L. (1996). Too sweeping and too narrow? *Psychological Inquiry, 7,* 25–28.

Bindra, D., & Scheier, I. H. (1954). The relation between psychometric and experimental research in psychology. *American Psychologist, 9,* 69–71.

Blum, K., Cull, J. G., Braverman, E. R., & Comings, D. E. (1996). Reward deficiency syndrome. *American Scientist, 84,* 132–145.

Boden, M. A. (1972). *Purposive explanation in psychology.* Cambridge, MA: Harvard University Press.

Bouton, M. E. (1994). Context, ambiguity, and classical conditioning. *Current Directions in Psychological Science, 3,* 49–53.

Brandon, T. H. (1994). Negative affect as motivation to smoke. *Current Directions in Psychological Science, 3,* 33–37.

Breland, K., & Breland, M. (1961). The misbehavior of organisms. *American Psychologist, 16,* 681–683.

Carver, C. S., & Scheier, M. F. (1996). Self-regulation and its failures. *Psychological Inquiry, 7,* 32–40.

Costa, P. T., Jr., & McCrae, R. R. (1992). *NEO-PI-R: Professional Manual.* Odessa, Fl: Psychological Assessment Resources.

Cronbach, L. J. (1957). The two disciplines of scientific psychology. *American Psychologist, 12,* 671–684.

Dashiell, J. F. (1939). Some rapprochements in contemporary psychology. *Psychological Bulletin, 36,* 1–24.

Dennett, D. C. (1987). *The intentional stance.* Cambridge, MA: MIT Press.

Dickinson, A., & Pearce, J. M. (1977). Inhibitory interactions between appetitive and aversive stimuli. *Psychological Bulletin, 84,* 690–711.

Digman, J. M. (1990). Personality structure: Emergence of the five-factor model. *Annual Review of Psychology, 41,* 417–440.

Elliot, A. J., & Sheldon, K. M. (1997). Avoidance achievement motivation: A personal goals analysis. *Journal of Personality and Social Psychology, 73,* 171–185.

Elliot, A. J., Sheldon, K. M., & Church, M. A. (1997). Avoidance personal goals and subjective well-being. *Personality and Social Psychology Bulletin, 23,* 915–927.

Emmons, R. A., King, L. A., & Sheldon, K. (1993). Goal conflict and the self-regulation of action. In D. W. Wegner & J. W. Pennebaker (Eds.), *Handbook of mental control* (pp. 528–551), Englewood Cliffs, NJ: Prentice-Hall.

Gibson, E. J. (1994). Has psychology a future? *Psychological Science, 5,* 69–76.

Gilovich, T. (1991). *How we know what isn't so: The fallibility of human reason in everyday life.* New York: The Free Press.

Goldberg, L. R. (1992). The development of markers for the Big-Five factor structure. *Psychological Assessment, 4,* 26–42.

Goleman, D. (1996, August 13). Brain images of addiction in action show neural basis. *New York Times,* pp. C1, C3.

Hogan, R. (1982). On adding apples and oranges in personality psychology. *Contemporary psychology, 27,* 851–852.

James, W. (1892). *Psychology: A briefer course.* New York: Holt.

Kimble, G. A. (1984). Psychology's two cultures. *American Psychologist, 39,* 833–839.

Kuhl, J. (1981). Motivational and functional helplessness: The moderating effect of state versus action orientation. *Journal of Personality and Social Psychology, 40,* 155–170.

Kuhl, J. (1992). A theory of self-regulation: Action versus state orientation, self-discrimination, and some applications. *Journal of Applied Psychology, 41,* 95–173.

Kuhl, J. (1996). Who controls whom when "I control myself"? *Psychological Inquiry, 7,* 61–68.

Kuhl, J., & Beckman, J. (1994). *Volition and personality: Action versus state orientation.* Seattle, WA: Hogrefe.

Logue, A. W. (1995). *The psychology of eating and drinking: An introduction.* New York: Freeman.

Logue, A. W. (1996). Self-control: An alternative self-regulation framework applicable to human and nonhuman behavior. *Psychological Inquiry, 7,* 68–71.

Meyer, M. F. (1933). That whale among the fishes—the theory of emotion. *Psychological Review, 40,* 292–300.

Mischel, W. (1990). Personality dispositions revisited and revised: A view after three decades. In L. A. Pervin (Ed.), *Handbook of personality: Theory and research* (pp. 111–134). New York: Guilford.

Naifeh, S., & Smith, G. W. (1995). *A stranger in the family.* New York: Dutton.

Nelson, P. (1994). *Defending the devil: My story as Ted Bundy's last lawyer.* New York: Morrow.

Ohman, A., & Soares, J. J. F. (1993). On the automaticity of phobic fear: Conditioned skin conductance responses to masked phobic stimuli. *Journal of Abnormal Psychology, 102,* 121–132.

Pervin, L. A. (1983). The stasis and flow of behavior: Toward a theory of goals. In M. M. Page (Ed.), *Personality: Current theory and research* (pp. 1–53). Lincoln: University of Nebraska Press.

Pervin, L. A. (1988). Affect and addiction. *Addictive behaviors, 13,* 83–86.

Pervin, L. A. (Ed.). (1989a). *Goal concepts in personality and social psychology.* Hillsdale, NJ: Lawrence Erlbaum Associates.

Pervin, L. A. (1989b). Psychodynamic-systems reflections on a social intelligence model of personality. *Advances in Social Cognition, 2,* 153–161.

Pervin, L. A. (1991). Goals, plans, and problems in the self-regulation of behavior: The question of volition. In P. R. Pintrich & M. L. Maehr (Eds.), *Advances in motivation and achievement* (pp. 1–20). Greenwich, CT: JAI.

Pervin, L. A. (1996). Does it take a gun to the head to assess problems of volition? *Psychological Inquiry, 7,* 72–73.

Polivy, J. (1996). Self-regulation failure: Can failure be successful? *Psychological Inquiry, 7,* 74–76.

Roney, C., Higgins, E. T., & Shah, J. (1995). Goals and framing: How outcome focus influences motivation and emotion. *Personality and Social Psychology Bulletin, 21,* 1151–1160.

Shapiro, D. (1996). The "self-control" muddle. *Psychological Inquiry, 7,* 76–79.

Singer, J. L. (1984). *The human personality.* New York: Harcourt, Brace.

Singer, J. L. (Ed). (1990). *Repression and dissociation.* Chicago: University of Chicago Press.

Singer, J. L., & Bonanno, G. A. (1990). Personality and private experience. In L. A. Pervin (Ed.), *Handbook of personality: Theory and research* (pp. 419–464). New York: Guilford.

Tiffany, S. T. (1990). A cognitive model of drug urges and drug-use behavior: Role of automatic and nonautomatic processes. *Psychological Review, 97,* 147–168.

Tomie, A. (1995). CM: An animal learning model of excessive and compulsive implement-assisted drug-taking behavior in humans. *Clinical Psychology Review, 15,* 145–167.

Tomie, A. (1996). Self-regulation and animal behavior. *Psychological Inquiry, 7,* 83–85.

Tomkins, S. S. (1970). Affects are the primary motivational system. In M. B. Arnold (Ed.), *Feelings and emotions: The Loyola symposium* (pp. 101–110). New York: Academic Press.

Wegner, D. M. (1992). You can't always think what you want: Problems in the suppression of unwanted thoughts. *Advances in Experimental Social Psychology, 25,* 193–225.

Wegner, D. M. (1994). Ironic processes of mental control. *Psychological Review, 101,* 34–52.

CONSCIOUSNESS AND PERSONALITY IN CONTEXT

Emotional Dissociation, Self-Deception, and Psychotherapy

George A. Bonanno
Hoorie I. Siddique
The Catholic University of America

> *When confronted with a series of unpleasant situations, the more extroverted or outgoing individual may simply shift attention rapidly around the room or towards different persons, with the result that there is little opportunity for the critical distressing imagery to reverberate long enough in the short-term memory system to be stored.*
> —Jerome L. Singer, *The Inner World of Daydreaming* (1966, p. 99)

As this quotation suggests, in this chapter we examine the dispositional or stylistic propensity to shift attention away from undesirable or unpleasant emotions, as well as the possible consequences such a style may hold for mental health and psychotherapy. Taking inspiration from Singer's lifelong devotion to the integration of clinical theory and basic experimental research, we begin by reviewing the historical progression of ideas inherent in the concepts of hysteria, repression and dissociation, and cognitive style. We then consider Bonanno and Singer's (1990) integration of various experimental and theoretical literatures in terms of the dialectic tension between the focus of attention inwardly, toward the self and private experience, versus the focus of attention outwardly, away from the self and toward other people and the external nonself-environment or field. We next consider the operational definitions of health and well-being in terms of the capacity to engage flexibly in both poles of this dialectic, and in the context of this definition, we review recent empirical findings about emotional dissociation, the repressive personality style, and self-deceptive enhancement. We then review some of our own recent

research illustrating the apparent adaptive functions of emotional dissociation and self-deception in the specific context of midlife conjugal bereavement. Finally, we discuss the implications these ideas may hold for
the psychotherapeutic process.

A BRIEF HISTORICAL REVIEW

The constellation of behaviors and experiences related to emotional dissociation and the reduced awareness of private experience can be traced
to the earliest observations of what eventually would become known as
hysteria. As far back as the 16th century B.C.E., medical texts had described
hysterical syndromes in terms of characteristic emotional difficulties, somatic complaints, and mysterious paralyses (Veith, 1965). By the 19th
century C.E., hysterical symptoms were generally thought to stem from a
dispositional weakness or failure of the nervous system (Jones, 1867),
primarily found among women (Carter, 1853). As the century progressed,
Benedikt in 1868 (as cited in Ellenberger, 1993) and later Charcot challenged these assumptions by demonstrating hysterical symptoms in hypnotized males and by linking these symptoms to hidden or dissociated
traumas or to secret experiences (Ellenberger, 1970).

Near the end of the 19th century, Janet (1889, 1893/1901) published
his groundbreaking conception of hysteria in terms of a subconscious *idée
fixe*, or fixed idea: an automated, organized pattern of thought, emotion,
and movement that represented dissociated aspects of the personality.
Janet chose the term subconscious to heighten the distinction between his
views and popular conceptions that circulated at the time of an inner,
mystical unconscious linked to 19th-century Romanticism (Hilgard, 1977).
Janet provided one of the first descriptions of individual differences in
attention and cognitive style, concluding that hysterical patients suffered
from a lack of psychological strength, an incapacity and superficiality of
attention, and a general narrowing or retraction of the field of consciousness. Janet also anticipated later dialectic models of attentional style by
contrasting the dissociative, superficial processing style of hysteria with
the more conscious, deliberate, and fixed ideas of obsessional disorders.
These observations were soon extended in James' (1890) popular and
remarkably integrative writings about the stream of consciousness. Although James was much taken with Janet's clinical descriptions, he nonetheless suggested a broader view of dissociation based on the ongoing
nature of conscious experience. In particular, James pointed to the normative, everyday dissociations that were unavoidably linked to the hierarchical structure of personality, as well as to the discontinuities of memory that tend to result from multiple social selves.

The advances by Janet, James, and others that soon followed (cf. Prince, 1906) clearly set the foundation for contemporary theories of consciousness and dissociation, and for many of the constructs that guide contemporary approaches to psychotherapy, such as schematic organization and automatic thoughts. For example, Janet (1889) proposed that it was not necessary for a patient to gain awareness of antecedent traumatic events, or for that matter of subconscious fixed ideas. Rather, a previously dysfunctional cognitive pattern could be altered simply by substitution—replacing a subconscious fixed idea with a more appropriate or more functionally workable construct—whether the patient was aware of this process or not.

The seminal and far-reaching implications of Janet's concepts brought him instant international fame (Ellenberger, 1970). Yet, somewhat remarkably, within just a few short years, these ideas were replaced by alternative, and in the long run perhaps less useful, perspectives about human functioning. The legitimacy of psychological inquiry into the nature of consciousness was first undermined by the obvious failure of the introspectionist approach to experimentation (Hothersall, 1995). The consciousness perspective was soon challenged with greater force by the call within academic psychology for a purely behavioral approach. However, even before the end of the 19th century, the displacement of a consciousness perspective was already evident in the rapid increase in popularity of Freud's inaugural psychoanalytic theorizing. In contrast to Janet's (1889) fluid descriptions of dissociated, fixed ideas that were available but "probably" occurred "below conscious awareness" (p. 438) and James' (1890) speculations about the transient dissociation of aspects of the self, Breuer and Freud (1895/1955) described repressed unconscious contents that were under normal circumstances completely unavailable to conscious awareness. Further, whereas Janet had minimized the role of sexual dynamics in hysterical cognition, Freud (1896/1962, 1898/1962) explicitly distanced himself from Janet by revisiting Benedikt's earlier suggestion that hysterical symptoms were the result of premature sexual stimulation during childhood. In the ensuing years, Freud moved rapidly away from the specific consideration of hysteric individuals to the sweeping conclusion that virtually all psychological and many physical symptoms could be traced to repressed sexual conflicts stemming from early childhood. In contrast to Janet's cautious statements about nonconscious processing, Freud (1917/1966) viewed his patient's symptoms as "the plainest indication of there being a special region of the mind, shut off from the rest . . . the unconscious in the mind" (p. 278).

Although Freud's many and far-ranging contributions to psychology can hardly be disputed, his insistence on the crucial importance of repressed memories ultimately appears to be of dubious merit (Bonanno,

1995; Bonanno & Keuler, 1998; Reviere, 1996; van der Hart & Nijenhuis, 1995). More to the point, Freud's theorizing shifted the focus of psycho-therapy away from the content or structure of subconscious fixed ideas, and from the nascent concepts of attention and cognitive style, toward an etiological search for repressed trauma and developmental fixation. Almost from the beginning, Freud's followers revolted against this trend. As a primary example, Jung (1971) introduced the concept of an atten-tional dialectic into psychoanalytic discourse with his seminal theorizing about the introversion–extraversion dimension. Jung's concepts were par-ticularly noteworthy for their emphasis on the tension between opposing poles of attention and experience. In a related manner, Horney (1939) broadened the psychoanalytic concept of character style, and recognized that "the connection between later peculiarities and earlier experiences is more complicated than Freud assumed: there is no such thing as an isolated repetition of isolated experiences; but the entirety of infantile experiences combines to form a certain character structure" (p. 9). Horney (1945) also extended Jung's dialectic approach, proposing that neurotic conflicts result from desires that "go in opposite directions" (p. 38). In Horney's view, the helplessness and isolation experienced during child-hood results in basic anxiety. The major dimensions of character structure grow out of the child's strategic attempts to cope with basic anxiety by either embracing, or rejecting and attacking, the interpersonal world. Finally, psychoanalytic discourse was firmly refocused from its original emphasis on the repression of childhood experiences toward enduring, stylistic habits of attention and consciousness with Shapiro's (1965) im-portant contribution to the literature about cognitive and defensive or neurotic styles.

> From our point of view, the neurotic person is no longer merely a victim of historical events . . . his way of thinking and his attitudes—his style, in other words—having also been formed by that history, are now integral parts of that neurotic functioning and move him to think, feel, and act in ways that are indispensable to it. (p. 21).

Interestingly, although Janet had been generally dismissed by this time as a mere precursor to Freud (cf. Woodworth, 1948, p. 160), Shapiro revealed an unmistakable debt to Janet in his suggestion that "hysterical cognition in general is global, relatively diffuse, and lacking in sharpness, particularly in sharp detail. In a word, it is *impressionistic*" (p. 111).

At this same time, experimental psychology was moving toward its so-called cognitive revolution and with it came a revitalized interest in normative processes related to a continuum of attentional foci. Singer and his colleagues extended the cognitive perspective into the clinical domain, while pioneering new methods for the empirical investigation of consciousness, private experience, and individual differences in imaginal processes (Antrobus & Singer, 1964; Huba, Aneshensel, & Singer, 1981; Klos & Singer, 1981; Singer, 1966, 1984; Singer & Pope, 1981). Witkin and his colleagues (Witkin, 1965; Witkin & Goodenough, 1981) extended the basic dialectic approach suggested in Jung's concept of introversion–extraversion in their extensive research program about field dependence–independence, or the dispositional propensity to attend to cues from the external environment or field versus the propensity to focus attention inwardly, independent of the field. This same attentional dialectic eventually manifested in research about self-focused attention and its dispositional manifestation in the continuum from high to low self-consciousness (Fenigstein, Scheier, & Buss, 1975).

THE DIALECTIC APPROACH TO HEALTH

Bonanno and Singer attempted to integrate these various theoretical and empirical observations in an encompassing model of attention, personality, and psychopathology (Bonanno & Singer, 1990, 1993; Singer & Bonanno, 1990). This approach was motivated in part by the apparent similarities between the basic internal–external attentional dialectic and Bakan's (1966) influential description of the tension, fundamental in all living things, between *agency*, the individuation and experience of the self, and *communion*, the minimization of the self through relatedness and affiliation with others. The dialectic nature of these overlapping attentional and motivational dimensions suggests their importance in the regulation of emotion and consciousness. Bonanno and Singer (1993) proposed that the internal, agentic aspects of the dialectic were characteristic of a more general type of reflective cognition while the external, communal aspects were characteristic of a more general type of perceptual cognition. Also, although both poles of the dialectic were assumed to represent different features of human experience, its was also assumed that individual differences would emerge in a dispositional propensity to favor one pole of experience over the other. Thus, the unique features of each pole of the dialectic may be associated with traitlike personality characteristics or, in extreme cases, different types of psychopathology. Personality manifestations were evidenced partly by the dispositional nature of the attentional construct (Lewis, 1976; Witkin & Goodenough, 1981) and partly in a related dimension of repressiveness versus sensitization in response to distress (Byrne, Barry, & Nelson, 1963). The psychopathological manifestations linked to these dimensions were apparent in dialectic theories of dysfunction, such as Blatt and Shichman's (1983) concept of anaclitic and introjective pathologies and Beck's (1983) observations of sociotropy and autonomy in depressive experience.

An important feature of this overarching attentional dialectic is that it provided an operational definition of physical health and psychological well-being in terms of the relative balance of the competing dimensions at the level of personality and cognitive style (Bonanno & Singer, 1990, 1993). More recently, Bonanno and Castonguay (1994) revised this approach by defining health and well-being in terms of the flexibility to engage in processes characteristic of each aspect of the dialectic. Thus, health is defined as the flexibility to allot greater attention internally, toward the self and private experiences, or externally, away from the self and toward other people or other stimuli in the environment, as mandated by the demands of specific situations.

The dialectic approach to health and well-being may be viewed as a heuristic in the explanation of the general pattern of findings about personality, attention, and normative functioning. Attention to one's private thoughts and feelings is generally acknowledged as an essential feature of normal self-regulation (Scheier & Carver, 1988). However, the relationship between excesses or rigidity in self-focus and emotional disorders has been well documented (Ingram, 1990; Pyszczynski & Greenberg, 1987; Wells & Matthews, 1994). A similar but less researched link to emotional dysfunction also appears to characterize the excessive or habitual focus of attention externally, away from the self (Bonanno & Singer, 1990, 1993). Importantly, however, the possible adaptive consequences of emotional dissociation and self-deception, which we discuss in detail, again underscore the crucial importance of attentional flexibility. Clearly, there are adaptive benefits that accompany the capacity to focus attention externally, away from private experience (e.g., avoiding nervous self-doubt while public speaking, increased vigilance when driving in dangerous weather conditions, etc.). Thus, individuals, who by disposition typically focus attention away from the self and private experience, will likely do well in such situations. However, these same individuals may also suffer untoward consequences in other situations for which private experience is more essential or informative. It is to this question that we devote the remainder of this chapter.

REPRESSIVE AVOIDANCE AND SELF-DECEPTIVE ENHANCEMENT

Perhaps the most widely researched dimension associated with reduced attention to the self is the repressor personality style (Weinberger, Schwartz, & Davidson, 1979). Bonanno and Singer (1990, 1993) characterized repressors as engaging less frequently in reflective, internally focused cognition in favor of a more superficial, externally focused, perceptual cognition. A considerable body of research has linked repressors with the dissociated awareness of distress. Repressors tend to report the same low levels of anxiety or distress as so-called "true low-anxious" individuals, but are distinguished from low-anxious individuals by their high scores on an indirect measure of defensiveness (Weinberger et al., 1979). Furthermore, during stressful tasks, they also tend to have elevated physiological arousal such as in verbal–autonomic response dissociation (Asendorpf, & Scherer, 1983; Newton & Contrada, 1992; Weinberger et al., 1979), and to show greater observer-rated distress (Asendorpf & Scherer, 1983; Fox, O'Boyle, Barry, & McCreary, 1989). When repressors' elevated levels of arousal are brought to their attention, they tend to doubt the accuracy of the autonomic equipment rather than revise their subjective appraisals (Weinberger & Davidson, 1994). In related research, repressors have evidenced a greater propensity to selectively attend away from threatening information (Fox, 1993), to report more interfering thoughts while attempting to focus attention in the presence of threat (Bonanno, Davis, Singer, & Schwartz, 1991), and they evidenced greater task interference when the selective avoidance of threatening stimuli was not possible (Dawkins & Furnham, 1989). Repressors also recalled fewer and less chronologically remote autobiographical memories of emotional events (Davis, 1987, 1990; Davis & Schwartz, 1987), and when tested in a signal-detection paradigm, showed genuinely poorer recognition (d') for emotional stimuli but showed no differences in (β) response criterion (Davis, Singer, Bonanno, & Schwartz, 1988).

Recently, the memory deficits associated with the repressor style have been linked to discrete or selective narrowing of attention at the point of encoding. For example, repressors performed better than other participants in a dichotic-listening paradigm in which they were required to repeat aloud or shadow words presented in a specified audio channel and ignore the words presented in the other audio channel (Bonanno et al., 1991). Repressors made fewer shadowing errors than other participants, and thus were able to more successfully narrow the focus of their attention to the designated channel, even when threatening words were presented in the to-be-ignored channel. Thus, by selectively narrowing the focus of their attention to nonthreatening information, repressors would be less likely to process, and subsequently recall, threatening information. Similar findings have been reported using visual stimuli. Repressors were found to appraise the emotional quality of faces more discretely—that is, they perceived the dominant emotions displayed in the faces similar to other participants, but perceived the blend of nondominant emotions less intensely than did other participants (Hansen, Hansen, & Shantz, 1992). In a related study using an induced-emotion paradigm, Egloff and Krohne (1996) found that, although participants in general reported the same amount of guilt, the dominant emotion after failure feedback in an anagram task, repressors reported experiencing less of the nondominant emotions: fear, sadness, and hostility (Egloff & Krohne, 1996).

The experimental evidence for attentional discreteness in repressors suggests an intriguing modification to the observations of Janet, Shapiro, and others regarding hysterical-obsessional dialectic. If repressors are considered exemplary of the hysterical pole of this attentional dialectic, as Bonanno and Singer proposed, then the superfical, impressionistic processing often associated with hysterical cognition may be more accurately viewed as the relative inattention to environmental cues, caused by the selective allotment of processing resources to specific, nonthreatening features of the environment. However, in contrast to the attentional rigidity characteristic of obsessional cognition (Shapiro, 1965), or the attentional priming often demonstrated in connection with anxiety disorders (Williams, Watts, MacLeod, & Mathews, 1988), repressive or hysterical cognition appears to involve attention to nonthreatening environmental features in the service of not attending to threatening cues.

This same type of selective narrowing of attention was illustrated recently in a study of sexually abused individuals diagnosed with Borderline Personality Disorder (BPD), a disorder linked to the same attentional dialectic (Bonanno & Singer, 1990). This study used a memory paradigm in which word stimuli were targeted as either to-be-remembered or to-be-forgotten (Cloitre, Cancienne, Brodsky, Dulit, & Perry, 1996). When BPD individuals who had suffered early parental abuse were compared with BPD individuals without abuse and to nonclinical controls, the three groups did not differ in their explicit recall of the to-be-forgotten words, therefore showing no differences in the capacity for intentional forgetting. Rather, the BPD individuals with abuse histories, relative to the other groups, had better recall for the to-be-remembered words, suggesting "enhanced attentional skills" (p. 209) related to the selective processing of benign information. Given that the salient group difference involved a history of parental abuse, Cloitre et al. (1996) noted the consistency of their findings "with reports of coping responses during sexual and physical abuse events in which conscious and effortful attention is given to 'neutral' material" (p. 209).

The repressor style also shares some features with the dispositional dimension of self-deceptive enhancement (SDE; Paulhus, 1984, 1991). The repressor and SDE measures use somewhat similar items (Paulhus, 1991) and have produced a relatively similar pattern of findings (Bonanno & Singer, 1993; Paulhus & Levitt, 1987; Paulhus & Reid, 1991). For example, both repressors and self-deceivers appear to be consistently low in self-focused attention (Bonanno & Singer, 1993; Ingram, Johnson, Bernet, Dombreck, & Rowe, 1992). Unlile the repressor personality, however, self-deceptive enhancement appears to be less focused on rejection or avoidance of the threatening information and more clearly directed toward a dogmatic confidence in one's own judgments and overly positive bias toward the positive (Paulhus & Reid, 1991). In addition, the SDE measure offers the added advantage of having been psychometrically distinguished both from denial and impression management, or the deliberate attempt to habitually appear favorably to others (Paulhus, 1984, 1991). Although few comparative data are available, recent evidence showed that repressors score high on both SDE and on impression management (Bonanno, Siddique, Keltner, & Horowitz, 1996). Thus, in contrast to the SDE scale, the repressor measure may be partially confounded with self-presentation effects.

THE QUESTION OF ADAPTATION
AND MENTAL HEALTH

The repressor style and its links to the dissociation of distress have been generally regarded as maladaptive responses to threat (Erdelyi, 1993; Shedler, Mayman, & Manis, 1993; Weinberger, 1990; Weinberger & Schwartz, 1990). Such an assumption is supported indirectly by evidence suggestive of a link between the repressive style, reduced immunocompetence (Jamner, Schwartz, & Leigh, 1988), greater basal salivary cortisol levels (Brown et al., 1996), and increased proneness to neoplastic disease (Eysenck, 1991; Jensen, 1987; Kneier & Temoshok, 1984). It is important to note, however, that competing empirical accounts are available, which also show that the repressor measure is unrelated to long-term health outcome (Cole, Kemeny, Taylor, & Visscher, 1996) and, in some cases, predicts a more benign disease course (Denollet, 1991; Denollet & DePotter, 1992).

These contradictory conclusions may be reconciled using the dialectic approach and its emphasis on the person–situation interaction. As discussed above, the dialectic approach suggests that in some situations repressive, emotionally dissociative, or self-deceptive habits may result in a maladaptive lack of insight into personal motivations, important emotional experiences, etc., while in other situations, the avoidance of private experience may be quite adaptive. Repressors' tendency to focus away from the self and private experience appears to be most pronounced in situations that threaten self-evaluation. For instance, repressors recalled fewer emotion words than low-anxious participants after receiving failure feedback after an analogy task, but recalled more emotion words after success feedback (Mendolia, Moore, & Tesser, 1996). Interestingly, however, repressors' capacity for attentional discreteness in the face of adversity has allowed them to perform better than nonrepressors do in some types of stressful laboratory tasks (Bonanno et al., 1991) and in the very real context of adjusting to the loss of a spouse (Bonanno, Znoj, Siddique, & Horowitz, in press). These findings are discussed in greater detail later.

Somewhat similarly, individuals high in SDE were found to perform better on difficult but solvable tasks when the contexts were ambiguous, while low SDE individuals were unaffected by context (Johnson, 1995). When provided with an excuse to explain poor performance on the task, however, self-deceivers performed at or above the level of participants who had enjoyed a successful experience. Self-deception also appears to serve an adaptive role in maintaining important interpersonal relationships. For example, individuals showing self-enhancement biases were also excessively optimistic about the futures of their close friends, but not about the future of a nonself-relevant other (Regan, Snyder, & Kassin, 1995). Similarly, idealization of a romantic partner was associated with greater perceived relationship satisfaction. The highest satisfaction ratings were given by both dating and married couples who perceived their partners more positively than their partners actually perceived themselves (Murray, Holmes, & Griffin, 1996).

Despite these findings, the possible long-term consequences of self-deceptive enhancement continue to be hotly debated. Taylor and Brown (1988, 1994) have persistently championed the normative and adaptive role of everyday, self-deceptive biases or positive illusions. Baumeister (1988) suggested an optimal margin of illusion and emphasized the dangers of too-extreme levels of self-deceptive enhancement. Other investigators have argued, however, that previous considerations of the adaptiveness of self-enhancement have failed to differentiate between individuals with relatively accurate, positive self-perceptions and those who inflate or defensively distort their self-perceptions in the positive direction (Colvin & Block, 1994; Shedler et al., 1993).

Although this criticism has already been addressed psychometrically in the dispositional measures—repressors have been distinguished from true low-anxious individuals and SDE has been distinguished from impression management—several investigators have attempted to explore enhancement biases in relation to judgments of trained observers and other presumably objective indices of mental health. Shedler et al. (1993) found that both clinical judges and undergraduate raters could distinguish a group of individuals who had described themselves as healthy on a self-report measure, but who nonetheless revealed their illusory mental health in responses to the Thematic Apperception Test (TAT) and other projective indices. Shedler et al. concluded that these individuals' reports of relative health were illusory largely because they had also exhibited elevated cardiovascular responsivity to several different stressful tasks. In a similar study, John and Robins (1994) found that individuals with enhanced or overly positive self-evaluations, relative to the evaluations of trained assessment staff, also scored higher on measures of narcissism. Finally, Colvin, Block, and Funder (1995) recently extended this paradigm by examining the relationship between self-evaluations and the assessments of trained evaluators during a 10-year period. Self-enhancers were consistently evaluated in the negative direction, regardless of whether assessments had been made 5 years prior or 5 years after the targeted self-evaluations.

A serious limitation of this approach, however, is that none of these studies actually provided an objective index of health or well-being. The increased cardiovascular response, cited as evidence for illusory health in the Shedler et al. study, was never linked explicitly to poor health. Indeed, this same type of dissociated arousal has been found to predict a relatively positive long-term outcome (Bonanno, Keltner, Holen, & Horowitz, 1995). Similarly, evaluations by trained assessment staff are not necessarily correlated with mental health. Neither of the studies that employed this approach (John & Robins, 1994; Colvin et al., 1994) had actually demonstrated an empirical link between the staff assessments and a more objective and concrete measure of health. Further, many of the dimensions (e.g., has social poise and presence) rated by the assessment staff were highly subjective in their own right, and may more accurately reflect the staff's own biases regarding mental health, a matter of no small importance given that the traditional criteria for mental health have strongly emphasized realistic or unbiased perceptions and the absence of illusion (Taylor & Brown, 1988). In other words, if an assessment staff-person had espoused the traditional view that self-enhancement is maladaptive, that staff person would also have been more likely to view the behavior and traits of self-enhancing participants as maladaptive, regardless of the actual appropriateness or consequences of the behavior or trait. Indeed, the possibility of bias in the staff ratings was sometimes glaringly evident. For example, female self-enhancers were rated by the assessment staff as less physically attractive than nonself-enhancing female participants—an evaluation that would not likely evidence a correlation with cognitive processes if a more carefully controlled measure were employed.

COPING WITH THE STRESS OF BEREAVEMENT

We recently examined the long-term consequences of emotional dissociation and self-deceptive enhancement in the specific context of midlife conjugal bereavement. The loss of a spouse has been listed among the most severe of stressor events (Holmes & Rahe, 1967). Coping with such a loss has generally been thought to require a concerted period of grief work involving the realistic review, expression, and disclosure of the cognitive and emotional meanings of a loss. The avoidance or minimization of grief work has been almost universally assumed to predict decreased health and well-being over time (Bonanno, in press; W. Stroebe & Stroebe, 1987). In contrast to these assumptions, however, we found that self-deception and emotional avoidance were consistently and robustly linked to a better outcome.

The study involved the longitudinal assessment of middle-aged individuals who had recently lost their spouses. Beginning approximately 3 months after the loss and continuing for the next several years, participants completed a series of questionnaire and interview measures. At the 6-month point in bereavement, participants were asked to describe their lost relationship—a procedure designed specifically to assess the experience, expression, and verbal disclosure of emotion related to the loss. Long-term outcome was assessed using self-reported somatic complaints and a structured clinical interview for grief-specific symptoms. The grief-symptom interview provided a relatively objective index of the degree that the loss impeded general functioning and well-being, and was validated against standardized measures of grief and depression, as well as against clinical ratings of grief severity made blindly and independently by a team of psychotherapists (Bonanno et al., 1995).

In the first study from this project, verbal–autonomic response dissociation was measured while participants discussed their losses using the standard method of comparing self-reported experience with autonomic arousal (Asendorpf & Scherer, 1983; Newton & Contrada, 1992; Shedler et al., 1993; Weinberger & M. Davidson, 1994; Weinberger et al., 1979). The assumption that low levels of emotion relative to autonomic arousal indicate a relatively automatic reduction in awareness or emotional dissociation was supported by convergence with clinician ratings of the Avoidance of Emotional Awareness. Discriminant validity for the verbal–autonomic dissociation score was evidenced in relation to a self-report measure of deliberate avoidance behaviors (e.g., deliberately trying not to talk about an event; Bonanno et al., 1995). In addition, the possibility that verbal–autonomic dissociation represents an enduring aspect of personality or cognitive style was supported by its relatively high test–retest correlation ($r = .63$) when measured over an 8-month span of bereavement.

Based on the assumed importance of grief work, it would be expected that emotional dissociation at 6 months of bereavement would lead to prolonged or delayed grief over time. A similar prediction is also suggested from the illusory mental health assumption, discussed previously (Shedler et al., 1993). In contrast to both assumptions, however, verbal–

autonomic dissociation at the 6-month point in bereavement predicted low levels of interviewer-rated grief symptoms through the 25 months measured in the study (Bonanno et al., 1995; Bonanno et al., in press). Further, this result was observed regardless of the participant's level of grief at the beginning of the study. There was some evidence for a physical cost of avoidance early during bereavement in that verbal–autonomic dissociation at 6 months was coupled with concurrent elevations in reported somatic symptoms. Importantly, however, over the long-term course of the study, verbal–autonomic dissociation predicted relatively low levels of somatic symptoms, and thus, was not linked to either a cumulative or delayed physical cost, as traditionally expected.

One potential limitation of these findings was that, because the verbal–autonomic data were obtained from the same 6-month interview, emotional grief work occurring at an earlier point in bereavement may not have been accounted for. This was addressed to a considerable extent by controlling for initial levels of grief. To address this question further, however, we also examined the grief course associated with the repressor style (Weinberger et al., 1979) and with self-deceptive enhancement (SDE; Paulhus, 1984, 1991). While these dimensions obviously cannot capture the entirety of a person's response to loss, their association with the habitual avoidance of unpleasant information clearly suggested that individuals scoring highly on these dimensions would not be likely to engage in cognitive or emotional processing of the loss at any point during bereavement. In addition, inclusion of these measures offered an alternative context for examining their actual longitudinal consequences and their presumed discordance with psychologically healthy functioning.

As expected, repressors were the only group to show verbal–autonomic response dissociation. SDE, on the other hand, was not clearly related to verbal–autonomic dissociation, and further suggested important differences between the two meaures. In support of the long-term or trait features of these dimensions, both repressor and SDE measures showed adequate test–retest reliability across 8 months of bereavement. As would be expected, repressors reported the same low levels of distress and somatic complaints as did so-called true low-anxious individuals. When the more objective, interviewer-rated grief score was considered, repressors showed earlier reductions in grief than all other participants, including the low-anxious group, and remained at low levels through 25 months (Bonanno, Siddique, Keltner, & Horowitz, 1996). The SDE findings were even more robust. SDE was associated with less distress, better perceived health, and fewer interviewer-rated grief symptoms across time, and these results remained significant when partialled for initial symptoms levels or the possible overlap with more general negative affectivity, in this case measured as trait anxiety. Thus, despite the previous findings linking self-enhancement with narcissism (John & Robins, 1994) and with relatively negative assessments by trained assessment staff (Colvin et al., 1995), the dispositional SDE scale predicted superior longitudinal adaptation to the stress of conjugal loss for each variable considered, including clinical interviewer ratings of grief symptoms.

A third study from this longitudinal project (Bonanno & Keltner, 1997) examined a different aspect of emotional responsivity, the expression of emotion in the face. Consistent with descriptions of emotion in the bereavement literature (Shuchter & Zisook, 1993), a range of both positive and negative emotions were evidenced in participant's facial expressions as they described their loss at the 6-month point in bereavement. When 6-month facial expressions were compared with the outcome variables through 25 months, the findings were similar to those observed for emotional dissociation. Facial expressions of negative emotion, exhibited while bereaved individuals described the loss at 6 months, predicted increased grief and decreased perceptions of health at later assessments. In addition, the overt expressions of positive emotion, typically associated in the bereavement literature with maladaptive denial, were predictive of decreased grief over time. Again, these findings remained significant when initial symptom levels and self-reported emotion were statisically controlled.

Emotional dissociation and facial expression variables continued to predict later symptom scores, even when partialled for initial symptom levels. This attests to the important mediating role of emotional regulation in long-term adaptation (Bonanno & Keltner, 1997). Additional evidence for the adaptive role of emotional regulation during bereavement was provided by the interrelationship among emotion variables. For instance, expressions of genuine laughter were more readily evidenced in those individuals who had also shown emotional dissociation, while individuals who did not evidence emotional dissociation tended to display only social (or nongenuine) laughter (Keltner & Bonanno, 1997).

Finally, in addition to these emotional and personality variables, we have recently investigated the role of verbal disclosure, as well as its relative absence, during bereavement (Bonanno & Eddins, 1997). Several variables related to verbal disclosure were coded from transcripts of the bereaved participant's descriptions of his or her lost relationship, including the frequency of disclosures of thoughts and emotions, the level of intimacy, and the affective valence of the disclosures. Consistent with the emotion findings, more frequent disclosure of negatively valenced thoughts predicted increased grief at later assessments, while more frequent disclosure of negatively valenced emotion predicted increased distress and somatic symptoms at later assessments. Again, as in the previous findings, these results were significant after initial symptoms levels were statistically controlled.

When considered together, these findings raise the important question of why minimizing emotion proved so adaptive in the particular context of conjugal loss. One possibility is that the ability or propensity to regulate the pain of a loss would allow bereaved individuals to more effectively maintain their ongoing responsibilities at work and in other life domains, and thus to reduce the generalized impact of the loss (Bonanno et al., 1995). This may be particularly true in light of the peak responsibilities often associated with midlife (Bumpus & Aquilino, 1995). Another possibility is suggested by the fact that these results were obtained in the social context of describing a loss to another person. In this case, minimizing or regulating the experience, expression, and disclosure of negative emotion may serve the function of maintaining a relatively normative social exchange between the speaker and the listener. Clearly, the experience of listening to a depressed or distressed individual can be quite stressful (Harber & Pennebaker, 1992; Silver, Wortman, & Crofton, 1990) and may drive potential avenues of support away (Coyne, 1976; Gottlieb, 1991; Pennebaker, 1993). Minimizing negative emotion may help reduce the burden or discomfort in the listener and foster the bereaved person's sense of ongoing affiliation with, and potential support from, that listener. The same may be true of positive emotional expression. Genuine positive emotions tend to be incompatible with, or attenuate, negative emotion (Levenson, 1988) and thus, may also foster prosocial exchanges (Bonanno & Keltner, 1997). For example, videotapes of bereaved individuals who did not smile or laugh at any time tended to induce significantly greater negative emotions in observers (Keltner & Bonanno, 1997).

IMPLICATIONS FOR PSYCHOTHERAPY

The findings reviewed suggest a number of implications for traditional concepts of therapeutic process and practice. First, it may be important to investigate the cultural assumptions inherent in the belief that emotional dissociation and self-deception are necessarily maladaptive. The principal emphasis on emotional experience and expression, typical of many psychotherapies and an essential feature of the traditional grief-work approach to bereavement, appears to be largely a Western–European construction (Bonanno, in press; M. Stroebe, M. Gergen, Gergen, & Stroebe, 1992). That is, in contrast to the psychologizing of Western cultures, non-Western cultures tend to de-emphasize or even discourage the experience and expression of emotion after difficult or traumatic events (Kleinman & Kleinman, 1985; Tseng, 1974). Prolonged attention to emotional distress is thought to have an adverse effect on health in many nonWestern cultures, including, for example, the Toraja in Indonesia

(Wellenkamp, 1995), African cultures generally (Opoku, 1989; Price & Price, 1991), and the Hopi Indians of the southwest United States (Mandelbaum, 1959). Also, in contrast to the grief-work assumption, mourning rituals in nonWestern cultures tend both to revolve around the community rather than around the particular experience of the individual, and to place a clear value on the importance of humor and dissociative fantasy rather than on realistic appraisal (Bonanno, in press).

Second, the theoretical and empirical data reviewed underscore the importance of considering both the adaptive as well as the maladaptive aspects of a therapy patient's habitual or stylistic responses to distress, as well as to his or her capacity for flexibility in response to the demands of different situational stressors. We have proposed a prescriptive framework for psychotherapy that involves matching the individual and the therapeutic approach in order to promote dialectic flexibility (Bonanno & Castonguay, 1994). Taking a person–situation interactive perspective, we proposed that during the initial therapeutic exchange, a patient will likely find therapy more desirable and more efficacious when the treatment approach matches his or her personality or cognitive style. Thus, individuals who typically focus attention inwardly, toward private experience, would likely benefit most from therapies that initially promote *intrapersonal* functioning—self-understanding, self-control, and autonomy—by exploration of implicit emotions and meanings, identification and challenging of distorted cognition, or the acquisition of problem-solving skills. Similarly, individuals who habitually focus attention externally, away from private experience and toward the social-environmental context, would likely benefit most from therapies that initially promote *interpersonal* functioning—the quality of important relationships—by sensitively reflecting, adjusting, and, when necessary, repairing the therapeutic dyad. We further proposed, in keeping with the emphasis on dialectic flexibility, that the later or more advanced phases of treatment must begin to challenge a patient's stylistic behaviors and move the patient essentially in the opposite direction, toward a dialectic balance. Thus, interventions that focus initially on private experience and intrapersonal functioning ultimately will need to be aimed toward social interaction and understanding, from within the context of an explicitly collaborative and sensitive therapeutic relationship. Interventions that initially focus on facilitating interpersonal functioning and the therapeutic exchange will ultimately need to be augmented with increased emphasis on self-awareness and self-reliant coping skills (e.g., self-control and problem-solving skills) that challenge the safety of the therapeutic bond.

Finally, the relative emphasis and timing of these different types of interventions will be informed by the specifics of the patient's situational difficulties. Let us return again to the example of a repressive or self-deceptive individual who has recently suffered the loss of a loved one. In contrast to the traditional grief-work assumption, which uniformly advocates intrapersonal exploration (Raphael, 1983), the dialectic model suggests that initial interventions for repressive or self-deceptive individuals should minimize intrapersonal examination and instead emphasize the development and maintenance of the quality of the external, therapeutic dyad. Consistent with this aim, the minimization of negative, grief-related emotion was linked to a more benign grief course, and this was especially true for repressive and self-deceptive individuals. If the ultimate aim of treatment is dialectic flexibility, however, the question becomes, "When does a therapist shift the emphasis toward increased self-awareness and intrapersonal functioning?" The answer to this question will, of course, depend on a thorough assessment of the patient's capacity to negotiate the stress of the loss or other related stressors. If a repressive therapy patient appears to have adapted to a loss reasonably well, it may be appropriate to direct the therapeutic dialogue more toward intrapersonal exploration and dialectic flexibility. If, on the other hand, a repressive or self-deceptive patient appears to be highly disturbed by a loss, then the dialectic model suggests the extreme importance of helping that patient restore or repair the disruption in his or her interpersonal world by attending to the safety and sensitivity of the therapeutic relationship.

CONCLUSION

These are but a few of the possible avenues to consider in examining the complex interplay of emotional dissociation, self-deception, and the psychotherapeutic process. In the tradition of Singer's wide-ranging and integrative achievements, we hope that our review has illustrated the importance of considering these variables in a broad, historically informed context, and of critically examining theoretical and cultural assumptions about both their maladaptive and potentially adaptive consequences.

REFERENCES

Antrobus, J. S., & Singer, J. L. (1964). Visual signal detection as a function of sequential task variability of simultaneous speech. *Journal of Experimental Psychology, 68*, 603–610.

Asendorpf, J. B., & Scherer, K. R. (1983). The discrepant repressor: Differentiation between low anxiety, high anxiety, and repression of anxiety by autonomic-facial-verbal patterns of behavior. *Journal of Personality and Social Psychology, 45*, 1334–1346.

Bakan, D. (1966). *The duality of human existence.* Chicago: Rand McNally.

Baumeister, R. F. (1988). The optimal margin of illusion. *Journal of Social and Clinical Psychology, 8,* 176–189.

Beck, A. T. (1983). Cognitive therapy of depression: New perspectives. In P. J. Clayton & J. E. Barrett (Eds.), *Treatment of depression: Old controversies and new approaches* (pp. 265–290). New York: Raven.

Blatt, S. J., & Shichman, S. (1983). Two primary configurations of psychopathology. *Psychoanalysis and Contemporary Thought, 6,* 187–254.

Bonanno, G. A. (1995). Accessibility, reconstruction, and the treatment of functional memory problems. In A. D. Baddeley, B. A. Wilson, & F. N. Watts (Eds.), *Handbook of Memory Disorders* (pp. 615–637). New York: Wiley.

Bonanno, G. A. (in press). The concept of "Working through" loss: A critical evaluation of the cultural, historical, and empirical evidence. In A. Maercker, M. Schuetzwohl, & Z. Solomon (Eds.), *Posttraumatic Stress Disorder: Vulnerability and Resilience in the Life-Span.* Seattle, WA: Hogrefe & Huber.

Bonanno, G. A., & Castonguay, L. G. (1994). On balancing approaches to psychotherapy: Prescriptive patterns of attention, motivation, and personality. *Psychotherapy, 31,* 571–587.

Bonanno, G. A., Davis, P. J., Singer, J. L., & Schwartz, G. E. (1991). The repressor personality and avoidant information processing: A dichotic listening study. *Journal of Research in Personality, 25,* 386–401.

Bonanno, G. A., & Eddins, C. (1997). *Verbal disclosure and the regulation of emotion: Correlates and consequences of talking about the loss of a spouse.* Manuscript submitted for publication, The Catholic University of America, Washington, DC.

Bonanno, G. A., & Keltner, D. (1997). Facial expressions of emotion and the course of conjugal bereavement. *Journal of Abnormal Psychology, 106,* 126–137.

Bonanno, G. A., Keltner, D., Holen, A., & Horowitz, M. J. (1995). When avoiding unpleasant emotion might not be such a bad thing: Verbal-autonomic response dissociation and midlife conjugal bereavement. *Journal of Personality and Social Psychology, 69,* 975–989.

Bonanno, G. A., & Keuler, D. (1998). Psychotherapy without repressed memory: A parsimonious alternative based on contemporary memory research. In S. J. Lynn, & N. Spanos (Eds.), *Truth and memory.* New York: Guilford.

Bonanno, G. A., Siddique, H. I. L., Keltner, D., & Horowitz, M. J. (1996). *Correlates and consequences of dispositional repression and self-deception following the loss of a spouse.* Manuscript submitted for publication. The Catholic University of America, Washington, DC.

Bonanno, G. A., & Singer, J. L. (1990). Repressive personality style: Theoretical and methodological implications for health and pathology. In J. L. Singer (Ed.), *Repression and dissociation,* pp. 435–470. Chicago: University of Chicago Press.

Bonanno, G. A., & Singer, J. L. (1993). Controlling the stream of thought through perceptual and reflective processing. In D. Wegner & J. Pennebaker (Eds.), *Handbook of Mental Control,* pp. 149–170. Englewood Cliffs, NJ: Prentice-Hall.

Bonanno, G. A., Znoj, H., Siddique, H., & Horowitz, M. J. (in press). Verbal-autonomic response dissociation and midlife conjugal bereavement: A follow-up at 25 months. *Cognitive Therapy and Research.*

Breuer, J., & Freud, S. (1955). Studies on hysteria. In J. Strachey (Ed.), *The standard edition of the complete psychological works of Sigmund Freud,* Vols. 4 & 5. London: Hogarth. (Original work published 1895)

Brown, L. L., Tomarken, A. J., Orth, D. N., Loosen, P. T., Kalin, N. H., & Davidson, R. J. (1996). Individual differences in repressive-defensiveness predict basal salivary cortisol levels. *Journal of Personality and Social Psychology, 70,* 362–371.

Bumpus, L. L., & Aquilino, W. S. (1995). *A social map of midlife: Family and work over the middle life course.* Unpublished manuscript. University of Wisconsin, Madison.

Byrne, D., Barry, J., & Nelson, D. (1963). Relations of the revised Repression-Sensitization scale to measures of self-description. *Psychological Reports, 13,* 323–334.

Carter, R. B. (1853). *On the pathology and treatment of hysteria.* London: Churchill.

Cloitre, M., Cancienne, J., Brodsky, B., Dulit, R., & Perry, S. W. (1996). Memory performance among women with parental abuse histories: Enhanced directed forgetting or directed remembering? *Journal of Abnormal Psychology, 105*, 206–217.

Cole, S. W., Kemeny, M. E., Taylor, S. E., & Visscher, B. R. (1996). Elevated physical health risk among gay men who conceal their homosexual identity. *Health Psychology, 15*, 243–251.

Colvin, C. R., & Block, J. (1994). Do positive illusions foster mental health? An examination of the Taylor and Brown formulation. *Psychological Bulletin, 116*, 3–20.

Colvin, C. R., Block, J., & Funder, D. C. (1995). Overly positive self-evaluations and personality: Negative implications for mental health. *Journal of Personality and Social Psychology, 68*, 1152–1162.

Coyne, J. C. (1976). Toward an interactional description of depression. *Psychiatry, 39*, 28–39.

Davis, P. J. (1987). Repression and the inaccessibility of affective memories. *Journal of Personality and Social Psychology, 53*, 585–593.

Davis, P. J. (1990). Repression and the inaccessibility of emotional memories. In J. L. Singer (Ed.), *Repression and dissociation.* Chicago: University of Chicago Press.

Davis, P. J., & Schwartz, G. E. (1987). Repression and the inaccessibility of affective memories. *Journal of Personality and Social Psychology, 52*, 155–163.

Davis, P. J., Singer, J. L., Bonanno, G. A., & Schwartz, G. E. (1988). Repressor personality style and response bias during an affective memory recognition task: A signal detection analysis. *Australian Journal of Psychology, 40*, 147–157.

Dawkins, K., & Furnham, A. (1989). The color naming of emotional words. *British Journal of Psychology, 80*, 383–389.

Denollet, J. (1991). Negative affectivity and repressive coping: Pervasive influence on self-reported mood, health, and coronary-prone behavior. *Psychosomatic Medicine, 53*, 538–556.

Denollet, J., & DePotter, B. (1992). Coping subtypes for men with coronary heart disease: Relationship to well-being, stress and Type A behavior. *Psychological Medicine, 22*, 667–684.

Egloff, B., & Krohne, H. W. (1996). Repressive emotional discreteness after failure. *Journal of Personality and Social Psychology, 70*, 1318–1326.

Ellenberger, H. E. (1970). *The discovery of the unconscious.* New York: Basic Books.

Ellenberger, H. E. (1993). *Beyond the unconscious.* Princeton, NJ: Princeton University Press.

Erdelyi, M. H. (1993). Repression: The mechanism and the defense. In D. Wegner & J. Pennebaker (Eds.), *Handbook of Mental Control* (pp. 126–149). Englewood Cliffs, NJ: Prentice-Hall.

Eysenck, H. J. (1991). *Smoking, personality, and stress: Psychological factors in the prevention of cancern and coronary heart disease.* New York: Springer-Verlag.

Fenigstein, A., Scheier, M. F., & Buss, A. H. (1975). Public and private self-consciousness: Assessment and theory. *Journal of Consulting and Clinical Psychology, 43*, 522–527.

Fox, E. (1993). Allocation of visual attention and anxiety. *Cognition and Emotion, 7*, 207–215.

Fox, E., O'Boyle, C. A., Barry, H., & McCreary, C. (1989). Repressive coping style in stressful dental surgery. *British Journal of Medical Psychology, 62*, 371–380.

Freud, S. (1962). The etiology of hysteria. In J. Strachey (Ed. and Trans.), *The standard edition of the complete psychological works of Sigmund Freud* (Vol. 3, pp. 191–221). London: Hogarth. (Original work published 1896)

Freud, S. (1962). Sexuality and the etiology of the neuroses. In J. Strachey (Ed.), *The standard edition of the complete psychological works of Sigmund Freud* (Vol. 3, pp. 261–289). London: Hogarth. (Original work published 1898)

Freud, S. (1966). Introductory lectures on psychoanalysis. In J. Strachey (Ed.), *The standard edition of the complete psychological works of Sigmund Freud* (Vols. 15 & 16). London: Hogarth. (Original work published 1917)

Gottlieb, B. H. (1991). The contingent nature of social support. In J. Eckenrode (Ed.), *Social context of stress*. New York: Plenum.

Hansen, C. H., Hansen, R. D., & Shantz, D. W. (1992). Repression at encoding: Discrete appraisals of emotional stimuli. *Journal of Personality and Social Psychology, 63*, 1026–1035.

Harber, K. D., & Pennebaker, J. W. (1992). Overcoming traumatic memories. In S.-A. Christianson (Ed.), *The handbook of emotion and memory: Research and theory* (pp. 359–387). Hillsdale, NJ: Lawrence Erlbaum Associates.

Hilgard, E. R. (1977). *Divided consciousness: Multiple controls in human thought and action* (3rd ed.). New York: Wiley.

Holmes, T., & Rahe, R. (1967). The social readjustment scale. *Journal of Psychosomatic Research, 11*, 213–218.

Horney, K. (1939). *New ways in psychoanalysis*. New York: Norton.

Horney, K. (1945). *Our inner conflicts*. New York: Norton.

Hothersall, D. (1995). *The history of psychology* (3rd ed.). New York: McGraw-Hill.

Huba, G. J., Aneshensel, C. S., & Singer, J. L. (1981). Development of scales for three second-order factors of inner experience. *Multivariate Behavior Research, 16*, 181–206.

Ingram, R. E. (1990). Self-focused attention in clinical disorders: Review and a conceptual model. *Psychological Bulletin, 107*, 156–176.

Ingram, R. E., Johnson, B. R., Bernet, C. Z., Dombreck, M., & Rowe, M. K. (1992). Vulnerability to distress: Cognitive and emotional reactivity in chronically self-focused individuals. *Cognitive Therapy and Research, 16*, 451–472.

James, W. (1890). *The principles of psychology, Vol. 1*. New York: Dover.

Jamner, L. D., Schwartz, G. E., & Leigh, H. (1988). Repressive coping predicts monocyte, eosinophile, and serum glucose levels: Support for the opioid-peptide hypothesis. *Psychosomatic Medicine, 50*, 567–577.

Janet, P. (1889). *L' Automatisme Psychologique*. Paris: Librairie Félix Alcan.

Janet, P. (1901). *The mental state of hystericals: A study of mental stigmata and mental accidents* (C. R. Carson, Trans.). New York: Putnam. (Original work published 1893)

Jensen, M. R. (1987). Psychobiological factors predicting the course of breast cancer. *Journal of Personality, 55*, 317–342.

John, O. P., & Robins, R. W. (1994). Accuracy and bias in self-perception: Individual differences in self-enhancement and the role of narcissism. *Journal of Personality and Social Psychology, 66*, 206–219.

Johnson, E. A. (1995). Self-deceptive coping: Adaptive only in ambiguous contexts. *Journal of Personality, 63*, 759–790.

Jones, C. H. (1867). *Clinical observations on functional nervous disorders*. Philadelphia: Lea.

Jung, C. G. (1971). Psychological types. In *Collected works* (Vol 6, pp. 1–486). New York: Pantheon.

Keltner, D., & Bonanno, G. A. (1997). A study of laughter and dissociation: Discrete correlates of laughter and smiling during conjugal bereavement. *Journal of Personality and Social Psychology, 73*, 687–702.

Kleinman, A, & Kleinman, J. (1985). Somatization: The interconnections in Chinese society among culture, depressive experiences, and the meanings of pain. In A. Kleinman & B. Good (Eds.), *Culture and depression: Studies in anthropology and cross-cultural psychiatry of affect and disorder* (pp. 429–490). Berkeley, CA: University of California Press.

Klos, D. S., & Singer, J. L. (1981). Determinants of the adolescent's ongoing thought following simulated parental confrontations. *Journal of Personality and Social Psychology, 41*, 975–987.

Kneier, A. W., & Temoshok, L. (1984). Repressive coping reactions in patients with malignant melanoma as compared to cardiovascular disease patients. *Journal of Psychosomatic Research, 28*, 368–378.

Levenson, R. W. (1988). Emotion and the autonomic nervous system: A prospectus for research on autonomic specificity. In H. L. Wagner (Ed.), *Social psychophysiology and emotion: Theory and clinical applications* (pp. 17–42). New York: Wiley.

Lewis, H. B. (1976). *Psychic war in men and women.* New York: International Universities Press.

Mandelbaum, D. G. (1959). Social uses of funeral rites. In H. Feifel (Ed.), *The meaning of death* (pp. 189–217). New York: McGraw-Hill.

Mendolia, M., Moore, J., & Tesser, A. (1996). Dispositional and situational determinants of repression. *Journal of Personality and Social Psychology, 70,* 856–867.

Murray, S. L., Holmes, J. G., & Griffin, D. W. (1996). The benefits of positive illusions: Idealization and the construction of satisfaction in close relationships. *Journal of Personality and Social Psychology, 70,* 79–98.

Newton, T. L., & Contrada, R. J. (1992). Repressive coping and verbal-autonomic response dissociation: The influence of social context. *Journal of Personality and Social Psychology, 62,* 159–167.

Opoku, K. A. (1989). African perspectives on death and dying. In A. Berger, P. Badham, A. H. Kutscher, J. Berger, M. Perry, & J. Beloff (Eds.), *Perspectives on death and dying* (pp. 14–23). Philadelphia: The Charles Press.

Paulhus, D. L. (1984). Two-component models of socially desirable responding. *Journal of Personality and Social Psychology, 46,* 598–609.

Paulhus, D. L. (1991). *Assessing self-deception and impression management in self-reports: The Balanced Inventory of Desirable Responding, version 6.* Unpublished manual. University of British Columbia, Vancouver, British Columbia, Canada.

Paulhus, D. L., & Levitt, K. (1987). Desirable responding triggered by affect: Automatic egotism? *Journal of Personality and Social Psychology, 52,* 245–259.

Paulhus, D. L., & Reid, D. B. (1991). Enhancement and denial in social desirable responding. *Journal of Personality and Social Psychology, 60,* 307–317.

Pennebaker, J. W. (1993). Social mechanisms of constraint. In D. M. Wegner & J. W. Pennebaker (Eds.), *Handbook of mental control* (pp. 200–219). Englewood Cliffs, NJ: Prentice-Hall.

Price, R., & Price, S. (1991). *Two evenings in Saramaka.* Chicago: University of Chicago Press.

Prince, M. (1906). *The dissociation of personality.* New York: Longmans Green.

Pyszczynski, T., & Greenberg, J. (1987). Self-regulatory perseveration and the depressive self-focusing style: A self-awareness theory of reactive depression. *Psychological Bulletin, 102,* 122–138.

Raphael, B. (1983). *The anatomy of bereavement.* New York: Basic Books.

Regan, P. C., Snyder, M., & Kassin, S. M. (1995). Unrealistic optimism: Self-enhancement or person positivity? *Personality and Social Psychology Bulletin, 21,* 1073–1082.

Reviere, S. L. (1996). *Memory for childhood trauma.* New York: Guilford.

Scheier, M. F., & Carver, C. S. (1988). A model of behavioral self-regulation: Translating intention into action. *Advances in Experimental Social Psychology, 21,* 303–346.

Shapiro, D. (1965). *Neurotic styles.* New York: Basic Books.

Shedler, J., Mayman, M., & Manis, M. (1993). The illusion of mental health. *American Psychologist, 48,* 1117–1131.

Shuchter, S. R., & Zisook, S. (1993). The course of normal grief. In M. S. Stroebe, W. Stroebe, & R. O. Hansson (Eds.), *Handbook of bereavement: Theory, research, and intervention* (pp. 23–43). Cambridge, England: Cambridge University Press.

Silver, R. C., Wortman, C. B., & Crofton, C. V. (1990). The role of coping in support provision: The self-presentation dilemma of victims of life crises. In B. R. Sarason, I. B. Sarason, & G. R. Pierce (Eds.), *Social support: An interactional view* (pp. 397–426). New York: Wiley.

Singer, J. L. (1966). *The inner world of daydreaming.* New York: Random House.

Singer, J. L. (1984). The private personality. *Personality and Social Psychology Bulletin, 10*, 7–30.

Singer, J. L., & Bonanno, G. A. (1990). Personality and private experience: Individual variations in consciousness and in attention to subjective phenomena. In L. Pervin (Ed.), *Handbook of personality theory and research* (pp. 419–444). New York: Guilford.

Singer, J. L., & Pope, K. S. (1981). Daydreaming and imagery skills as predisposing capacities for self-hypnosis. *The International Journal of Clinical and Experimental Hypnosis, 29*, 271–281.

Stroebe, M., Gergen, M. M., Gergen, K. J., & Stroebe, W. (1992). Broken hearts or broken bonds: Love and death in the historical perspective. *American Psychologist, 47*, 1205–1212.

Stroebe, W., & Stroebe, M. (1987). *Bereavement and health: The psychological and physical consequences of partner loss.* Cambridge, England: Cambridge University Press.

Taylor, S. E., & Brown, J. D. (1988). Illusion and well-being: A social psychological perspective on mental health. *Psychological Bulletin, 103*, 193–210.

Taylor, S. E., & Brown, J. D. (1994). Positive illusions and well-being revisited: Separating fact from fiction. *Psychological Bulletin, 116*, 21–27.

Tseng, W. S. (1974). The development of psychiatric concepts of Chinese medicine. *Archives of General Psychiatry*, 569–575.

van der Hart, O., & Nijenhuis, E. (1995). Amnesia for traumatic experiences. *Hypnosis, 22*, 75–86.

Veith, I. (1965). *Hysteria: The history of a disease.* Chicago: University of Chicago Press.

Weinberger, D. A. (1990). The construct validity of the repressive coping style. In J. L. Singer (Ed.), *Repression and dissociation* (pp. 337–386). Chicago: University of Chicago Press.

Weinberger, D. A., & Davidson, M. N. (1994). Styles of inhibiting emotional expression: Distinguishing repressive coping from impression management. *Journal of Personality, 62*, 587–613.

Weinberger, D. A., & Schwartz, G. E. (1990). Distress and restraint as superordinate dimensions of self-reported adjustment: A typological perspective. *Journal of Personality, 58*, 381–417.

Weinberger, D. A., Schwartz, G. E., & Davidson, J. R. (1979). Low-anxious and repressive coping styles: Psychometric patterns of behavioral and physiological responses to stress. *Journal of Abnormal Psychology, 88*, 369–380.

Wellencamp, J. (1995). Cultural similarities and differences regarding emotional disclosure: Some examples from Indonesia and the Pacific. In J. W. Pennebaker (Ed.), *Emotion, disclosure, and health* (pp. 293–311). Washington, DC: American Psychological Association.

Wells, A., & Matthews, G. (1994). Self-consciousness and cognitive failures as predictors of coping in stressful episodes. *Cognition and Emotion, 8*, 279–295.

Williams, J. M. G., Watts, F. N., MacLeod, C., & Mathews, A. (1988). *Cognitive psychology and emotional disorders.* New York: Wiley.

Witkin, H. A. (1965). Psychological differentiation and forms of pathology. *Journal of Abnormal Psychology, 70*, 317–336.

Witkin, H. A., & Goodenough, D. R. (1981). *Cognitive styles, essence and origins: Field dependence and field independence.* New York: International Universities Press.

Woodworth, R. S. (1948). *Contemporary schools of psychology.* New York: Ronald Press.

Modes of Conscious Representation and Their Exploration Through Psychotherapy

Mardi Horowitz
University of California, San Francisco

Jerome Singer's contributions to psychology have been priceless. His work with consciousness, image formation, daydreaming, social meanings, and mental processes has broadened the field and influenced my work. In this chapter, I would like to honor this outstanding scholar by discussing themes of conscious representation that both stem from and tie into his research.

MODES OF REPRESENTATION

Ideas and feelings are represented by enactive, image, and lexical modes of reflective consciousness. These different modes are formed from many unconscious operating systems that process information. The following everyday examples illustrate thought representations in images and en-actions: Planning a picnic often involves word lists of food, but the appetite is whetted by visual images of colorful fruits and an assortment of sandwiches. A child absorbed in a daydream dances about the room according to her unfolding inner fantasy; during this enaction of an inner drama, changing emotional expressions flicker over the child's face. Modes of representation are important phenomena in psychotherapy. Analyzing defensive controls of emotion is essential to uncovering warded off but conflictual themes. Efforts to increase expression often involve attention to nonlexical modes.

People seldom notice the divisions between modes of representation; they usually have seamless experiences. However, stress and conflict can make the divisions between modes more apparent. Defensive control processes can inhibit expression in one or all modes, and can also inhibit translations of thought and feeling across modes in order to check excesses of emotion. Sometimes a volitional shift from one mode to another can alter avoidance and facilitate a shift to a mental state of intense emotional expression.

Inhibition of translation of ideas and feelings across modes frequently occurs when someone feels uncomfortable about a given theme or topic that is being contemplated. For example, a man might have a vivid image of destroying a rival's car with a sledge hammer, but his passionate hostility could remain verbally untranslated by using such diluted words as, "I am just a bit irritated with him." In psychotherapy, fuller verbalization would need to be encouraged to clarify and directly confront the problem.

Ideas are expressed differently in particular modes. In the previous example, the visual image of smashing a car expresses a social relationship where the self furiously attacks something of value belonging to a specific person. In addition, the individual might portray the magnitude of his rage with an enactive bodily tension: red face, clenched jaw, glaring eyes, and balled fists. And words like, "He took what I deserved! I hate him and I will get my revenge!" would narrate the emotional state with clarity.

In order for individuals to be able to recognize, to understand, and to utilize the different properties from different modes, it is helpful to describe categories and connections between categories. Bruner (1964) and Horowitz (1970) selected and described enactive, image, and lexical modes of conscious representation. These three modes are summarized in Table 11.1 and illustrated in Fig. 11.1.

The Enactive Mode

The intrapsychic recognition of muscle tension is an important conscious representation. These tensions result from changes in both striated and smooth (visceral) muscles. Such physical reactions to various stimuli can be emotional clues (Zajonc, 1980; Zajonc and Markus, 1984). Facial expressions and bodily gestures are the communicative forms of enactive representation. In most cases, a smile is instantly recognizable as an expression of happiness, and a downward gaze and drooping shoulders usually signify unhappiness. Some bodily enactions are also self-observed. The observing self recognizes unhappiness, perhaps, when the experiencing self is physically downcast with heavy lids and sagging shoulders. People also recognize gut feelings, which they might refer to as the "butterflies in my stomach" or the "frog in my throat." Weak knees, a

TABLE 11.1
Modes of Conscious Representation of Ideas and Feelings

Conscious Representation Mode	Subsystems	Organizational Tendencies	Sample Organizing Statements	Sample Derivatives
Enactions	Musculature Autonomic nervous system	Sequences and combinations of actions	X does this. X and Y happen together like this.	Facial expressions Gestures Postures
Images	Visual Tactile Olfactory Gustatory Auditory	By spatial relationships; shape similarities and differences; simultaneous topographies	X is like this. X is like Y. X is here, and Y is there.	Dreams Daydreams Self-images
Words and numbers	Different languages	Grammar, syntax and sequence; by hierarchical categorization; by rules	If X and Y then Z because $X + Y = Z$.	Phrases Lists Logical deductions

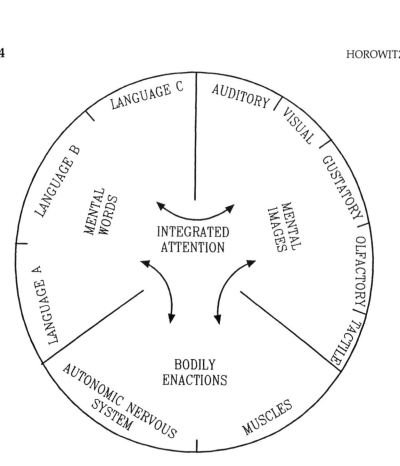

FIG. 11.1. Modes of representation.

pounding heart, a constricted throat, and a tightness across the upper back may be consciously felt and translated into semantic meanings such as, "I am afraid of something!"

The following examples of enactive representation clarify this aspect of conscious recognition of ideas and emotions: a pianist taps her fingers on a table while recalling a phrase of music; a dancer moves her hands and feet while recalling a choreographic phrase; and in anticipation of a coming tennis match, a woman notes that she makes various slight muscle tensions and micromovements. A wish–fear dilemma is enactively represented when a little boy wants some candy, but he has been emphatically told not to touch it. As he tentatively reaches for it with his right hand, he makes a stern, reproving face and grasps his right hand with his left. Translating these enactions into words and images clarifies what is happening, but sometimes conscious thought can only proceed through a series of motor impulses. If so, that occurs in peripheral awareness rather than reflective, self-observing awareness. Most of the time, consciousness is a reasonably harmonious blend across modes. For example, kinesthetic sensations—those of a pattern of moving—are often a synthesis of muscle sensations and tactile imagery.

These blends are a fascinating aspect of the mind–body problem. At the level of cognitive neuroscience, we know that each mode has its own modular brain systems. Conscious experiences are a high-level combination of many parallel processors. How are coherent meanings organized in constructing these experiences? We do not know the neuroscience answer to that, but a discussion of the psychological level construct of schemas will be helpful.

The Image Mode

There are various types of image representation that correspond to the various senses: visual, auditory, olfactory, gustatory, and tactile. Touch blends with enactive kinesthetic representations or concepts of moving in a certain way. Auditory and visual images blend into lexical representations when words are spoken or read, or when words are imagined as spoken or read. Writing words, really or imaginatively, also blends across modes of representation, and requires some kind of organization of meanings across neuronal networks.

Image formation allows an individual to review information for new meanings. Objects can be contemplated even in their absence. Just as the tensing of muscles can be called thought by trial action, images may be called thought by trial perception. As Singer (1966, 1973) demonstrated, children use imagery and fantasy for rehearsal of various skills and roles associated with maturity and adulthood. Adults also use daydreaming. The contents and forms of daydreaming change, and Singer showed that this is a development during the lifecycle.

The formation of images is a constructive process: one combines, compares, and recombines sets of information from perception and inner knowledge. This combination of external stimuli and internal biases means that images can rarely be deemed objective or correct. The visualization of a two-dimensional drawing as a three-dimensional room is one example of this overlap between sources. The conscious representation is forged from both information in the drawing and prior knowledge about the structure of a room.

One is not often consciously aware of which aspects of a perception come from the outside world and which come from the inside. We might see a stranger's face and believe for a moment that we are seeing a long-lost friend. This combination of perception and expectation is called an *illusion*. When we have a perception that is only derived from internal sources, yet we believe in the external reality of the situation, we call it an *hallucination*. If the perception is vivid but known to be unreal, it is a *pseudohallucination*.

This flexibility of perception can be advantageous; in fact, it is necessary in some situations because it allows for creativity and invention. Architects, painters, and surgeons employ the conceptual manipulation and formation of visual images. Skill at auditory image formation is useful in poetry and music; kinesthetic blends of spatial visual images, touch and bodily enactions are useful in dance; and olfactory and gustatory imagery is useful in cooking.

In addition to increasing creativity, image formation can circumvent some defensive controls that block the other two modes (Singer & Pope, 1978; Horowitz, 1998). Analysts, including Freud (Breuer & Freud, 1895; Freud, 1900, 1915), Jung (1939, 1959), and Kubie (1943), once suggested that their patients amplify free association by consciously forming visual images. Abreactive phenomena could occur when vivid imaging of past traumas led to an intensely emotional sense of reliving the experience. These techniques helped patients gain access to previously repressed memories and unconscious fantasies. The results of these clinical interventions indicated that images may evoke stronger emotional states than do purely verbal representations of difficult topics (Ferenczi, 1950; Jung, 1939, 1959).

Because visual images can evoke intense emotion, one can, by forming specific images, modify or transform an existing emotional state: a sense of danger can be activated by the formation of threatening images; sexual desire can be increased by erotic images; and anger can be fostered by images of bestial men attacking the innocent. A person may form anger-provoking images in order to become enraged and thereby ward off the experience of more threatening emotional states, such as fear or guilt (Jones, 1929).

Like other systems, visual images are constructed from multiple inputs. Figure 11.2 shows inputs into what Baars (1992) and Kosslyn (1990) have called the visual workspace. To the left of the figure is the entrance of information, bits from internal and external perceptual stimuli. External sensations are what one usually thinks about when talking of perceptual stimuli, but the eye itself can contribute stimuli from, say, the debris floating in the fluid of the eyeball or from the shadow of small blood vessels lying between light from the pupil and the photosensitive nerves of the retina. Experiences from these sensations are called *entoptic phenomena*. They are sometimes elaborated into illusions (Horowitz, 1998).

Information from other sources also flows into a representational system. One source, shown entering at the top of Fig. 11.2, involves memory of prior perceptions and conscious images. Usually, this is from short-term memory. Other sources of information, shown entering from the right of the figure, include activated ideational and emotional associations and schemas.

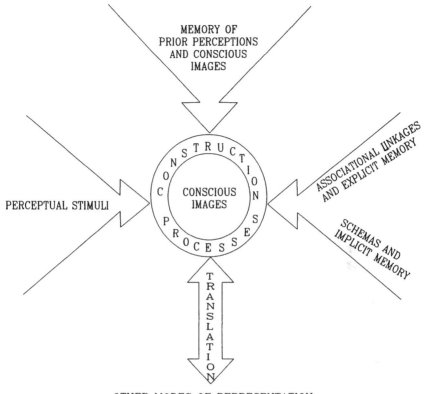

FIG. 11.2. Forming an image.

A consciously experienced visual image may contain elements of what was seen, but seeing itself is a constructive process. Some information is derived from internal knowledge, as in expectations of what might be seen. Some information is a priming of associational networks because of needs or motivational states, as in anticipation of desired or dreaded objects. The conscious experience is a best-fitting composite constructed from these diverse inputs.

The calculations and processes of input control in image formation are not conscious. Schemas organize perception and recollection; these cognitive maps are nonconscious, only derivatives are represented, and only derivatives can be reported. The schemas referred to here include both smaller and larger order schemas. Smaller schemas are those that allow a person to decipher the external world by organizing it into meaningful small wholes (Singer & Salovey, 1991). Larger schemas are those that establish perceptions of the self, as in body images, and establish a sense of overall identity and roles vis-à-vis others in the world. These may include person schemas (Horowitz, 1991). For example, small schemas might organize percepts into recognition of an eye, large schemas would combine eyes, nose and mouth, and yet larger schemas would recognize a whole person.

At the bottom of Fig. 11.2 we find entry of another source of input: the translation of information being expressed in other co-occurring modes of representation. Other image systems such as auditory image representation may contain information that can be cross-translated into visual image meanings such as when one listens to a story. Some people, when reading a number, have a certain hue in their visual images representing system. Color hearing is another relevant phenomenon: some persons, when hearing certain tones, also see certain colors—a translation across modes that is called *synesthesia*. Verbal systems such as reading a book may influence visual image formation, and enactive conscious representations may also be transformed into visualizations. One can feel a shape by moving one's finger around it, can translate that tactile sense into an enaction or kinesthetic sensation, and can end by labeling the felt object with words: "It is a baby's shoe."

The Lexical Mode

At birth, babies use simple sounds and then babbling to communicate with their caretakers. However, when babies first establish a connection between words and the objects and actions that they signify, they enter a new level of conscious thought. At this stage, children become more competent at abstract generalizations, at semantic reasoning, and at planning complex and orderly sequences. They learn temporal ordering in the process of sentence construction, just as they learned spatial ordering in the process of visual representation. Lexical expression opens up new worlds of understanding for the self and its environment.

Pure lexical representation would be actionless (no sub-vocal speech) and imageless (no auditory, visual, or kinesthetic accompaniments). Such purity is seldom found; consciousness is usually a blend as shown in the center of Fig. 11.1. However, some states of mind are characterized by many words and few images, others by vivid images and few words. Also, as Singer has shown, people vary in their trait-like use of different modes, and a few seldom experience vivid images in their mind's eyes, and report that they think entirely in words.

The lexical mode has its own preconscious information-processing modules. Generative grammar is one example. Like the other systems, these parallel processors are specialized networks for associating and reconfiguring both external and internal sources of information. As in the diagram for visual input (Fig. 11.2), the lexical system uses memory knowledge, grammatical schemas, and data derived from translations of meaning from other systems such as visual or auditory images of words. All these processors operate to some extent simultaneously, operating in different channels. The output of parallel processors is combined; smaller subsystems assemble meanings and then larger systems assemble more complex integrations.

Blending

Several modes of representation have now been discussed and we can turn to the interesting question of blending and harmonization across modes touched upon earlier. Some supraordinate schematic organization must allow coordination across modes, even though each mode might be formed using its own modules and subordinate schemas for unconscious processing of information.

Each mode or submode uses a specialized network of associated bits of information. Each module is served by several information processors operating in parallel. Separate memory storages and separable cognitive maps serve each parallel processor. Supraordinate schemas must help organize information across different parallel modules.

Selection of which possible schemas might assemble a set of information is regulated by control processes as well as by associational relevance to incoming stimuli. Control of supraordinate schemas influences all the subordinate schemas contained in the associational matrix. Such a transactive matrix could lead to blends or to seamless experiencing of a harmony of meanings across representational systems. This model of control of organizational forms is illustrated in Fig. 11.3. For simplicity, only some systems are considered: those for shape, grammar, and movement.

Schemas are abstract concepts akin to cognitive maps. Clinicians focus on person schemas in order to understand phenomena of identity experiences and of repetitive maladaptive interpersonal patterns (Horowitz, 1991, 1997; Singer & Salovey, 1991). The idea of an individual having a varied repertoire of person schemas can be illustrated with an example that links to issues of motivation and control.

Susan

Susan is preparing to give a lecture and she wants to dazzle her audience with a daring new approach. She is motivated to try for a great success and activates a hopeful schema that leads to visual images of a rapt audience, enthralled by her outstanding performance. She imagines herself in triumph. Schemas organize her conscious reflections about her professional competency.

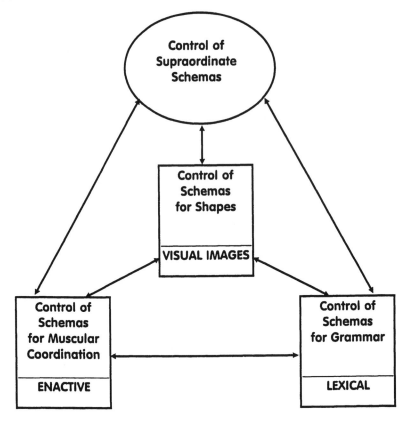

FIG. 11.3. Supraordinate control systems may coordinate subordinate schemas that are module-specific (only some modules are illustrated).

Then controls shift schemas. A dreaded state of shame is imagined as she has contrary images of a bored, disgusted audience. Her quest for a novel approach could lead to a humiliating disaster. She can anticipate and feel the sweat on her palms and the turmoil in her stomach before the event. Her identity experience is one of tremulous weakness and of being swallowed by the earth.

Late at night, Susan is tired and enters into this fearful state. She has bodily enactions of trembling. She thinks of negative words like failure and disaster. As a symbol of her fear of being reckless, she has intrusive images of a car speeding out of control. Somehow, she sleeps. In the morning, she realistically plans a novel, but not too risky, approach, organized by a competent sense of self. She imagines new slides for her data, she thinks of phrases like think it through, and plan it carefully, in order to help regulate her planning tasks.

Susan could contemplate her idealized, dreaded, and realistic scenarios, each organized by different roles of self. Using a split between her experiencing self and her observing self, Susan had an option of exerting conscious control over the unconscious operation of these schemas. If she focused her attention mainly on failure themes, she could prime and so increase a self-schema as an incompetent professor. If she focused mainly on fantasies of novelty and startling megasuccesses, she could activate (and even come to rely on) an excessively grandiose self-schema. If she focused reflective awareness on a realistic plan, she could activate a competent self-schema. Knowing the spectrum of possible selves gave her a sense of courage to try a new approach with a resolve to consider and practice it well before the event.

This example of Susan illustrates how activation and inhibition of person schemas can lead to formation of certain conscious representations and identity experiences, and not others. It also illustrates a split between self-experiencing and self-observing in reflective consciousness. Such consciousness can utilize several modes of representation. The modes can interact in both content and regulation of contents or forms.

In considering the formation of contents of consciousness, the historically emphasized psychology has been that of memories, and how active memories are retained from perceptions or primed from memory storages, as shown in the left part of Fig. 11.4. The middle part of that figure models the regulatory processes that are influenced by emotion systems and prior associations. To these classical models, contemporary theoreticians add cognitive maps, the kind of organizers shown as schemas on the right side of Fig. 11.4. Controls can affect associational networks by priming

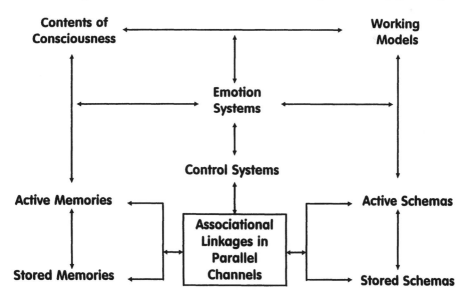

FIG. 11.4. Emerging contents and parallel processing.

or by inhibition. This can alter the activity of schemas, as well as alter episodic memories.

Schemas are shown in Fig. 11.4 as enduring, stored schemas. Working models of a current situation are influenced by both perceptions and active schemas primed from stored repertoires. Schemas, especially supraordinate schemas, can harmonize the contents of consciousness across the several modes of representation. They can do so by effecting parallel processors for the information that will enter or be augmented in each mode.

This theory is an associationist model, because schemas are complex associational networks just as are less generalized, mapped, or repackaged memories. To emphasize associational linkages, they are boxed in Fig. 11.4 as the heart of connections between meanings and forms.

Therapeutic Use of Multiple Modes of Conscious Representation

Therapists can teach patients how best to use each mode and to translate information across modes, a current interest of Singer (in press). Sometimes, work to reduce defensive inhibitions of a mode is indicated. This can reduce repression and dissociation, also interests of Singer (1990). Such work is typically part of both interpretive–exploratory techniques and supportive ones. Some examples are shown in Table 11.2. The examples of Fred and Paul will illustrate use of multiple modes of representation to advance stress mastery and personal development.

Fred: An Example of Mastery Over Unbidden Images After a Stressor Life Event

States of intrusion and denial numbing are typical deflections from ordinary consciousness after stressful life events. An intrusive state of mind often contains conscious representations of topics warded-off from expression during a denial state.

Fred, a young man at the peak of beginning his career, had pseudo-hallucinations after the suicide of a friend. A few days before the death, Gregory had called Fred and asked him to come over. Even though his friend had sounded depressed, Fred had replied that he was too busy. When he later heard that Gregory had committed suicide, Fred said to himself, "I refuse to feel guilty about that!" and tried to put thoughts of Gregory out of his mind.

A week later, Fred started seeing intrusive images of Gregory's face whenever he shut his eyes. He could not sleep with the lights off because the darkness would evoke more images. These images were so threatening

TABLE 11.2
Techniques to Foster Cross-Modal Representation

Observed Phenomenon	Sample of an Interpretative Intervention	Sample of a Suggestive Intervention
Images not associated with word meanings	You do not let yourself describe the images you are having because you are afraid to think about them clearly and you are afraid to tell me about those ideas.	Describe your images to me in words. Tell me what that image means.
Lexical representations not translated into images	You do not let yourself think that idea visually because you are afraid of the feelings that might occur if you did.	Let yourself think in visual images and report whatever you experience to me.
Vague images not intensified into reflective consciousness	You are afraid to let that fleeting image become really clear in your mind because you are afraid you will feel or act badly if you do.	Try to hold onto those images and tune them up.
Enactive representations not translated into images	You are afraid to picture in your mind the implications of your present posture and facial expression; you are afraid the self-image that would result would shame you.	Try to sense your posture and the expression on your face, and form a picture in your mind of what it would look like.

283

that he even changed the way that he washed his face in order to avoid closing his eyes.

Fred was treated with psychotherapy. Inhibition of lexical representation for the theme of Gregory was reduced. Issues of self-blame were then examined verbally. When the issues were resolved, the ghost-like intrusions abated.

Paul: An Example of Increasing Use of the Lexical Mode

In high school, Paul began to steal, drink, and cut class. His parents and psychotherapist tried to help him stop, but their efforts had no effect. Because his problems seemed to spring from psychological conflicts rather than from criminal intent, he was eventually placed in an adolescent daycare facility rather than prison.

Even though Paul was tactful and cooperative at first, he quickly began to break the rules. He tried to provoke the staff's enmity by lying, bringing a bottle of wine to the unit, and by breaking other assorted rules. He taunted the staff, making them either helplessly enraged or prone to react in a harsh, authoritarian manner. Unfortunately, Paul worked to enhance any hostility he found in this social context. If a woman on the staff scolded and restricted him, he would go to a man on the staff and describe the woman as unfairly overreacting. Apparently, this pattern replicated his family life.

Paul's mother oscillated between over-controlling, harshly punitive efforts and fluttering helplessness when she demanded that Paul's father punish him. His father vacillated weakly between an alliance with Paul or with his wife. Underneath Paul's manifest toughness and attempts to ally himself with the men around him, he had a weak self-concept. He was angry with his father for being weak.

The staff eventually recognized and discussed Paul's pattern of provocation. In the course of their discussions, they started understanding his problems, and they developed a consistent approach to help him. They patiently called Paul's actions to his attention by labeling them with the same words over and over. In addition, they calmly and repeatedly asked Paul about the meaning of his actions. This dialogue surprised Paul, geared as it was toward establishing verbal representation and planned (self-controlled) communication. He had expected punishment or abandonment, and was unaccustomed to translating his feelings into words.

Paul felt increasingly uneasy at the staff's unexpected reactions. He tested them to see how far he could go before they would retaliate by abusing or rejecting him. Then he began to like members of the staff and opened up to them. He started speaking about his fear of weakness, his anger toward his parents, and his fear of growing up and having to leave his home.

As Paul learned to analyze his actions for intentions, he gained conceptual skills. He also learned to consciously translate his aims into images and words rather than to act them out as behaviors with meager conscious planning. As he learned to better communicate his emotions, especially his urgent, angry sense of frustration, he felt more in control. His fear of his impulses lessened. His increased sense of capacity for this type of adult behavior helped him bolster a new, competent self-concept.

CONCLUSION

Consciousness is a combination of ideas and feelings, of memories and fantasies, and of realities and imaginings. It is a construction that melds multiple channels for unconscious processing. Multiple organizers, such as person schemas, can bring a sense of coherence in experience, and can blend the meanings that arch across many modes. Schemas, especially supraordinate schemas, provide an associational network that can integrate ideas and feelings across the many processors that feed information into separate modes for representation.

Understanding person schemas expands and clarifies theories about how defenses may operate. In addition to modifying entry at the portals or gates of representation, defensive control processes can shift the schemas that organize information processing. Person schemas can best be understood at the psychological level, because they are probably too complex as associational networks to reduce to neurobiology. As Singer and Kety have agreed, we may yet gain a biology of memory, but not of memories (including generalized memories). Like Singer, many of us should focus on the psychology of consciousness and its unconscious formative processes.

Psychotherapists need to focus on how conscious representation occurs. They can modify controls and help people experience new connections between meanings. They can teach people how conscious intentions can override unconscious defensive controls, even habitual ones. The result may be heightened use of enactive, image or lexical representations, or may be better integration of meanings across the modes. Insight can occur as meanings are cross-translated, using techniques as described by Singer (1974, in press). New decisions, based on enhanced attention and revised purposes, can be practiced over and over. This procedure can both reschematize self-concepts and lead to new identity experiences.

REFERENCES

Baars, B. J. (1992). Divided consciousness or divided self? *Consciousness & Cognition: An International Journal, 1*(1), 59–60.

Breuer, J., & Freud, S. (1895). Studies on hysteria. In *The standard edition of the complete psychological works of Sigmund Freud* (Vol. 2). London: Hogarth Press.

Bruner, J. S. (1964). The course of cognitive growth. *American Psychologist, 19*, 1.

Ferenczi, S. (1950). *Further contributions to the therapy and techniques of psychoanalysis*. London: Hogarth Press.

Freud, S. (1900). The interpretation of dreams. In *The standard edition of the complete psychological works of Sigmund Freud* (Vol. 4, pp. 1–320; Vol. 5, pp. 1–630). London: Hogarth Press.

Freud, S. (1915). The unconscious. In *The standard edition of the complete psychological works of Sigmund Freud* (Vol. 14, pp. 161–204). London: Hogarth Press.

Horowitz, M. J. (1970). *Image formation and cognition*. New York: Appleton-Century-Crofts. (Third edition now available as *Image formation and psychotherapy*. Northvale, NJ: Aronson, 1988.)

Horowitz, M. J. (Ed.). (1991). *Person schemas and maladaptive interpersonal patterns*. Chicago: University of Chicago Press.

Horowitz, M. J. (1997). *Formulation as a basis for planning psychotherapy*. Washington DC: American Psychiatric Press.

Horowitz, M. J. (1998). *Cognitive psychodynamics: From conflict to character*. New York: Wiley.

Jones, E. (1929). Fear, guilt and hate. *International Journal of Psycho-Analysis, 10*, 383–97.

Jung, C. G. (1939). *The integration of personality*. New York: Farrar & Rinehart.

Jung, C. G. (1959). *The archetypes and the collective unconscious*. New York: Pantheon.

Kosslyn, S. M. (1990). Mental Imagery. In S. Osherson, S. Kosslyn, & J. Hollervach (Eds.), *Visual cognition and action: An invitation to cognitive science* (Vol. 2). Cambridge, MA: MIT Press.

Kubie, L. S. (1943). The use of induced hypnotic reveries in the recovery of repressed amnesic data. *Bulletin of the Menninger Clinic, 7*, 172.

Singer, J. L. (1966). *Daydreaming*. New York: Random House.

Singer, J. L. (Ed.). (1973). *The child's world of make-believe*. New York: Academic Press.

Singer, J. L. (1974). *Imagery and daydreaming: Methods in psychotherapy and behavior modification*. New York: Academic Press.

Singer, J. L. (in press). *Imagery techniques and psychotherapy*. Washington, DC: American Psychological Association.

Singer, J. L., & Pope, K. S. (1978). *The power of human imagination*. New York: Plenum.

Singer, J. L., & Salovey, P. (1991). Organized knowledge structures and personality: Person schemas, self-schemas, prototypes and scripts. In M. J. Horowitz (Ed.), *Person schemas and maladaptive interpersonal patterns*. Chicago: University of Chicago Press.

Singer, J. L. (Ed.). (1990). *Repression and dissociation*. Chicago: University of Chicago Press.

Zajonc, R. B. (1980). Feeling and thinking. *American Psychologist, 35*, 151–75.

Zajonc, R. B., & Markus, H. (1984). Affect and cognition: The hard interface. In C. E. Izard, J. Kagan, & R. B. Zajonc (Eds.), *Emotions, cognitions and behavior*. Cambridge, England: Cambridge University Press.

Jack Kerouac: The Pulse of Memory

Delmont Morrison
University of California, San Francisco

INTRODUCTION

Although it is recognized that creative imagination can be nourished in a supportive, relatively conflict-free family environment, the focus in this chapter is the child's experience as the family endures the stress caused by the death of an important family member. The anxiety and conflict experienced by the child in this stressful life event, in combination with an enduring lack of conscious resolution, results in chronic preoccupations and affective states. In these situations the event has immediate effects but can also have an enduring influence on the individual's cognitive organization and future personal relationships. These psychological conditions may motivate the individual's persistent creative attempts to reconstruct and understand the original trauma. This model may be useful in understanding the development of creativity in other modalities such as the visual arts or science, but is used here to examine literature. The life and fiction of the late author Jack Kerouac are examined in the context of his reaction, as a child, to the death of an idealized older brother.

JACK KEROUAC: MEMORY AND CREATIVITY

Jack Kerouac did not learn to speak and write English until he was 5 years old, and he used his native French-Canadian language throughout his life. At about the time he was learning English at his Catholic school, he was going through a major reaction to the death of his 9-year-old brother, Gerard. Gerard was considered a saint by his mother and by the nuns who taught Gerard and Jack. His death from rheumatic heart disease was long and painful and was fully witnessed by Jack. The family never recovered from this death. As Jack later wrote, his mother Gabrielle lost all of her teeth, and his father Leo lost his Catholic faith. Working through his own mourning and tremendous sense of guilt, Jack, as a child, developed the Great Worlds' Snake fantasy and the sense that he was Judas to the Christ-like figure of Gerard. The evil serpent's purpose in life was to come from the dead, find Jack, and destroy him. He struggled with these images of himself while attempting to reduce his parent's grief by becoming the idealized Gerard. He tried especially hard to be the successful son his unsuccessful father needed, and became something of a high school hero in his native Lowell, Massachusetts. Although his own memories of this time describe his guilty sexual preoccupation and obsession with death, outwardly he was a star high school football running back and an admired intellect among his blue-collar friends. The severe tensions between self and ideal culminated after he received a football scholarship to Columbia University to be coached by the famous Lou Little. Drawn more to the escape of movies and literature than to the classroom and competitive sports, Jack soon dropped out of school.

This event marks a major shift in Jack's life because in quick succession he had a failed marriage, was discharged from the Navy after a psychiatric hospitalization, and began a lifelong habit of substance abuse. At this time he also became close friends with Neal Cassady and William Burroughs, who were, along with Jack, to have a major influence in the Beat literary movement. Cassady and Burroughs introduced Jack to people different from those he had known before. They had frequent encounters with the law, and also with drugs and alternative lifestyles, including homosexuality. Jack thought of Cassady as a brother and attempted to emulate his lifestyle and his writing style. The relationship between the two is expressed in *On the Road* (Kerouac, 1957) and *Visions of Cody* (Kerouac, 1993). Jack recognized Burroughs as a major influence and he was part of the character *Doctor Sax* (Kerouac, 1959). Kerouac's creativity came from his depression and preoccupation with his idealized images of Gerard. He sought resolution of these conflicts in relationships with idealized people such as Cassady and Burroughs, which also fed his creativity.

In contrast to many studies of affect and creativity, an examination of Kerouac's personal relationships and life indicate that his unresolved conflicts and affect-laden memories compelled him to write, and as in childhood play, to understand and to master his past experiences. These obligatory thoughts (Noy, 1979) reflected Kerouac's arrested mourning process for Gerard (Pollack, 1978) and were signs of the splitting of self

(Pine, 1985, chap. 9). His efforts to resolve his conflicts through his relationships, such as the ones with Cassady and Burroughs, is seen as a narcissistic extension of self with a corresponding inability to relate to the idealized person on a more reciprocal basis (Morrison & Morrison, 1989; Schniderman, 1995–96). This view of the source of creativity is an extension of current psychoanalytic–cognitive theory and differs significantly from major contemporary views of the contribution of affect to creative thought (Rothenberg, 1990; Russ, 1993).

AFFECT AND THE DEVELOPMENT OF CREATIVE THOUGHT

Affect is motivational as it is associated with varying levels of psychological tension and typically includes identifiable states such as anxiety, depression, anger, and affection. The interaction of these affective states and cognition is the subject of much current research about the development of creativity (Russ, 1993, chap. 2). Affective states can contribute to cognitive functioning by making an individual's thoughts richer and more diversified. For example, access to affect-laden states and openness to affective states in an individual is associated with an openness to experience, tolerance of ambiguity, self-confidence, and a preference for challenge. The excitement and tension involved in identifying and solving a problem create an affective pleasure that also contributes to creative thinking, if there is an appropriate modulation of affect, and integration of affect and cognition.

Affective states and thought have been the subject of intense study by psychoanalytic theorists and researchers (Holt, 1977; Noy, 1979). Primary-process thought describes two interrelated components that occur in the child's earliest representation of experience. A major content component is associated with affect-laden aggressive and libidinal wishes that are directed at objects that are differentiated from other objects at various levels. A second component is organized by formal qualities of primary-process thought, including illogical thinking, fusion of separate images, and loose associative links dominated by the expression of the wish. In the creative individual, primary-process thought is integrated with secondary process and both are available for the creative process. Thus, there is a richness in the individual's memory, associations, and divergent thinking, with a discovery of unique relationships and images advancing both the creative individual's and society's understanding of the domain that is of concern to the artist.

Studies with adults using the Rorschach procedure have shown that a measure of adaptive regression, indicating intensity of primary process material and effectiveness of integration, relates to a number of independent measures of creativity and problem-solving skills. The creative effort is a function of the interaction of both affective and cognitive components, and considerable literature indicates a close relationship between primary process, cognitive integration, and creativity in adults and children (Russ, 1993, chap. 2).

DYSFUNCTIONAL FAMILIES AND CREATIVITY

Although stable family relationships and the parents' respect for the child's imagination and personality are related to creativity (D. Singer & Singer, 1990, chap. 7), there are indications that creative individuals also grow up in families that do not always provide such a nurturing environment. Studies have shown that creative adults frequently come from families that are seen as emotionally distant, have considerable marital instability, and have family conflict. One of the earliest studies of eminent 20th-century individuals (Goertzel & Goertzel, 1962) found that 85% came from families demonstrating significant problems. The issue may be how these families cope with the commonly occurring stressors of life such as illness, birth, economic reversals, divorce, and death. Although the stressors may be shared by the family, coped with, and ultimately lead to a strengthening of family unity, these same stressors may disrupt a family that is poorly organized as a unit in the first place. The early experience of the death of a family member has been linked to later creativity.

Studies of individuals eminent in the arts, humanities, and military have shown that these creative individuals had lost a parent early in their life more frequently than expected in the population in general, while in a study of poets and distinguished writers, more than half had lost a parent before age 15 (Albert, 1978). The loss of a sibling in early childhood had also been noted in the lives of creative authors and artists (Pollack, 1978). What is the possible link between early loss and later creativity? Possible associations are in the stress created in the vulnerable family and in the child's unique emotional–cognitive organization at the time that greatly influenced his or her experience of the event.

EARLY LOSS AND THE MOURNING PROCESS

The child's initial understanding of death is that it is a transitory state such as sleep. Understood in this way, it is like something experienced and therefore knowable; loved ones, including pets, can return. Eventually, the child knows that it is a permanent state beyond experience and that no one really returns. This knowledge is the beginning of the child's awareness of his or her vulnerability and existential link with all of nature. The immediate effect of the child's experience of the death of a family member is an individual matter and depends on other variables such as the one who dies, the culture and religion of the family, and the circumstances of the death (Cain, Fast, & Erickson, 1964). Children react differently to the death of a parent (Pollack, 1962) and the death of a sibling (Pollack, 1978). The latter often generates ambivalent feelings of loss as well as some satisfaction in the removal of a rival for parental affection. As was true of Kerouac's experience, a prolonged serious illness of a sibling may require that parents devote time caring for the sick child, and because of the possibility of death, the child's value to the parents increases and more open demonstrations of love are displayed. Meanwhile, the child who is well may get less attention and is responded to in the routine manner of everyday life. After the death, the parents' view of the remaining children shifts, as future goals and anticipation, once focused on the dead child, may be transferred to them.

For the remaining children this early adaptation to change and loss is probably the first experience of the mourning process. A successfully completed mourning involves coming to terms with the loss psychologically with an exploration of the full range of affect involved. This can be a long-term process with the goal of freeing one from a person and event that only exists in memory. A successful outcome of the mourning process is a reduction of anxiety and sadness so that the memory of the event can be recalled and understood without intrusive, obligatory thoughts, such as guilt.

Brothers and sisters are often the objects of open expression of intense feelings of both affection and hostility that could not be expressed toward a parent. Although siblings may be seen as competitors, they are also models for learning, identification, and definition of self. The child knows and evaluates the sibling based on his or her own experience with that sibling, but also through the evaluation expressed directly and indirectly by a parent. This was true of Kerouac's experience of his older brother, and the discrepancy between his parents' experience, especially his mother's, and his own. Kerouac's mother idealized Gerard before and after his death, and was unable throughout Kerouac's life to let him forget his sainted dead brother. Idealization of the dead, which cannot be corrected by experience, is critical in making the mourning process pathogenic (Pollack, 1978). Kerouac's loss of an older brother also illustrates the importance of birth order if the older sibling for particular reasons, such as a serious illness, acquires an authority that rivals that of the parents.

Anxiety and Reflective Thought

Probably the most important variables in the disruption of cognitive–affective development due to the loss of a sibling are the cognitive maturity of the child at the time of the loss and the amount of stress and anxiety experienced at the time. Contemporary theory (Noam, 1985; Noy, 1979) and research (Harter, 1986; Nannis & Cowan, 1987) about the interrelationship of the development of cognition and self indicate that the cognitive capacity to integrate the awareness of self and awareness of others is a gradually evolving process, not adequately achieved until the beginning of adolescence. As Piaget (1952) observed, there is a perpetual confusion between the internal and external basis of understanding until representational and reflective thought develop to the point that the child can differentiate and accommodate to the two sources of information. Preoperational thought (Piaget, 1952), or primary-process thought (Noy, 1979), is important because it is the dominant cognitive system that the child uses to represent and organize early experience. The child's first representational systems are organized by egocentric motives at a stage when a cognitive system incorporating information regarding the discrimination between self and other is developing (Morrison & Morrison, 1988). Probably the most detailed description of the formal characteristics of this first representational system is the one described by Piaget (1952) as preoperational thought, while the evolving representation of self—developing from this system, which was ignored by Piaget—is discussed most fully in object relations theory (Pine, 1985, chap. 5) and in research on the development of the self-concept (Harter, 1986).

The first ways of organizing experience are affectively charged, preverbal, and metaphorical with mental representations that are egocentric. The initial representation of self develops mainly from interpersonal experience, while the self-concept as a cognitive system becomes more differentiated as a conceptual self, and later incorporates more socially shared systems. Mature thought regarding self is characterized by an always-evolving representational system that has access to memory and a capacity to explore new experiences, with an adequate balance between experiential and objective representations. A crucial aspect in this balance is the individual's ability to incorporate memory and to evaluate various operations of thought in the light of his or her results. Autonomous thought is subject to conscious control and is not dominated by either memory or affect, but can be enriched through the individual's capacity for reflective thought. The capacity for the self to reflect on itself is the major characteristic of autonomous thought.

INTRUSIVE MEMORY AND CREATIVITY

This description of the balanced personality, which has access to memory and affect in the context of autonomous thought, relates to the earlier discussions of the creative personality (Russ, 1993) and of the parent who encourages creativity in his or her child (D. Singer & Singer, 1990). However, creativity can also evolve in the child who does not develop such a balance. Because of chronic anxiety and conflict regarding self, he or she is compelled to repeat the unmastered events that were the source of the original conflict. Memory of experience that was a threat to the evolving self can become associated with anxiety that disrupts cognitive and emotional development. The images generated by such events become laden with anxiety and cannot be comfortably reflected upon and explored in terms of their meaning to self (Morrison & Morrison, 1988; J. A. Singer & Salovey, 1993, chap. 6). As the child develops, these images take on particular characteristics unlike anxiety-free images of experience. Because they are less accessible to reflective thought they do not go through the usual developmental transformation and synthesis, but remain represented by images acquired during a less differential period of cognitive development. Because of anxiety, reflective thought does not function adequately with these isolated memories, and consequently autonomous thought is not required for these events. Another characteristic of these images is that they became obligatory and intrusive, and the individual is compelled to explore them repeatedly through actions and preoccupation with inadequate reduction of the anxiety and unsatisfactory resolution of the conflicts (Terr, 1990, chap 12).

Because the individual's sense of historical self is determined by events that cannot be reflected upon, or explored and modified, a part of the self is unconscious and the self is functionally psychologically divided (Noam, 1985). The sense of an autonomous self does not develop, and the traumatized individual may seek to regain or establish self-confidence through association and identification with individuals who he or she perceives as having characteristics he or she needs but feels he or she does not have. The traumatized individual often attempts to establish a sense of trust in these relationships that was not available from important individuals who were physically present at the initial traumatic event, but were not available emotionally for the child (Brothers, 1995). Interpersonal events generating anxiety and disruption in development of self are multiple, but the death of a sibling, followed by experience that does not allow this event to be the subject of reflective thought and incorporated into consciousness, can result in the event continuing to be known essentially as the child originally understood it. In this situation, affect-laden memory intrudes on new experiences as the maturing individual attempts to understand his or her past and to create a different definition of self. Kerouac understood his past and present in terms of his memories of Gerard, and he attempted to reconstruct his future through relationships such as his enduring friendships with Cassady and Burroughs.

JACK KEROUAC'S MEMORY OF GERARD

Kerouac had recently lost his father, Leo, when he first met Cassady. Kerouac tried to express his complex feelings regarding Leo in his first published book, *The Town and the City* (Kerouac, 1950). The book was an idealized memory of his boyhood and was not a success. Whereas Kerouac struggled to express his own ideas and found himself uncomfortable with females and with people in general, Cassady appealed to Kerouac because he had none of those difficulties. When Kerouac first met Cassady he saw him as a Nietzschean intellectual hero without a formal education (Nicosia, 1994). He was also impressed with Cassady's sexual prowess and way with women. Whereas Kerouac was preoccupied with guilt and ideas of right and wrong, Cassady had a long history of arrests for acts such as stealing cars. Most importantly, Cassady could verbally express his experiences and his ideas about creativity in an incisive manner.

In November 1950, Kerouac was struggling to begin his next novel when he received a letter from Cassady in which he tells the story of a Christmas in 1946 in Denver with his girlfriends Joan Anderson and Cherry Mary. The two men had known each other for approximately 4 years, and had already shared the travels that were to become *On the Road* (Kerouac, 1957). Kerouac immediately read the story and was profoundly moved. He was particularly impressed with Cassady's ability to describe his experience in honest terms. He quickly wrote a series of letters to Cassady that demonstrate how influential Cassady's style of writing became for Kerouac. As he said, he needed to confess to Cassady his own hypocrisy and dishonesty with himself while he authored what was to be his lifework (Charters, 1995, p. 243). In the first of a series of long letters to Cassady, Jack attempted to "proceed to the actual truth" of his life.

He begins with his memory of his own birth and the images of red air and sadness. Remembering himself in a wicker-basket baby carriage, he thinks that somewhere during that time his sin began because he knew that a Great World Snake was worming its way toward him. In this context, Kerouac moves on to describe Gerard, his dead brother. Although he describes mankind as "covered with sin and self disgrace," Gerard is a beautiful, angelic boy who, according to Jack, looks like himself in his earliest photographs. He writes that Gerard could not understand or tolerate violence of any kind. At one time Gerard lectured their cat for eating a mouse Gerard was nursing after it was caught in a trap. Kerouac tells of his mother repeating such stories of Gerard to him a million times and confesses to Cassady that he is convinced that Gerard was a saint. Gerard's love of birds was powerful, and every act of love he made was recorded in their mother's memory forever. The impact of Gerard's life and death is beyond his understanding, as is evidenced in this letter to Cassady, "Neal, the death of this child was a loss that must be impossible for you and I to calculate in the souls of my mother and father" (Charters, 1995, p. 253).

These letters to Cassady continued for approximately 2 months and not only served as a confession for Kerouac, but also were the basis of two major books he would write, *Visions of Gerard* (1961) and *Doctor Sax* (1959). Each book is a memory of Gerard's death. Kerouac's memories illustrate the richness of affect and evolving definition of self, in the context of death and guilt that were to be his lifelong characteristics. These autobiographical memories defined Kerouac's personality and influenced much of his creativity.

One night in 1955 Kerouac was visiting Cassady and his current girlfriend at her apartment in San Francisco. Natalie Jackson was very much part of the group of people who frequented North Beach at that time and was known to have serious emotional problems. Cassady frequently left Kerouac alone with his girlfriends, and he did so that night as well. Natalie became very angry and depressed, threatening suicide. Kerouac was trying to incorporate the teachings of Buddha into his concept of Catholicism at the time and dealt with her by explaining Buddhism. The actual sequence of what happened and exactly when it happened has been lost, but Natalie either fell or jumped to her death from the roof of the apartment building (Clark, 1990, pp. 141–42). Kerouac reacted by immediately leaving for his sister's home in North Carolina, where his mother was staying. However, when he arrived, his mother and sister had commitments, and he was left alone. One night he had a vision of his own death and began writing down his memory of Gerard:

> For the first four years of my life, while he lived, I was not Ti Jean Dulouz, I was Gerard, the world was his face, the flower of his face, the pale stopped disposition, the heartrearingness and the holiness and his teachings of tenderness to me . . . (Kerouac, 1961, p. 2)

This memory of his fusion with Gerard, which is the opening paragraph of *Visions of Gerard*, indicates the intensity of Kerouac's identification with the figure his mother saw as a saint. The story contains many examples of Gerard's Christlike life and acts of love and kindness. Another theme is sin, and in the book even Gerard has sins: He confesses he has pushed one boy and looked at another boy's penis. The heavy burden of sin, original or acquired, dominates the story.

Gerard's Death: Other Memories

In *Visions of Gerard* (Kerouac, 1961) the memory of Gerard is the one endorsed by Gabrielle and the nuns who loved the suffering Gerard as a Christlike figure. Kerouac does comment that in his memory he recalled not having his needs met because of the needs of Gerard, but he manages to mitigate the angry frustration by understanding how selfish his needs are compared to the needs of the suffering Gerard. He states that he knows his mother loved Gerard more than she loved him. Kerouac's lifelong preoccupation with "falling from grace" begins as a 4-year-old "who basked in Gerard's eternal bliss and made to appreciate it as a fallen angel." The exploration of jealousy and anger as part of grief does not occur in the memory.

In his confessional letters to Cassady, Kerouac explores the more puzzling and mysterious memories of Gerard. In *Visions of Gerard* he describes the Erector set that Gerard received on Christmas, and remembers it in the context of love. As Kerouac watches Gerard with the set he expresses these feelings, ". . . in the action of his hands and the working of his face as he thinks, and I marvel at my love for him" (Kerouac, 1961, p. 66). He describes a different memory of the Erector set to Cassady. It was just before Gerard died, and while he was working with the set, that the 4-year-old Jack knocked down part of the structure. Gerard in "understandable rage" slapped him in the face. Even to Cassady, Kerouac can only remember his guilt and sadness as a reaction to this incident, which he reports as the last thing he remembered before Gerard's death, "Gray vultures of gloomy day were feeding at the rooftops of time, I could see outside the curtains. Gloom, grayness, faucet-ticking . . ." (Charters, 1995, p. 259).

An enduring image for Kerouac throughout his life was the Great World Snake. This morbid image was intimately related to Gerard's life and death. When Jack was 3 or 4 years old, the family moved into a house that was allegedly built over an ancient, sunken cemetery. One night, lights began flashing in his bedroom. Kerouac associated this with other strange happenings in the house, such as plaster falling from the ceiling, as notification that the souls of the dead were shaking in their graves because the living had built a house on their cemetery. When Kerouac asked Gerard about the flashing light he replied that it was the souls of the dead. A few nights later Jack remembers a figure standing above his crib. Even in the letter to Cassady, Kerouac is confused about whether it was the soon-to-be-dead Gerard risen like a ghost from his bed of miseries to haunt him, or a ghost from the disturbed cemetery. Kerouac's difficulties in understanding his feelings for Gerard are expressed to Cassady in his view that Gerard died because they lived above the cemetery and the ghost was Gerard, who probably hated him.

During a time when Kerouac was aware of Gerard's impending death, he remembers believing that a house nearby was haunted by an evil old man. This was the "Mighty Snake Hill Castle." This image is closely interrelated with the Dr. Sax figure, and the Great World Snake that had searched for Jack since he was an infant when his "sin" began: "Worming its way up from the middle of the world, devouring dirt, excreting dirt, inch by inch arriving, to find me in poor Lowell . . ." (Charters, 1995, p. 250).

It is unclear what Kerouac thinks his sin is. It seems vaguely related to Gerard and to guilt. He cannot say he just loved Gerard as a person, but can only describe the relationship as he remembers as a child: admiration, love, guilt, and sadness. Gerard could be seen as a saint in *Visions of Gerard*, but not as a total person because of Kerouac's difficulty in exploring and understanding his own jealousy and hostility. In Kerouac's letters to Cassady, he says that Gerard's death was the beginning of his own mysteries. His sense of guilt and of being a fallen angel became concretized with the fantasy of the Great World Snake, the basis of *Dr. Sax*. However, there is no Gerard nor any Catholic family morality to order experience for Kerouac in *Doctor Sax*. The image of Doctor Sax is part Leo, Kerouac's father, part W. C. Fields, part the Shadow, and part Burroughs. The first three are memories from the past. Burroughs is a contemporary vision of an alternative route to escape the memories of the past.

The Herb Didn't Work: William Burroughs

Although Kerouac discussed his preoccupation with the Great World Snake in earlier letters to Cassady, it was almost 3 years later, when he was 30 years old and living with Burroughs in Mexico, that he wrote *Dr. Sax*. Published years later (Kerouac, 1959), *Dr. Sax* is an elaborate fantasy of that preoccupation. Having externalized the source of his conflict in the fantasy of the snake, Kerouac attempts, with the character of Dr. Sax, to find an external solution. It is the failure of this solution in the book and in his life that is significant.

Burroughs' influence on Kerouac was twofold: relating to intellectual interests and drug use. Kerouac and Burroughs were both living near the campus of Columbia University when they met. Kerouac was in a major personality crisis involving his failures in college, football, the Navy, and marriage. Burroughs exuded personal and intellectual confidence at the time. Whereas Kerouac came from a lower middle-class background, Burroughs' family had considerable money and social position. Burroughs helped introduce Kerouac to drugs. Although Kerouac was involved in homosexual relationships and heavy drug use, in his relationship with Burroughs there are indications he felt guilty about that lifestyle. Most importantly, at the time, and throughout their relationship, Kerouac saw Burroughs as his great teacher. Burroughs was an addict and saw heavy drug use as an acceptable part of life. Kerouac brought drugs with him when he arrived at Burroughs' place in Mexico, and both used marijuana and frequently shot up on morphine during the visit (Clark, 1990, pp. 109–110; Nicosia, 1994, p. 390). Kerouac was also experimenting with a new nonlinear form of writing he had developed under the influence of Cassady. Kerouac described this act of creativity as his mind exploding to say something about every image and every memory that would be expressed in a form beyond the confines of a story (Nicosia, 1994, p. 392).

The book is about growing up, and events, dreams, childhood impressions, and memories are intermixed. The earliest memories are of death and include Gerard and a host of others: "Catholic childhood of Centraville-deaths, funerals, the shroud of that, the dark figure in the corner when you look at the deadman coffin in the dolorous parlor of the open house with a horrible purple wreath on the door" (Kerouac, 1959, p. 76).

To reduce the anxiety and depression of his boyhood, Kerouac and his friends engaged in sexual stimulation, masturbation, and fantasies of girls. The press of sex pushed Kerouac toward engagement, but the move toward adulthood in his mind is equated with the loss of a favorite toy, a ballbearing in the mud of a neighbor's yard: "But doom came like a shot, when it did, like the foreboding said, and like implied in the laugh of Dr. Sax as he glides among the mud where my ballbearing was lost . . ." (Kerouac, 1959, p. 76).

The ballbearing loss is significant because it was also an important part of an enduring and elaborate paracosmic game (Morrison & Morrison, 1988; Silvey & MacKeith, 1988) using marbles that Kerouac actually developed not long after Gerard's death. In this game Kerouac was able to control his chaotic, fearful experience by using marbles as racehorses and handicapping them by chipping their surfaces. Generally, the book's mood is depressed, and is dominated by images such as the description in Part 4 of the man with the watermelon who died on the Moody Street Bridge in Kerouac's presence. The one potential positive force is the character of Dr. Sax. The images of Dr. Sax, the Great World Snake, and Kerouac's guilt and evil dominate the conclusion of the book.

The Image of Dr. Sax

Probably the first articulate fantasy of Sax developed from *The Shadow* radio shows and comic books that Kerouac loved when he was 8 to 10 years old. As an adolescent, he wrote short stories of *The Shadow*, and the image of the dark figure and his hat, cape, and invisibility is expressed in his adult imagination. *The Shadow* was also associated with W. C. Fields. The consistently male figure knows what the mystery is, and although he may be a guide through the fear and anxiety, "his knowing laugh strikes terror in your heart." In the beautifully written dream in *Dr. Sax*, Kerouac brings together the collected memories of Sax, beginning with a scene in the alley where Leo had his business. Multiple memories of movies seen as a child are fused with memories of real events and with dreams culminating in the flooding of the Merrimac River in Lowell in 1936, and the destruction of Kerouac's world.

At this moment the figure of Dr. Sax, who has never fully appeared in the book, now comes to save Kerouac. He is dressed like the Shadow and has a W. C. Fields mask. Kerouac defends himself against his genuine feeling of evil and death by portraying Sax and himself as stumbling over each other and bumping into each other like the Three Stooges or the Marx Brothers. Sax has received a secret powder from a dark eagle and Jack admits that they are both crazy. At this point he is writing fully in stream-of-consciousness and they explore and know various events in his childhood, finally arriving at the castle on Snake Hill where the confrontation with the Great World Snake takes place. The scene is one of judgment day complete with angels. A snake, as the symbol of evil, rises from the pit of the castle to claim Kerouac: "I leaned on a stone, the Pit yawned below, I looked down to face my horror, my tormentor, mad-face demon of myself" (Kerouac, 1959, p. 238). Sax squeezes a vial of one of his secret potions on the snake and the potion is so powerful that it causes the very earth to shake, but the snake continues to pursue Kerouac. At that point, Sax is transformed again, this time to the common everyday figure who can only be Burroughs, who says simply, "The herb didn't work" (Kerouac, 1959, p. 240). Kerouac's memory and anxiety are his, and no external source such as a drug will change that.

CONCLUSION

At times, at some conscious level, Kerouac recognized his resentment and hostility toward his brother, but he never resolved his conflicts involving his brother, his father, and his mother. Leo was on his deathbed when he told Kerouac that Burroughs would destroy him someday (Clark, 1990, p. 69). Kerouac always went back to Gabrielle, who never approved of his life, and was openly hostile to Burroughs. At the same time, Kerouac needed Burroughs and saw him as his great teacher. He introduced Kerouac to drugs as a way of expanding his consciousness and creativity. Kerouac was becoming a substance abuser before *Doctor Sax* and began a steady decline afterward, finally dying from the effects of alcoholism at the age of 47 in a home he shared with Gabrielle.

Alcohol and drugs, as Burroughs said as Doctor Sax, did not work to reduce Kerouac's conflict, self-doubts, and sense of failure. His abuse only added to his depression. Obsessed with his memories of the past, he also tried to resolve the conflicts of self through his relationships and his creativity. His relationships with Cassady and Burroughs failed to provide him with satisfaction. His close relationships were generally based on

early narcissistic injuries to self and his attempts to reconstruct what he
felt he had failed to obtain when "the mysteries began" with Gerard's
death. What gave him some satisfaction, at least initially, was his creativity. His capacity to express these early images and his attempt to weave
them into his life to create something beyond his past was his art. At
times, he succeeded as perhaps no one else from his generation has.
Kerouac's memory of the flooding of the Merrimac River in Lowell, which
he witnessed when he was 14 years old, demonstrates that he could write
visions:

> By moonlight night I see the Mighty Merrimac foaming in a thousand white
> horses upon tragic plains below. Dream: wooden sidewalk planks of Moody
> Street Bridge falls out, I hover on beams over rages of white horses in the
> roaring low, moaning onward, armies and cavalries in charging Euplantus
> Eudronicus King Grays loop'd and curly like artists' work, and with clay
> souls' snow curlicue rooster togas in the forefront (Kerouac, 1959, p. 8–9).

REFERENCES

Albert, R. S. (1978). Observations and suggestions regarding giftedness, family influence
    and the achievement of eminence. *Gifted Child Quarterly, 22*, 201–211.
Brothers, D. (1995). *Falling backwards.* New York: Norton.
Cain, A., Fast, I., & Erickson, M. E. (1964). Children's disturbed reaction to the death of a
    sibling. *American Journal of Orthopsychiatry, 34*, 741–752.
Charters, A. (1995). *Jack Kerouac: Selective letters.* New York: Viking.
Clark, T. (1990). *Jack Kerouac.* New York: Paragon House.
Goertzel, V., & Goertzel, M. (1962). *Cradles of eminence.* Boston: Little Brown.
Harter, S. (1986). Cognitive-developmental processes in the integration of concepts about
    emotions and the self. *Social Cognition, 4*, 119–151.
Holt, R. R. (1977). A method of assessing primary process manifestations and their control
    in Rorschach responses. In M. Rickers-Ovsiankiua (Ed.), *Rorschach psychology.* New York:
    Wiley.
Kerouac, J. (1950). *The town and the city.* New York: Harcourt Brace.
Kerouac, J. (1957). *On the road.* New York: Viking.
Kerouac, J. (1959). *Dr. Sax.* New York: Grove Weidenfield.
Kerouac, J. (1961). *Visions of Gerard.* New York: Penguin.
Kerouac, J. (1993). *Visions of Cody.* New York: Penguin.
Morrison, D., & Morrison, S. (1988). The development of romantic ideation & J. M. Barrie's
    image of the lost boy. In D. Morrison (Ed.), *Organizing early experience.* Amityville, NY:
    Baywood.
Nannis, E., & Cowan, P. A. (1987). Emotional understanding: A matter of age, dimension
    and point of view. *Journal of Applied Developmental Psychology, 8*, 289–304.
Nicosia, G. (1994). *Memory babe.* Berkeley: University of California Press.
Noam, G. (1985). Developmental psychopathology: An introduction. *McLean Hospital Journal,
    10*, 12–14.
Noy, P. (1979). The psychoanalytic theory of cognitive development. *Psychoanalytic Study of
    the Child, 34*, 169–215.

Piaget, J. (1952). *The origins of intelligence in children*. New York: International Universities Press.

Pine, F. (1985). *Developmental theory and clinical process*. New Haven, CT: Yale University Press.

Pollack, G. H. (1962). Childhood parents and sibling loss in adult patients: A comparative study. *Archives of General Psychiatry, 7*, 295–305.

Pollack, G. H. (1978). On siblings, childhood sibling loss, and creativity. *The Annuals of Psychoanalysis*, Vol. VI. New York: International Universities Press.

Rothenberg, A. (1990). *Creativity and madness*. Baltimore: Johns Hopkins University Press.

Russ, S. W. (1993). *Affect and creativity*. Hillsdale, NJ: Lawrence Erlbaum Associates.

Schniderman, L. (1995–96). Cynthia Ozick: Diverse functions of transitional objects in fiction. *Imagination, Cognition and Personality, 15*, 207–222.

Silvey, R., & MacKeith, S. (1988). The paracosm: A special form of fantasy. In D. Morrison (Ed.), *Organizing early experience*. Amityville, NY: Baywood Publishing Company.

Singer, D., & Singer, J. L. (1990). *The house of make believe: Children's play and the developing imagination*. Cambridge, MA: Harvard University Press.

Singer, J. A., & Salovey, P. (1993). *The remembered self: Emotion and memory in personality*. New York: The Free Press.

Terr, L. (1990). *Too scared to cry*. San Francisco: Harper & Row.

Imaginative Play and Television: Factors in a Child's Development

Dorothy G. Singer
Yale University

> *The medium of make-believe in childhood, internalized by middle childhood into a richly elaborated fantasy capacity, becomes eventually a major functional system through which all of us can entertain opportunities and possibility for warmth, closeness, and communion with others while still sustaining our sense of individuality and privacy.*
> —J. L. Singer (1996, p. 211)

DAYDREAMING AND THE ROOTS OF IMAGINATION

Poppy Ott, a character in a series of boys' books, emerged as a hero for Jerome Singer in his preadolescent and early adolescent years. Poppy Ott was clever, intellectually gifted, and in Singer's fantasies became a football superstar, although the original stories had nothing to do with the game. Other fantasy figures of his, the distinguished senator and the great composer, helped fill Singer's idle moments through the use of his vivid imagination and elaborate daydreaming. With detailed drawings and scribblings in his notebooks, he depicted these figures as well as an assortment of associated characters.

Pleasure and excitement accompanied these rich fantasies, but Singer realized quickly that his fantasy life needed to be kept private and circumspect in order to avoid embarrassment. Fortunately for psychology, Singer's innate curiosity about his own rich inner life led him in later years to examine the phenomenon of daydreaming in a systematic way, and to lay the groundwork for numerous investigations that followed. Before J. L. Singer's book *Daydreaming* (1966) appeared, daydreaming had been considered a trivial epiphenomenon, and along with consciousness in general, had seldom been the topic of systematic research. *Daydreaming*'s presentation of his own fantasies, questionnaires such as the Imaginal Processes Inventory (IPI) for adults (adapted for children by McIlwraith & Schallow, 1982–83, and Rosenfeld, Huesman, Eron, & Torney-Purta, 1982), interview data, and numerous experimental studies heralded a rich body of research carried out by Singer's laboratory and other researchers whom his work inspired.

When one studies daydreaming, it is natural to ask how it begins and why it happens. Singer's curiosity led him to examine children's play and the roots of imagination. Accepting White's (1959) notion of competence, Singer argues that a baby achieves pleasure and control through the early game of peek-a-boo. Eventually, a baby learns that objects or people disappear and reappear, and that this game can be played by baby as well as by the adult. This capacity for control and self-actualization helps children to differentiate themselves from their environment and further their willingness to explore other types of play. Play for its own sake, the joy and sense of pleasure and efficacy that comes from a feeling of control over self and environment, paves the way for symbolization, imagery, and for the "attitude toward the possible" (Goldstein, 1940).

Both White's and Singer's positions are close to that of Piaget, who was intrigued by a child's fundamental role of curiosity. Just as Piaget proposed, Singer also asserted that much of a child's striving to understand the world is part of the normal motor and cognitive development of an individual's feeling of competence. Piaget's careful observations and recordings of his children's play behaviors reinforced his belief that a child processed information differently at each stage due to biological structures or to hereditary adaptation (Piaget, 1952, 1962). Added to Piaget's theory is Singer's stress on the importance of emotion and human interaction as impetus for play. The mother's face with its smile, for example, will be one of the first stimulus sources for the baby's responses and ability to interact with the environment.

Although Singer recognizes the various forms of play such as sensorimotor play of babies, or the later forms of play such as games involving physical skills or rule games, his main emphasis and chief interest throughout his studies have been on make-believe play, play that is "not obviously associated with direct satisfaction of biological needs. . . . or the overcoming of immediate obstacles in one's life situation. It is relatively free of any effort to meet standards set up by society. At least the standards of play, one might say, are established by the player himself within a context that need not be the same as those ordinarily observable in society" (Singer, 1973, p. 11).

In keeping with his interest in the origins of make-believe play, Singer's book, *The Child's World of Make-Believe* (J. L. Singer, 1973), is a thorough compilation of empirical studies of make-believe play and its implications for the emotional and cognitive life of the child. In this book, Singer departs from the narrow psychoanalytic model of drive reduction as a basis for fantasy and make-believe. He and his collaborators accept Berlyne's (1969) theory of curiosity and exploration as inherent drives. As Singer puts it, "imaginative play of children represents an effort to organize available experience and at the same time utilize motor and cognitive capacities to their fullest" (J. L. Singer, 1973, p. 23). Using Tomkin's (1962) cognitive–affective model, Singer proposes that to the extent a child interacts successfully with novel material, interest, alertness, and positive emotions will ensue. As the toddler or preschooler becomes increasingly familiar with a toy or game, more joy and laughter will be forthcoming.

Through the development of observation techniques, questionnaires and rating forms, Singer was able to empirically test his assumptions that play led to joy and laughter. Toward this end, I began to join him in the play aspects of research in the early 1970s after a fruitful collaboration for the *Annual Review of Psychology* about the topic of personality (J. L. Singer & D. G. Singer, 1972). Focusing on make-believe play and imagination, an area of interest to both of us, we began the design of numerous experiments and instruments that would help us to carry out more systematic studies of this common activity of children, and as we found through our work, there is a continuation of the playful spirit and play itself throughout the life cycle.

One of our first joint projects involved a study of the play of preschoolers. Using an observation form that we developed, we trained students to do continuous 10-minute samplings of play of specific children during free play in their recreation rooms, and during structured play with specific materials such as arts and crafts. Children were rated on a 5-point scale for imagination, positive affect, and concentration, as well as on moods such as anger, fear, elation, fatigue and aggression (J. L. Singer, 1973). Our results were consistent with Pulaski (1973), who found that children played more imaginatively in free play with unstructured materials and toys (blocks, puppets) than in controlled play settings with structured toys (battery-operated toys). In addition to the Pulaski experiment, other research studies carried out by students of Singer and presented in *The Child's World of Make-Believe* (J. L. Singer, 1973) also attest to the power of spontaneous imagination and fantasy.

The questionnaire, The Imaginative Play Predisposition Interview (IPPI), also discussed in the book, sought to determine differences among children's responses to such items concerning their favorite toys, favorite games played, ways they played, and whether or not they had a make-be-lieve friend. J. L. Singer (1961) earlier had used a version of this question-naire to test whether there would be a difference between high- and low-fantasy groups in their ability to sit still in a rocket ship game. Forty children between the ages of 6 and 9 years were told that experimenters were looking for astronauts of the future. Children were asked to sit quietly in chairs for as long as they possibly could. The experimenters were careful to inform the participants that no selections actually would be made, but they wanted the children to see what kinds of conditions were necessary for a space flight. Two conditions were included; in one, children could indicate when they wanted to get up, and in the second, they were asked to remain seated for 15 minutes. Results found that high-fantasy children were able to sit in place longer than children who had reported little indication of daydreams or of make-believe play. The high-fantasy children used some motor activity and vocalizations as they sat in their chairs, suggestive of some pretense at flying. A further result found differences in creativity of stories they told as rated by judges who were unaware of the experimental objectives or of the differences of fantasy production on the questionnaire. A replication of this procedure years later with preschoolers yielded similar results (J. L. Singer & D. G. Singer, 1981).

Interestingly, Rosenfeld et al. (1982) found that data from her adaptation of the Imaginal Processes Inventory (IPI) correlated with the IPPI. She identified three patterns or factors that characterized children's fantasy styles. Factor I was labeled Dysphoric or Unpleasant–Aggressive Style, Factor II was Forceful–Intense Style, and Factor III was labeled the Active–Intellectual Style. These styles are similar to those found for adult daydreams.

The IPPI sought to determine whether children ever had pictures in their heads, or what sorts of things or pictures they thought about. An additional set of questions probed for information about the games they played with their parents and whether their parents read to them or told them stories. We added two questions about television, although at that time neither we nor others recognized the tremendous influence this medium would exert on children. We added more instruments and more variables relating to this medium as our work in the area of imagination continued, and in later years, we replicated and expanded on our research about play and television in the numerous other studies reported in *The House of Make-Believe* (D. G. Singer & J. L. Singer, 1990).

The Metarepresentational Mode

As research progressed, many questions about the origins of make-believe play emerged. In the preverbal stage we do not know if the baby is using imagery extensively, but through observations of a toddler, we do see some imagery storage capacity manifested by the simple words, phrases, or movements of the child as he or she plays in the crib or on the floor. As the child matures and more information is stored, more schemata or plans are formed about the environment. Thus, this accommodation–assimilation process allows the child to adjust and to adapt to the environment more easily. Singer suggested that preschoolers' play involves both a rapid sequence of motor interactions with their environment and bits and pieces of conversation from the stories they have heard or assimilated from the television medium. Singer stated, "A child confronts an environment which consists in part of memory material as well as material directly presented to the senses. The very young child may make no clear distinction between these two sources of stimulation interweaving them seemingly in a random fashion. Gradually, the combinations of the momentary concerns and problems of the child as well as the predisposition set which the child is already beginning to acquire toward make-believe in imagery, may begin to assert themselves" (J. L. Singer, 1973, p. 197).

To enhance imagery formation and make-believe further, Singer (1973) proposed the following to help a child process and reprocess stored material and to develop a set or predisposition toward attending to this material: (a) a child must have the opportunity for privacy and for the practice of imagery; (b) there must be available materials such as playthings, books, and stories; (c) there must be freedom from interference by adults or peers who demand immediate responses or reactions; and (d) there is a need for older children or adult models who encourage, sanction, and accept make-believe without the teasing or putting down that many people do unwittingly.

Such opportunities for play can help a child to engage in a meta-representational mode of thought that Leslie (1987) has deemed necessary for the development of a *theory of mind*, an awareness of one's own thoughts. Leslie has proposed that through play the child forms a set of perceptual images of objects, persons, or situations into a new set of symbols or mental representations that become part of an entire system of thought. The child on his or her own, or with the help of an adult, develops this ability to transform or change representations into metaphors. This theory of mind suggests that human beings are capable, through the metarepresentational system, of making inferences about causes and predictions about future events. As J. L. Singer (1996) has asserted, they can "recognize the consequences of ignorance, distinguish reality from fantasy, acquire a language of words and phrases depicting mental experiences or states, and infer motivations" (p. 207). Recently, research in our center, following up on false-belief experiments, found that greater verbal ability and language skills enhanced a child's development of metarepresentation. Results indicate that children who had a larger receptive vocabulary performed better on both appearance–reality and false-belief tasks, and were more likely to engage in jointly constructed sociodramatic play than were children with less verbal facility (Rosen, Schwebel, & J. L. Singer, 1997; Schwebel, Rosen, & J. L. Singer, in press).

By the end of the second year of a toddler's life, pretend play and the beginning of a metarepresentational system can be identified. Fein (1981) has demonstrated that some infants, as early as 18 months of age, can pretend to drink from a cup, and soon after can offer a drink to a toy animal. As the child's cognitive capacities emerge through development of the brain and through increased social experiences, further and more complex imaginative play emerges. By 3 to 4 years of age, children are evidencing the ability to recognize and to effectively signal play and nonplay states. By 5 years of age they are able to develop more play themes, to organize rules, and to use pretense more elaborately than their younger friends (Takahashi, 1989). Play becomes more social and cooperative as the child advances in age. The simple social play of the toddler becomes social pretend play with the changes of voice, settings, roles, and more intricate plots.

Factor-Analytic Studies of Play

Both in an invited address to the Division of Educational Psychology (August 1976, American Psychological Association, Washington, D.C.), and in an article, Singer presented some of the specific potential advantages of make-believe play for growth and learning (J. L. Singer, 1977). Many of these benefits have been proposed by other researchers, but few have studied the advantages of play as systematically as Singer. He has found that children who play at make-believe smile more, are happier, give evidence of empathy, appear more interested in their surroundings and in activities, and are less likely to engage in aggressive behavior. In terms of self-control and waiting behaviors, children who reported more make-believe behavior as part of their daily play are able to sit still for longer periods of time and resist temptations to touch a toy. There appears to be a relationship between greater restraint and self-control and make-believe play. Children who play make-believe are able to cooperate, share, take turns, and in general, to behave in a more civil manner than children who do not play pretend games. These children, the make-believe players, tend to be creative, divergent thinkers (D. G. Singer & J. L. Singer, 1976, 1990; J. L. Singer, 1973). Make-believe play seems to be a very important form of preparation for school readiness as conceptualized by early education specialists. The studies described below attempted to delineate the relationship among variables related to make-believe play.

A major project involved following 141 children from eight nursery schools over 1 year's time. Pairs of observers watched a given child for a period of time during 2 consecutive weeks, repeating this pattern a few months later. This resulted in eight observations of the sample spread across the year. The children were rated on similar variables used in earlier work such as positive and negative emotions, imagination, cooperation with peers, ability to concentrate, and overt aggression. Results indicated that positive emotions such as joy and liveliness were positively related to imaginative play. Those children who displayed positive affect made more transformations during play and were less likely to engage in overt aggressive acts. When we controlled for language usage, such as number of words used, the relationship between imaginative play and positive emotions remained (D. G. Singer & J. L. Singer, 1980; J. L. Singer & D. G. Singer, 1981). This suggests that even without an extensive vocabulary, a child's predisposition to fantasy is crucial as a precursor to make-believe play.

During the year, we also were able to plot systematically the kinds of play children used, including sensorimotor play, make-believe or symbolic play, physical play, arts and crafts use, whether children played alone or with others, what major play themes ensued, and the degree of transformations in pretend play. From these play protocol analyses, seven statistical factors of play emerged: Adventurous Fantasy Play, Domestic Play, Gross Physical Activity, a General Emphasis on Make-Believe Play Pervading All Forms of Play, Ritual Games or Dancing and Singing, Play With Pet Animals, and Games With Rules. (For examples of the protocols see J. L. Singer & D. G. Singer, 1981.)

Major findings from these early studies of preschoolers showed that children who were highly imaginative engaged in more social play and were less likely to play alone. They enjoyed participating in ritual games and in singing. Over the year's time, more interest in art appeared and more social interaction was evident. Children who were heavy television viewers and who were low in fantasy play tended to be the most aggressive of the sample (J. L. Singer & D. G. Singer, 1981). These findings were replicated in later research. In one longitudinal study, for example, we found that early television viewing predicted less imagination in children several years later, even when family variables were included and examined (J. L. Singer, D. G. Singer, & Rapaczynski, 1984a).

J. L. Singer, D. G. Singer, and Sherrod (1980) examined the ongoing play behavior of 87 three- to four-year-olds during free play periods on eight separate occasions over 1 year's time. This factor analytic study of play behavior performed on 33 variables yielded three factors along which preschoolers' play could be measured. The first factor described a general good-humored playfulness or elation. The second factor indexed a relationship between preschoolers' aggressive interactions and home television viewing. The third factor measured the inner imaginative tendencies and prosocial behaviors of the preschooler. This factor was stable over the year and across several different analyses. The first factor involved imagination, language, social interaction, positive affect, mood, and activity level. The second factor involved the frequency of television viewing and pattern of viewing (especially the action shows), and related positively to anger and aggression. Factor 3 described the cooperative and creative capacity of the preschooler and demonstrated high loadings on such variables as peer prosocial behavior, persistence, imaginative predisposition, mature language usage, and viewing of educational television programs.

The factor-analytic procedure suggested that certain basic dimensions of spontaneous play of preschoolers could be measured. An important result was that imaginative play appeared from these data to be part of a more general pattern of good-humored playfulness and social interaction. Imagination, then, is not only a useful function in the good-natured, constructive quality of play, but is an essential part of the creative, intellectual, inner tendencies of the child and his or her external social capacities as well.

Make-believe play or imaginative ability appears to involve at least five components (Sherrod & J. L. Singer, 1989, p. 5):

1. The ability to form images
2. Skill in storing and retrieving images already formed
3. A store of images (quantity and quality)
4. Skill in remembering, integrating, and so forth—generally employing these images as a source of internal stimulations—and divorcing them from reality, and
5. Reinforcement for skillful processing as described in 4. When children develop these capacities, they are better able to exercise these skills in cognitive tasks such as paired-associate learning, immediate story recall, verbal fluency, and Piagetian tasks of conservation.

Imaginary Playmates: A Feature of Make-Believe Play

Children like to cuddle soft clothes, blankets, or furry toys. These transitional objects reflect the warmth and closeness of the mother, but are now under the child's control and represent a significant step away from self as fused with mother (Benson & Pryer, 1973; Klein, 1985). The child's attachment to the favorite object gradually wears off and the child eventually casts the teddy bear or other stuffed animal aside. According to Singer, the imaginary companion is a normal phenomenon and occurs when thought, rather than the use of a palpable object, can serve as a soothing activity. Thus, Singer states that the imaginary playmate is one manifestation of the internalizing process. The imaginary companion can help a child deal with loneliness, helplessness, and fear of the dark or of the unknown. On a more positive note, the imaginary friend also serves to aid children in constructive, adaptive ways by enabling them to be creative, sensitive, and to elaborate on themes and story plots when there is no actual friend available (D. G. Singer & J. L. Singer, 1990).

Because Singer believed so strongly in the positive aspects of the use of the imaginary playmate, he inspired a research project using the IPPI with 141 children and a questionnaire with 111 parents of low- and middle-class socioeconomic status. Sixty-five percent of the children reported having an imaginary friend while 55% of the parents answered in the affirmative (Caldeira, J. L. Singer, & D. G. Singer, 1978). Some parents may actually fail to be aware of these imaginary friends or may perhaps suppress this information because earlier clinical studies tended to emphasize the conflict-related defensive or compensatory aspects of this phenomenon.

In general, data from this study and from previous research found that children with no siblings reported more imaginary playmates, and that girls tended to have more such playmates than did boys. Children with these playmates, when observed and rated in their classrooms by research assistants unfamiliar with their answers to the IPPI, were found to be more imaginative in their spontaneous play, more positive in their emotions during play, and somewhat more cooperative with adults. In terms of sex differences, boys almost invariably chose male imaginary playmates while girls were likely to choose both male and female friends. When language data were examined in this study, boys with imaginary playmates spoke significantly more words ($M = 112$) during spontaneous play than did boys without imaginary playmates ($M = 70$). The same trend was apparent in girls but was not significant.

A major implication of this study seems to be that reports of imaginary playmates indicate a likelihood that children will engage in spontaneous imaginative play in other settings than home, will show more positive emotionality, will be absorbed in their play, and will manifest longer periods of concentration. These children are also more socially cooperative. According to Singer, this may be a pervasive personality or cognitive disposition that is identifiable even in a preschooler. The more developed language also suggests that self-entertaining play may improve imagery and language skills through the active rehearsal with the imaginary friend. The children with the imaginary friends seem to display the numerous benefits of play that were described above. Rather than viewing imaginary playmates as a cause of concern, psychologists are beginning to recognize the positive and constructive role that such early fantasy play has in the development of childrens' later capacities for continued imaginative growth.

PLAY TRAINING

Scientists have been able to demonstrate that a correlation exists between a juvenile animal's period of greatest playfulness and the time when brain cells are most active in forming connections in the cerebellum, the part of the brain that regulates movement and posture (Angier, 1992). Play is profoundly important for an animal's physical and mental growth. One of the most important distinctions between humans and the rest of the animal kingdom is the fact that while play is usually initiated by the young animal, among humans, the parent must take the first step in play. Parents need to begin the game, give structure and direction to play, and know when to withdraw and allow the child to continue the game alone. Shmukler's (1984) pioneering work with preschoolers in South Africa found, for example, that children engaged in more imaginative play when mothers introduced a game, helped them get started, and then stepped aside. For this reason, we began to work with parents of children who participated in our studies, attempting to teach these parents to play and to offer suggestions about childrearing.

Based on Singer's four criteria (listed previously) for the elements conducive to the enhancement of make-believe play, we began a simple form of community intervention with parents of low socioeconomic status. These were the parents of children who had participated in one of our first studies about the effects of a TV program on a child's imagination and emotions. We met over the course of a year with these modestly educated young parents, offering them help in parenting skills and supplying them with information to aid in controlling their children's TV habits (J. L. Singer & D. G. Singer, 1976a). This experience led to a more systematic series of play training sessions for parents of children who were involved in a later, more comprehensive longitudinal study. Parents attended workshops over a 3-week period, each lasting 2 hours. Included were information about developmental stages, discussion about various kinds of play, and the actual modeling and hands-on opportunities to engage in make-believe play activities. Films were shown to demonstrate concepts, reference lists were prepared, a packet of play ideas was distributed. The materials formed the basis of two books, *Partners in Play* (D. G. Singer & J. L. Singer, 1977) and later a revised edition, *Make-Believe: Games and Activities to Foster Imaginative Play in Young Children* (D. G. Singer & J. L. Singer, 1985).

Singer's interest in play and in play training not only involved normal children, but touched on the lives of emotionally impaired children as well. His research with children in a state psychiatric hospital indicated that training in imaginative play techniques could help them gain more of a sense of self and feelings of competence (Nahme-Huang, D. G. Singer,

J. L. Singer, & Wheaton, 1977). Earlier, his interest in the daydreams and imagination of the blind resulted in a joint study with one of his students. Using a structured interview with normal sighted and blind children, the experimenters were seeking to determine the play habits, daydreams, and night dreams of their subjects. The nature and degree of parental contact was also considered, as was the children's involvement with imaginary playmates, favorite games, thoughts before going to sleep, and conversations with self.

Results indicated that congenitally blind children do engage in daydreams, night dreams and make-believe play. Their dreams, both day and night, are more concrete and are more clearly related to personal experience than those of sighted children. In one area, imaginary companions, the blind children surpassed the sighted children in fantasy disposition. They reported more imaginary companions than did their sighted counterparts, and their companions were described as more capable than they were (J. L. Singer & Streiner, 1966).

Play training of parents and teachers continues to be an important facet of Singer's work. Influenced by Boyer's report (1991) wherein he outlined seven mandates that challenged our nation to concern itself with school readiness, we were especially interested in one mandate that specifically urged the television industry to become an active partner in the national effort to support readiness-to-learn programs directed to children, families, and caregivers. A first step was to determine the television and VCR usage among family home-care providers and day-care centers in Connecticut. With funding from the Corporation for Public Broadcasting (J. L. Singer & D. G. Singer, 1993), a telephone survey was conducted. Results indicated that 95% of 61 home-care providers and 5% of 54 day-care centers used television some part of the day. In terms of VCR usage, 58.6% of home-care providers used videotapes compared to 23.5% in day-care centers. Home-care providers tended to use their VCRs in the morning, while day-care centers used their VCRs in the afternoon. TV was used as a sitter during transitional periods (children arriving or leaving day care). Programs were used primarily for entertainment rather than for education, although home-care providers, more so than day-care providers, stated that if they had ancillary materials, they would use TV in a more constructive way.

Under the auspices of the Connecticut Public Broadcasting (D. G. Singer & J. L. Singer, 1995) and the Yale University Family Television Research and Consultation Center we conducted four workshops in Connecticut. All workshops were open to family home-care providers, day-care center directors, and parents of preschoolers (D. G. Singer & J. L. Singer, 1995).

The purpose of these workshops was to acquaint the participants with materials and articles prepared by PBS stations around the country. These materials used ideas from TV programs that could encourage parents and educators to use TV in a more active way with their children. Many of the materials emphasized cognitive as well as prosocial themes. Our goal was that through workshops, parents and educators could be acquainted with the learning potential of television, with emphasis on imagination. Currently, many stations continue to provide lesson plans and manuals for use in the home or at day-care centers.

TELEVISION AND IMAGINATION

The interest in television emerged from Singer's involvement in tracing the origins of adult consciousness and imagination back to early manifestations of children's make-believe play and to the cognitive–developmental influences on the emergence of fantasy. Through the many direct observations of children at play, or in talks with parents and nursery school educators, it became apparent that many of the play themes and conversations of young children were drawn from the television programs they viewed. Preschoolers watch TV on the average of 2½ to 3 hours per day, almost one third of the waking day.

Special properties of American television are its fast pacing, rapid shifts of scene, constant changes in sound level, and numerous intercuttings and interruptions. Directors use interesting camera angles, lighting, music, new or unusual characters, and a variety of special effects in order to keep a viewer's attention to the screen. American children have grown up with this pattern of stimulation and are experiencing a perceptual environment never before part of a child's cognitive system. The television medium has an especially powerful appeal. The human brain is organized to respond to movement, a survival of adaptive evolutionary self-defense for hunting tendencies. Thus, both children and adults find the moving picture difficult to ignore. The television medium is also a small social world providing stories and characters to keep us company. The material can also elicit a range of emotions, both positive and negative. Television also has power to distract us from our mundane chores and daily concerns. In this way, the medium may be a substitute for our daydreaming and fantasy-producing capacities. As Singer puts it,

> The TV set attracts us by movement, by conversation and music, by presenting us chiefly with that most significant of all environmental stimuli, the human face (or its caricatured exaggeration in the cartoons for children). It plays upon our orienting response and the inherent pleasure we get from manageable doses of novelty, neatly packaged in a small box. (J. L. Singer, 1980, p. 48).

If we feel threatened or bored, we can always turn the set off. Unfortunately, many people choose to keep the TV set on all day as a constant companion or source of stimulation. The average American household has the TV set on more than 7 hours per day. The average elementary-school aged child watches about 5 hours of TV daily, and poor children watch more.

It is important then, to ask how television is affecting the cognitive, emotional, and behavioral development of children in this country. Does television enhance or impede a child's imaginative capacity? Does television impede or promote a child's language ability, reading acquisition, concentration efforts, and self-control? What does television do to a child's ability to control anger and aggression?

During the past 20 years, we have attempted to answer these questions through numerous studies. Beginning with grants from the Yale Child Study Center, the Yale Institute of Social and Policy Studies, and Family Communications, Inc. we were able to carry out an experimental study of the effects of television on the imagination and emotions of nursery-school aged children (J. L. Singer & D. G. Singer, 1976a). One of the main results of that early study demonstrated that preschoolers could benefit from watching a carefully produced program such as *Mister Rogers' Neighborhood* (the program used in the study) if adult mediation were available. Interestingly, this first study was reconfirmed many years later when we examined the effects of *Barney & Friends* on young viewers (J. L. Singer & D. G. Singer, 1998). The groups of preschoolers that made most cognitive and social awareness gains were those whose teachers reinforced the television content through simple activities designed to complement each program.

Traditionally more attention has been focused by the general public and press on television and aggression than on television and imagination and prosocial behaviors. The report issued by the National Institute of Mental Health (NIMH) provided evidence that children who watch violent, aggressive television programs are more apt to imitate and engage in aggressive acts than children who watch less of that kind of material (Pearl, Bouthilet, & Lazar, 1982). Our own studies (J. L. Singer & D. G. Singer, 1986) added support to the major findings in the NIMH report. Early heavy viewing of television, especially viewing of programs with high action, fast pacing, or aggressive content are consistently linked in children to signs of overt aggression, and to the emotion of anger or to motor restlessness. The importance of the parents' roles in controlling their children's television viewing, or in mediating or explaining program content to help mitigate the negative effects of the medium, was also clear. As a result, we began to focus more of our research efforts toward this end.

Family Mediation Studies

Not long after finding that television played an important role in a young child's life (J. L. Singer & D. G. Singer, 1976b) we took a more sophisticated approach concerning the effects of television on a child's cognitive and social behaviors. A grant from the National Science Foundation in 1976 enabled us to continue to explore facets of make-believe combined with our increasing involvement in the television medium. Table 13.1 presents

TABLE 13.1

Home Influences (Independent Variables) and Cognitive or Behavioral Measures (Dependent Variables) in a Longitudinal Study

Home Influences	Cognitive and Behavioral Measures
1. Family characteristics	1. Cognition
parents' self-described values (e.g. resourcefulness, imagination, curiosity, adventurousness, creativity)	reading scores (recognition and comprehension) language use academic adjustment beliefs ("mean world")
parents' attitudes toward discipline & childrearing (e.g. power-assertive vs. inductive methods)	2. Imagination
parents' belief-systems: "mean & scary world" test	inkblots, interview, block play, birthday party script
family structure and stress level (e.g. single-parent family, etc.)	3. Comprehension of TV content
daily lifestyle sleep patterns organized daily routines diverse cultural activities vs. limited outside activities emphasis on outdoor sports	plot commercials
	4. Waiting ability
	delaying ability motor restlessness during spontaneous waiting period.
2. Television environment	5. Aggression
average weekly viewing	6. School behavioral adjustment
type of programming (e.g. action-adventure [realistic or fantasy], cartoons)	
home emphasis on TV (e.g. parent-viewing, cable, paid programming, number of sets, attempts to control child's viewing)	

the independent and dependent variables that we have used in a variety of studies, both short term and longitudinal. We have examined these variables with different samples of children of lower-class, lower-middle-class, and middle-class socioeconomic status. Our home variables encompass a broad array of influences that may affect a child. We have not systematically studied the mediating role of older siblings or peer groups in our sample, but we do regard these parental variables as reasonably comprehensive potential influences on how a child forms his or her concepts of the world, learns how to use language, learns to pretend, and learns to control motor activity or aggressive behavior. Research by Tower (1980) has indicated, for example, that parents' own values along three dimensions, *resourcefulness* (imagination, creativity, curiosity, etc.), *reliability* (efficiency, competence, punctuality) and *relationships* (friendly, generous, sincere, likable) are differentially reflected in the spontaneous play or school behavior of children as early as the preschool level.

Our chief interest was whether television-viewing patterns of the children might have a special influence beyond the family inputs on development. Multiple regression analysis sought to determine the combination of independent variables yielding the highest prediction of the child's cognitive and behavioral patterns. This procedure also permitted us to estimate whether or not family or television variables made independent contributions to predicting child outcomes. For example, could television viewing habits predict children's behavior, even when general family orientations (e.g., children from certain familes like more TV) were partialled out?

A series of studies began to explore the extent to which the patterns of parental mediation might predict aspects of a child's later emotional and behavioral tendencies. We viewed parental mediation as a critical process through which caretakers could filter the complex environment into manageable information, thus providing children with a differentiated cognitive structure about events, people, and places. Parents could also help children deal with their worlds through the provision of verbal tools. Families mediate by offering verbal approval or disapproval of TV content, by paralanguage (e.g., "Ugh!" or nonverbal gestures) used when a scene or commercial is irritating, by judgmental comments, through explanation of the characteristics of a program, or the conventions of program production, through comments on morality of characters or the suitability of characters as role models, through their affective reactions to a program, and finally through rule setting and discipline.

Data from a number of our studies indicated that a child's reading readiness and achievement were best predicted by an independent combination of family and television-viewing variables. When parents viewed the world as a hostile, scary place, were from a lower social class, and when children watched more television, children had poorer reading scores and less general information. Additionally, children who were heavy TV viewers (especially of the more violent, aggressive shows) were more apt to believe that the world is a hostile, scary place, to have difficulty discriminating real from fantasy occurrences, and were more restless, impulsive, and aggressive.

Parents who imposed rules concerning TV, who reported less fearful views of the world, and who rated themselves as imaginative and resourceful had children who were generally more imaginative, less aggressive, used more complex language, and scored higher on general information. Heavier viewing of violent programming or of television in general by parents, and more emphasis by parents on physical discipline and power assertion predicted greater aggressive behavior by the children (Desmond, J. L. Singer, D. G. Singer, Calam, & Colimore, 1985; D. G. Singer & J. L. Singer, 1984; J. L. Singer & D. G. Singer, 1983b; J. L. Singer & D. G. Singer, 1986; J. L. Singer, D. G. Singer, Desmond, Hirsch, & Nicol, 1988; J. L. Singer, D. G. Singer, & Rapaczynski, 1984a; J. L. Singer, D. G. Singer, & Rapaczynski, 1984b).

A parental mediation style of discussion (explanation, pointing things out, allowing children to participate in discussions) rather than one of moral judgment and discipline seemed to be the most important independent variable across the array of cognitive and behavioral dependent variables used in our mediation studies. Home observations and interviews with children and parents suggested that family mediation is a critical feature of parenting. Our data pointed repeatedly to the fact that those parents who are heavy viewers, who lack other interests, and who do not exert efforts to establish rules about television viewing may provide a home atmosphere that puts their children at risk for fears about daily dangers, for greater restlessness, and for a proneness to aggression. Children may model their parents' own emotionality or may react to power-assertive discipline in addition to reflecting the heavy dose of frightening or aggressive content that makes up television programming.

When parents do control TV viewing, and are involved in explaining content to their children, the children tend to comprehend the programs more readily, are less aggressive or restless, and are more imaginative. Imaginativeness in older children tracked in our samples is best predicted by less preschool television viewing, less recent viewing of realistic action-adventure programming, greater self-description by both parents as imaginative and creative, and less parental emphasis on power-assertive disciplinary measures.

The prosocial effects of quality television have been documented by us (D. G. Singer, J. L. Singer, & Zuckerman, 1990; J. L. Singer & D. G. Singer, 1998) and by numerous researchers, some of whom are represented in books edited by Berry and Asamen (1993), and by Zillman, Bryant and Huston (1994). A recent study of preschoolers' viewing habits of educational television and its effects on academic skills, school readiness, and school adjustment (Wright & Huston, 1995) also presents the positive benefits of selected television viewing.

Barney & Friends—A Model for Prosocial Television

President Clinton signed a bill in 1996 stating that broadcasters must provide at least 3 hours a week of children's programming that is educational and not merely entertaining. Although the Federal Communications Commission has not presented explicit criteria for educational programming, there are numerous national organizations that have suggested guidelines for television shows that could enhance the learning potential of young children. Our report to the Corporation of Public Broadcasting in 1993 outlined potential learning dimensions that could help children prepare for effective school entrance and subsequent performance. A series of studies of *Barney & Friends* (J. L. Singer & D. G. Singer, 1998) reflected an effort to evaluate an extremely popular television series to determine how it could contribute to the national ready-to-learn goals for children's programming. Three steps were involved: (a) analysis of the dimensions of experience required to prepare children for effective school entrance and subsequent performance, (b) an assessment of specific elements of 68 episodes of the *Barney & Friends* television series that might reflect such dimensions, and (c) a series of experiments to determine whether preschool children would actually make gains if exposed to a daily in-school diet of 10 episodes chosen as richest in potential from the *Barney* series.

Table 13.2 presents the six major areas that were utilized in carrying out the content analyses of the 68 *Barney* episodes. Only those elements that were clearly explained, modeled, or defined on the program by the children or by Barney were included as part of the lesson plans we developed, or as part of the assessment procedures we used in the various studies.

Beginning with a lower middle-class sample of suburban preschoolers, we eventually also studied poor and inner-city preschool children from five U.S. cities. We also studied a sample of kindergarten children from a small industrial city. Our goal was to determine how children behaved as they watched each episode. At the end of 2 weeks of viewing, we assessed whether they showed gains (compared to nonviewing closely matched control groups) on a series of measures of the cognitive, social, emotional, physical health and safety, and multicultural dimensions we had identified as the teaching elements in the *Barney* series. A further study was conducted of the responses of toddlers, both to watching the 10 episodes and in their subsequent spontaneous school behavior.

TABLE 13.2
Variables Used in Content Analysis of
80 *Barney & Friends* Television Programs

1. Cognitive

new vocabulary	colors	sequencing
alphabet	shapes	science/nature
numbers	concepts	achievement
imagination	sorting	riddles, metaphors

2. Emotional awareness

joy, approval	anger	fear, tension
surprise & excitement	shame, shyness	crying, sadness
interest & curiosity	disgust	pain
empathy & sympathy	jealousy/envy	

3. Social/Constructive attitudinal

sharing	self-restraint/control	disciplining
turn taking	interpersonal skills	
cooperation	helping/teaching	

4. Physical

fine motor skills	nutrition & health	personal grooming
large motor skills	handicaps	
eye/hand coordination	injury	

5. Music and entertainment

song related to	song & dance	singing alone
instructional	combined	musical instruments
incident	dancing alone	games

6. Multicultural exposure

language	dancing	reference to ethnic group
custom	name of country	ethnic guest
food	discussion of country	
song		

Results indicated impressive evidence that exposure of hundreds of 3- to 5-year-old preschool children to 10 episodes of *Barney* in their day-care settings was followed by gains in vocabulary, counting and other cognitive skills, and awareness of socially constructive behaviors. These gains were especially apparent in conditions wherein trained preschool caregivers followed TV viewing with games or exercises based on lesson plans relevant to the episode. Such learning was not found for kindergarten students, however, perhaps because the teaching material of the series was better suited to the younger age groups. The kindergarten children were already familiar with the many cognitive elements presented on *Barney*, and therefore made insignificant gains from pre- to posttest measures. Toddlers averaging 27 months of age who watched 10

10 episodes of *Barney* in day-care settings subsequently showed more early signs of imagination, somewhat more socially appropriate behavior and especially strong indications of less aggression or angry moods when compared with a matched group who had not watched the episodes.

We found a striking association between what children retained from a *Barney* episode just watched and the number of cognitive teaching elements that our panel had assigned to the same episode. This finding strongly supports the value of adult panel ratings. It also particularly emphasizes the importance of including clear examples of carefully defined words, counting procedures, or other cognitive skill elements which may then enhance children's abilities to retain and reproduce story content (J. L. Singer & D. G. Singer, 1998).

Our outreach efforts using *Barney*-derived lesson plans with day-care workers, nursery school teachers, and parents were enthusiastically received. It seems likely that wider availability of TV-related teaching material can play a significant role in fostering the ready-to-learn national goals for preschoolers.

Social Policy—Media Literacy

The outreach programs initiated by the Yale Television Center are only one part of Singer's efforts to communicate research findings to the general public. Meetings with the Chair of the Federal Communications Commission (FCC) concerning the Telecommunications Act of 1996, and with Vice President Gore concerning the V chip (device used to block out violent programs) and children's educational television are examples of Singer's commitment to intervention strategies in television. Singer has served as an advisor, along with other psychologists, in the drawing up of industry self-regulation guidelines concerning advertising for the Council of Better Business Bureau's Children's Review Unit, which oversees advertising on broadcast and print media.

Singer also served on the National Institute of Mental Health's (NIMH) committee that updated the research about television and behavior (Pearl, Bouthilet, & Lazar, 1982). He has testified before the FCC on cognitive development and the importance of age-specific programming for children, and has met directly with producers and writers to discuss programming possibilities for children. Singer consults with government agencies and with producers, both in this country and in foreign countries, reviewing manuscripts and pilot television programs geared to young children and to adolescents. Currently, he is on the advisory board of *Zillions TV*, a television series produced by Consumer Reports Television, a division of Consumers Union. These programs educate consumers about products advertised on television, how to become educated shoppers, and how to become more aware of hazards to health and safety when making purchases.

One of the most important aspects of outreach activities is Singer's involvement in media literacy. With colleagues and with me, he has developed curricula, for children from kindergarten through high-school age, focusing on teaching children to become critical, intelligent viewers of the television medium (Rapaczynski, D. G. Singer, & J. L. Singer, 1982; D. G. Singer & J. L. Singer, 1990; D. G. Singer & J. L. Singer, 1994; D. G. Singer, J. L. Singer, & Zuckerman, 1981).

Lessons and videos that are age appropriate have been prepared with the following objectives in mind:

- To raise students' awareness of their television viewing habits
- To be able to identify the different formats of programs and basic scheduling strategies
- To develop an understanding of the many possible career choices there are in television
- To understand the conventions and formal features of TV
- To be able to differentiate between the different elements of fantasy and reality
- To learn to recognize various effects used to distort reality or arouse excitement, suspense, and interest
- To help students identify some of the different styles and forms of advertising and to adopt a critical approach to analyzing and even appreciating commercials
- To understand how television may influence our social customs and attitudes, confront the possible anti-social values portrayed on TV, and assist students in thinking through some of their own ethical values in comparison with those presented on TV
- To give students some understanding about how TV conveys both positive and negative messages about such issues as nutrition, alcohol consumption, cigarette smoking, and AIDS
- To explore how TV can be useful in promoting information about the environment

The curricula are in use throughout the country and are part of the current national media literacy movement. From theory to practice, Singer has truly been one of the leaders in the field of television research.

SUMMARY

J. L. Singer continues to pursue his lifelong interest in imagination and play. His curiosity leads him to carry out numerous systematic investigations of children's involvement in the area of make-believe and fantasy.

His studies offer evidence for the many benefits of play, particularly the relationships among imagination, positive affect, and prosocial behavior. The development of rigorous techniques that enable researchers to study fantasy in children, whether through observations, questionnaires or interview methods, has added considerably to the scientific knowledge in this field.

His interest in imagination led inevitably to the study of the effects of television on children's cognitive, social, and behavioral development. Dozens of experiments were carried out by Singer and colleagues using large samples of children from all socioeconomic groups. A concomitant area of study involved his work about parental and teacher mediation of television. The important report to the Corporation of Public Broadcasting (J. L. Singer & D. G. Singer, 1993) included recommendations suggesting that television be used as an educational tool for parents and teachers with programs about parenting, literacy, and the modeling of how to use material from programs to enhance children's readiness to learn.

Singer has been personally involved in training children and parents how to play and in training parents and educators in use of television as an adjunct to educating children. He has been a strong advocate for quality children's programming through his work with the Federal Communications Commission and the Children's Review Unit of the Better Business Bureau and as an advisor to producers and writers of children's TV programs both in the United States and Europe.

Numerous students in this country and abroad have benefited from Singer's inspiration in the areas of fantasy, play, and television. Researchers in many countries including China, Liu Yan; England, Rachel Calam; Holland, Jeffrey Goldstein and Joop Hellendoorn; Israel, Shlomo Ariel and Itzak Levine; Japan, Tamaki Takahashi; South Africa, Diana Shmukler; and the United States, Brian Sutton-Smith have acknowledged him as their mentor and inspiration, and in some instances have written articles with him about the study of play and about unconscious processes. On a personal note, I have found my years of collaboration with him to have been fruitful and exciting. I have learned much from him and I feel fortunate to have added something to his adventures in the world of make-believe.

REFERENCES

Angier, N. (1992, October 20). The purpose of playful frolics: Training for adulthood. *The New York Times, Science Times*, p. C1.

Benson, R., & Pryer, D. (1973). When friends fall out: Developmental interference with the function of some imaginary companions. *Journal of the American Psychoanalytic Association, 21*, 457–468.

Berlyne, D. E. (1969). Laughter, humor, and play. In M. Lindzey & E. Aronson (Eds.), *The Handbook of Social Psychology, Vol. 3* (2nd ed., pp. 795–852). Reading, MA: Addison-Wesley.

Berry, G. L., & Asamen, J. K. (1993). *Children and television: Images in a changing sociocultural world.* Newbury Park, CA: Sage.

Boyer, E. (1991). *Readiness to learn: A mandate for the nation.* Princeton, NJ: The Carnegie Council for the Advancement of Teaching.

Caldeira, J., Singer, J. L., & Singer, D. G. (1978, March). *Imaginary playmates: Some relationships to preschoolers' spontaneous play, language, and television viewing.* Paper presented at the meeting of the Eastern Psychological Association, Washington, DC.

Desmond, R. J., Singer, J. L., Singer, D. G., Calam, R., & Colimore, K. (1985). Family mediation patterns and television viewing: Young children's use and grasp of the medium. *Human Communication Research, 11*(4), 461–480.

Fein, G. (1981). Pretend play in childhood: An integrative review. *Child Development, 52,* 1095–1118.

Goldstein, K. (1940). *Human nature in the light of psychopathology.* Cambridge, MA: Harvard University Press.

Klein, B. R. (1985). A child's imaginary companion: A transitional self. *Clinical Social Work Journal, 12,* 272–282.

Leslie, A. M. (1987). Pretense and representation: The origins of "theory of mind." *Psychological Review, 94,* 412–426.

McIlwraith, R. D., & Schallow, J. R. (1982–83). Television viewing and styles of children's fantasy. *Imagination, Cognition and Personality, 2,* 323–331.

Nahme-Huang, L., Singer, D. G., Singer, J. L., & Wheaton, A. B. (1977). Imaginative playtraining and perceptual-motor interventions with emotionally-disturbed hospitalized children. *American Journal of Orthopsychiatry, 47,* 238–249.

Pearl, D., Bouthilet, L., & Lazar, J. (Eds.). (1982). *Television and behavior: Ten years of scientific progress and implications for the eighties* (Vol. 1 & 2). Washington, DC: U.S. Government Printing Office.

Piaget, J. (1952). *The origins of intelligence in children.* New York: Norton.

Piaget, J. (1962). *Play, dreams, and imitation in childhood.* New York: Norton.

Pulaski, M. A. (1973). Toys and imaginative play. In J. L. Singer (Ed.), *The child's world of make-believe* (pp. 74–103). New York: Academic Press.

Rapaczynski, W., Singer, D. G., & Singer, J. L. (1982). Teaching television: A curriculum for young children. *Journal of Communication, 32,* 46–55.

Rosen, C. R., Schwebel, D. C., & Singer, J. L. (1997). Preschoolers' attributions of mental states in pretense. *Child Development, 68*(4), 1133–1142.

Rosenfeld, E., Huesman, L. R., Eron, L., & Torney-Purta, J. V. (1982). Measuring patterns of fantasy behavior in children. *Journal of Personality and Social Psychology, 42,* 347–366.

Schwebel, D. C., Rosen, C. S., & Singer, J. L. (in press). Preschoolers' pretend play and theory of mind: The role of jointly constructed pretense. *British Journal of Developmental Psychology.*

Sherrod, L. R., & Singer, J. L. (1989). The development of make-believe play. In J. H. Goldstein (Ed.), *Sports, games and play: Social and psychological viewpoints* (2nd edition, pp. 1–37). Hillsdale, NJ: Lawrence Erlbaum Associates.

Shmukler, D. (1984). Imaginative play: Its implications for the process of education. In A. Sheik (Ed.), *Imagery and the Educational Process* (pp. 39–62). New York: Baywood.

Singer, D. G., & Singer, J. L. (1976). Family television viewing habits and the spontaneous play of children. *American Journal of Orthopsychiatry, 46,* 496–502.

Singer, D. G., & Singer, J. L. (1977). *Partners in play.* New York: Harper & Row.

Singer, D. G., & Singer, J. L. (1980). Television viewing and aggressive behavior in preschool children: A field study. *Annals of the New York Academy of Science, 347,* 292–203.

Singer, D. G., & Singer, J. L. (1984). Parents as mediators of the child's television environment. *Educational Media International, 4,* 7–11.

Singer, D. G., & Singer, J. L. (1985). *Make believe: Games and activities to foster imaginative play in young children.* Glenview, IL: Scott, Foresman.

Singer, D. G., & Singer, J. L. (1990). *The house of make believe: Children's play and the developing imagination.* Cambridge, MA: Harvard University Press.

Singer, D. G., & Singer, J. L. (1994). *Creating critical viewers.* Denver, CO: Pacific Mountain Network.

Singer, D. G., & Singer, J. L. (1995). *Readying children for school through brief exposure to television segments from* Barney & Friends, Mr. Rogers' Neighborhood *and* Sesame Street: *A report on workshops for daycare teachers and family home care providers.* New Haven, CT: Yale University Family Television Research and Consultation Center.

Singer, D. G., Singer, J. L., & Zuckerman, D. M. (1981). *Getting the most out of TV.* Santa Monica, CA: Goodyear.

Singer, D. G., Singer, J. L., & Zuckerman, D. M. (1990). *The parent's guide: Use TV to your child's advantage.* Reston, VA: Acropolis.

Singer, J. L. (1961). Imagination and waiting ability in young children. *Journal of Personality, 29,* 396–413.

Singer, J. L. (1966). *Daydreaming: An introduction to the experimental study of inner experience.* New York: Random House.

Singer, J. L. (1973). *The child's world of make-believe: Experimental studies in imaginative play.* New York: Academic Press.

Singer, J. L. (1977). Imagination and make-believe in early childhood: Some educational implications. *Journal of Mental Imagery, 1,* 127–144.

Singer, J. L. (1980). The power and limitations of television: A cognitive-affective analysis. In P. H. Tannenbaum (Ed.), *The entertainment functions of television* (pp. 32–65). Hillsdale, NJ: Lawrence Erlbaum Associates.

Singer, J. L. (1996). Cogntive and affective implications of imaginative play in childhood. In M. Lewis (Ed.), *Child and Adolescent Psychiatry: A Comprehensive Textbook* (2nd ed., pp. 202–212). Baltimore, MD: Williams & Wilkins.

Singer, J. L., & Singer, D. G. (1972). Personality. In P. H. Mussen & M. R. Rosenweig (Eds.), *Annual Review of Psychology, 23,* (pp. 375–412). Palo Alto, CA: Annual Reviews.

Singer, J. L., & Singer, D. G. (1976a). Can TV stimulate imaginative play? *Journal of Communication, 26,* 74–79.

Singer, J. L., & Singer, D. G. (1976b). Imaginative play and pretending in early childhood: Some experimenal approaches. In A. Davids (Ed.), *Child Personality and Psychopathology* (pp. 69–112). New York: Wiley.

Singer, J. L., & Singer, D. G. (1981). *Television, imagination, and aggression: A study of preschoolers.* Hillsdale, NJ: Lawrence Erlbaum Associates.

Singer, J. L., & Singer, D. G. (1983a). Learning how to be intelligent consumers of television. In M. Howe (Ed.), *Learning from television* (pp. 203–222). London: Academic Press.

Singer, J. L., & Singer, D. G. (1983b). Psychologists look at television: Cognitive, developmental, and social policy implications. *American Psychologist, 38,* 826–834.

Singer, J. L., & Singer, D. G. (1986). Family experiences and television viewing as predictors of children's imagination, restlessness and aggression. *Journal of Social Issues, 42,* 107–124.

Singer, J. L., & Singer, D. G. (1993). *A role for television in the enhancement of children's readiness to learn.* In preparation for a report by the Corporation for Public broadcasting to the Congress of the United States. New Haven, CT: Yale Unversity Family Television Research and Consultation Center.

Singer, J. L., & Singer, D. G. (1998). *Barney & Friends* as entertainment and education: Evaluating the quality and effectiveness of a television series for preschool children. In

W. K. Asamen & G. Berry (Eds.), *Research paradigms in the study of television and social behavior* (pp. 305–367). Beverly Hills, CA: Sage.

Singer, J. L., Singer, D. G., Desmond, R., Hirsch, & Nicol, A. (1988). Family mediation and children's cognition, aggression, and comprehension of television: A longitudinal study. *Journal of Applied Developmental Psychology, 9,* 329–347.

Singer, J. L., Singer, D. G., & Rapaczynski, W. (1984a). Family patterns and television viewing as predictors of children's beliefs and aggression. *Journal of Communication, 34,* 73–89.

Singer, J. L., Singer, D. G., & Rapaczynski, W. (1984b). Chidren's imagination as predicted by family patterns and television viewing: A longitudinal study. *Genetic Psychology Monographs, 110,* 43–69.

Singer, J. L., Singer, D. G., & Sherrod, L. R. (1980). A factor analytic study of preschooler's play behavior. *Academic Psychology Bulletin, 2,* (pp. 143–156).

Singer, J. L., & Streiner, B. F. (1966). Imaginative content in the dreams and fantasy play of blind and sighted children. *Perceptual and Motor Skills, 22,* 475–482.

Takahashi, T. (1989). *Imagination and reality: The child's world of pretend play.* Tokyo: Doshin.

Tomkins, S. (1962). *Affect, imagery, consciousness* (Vol 1). New York: Springer.

Tower, R. B. (1980). *The influence of parent's values on preschool children's behavior.* Unpublished doctoral dissertation, Yale University, New Haven, CT.

White, R. W. (1959). Motivation reconsidered: The concept of competence. *Psychological Review, 66,* 197–333.

Wright, J. C., & Huston, A. C. (1995). *Effects of educational TV viewing of lower income preschoolers on academic skills, school readiness, and school adjustment one to three years later.* Lawrence, KS: Center for Research on the Influences of Television on Children, Department of Human Development.

Zillman, D., Bryant, J., & Huston, A. C. (1994). *Media, children and the family.* Hillsdale, NJ: Lawrence Erlbaum Associates.

Author Index

Subject Index

SUBJECT INDEX

345

Late-selection theory, 8, 10
Learning, *see also* Cognition; Information, assimilation
  brain imaging studies, 17–19
  emotion effects, 86–87
  experiential system for, 55–58, 56*t*, 76
  of task performance, 11–26
Lexical representation, 273*t*, 274*f*, 278–279, 284–285
Listening, *see* Attention

M

Machiavellianism, 151, 162, 163*t*, 166
Markov response organization, 30
Marriage, 21–22
MAXCOV procedure, 160
Meaning
  dimensions of, 187–192
  functions of, 184–186
  intentional, 31
  semantic, 31
Meaning assignment process, 107, 184
Meaning complexes, 31–32
Meaning profiles of tasks, 182
Meaning system
  cognition and, 179, 181–184
    dynamic relations, 187–192
  consciousness generation from, 192–197
  defined, 179–180, 196
  dynamic, 182–183, 187–192
  interpersonal mode, 180, 197–200
  modes
    analogy, 191–192
    per relation types, 198–201
  organizational transformation, 189–197
  personal mode, 180, 197–200
  properties of, 186–187
  static, 182–183
  types of, 180
  variable sets, *see* Meaning variables
Meaning Test, 180–181
Meaning variables
  cognition role, 181–184
  emotions and, 185–186
  forms of expression, 181, 202
  forms of relation, 180, 202
  meaning dimensions, 180, 201
  organizational changes, 189–192

personality and, 185–186
referent shifts, 180–181, 202
self-concept and, 185
types of relation, 180, 201
  meaning modes from, 197–201
value changes, 187–188
Media, 24–26, *see also* Television
Memory representation
  consciousness relationship, 176–177
  creativity from, 287–289, 292–299
  in dreams, 58–61, 63
  interpersonal associative linkages, 119–122
  intrusive, 292–299
Memory retrieval
  cognitive interference and, 35–36
  emotion impact, 38, 86–87, 195
  by repressors, 255–257
  of significant others, 119–121, 126–128
  top-down, 25–26
Memory structures, 116*n*, 124–125, *see also* Knowledge
Me-ness, *see* Private experiences
Mental content
  continual flow patterns, 35
  segmentation
    behavioral, 31–32
    conscious, *see* Thought flow
Mental health
  adaptation and, 257–259
  defined, 254
  dialectic approach, 253–254, 257, 264
  illusory, 258–259
  imaginal thought role, 3–4
  traditional criteria, 259
Mentation, 29, *see also* Mental content
Metacognitions, 115
Metaphors
  in dream interpretation, 61–62
  in meaning assignment, 195, 200
Military policies, 220–222
Mindsets
  deliberative, 42
  evaluative, 42
  implementational, 42
  thought content effects, 41–42
Mindwandering, 5, 9
MMPI personality test, 156*t*, 157
Motivation
  in transference, 111–113, 125